Sport and the Social Significance of Pleasure

This innovative text's critical examination foregrounds the prime reason why so many people participate in or watch sport—pleasure. Although there has been a "turn" to emotions and affect within academia over the last two decades, it is somewhat remiss that pleasure, as an integral aspect of human life, has not received greater attention from sociologists of sport, exercise and physical education. This book addresses this issue with an unabashed examination of sport and the moving body via a "pleasure lens." It provides new insights about the production of various identities, power relations and social issues, and the dialectical links between the socio-cultural and the body. Taking a wide-sweeping view of pleasure—dignified and debauched, distinguished and mundane—it examines topics as diverse as aging, health, fandom, running, extreme sports, biopolitics, consumerism, feminism, sex and sexuality. In drawing from diverse theoretical approaches and original empirical research, the text reveals the social and political significance of pleasure and provides a more rounded, dynamic and sensual account of sport.

Richard Pringle is an Associate Professor in the School of Curriculum and Pedagogy in the Faculty of Education at the University of Auckland.

Robert E. Rinehart is Associate Professor in Sport and Leisure Studies at the University of Waikato.

Jayne Caudwell is Reader in Sport, Gender and Sexualities at the University of Brighton.

Routledge Research in Sport, Culture and Society

For a full list of titles in this series, please visit www.routledge.com

11 Ultimate Fighting and Embodiment
Violence, Gender and Mixed Martial Arts
Dale C. Spencer

12 The Olympic Games and Cultural Policy
Beatriz Garcia

13 The Urban Geography of Boxing
Race, Class, and Gender in the Ring
Benita Heiskanen

14 The Social Organization of Sports Medicine
Critical Socio-Cultural Perspectives
Edited by Dominic Malcolm and Parissa Safai

15 Host Cities and the Olympics
An Interactionist Approach
Harry Hiller

16 Sports Governance, Development and Corporate Responsibility
Edited by Barbara Segaert, Marc Theeboom, Christiane Timmerman and Bart Vanreusel

17 Sport and Its Female Fans
Edited by Kim Toffoletti and Peter Mewett

18 Sport Policy in Britain
Barrie Houlihan and Iain Lindsey

19 Sports and Christianity
Historical and Contemporary Perspectives
Edited by Nick J. Watson and Andrew Parker

20 Sports Coaching Research
Context, Consequences, and Consciousness
Anthony Bush, Michael Silk, David Andrews and Hugh Lauder

21 Sport Across Asia
Politics, Cultures, and Identities
Edited by Katrin Bromber, Birgit Krawietz, and Joseph Maguire

22 Athletes, Sexual Assault, and "Trials by Media"
Narrative Immunity
Deb Waterhouse-Watson

23 Youth Sport, Physical Activity and Play
Policy, Interventions and Participation
Andrew Parker and Don Vinson

24 The Global Horseracing Industry
Social, Economic, Environmental and Ethical Perspectives
Phil McManus, Glenn Albrecht, and Raewyn Graham

25 Sport, Public Broadcasting, and Cultural Citizenship
Signal Lost?
Edited by Jay Scherer and David Rowe

26 Sport and Body Politics in Japan
Wolfram Manzenreiter

27 The Fantasy Sport Industry
Games within Games
Andrew C. Billings and Brody J. Ruihley

28 Sport in Prison
Exploring the Role of Physical Activity in Penal Practices
Rosie Meek

29 Sport and Nationalism in China
Lu Zhouxiang and Fan Hong

30 Rethinking Drug Use in Sport
Why the war will never be won
Bob Stewart and Aaron Smith

31 Sport, Animals, and Society
Edited by James Gillett and Michelle Gilbert

32 Sport Development in the United States
Edited by Peter Smolianov, Dwight Zakus and Joseph Gallo

33 Youth Olympic Games
Edited by Dag Vidar Hanstad, Barrie Houlihan and Milena Parent

34 Safeguarding, Child Protection and Abuse in Sport
International Perspectives in Research, Policy and Practice
Edited by Melanie Lang and Mike Hartill

35 Touch in Sports Coaching and Physical Education
Fear, Risk, and Moral Panic
Edited by Heather Piper

36 Sport, Racism and Social Media
Neil Farrington, Lee Hall, Daniel Kilvington, John Price and Amir Saeed

37 Football and Migration
Perspectives, Places, Players
Edited by Richard Elliott and John Harris

38 Health and Elite Sport
Is High Performance Sport a Healthy Pursuit?
Edited by Joe Baker, Parissa Safai and Jessica Fraser-Thomas

39 Asian American Athletes in Sport and Society
Edited by C. Richard King

40 Pierre Bourdieu and Physical Culture
Edited by lisahunter, Wayne Smith and elke emerald

41 Reframing Disability?
Media, (Dis)Empowerment, and Voice in the 2012 Paralympics
Edited by Daniel Jackson, Caroline E. M. Hodges, Mike Molesworth and Richard Scullion

42 Sport and the Social Significance of Pleasure
Richard Pringle, Robert E. Rinehart and Jayne Caudwell

Sport and the Social Significance of Pleasure

Richard Pringle, Robert E. Rinehart
and Jayne Caudwell

NEW YORK AND LONDON

First published 2015
by Routledge
711 Third Avenue, New York, NY 10017

and by Routledge
2 Park Square, Milton Park, Abingdon, Oxon OX14 4RN

*Routledge is an imprint of the Taylor & Francis Group,
an informa business*

© 2015 Taylor & Francis

"The Force That Through the Green Fuse Drives the Flower" By Dylan
Thomas, from *The Poems of Dylan Thomas*, copyright ©1939 by New
Directions Publishing Corp. Reprinted by permission of New Directions
Publishing Corp. UK: *The Collected Poems of Dylan Thomas: The New
Centenary Edition*, copyright ©2004 by Orion Publishing Group. Reprinted
with permission from David Higham Associates Limited.

"Do Not Go Gentle Into That Good Night" By Dylan Thomas, from *The
Poems of Dylan Thomas*, copyright ©1952 by Dylan Thomas. Reprinted by
permission of New Directions Publishing Corp. UK: *The Collected Poems
of Dylan Thomas: The New Centenary Edition*, copyright ©2004 by Orion
Publishing Group. Reprinted with permission from David Higham Associates
Limited.

The right of Richard Pringle, Robert E. Rinehart and Jayne Caudwell to
be identified as authors of this work has been asserted in accordance with
sections 77 and 78 of the Copyright, Designs and Patents Act 1988.

All rights reserved. No part of this book may be reprinted or reproduced or
utilised in any form or by any electronic, mechanical, or other means, now
known or hereafter invented, including photocopying and recording, or in any
information storage or retrieval system, without permission in writing from
the publishers.

Trademark Notice: Product or corporate names may be trademarks or
registered trademarks, and are used only for identification and explanation
without intent to infringe.

Library of Congress Cataloging-in-Publication Data

Pringle, Richard, 1964–
   Sport and the social significance of pleasure / by Richard Pringle, Robert E.
Rinehart and Jayne Caudwell.
      pages cm. — (Routledge research in sport, culture and society ; 42)
      Includes bibliographical references and index.
   1. Sports—Sociological aspects.   2. Pleasure.   I. Rinehart, Robert E.,
1951–   II. Caudwell, Jayne.   III. Title.
      GV706.5.P75 2015
      306.4'83—dc23
      2015005069

ISBN: 978-0-415-88510-2 (hbk)
ISBN: 978-1-315-71963-4 (ebk)

Typeset in Sabon
by Apex CoVantage, LLC

Contents

List of Figures		ix
Acknowledgments		xi
1	Proem: Sport and the Social Significance of Pleasure RICHARD PRINGLE, ROBERT E. RINEHART AND JAYNE CAUDWELL	1
2	Pleasures Small and Large ROBERT E. RINEHART	12
3	A Short History of Pleasure RICHARD PRINGLE	29
4	Theorizing Sporting Pleasures across the Disciplines RICHARD PRINGLE	41
5	Studying Sport, Feminism and Pleasure JAYNE CAUDWELL	64
6	Aging Bod(ies) and Pleasure: Poetic Orientations ROBERT E. RINEHART	80
7	Running for Pleasures JAYNE CAUDWELL	97
8	When the Pleasurable Is Political: An Affective Analysis of Viewing the Olympics RICHARD PRINGLE	116
9	'I Just Love Watching Football' JAYNE CAUDWELL	133

viii *Contents*

10 Aesthetic Pleasure and Sport: The Case of *Love + Guts: Skateboarding Killed the Art Show*   151
ROBERT E. RINEHART

11 Anhedonia and Alternative Sports   180
ROBERT E. RINEHART

12 Be Happy, Play Sport?: Governing Happiness via the Promotion of Sport   195
RICHARD PRINGLE

Authors   209
References   211
Author Index   235
Subject Index   239

Figures

7.1	Bogor, nr. Jakarta, Java, Indonesia	104
10.1	Outside Manky Chops Gallery	166
10.2	'Solitude'	167
10.3	'Forever Rolling' and 'Mike's Will'	168
10.4	'Drain it, ride it'; 'Early Release'; 'Dive In'; 'Dive In'; 'Early Release'; 'Drain it, ride it'	170
10.5	'Get rotten'	171
10.6	'Adro hand'	173
10.7	'Untitled'	174
10.8	'Drawings'	175
10.9	'Non Compliance' and 'Six Fingers'	176

Acknowledgments

RICHARD PRINGLE

My contributions to this text have been enriched through discussions with Doug Booth, Mark Falcous—my erudite doctoral students Anita Harman and Gōran Gerdin—and, of course, Dixie, Zachary and Luke (who have taught me a lot about pleasure). I have also appreciated the experience and learned considerably through writing with Bob and Jayne: your collective intellect, wit and friendship are warmly regarded.

ROBERT E. RINEHART

I wish to acknowledge Richard and Jayne, whose work continues to inspire me. Our affective negotiations regarding the directions, foci and integration of our creative endeavors were highly pleasurable: good colleagues, co-authors and friends always raise (hopefully) one's game. As always, I also want to thank my grown children—who are now young adults—Nick and Aly. They continually delight me and make me proud to be their dad. I thank this wonderful island-nation, Aotearoa, for allowing me to live here, and I thank the people, both Indigenous and otherwise, who live here, for graciously co-existing with me. I would be remiss if I didn't thank my colleagues at the University of Waikato. We often naturalize our daily workings, and glamorize other places ('the grass is always greener') but, on the whole, it is a totally 'rad' place to work and play.

I dedicate my part of this volume to my childhood friend, Brian E. Hunt.

JAYNE CAUDWELL

Many people help shape a creative project such as a book. I thank my family, friends and work colleagues for their on-going encouragement and support. Especially, I thank Richard and Bob for the many happy times we have

xii *Acknowledgments*

shared during the process of writing. These include focused and unfocused meetings, numerous quirky and witty e-mail correspondences, earnest metaphysical questioning and the explicit appreciation of each other's points of view. I will miss the pleasures of our collaborations, especially as our academic worlds are becoming more individualized.

I dedicate this pleasure book to Keri Allen (22.7.63–19.8.12)

1 Proem
Sport and the Social Significance of Pleasure

Richard Pringle, Robert E. Rinehart and Jayne Caudwell

This is a book about sporting pleasures. It is not a text on how to maximize experiences of pleasure in sport settings, but a critical socio-cultural examination of the significance of pleasure in the constitution of the sporting world, identities and sets of relations of power. The multiple pleasures derived from sport are productive in constituting subjectivities, social belongings, nationalistic fervor and, for some, even reasons for living. However, the examination of sport pleasure has not been a central topic of examination within sport sociology. Given that sport centers on embodied action and the pursuit of excitement, Joseph Maguire (1992) noted it is strange that pleasure, as an integral aspect of human life, has not received greater attention from sociologists of sport.

Within this text we, accordingly, aim to examine the social significance of sport pleasures and promote it as a topic worthy of extensive consideration. Through this examination of sporting pleasures we reveal the importance of pleasure in human lives, and how pleasure is integral to prime sociological issues such as identity formations, power relations and social transformation. In this manner, we gain greater understanding not only of sport, but also of contemporary cultures, humans and social issues.

We view sporting pleasures as productive or constitutive in many of the same ways that Foucault (1990) viewed the workings of power. Foucault did not view power as primarily coercive, but as the inspirational force that underpinned the production of actions, relations, identities and ways of living. Power and pleasure, in this respect, can be understood as discursive, enacted and embodied. We, correspondingly, signal our linkages to post-structural and postmodern theorizing, but stress that we examine pleasure through multiple theoretical and methodological approaches throughout the text.

Our interest in examining pleasure arose in part from our recognition that the sociological study of sport had been predominantly focused on issues and problems, such as the critical excavation of racism, sexism, nationalism, violence and homophobia. We applaud such examinations, yet also recognize that humans primarily play or watch sport in pursuit of pleasure. Our concern was not simply that sporting pleasures have been

2 *Richard Pringle et al.*

typically marginalized as a topic of examination, but that they have not been widely understood as playing an important role in constituting sporting contexts, politics and identities. As critical sociologists with a desire to transform rather than just know the social world, it became apparent to us that it is also important to examine how sporting pleasures are connected to the development and maintenance of various sporting problems. We tentatively suggest, as examples, that the sexualization of sportswomen in the media is likely produced in relation to the instrumental pleasures of objectification and voyeurism (see Chapter 5), that the tight restrictions associated with performing gender and sexuality in sport are linked to the rewards of social acceptance and normalization (see Chapter 9) and that the risk of sporting pain and injury is negotiated in relation to the potential of experiencing a diverse array of pleasures (e.g. the rush of BASE jumping, the production of a comforting sense of self via continued sport participation, the friendship of teammates, the stoke of surfing, the joy of burning muscles after a workout or the freedom of thought that the banality and aesthetics of jogging can produce). Each of these forms of sporting pleasure, given the social dynamics that they constitute and are constituted by, deserves in-depth examination.

Within the last two decades there has been what some have called a turn to emotion and affect within academia. This turn has spurred the development of new fields of study (e.g. hedonic psychology, happiness studies), theorizing (e.g. affect theories, life satisfaction theories, the concept of subjective wellbeing) and political actions. The United Nations (UN) has recently adopted, as an example, a resolution for all member states to give greater consideration to happiness in their economic and social development policies. In relation to this resolution, the UN proclaimed March 20 the International Day of Happiness with the aim that this day will be observed in an appropriate manner, via education and public awareness-raising activities, to promote happiness, wellbeing, poverty eradication and sustainable development.

Although the topics of pleasure and happiness are currently receiving increased attention within academia (including sport studies), these topics have been of interest to a diverse range of distinguished scholars, religious leaders and politicians for centuries. Aristotle, Jeremy Bentham, Sigmund Freud and the Dalai Lama, as diverse examples, all agreed that the attainment of happiness was the prime goal and purpose of life. Thomas Jefferson justified the need for government, in part, by his belief that the pursuit of happiness is an inalienable right. Transnational corporations are also well aware of the marketing importance of pleasure and happiness. The Coca-Cola Company has long striven to connect the consumption of their products with the apparent pleasures of youthful, active, athletic bodies that are (perhaps ironically) toned, thin and fit. The company's recent global marketing campaign simply advises consumers that they can 'open happiness'. In neoliberal times, happiness and pleasure are states of mind that can seemingly be purchased. Indeed, consumers are routinely 'informed' that their lives will be better, happier and more pleasurable if they drink a certain beer, drive a particular car, join a gym, lose weight, have whiter/straighter teeth or support the (men's) national or regional sporting team. Yet if we fail in our pursuit of pleasure we are still told 'don't worry, be happy'. The ubiquitous happy face '☺' now populates the ends of text messages and emails. Happiness, as such, has become an imperative for (post)modern life and irrespective of our inner state of mind, there is increased pressure on people to at least appear happy. Despite such moral imperatives, official rates of depression have grown in recent years.

Although there is much agreement that humans strive for happiness and are motivated by pleasures, there is also considerable debate about how to achieve these emotional/affective states. Socrates, for example, argued for the higher pleasures of the intellect, whereas the Cyrenaics (an ultra-hedonist Greek school of philosophy) countered by asserting that bodily pleasures, being easier to attain and more vivid, were superior (Internet Encyclopedia of Philosophy, 2013). The Cyrenaics even encouraged 'living for the moment' rather than worrying about the future and, thus, advocated the pursuit of whatever caused the greatest pleasure now. Needless to say, this crude form of hedonism that countered mainstream Greek ethics did not have a long existence, yet it can be considered as a precursor to Epicureanism, which has had more lasting impact. Indeed, many notable figures have identified with Epicureanism, including Thomas Jefferson, Jeremy Bentham, Christopher Hitchens and French philosopher Michel Onfray.

Regardless of these lifestyle/pleasure debates there appears a widespread, but typically unquestioned, agreement that playing sport is an important activity that can produce pleasure and create social and physical benefits. Indeed, many parents/guardians encourage their children to play sport due to these beliefs. Yet, somewhat erroneously, the first question they often ask their children upon returning from sport is 'did you win?' as opposed to 'did you have fun?', thus emphasizing the benefits of competition rather than the potential joys of movement. Many governments (e.g. England, Scotland, New Zealand, Australia, Canada) now also promote sport participation as a biopolitical strategy to allegedly enhance their population's level of well-being and happiness (see Chapter 10). Sport Scotland, for example, primarily aims to help more people *enjoy* the benefits of sport.

Whether or not playing sport is a prudent strategy for attaining pleasure and happiness, we acknowledge that scholars of sport and physical education—such as biomechanists, exercise physiologists or sociologists—have all been typically seduced by the pleasures of sport at some stage within their life trajectories. These pleasures have subsequently shaped their identities, lifestyles, educational and career pathways. Douglas Booth (2009: 133) even contended that pleasure can be understood 'as a potential pillar of disciplinary coherence in physical education', as sporting pleasures act as a glue to connect interdisciplinary scholars of disparate beliefs.

4   *Richard Pringle et al.*

Some critical sociologists of sport also appear to be sport fans. At a relatively recent conference for the North American Society for the Sociology of Sport (NASSS) it was announced that a professional ice hockey match was being played that evening and if anybody wanted to attend that transport was being arranged. A palpable buzz subsequently circulated among some of the delegates. Yet this announcement seemed somewhat out of place, as the day's program of papers had overwhelmingly revolved around densely theorized critiques of sport. Concerns, for example, had been raised about the connections between violence on and off the field of play, various problems within National Collegiate Athletics Association (NCAA), inequitable gendered relations of power and even the need for greater political activism among sport sociologists. Hence, the encouragement to attend a 'men's only' professional ice hockey match, no doubt replete with acts of violence, seemed to be in opposition to the underpinning politics of the conference program. We do recognize, however, that one can be a social critic of sport but still enjoy participating in or watching it. George Sage (1990), paraphrasing US Senator J. William Fulbright, even argued that he was critical of sport because he cared for and wanted to improve it. Sage accordingly portrayed critical analyses of sport as acts of redemption in the service of sport.

The writing of this text would not likely have eventuated if it were not for our own formative experiences of sporting pleasure. Richard acknowledges that it was his identity-affirming experiences on the rugby field as a ten year-old, in his red colored jersey for Tahunanui School, that eventually led him to study physical education at university. Although now a stern critic of rugby, he still gains pleasure (and pain) on the tennis court. Robert swam competitively from age six, broke his collarbone twice playing 'pick-up' football with his brothers' friends, loved the aggression, the joy of physical contact and tackling, and yet ended up concentrating on swimming and more solitary pursuits, like training for (running) marathons. Jayne has a long-term, often intense and troublesome, love affair with numerous forms of physical activity. Over many years, she struggled to disengage from the competitive nature of human movement and now finds solace in the non-serious and playful aspects of sport.

EXPLAINING HOW WE WROTE THE BOOK OF PLEASURE

Despite growing up and living most of our lives in different parts of the world (Jayne in England, Richard in Aotearoa New Zealand and Robert in California), we developed similar research interests, approaches and axiologies. Although our topics of examination were different, we all drew from qualitative research methods, adopted postmodern and/or poststructural sensibilities and had an interest in critical analyses of sport that we hoped would challenge injustices and inequities. It was somewhat serendipitous, therefore, that in 2010, when Jayne was on leave from the University of

Proem 5

Brighton, we found ourselves living in close proximity to each other in Aotearoa New Zealand. Robert had recently begun work in Hamilton at the University of Waikato, Richard was based 'up the road' at the University of Auckland and Jayne was in Raglan, a town with a renowned left-hand surf break within a 30 minute drive of Hamilton. We subsequently had an opportune get together at a party held in Raglan, and eventually found ourselves talking about the sociological significance of sporting pleasures. Not long after, we came to a general agreement to write this book.

Discussions concerning the writing of this text took place at each other's places of residence, in various cafes, at conferences and via Skype. Within the initial meetings we debated, among other factors, whether we wanted to produce a text akin to a handbook of the sociology of sporting pleasure (with various chapters exploring topics such as sporting pleasures and the media, politics, gender and identity formation) or a text that better represented the 'feel' and malleable nature of pleasures. Inspired by Susan Bordo (1999: 29), who claimed that 'cultural interpretation is an ongoing, always incomplete process, and no one gets the final word', we opted for the latter style, and subsequently developed a text that reflected the somewhat chaotic and, at times, contradictory nature of pleasure. As authors, we had noted, for example, how we had each gained differing sporting pleasures in pursuits that were often painful or repetitive, from running marathons (Jayne), playing rugby (Richard) or staring at the bottom of the pool in swimming lap after lap (Robert).

We also discussed whether the book should be underpinned by one or multiple theoretical approaches. At first we thought there would be greater coherence within the text if one theoretical approach dominated. Yet we eventually decided that there was value in examining pleasure from multiple perspectives. We accordingly drew on diverse theories, concepts and research approaches to examine and reveal the multifaceted, varied and changing nature of sporting pleasures. We also drew from differing disciplines (e.g. philosophy, history, psychology and even biology) yet our prime interests remain grounded in sociology and cultural studies.

We also debated whether to present the chapters as co- or individually authored. Given that our understandings of pleasure had been shaped by our differing lived experiences and theoretical lenses, and that we each have different writing styles, we agreed to write the chapters as individuals. We did, however, carefully read, discuss and debate each other's chapters and, at times, ideas/paragraphs or sections were swapped into other chapters. In this respect, the various chapters reflect a combined effort, but we decided to state that the chapters were 'primarily' written individually. With reflection, we agree that our different interests, writing styles, philosophies and theoretical underpinnings have helped produce a rich, diverse and, hopefully, pleasurable text.

Our examination of pleasure, as such, might seem 'messy', yet we believe that this is an apt representational style given that we were examining an

6   *Richard Pringle et al.*

intangible, often ephemeral feeling that is often taken for granted and difficult to define, but is of considerable social significance. We use the word messy in relation to John Law's (2004) ideas on messiness in social science research. He argued that social science researchers have developed robust ways of examining some relatively 'stable realities' (p. 2), such as income distributions and terms of trade, yet the traditional methods have not worked well to capture the realities of more slippery phenomena such as 'pains and pleasures, hopes and horrors, intuitions and apprehensions, losses and redemptions, mundanities and visions . . . things that slip and slide, or appear or disappear, change shape or don't have much form at all . . .' (p. 2). Pleasure is clearly one of these slippery phenomena, as last night's 'pleasure' can be this morning's 'horror'. Law argues that when social scientists try to simplify the realities of messy phenomena they make more of a mess, as they oversimplify and do not capture the fluid complexities. He accordingly advocates methods that do not provide tidy conclusions or single answers and encourages greater methodological variety, the blurring of disciplinary boundaries and innovative ways of knowing, such as forms of knowing via embodiment, 'private' emotions and poetics. Our text subsequently employs a variety of methods, the use of poetics and autoethnography, and boundary crossing in its examination of sport pleasures. A recognized advantage of a messy text is that it can work in an ethical and political manner to reflect 'diverse and potentially contradictory experiences—rather than reducing them to a singular Truth or voice' (Avner et al., 2013: 2).

INTRODUCING THE TEXT

Our broad aim in co-writing this text, as already stated, was to reveal and promote the social significance of pleasure. Yet we also wanted to illustrate that by examining sporting issues via a focus on pleasure, one can gain a new way of looking at these issues. In other words, we wanted to show how a 'pleasure' lens could encourage ways of seeing things afresh. A pleasure lens in this sense could be understood as akin to a theoretical tool, as it can direct our attention and change our social and sociological imaginations (cf. Mills, 1959), allowing new insights and possibilities.

To achieve these broad aims we decided to examine the importance of sporting pleasures by linking them to an array of diverse topics. We explored the ubiquitous ability of pleasure to shape human lives by connecting the relevance of pleasure to topics as diverse as biopolitics and the governing of active citizens and sexuality pleasures within sporting contexts. We also illustrated the importance of lived experiences of pleasures, those that are perhaps the most tangible, by examining the pleasures of moving (running) and consuming mediated sport (watching the Olympics). We also complicated the place of pleasure by examining topics that some might mistakenly believe have little connection to sporting pleasures: feminism and aging.

Proem 7

In order to do justice to this diverse array of topics, the first section of the book introduces and examines the concept of pleasure. This is a concept that many feel needs no introduction, as people know 'pleasure' when they feel it or live it. Yet there is overlap, and at times confusion, between synonyms such as pleasure, joy, fun, happiness, ecstasy, jouissance (cf. Barthes, 1975) and satisfaction. This blurring of terms exists not only in the literature but also within people's life trajectories, as Aristotle explained: a life of gratification and pleasure does not necessarily constitute a life of happiness, yet a happy life can be pleasant.

In **Chapter 2**, Robert delves deeper into the concept of pleasure by illustrating its complex and diverse nature and its dis/connections to hedonism, happiness, delight and even shame and guilt. He provocatively notes that pleasure requiring a detailed introduction 'speaks volumes to our Western, hegemonic Judeo-Christian approach to the subject'. In other words, he argues that the influence of religion in Western societies has contributed a sense of shame to select bodily pleasures (e.g. dance, sport, alcohol and sex) and that this shame is one reason why pleasure has been marginalized as scholarly topic of analysis. Robert subsequently contends that as pleasure can be regarded as a prime mover within human life, we should strive to make pleasure the default setting so that the quality of pleasure becomes a key focus of examination and the development of social policies. Robert concludes by drawing from Foucault to suggest that the prime task of the book is to prompt awareness of the social significance of pleasure by luring 'pleasure' out into the open.

The introduction to the concept of pleasure continues in **Chapter 3**, with Richard providing a short history of the places of pleasure in Western cultures and its tangential links to issues within contemporary sport. The inspiration for the chapter was Huizinga's (1970/1938) contention that play has been significant in the development of human civilizations. The chapter's selective history correspondingly examines this contention by drawing from the writings of various scholars and traversing time from the Ancient Greeks (via the writings of Aristotle, Foucault and Nietzsche) to studies of the medieval (Bakhtin), to the enlightenment (John Locke, Jeremy Bentham, Mary Wollstonecraft) to, finally, the 20th century, with help from Sigmund Freud and Herbert Marcuse. This historical sketch of pleasure allows insight into its somewhat amorphous nature, given it has been conceptualized as constitutive and destructive, embodied and disembodied, natural and socially constructed, political and subjective, serious and insignificant, and good and evil. Perhaps the prime lesson learned from this historical analysis is that although humans have long been concerned about pleasure and happiness, the civilizations they have constructed and their associated leisure pursuits, such as sport, have not necessarily solved the issue of how to attain pleasure and happiness.

The diverse characteristics of pleasure, as illustrated in Chapters 2 and 3, and the associated links between pleasure and the body (e.g. adrenaline rush,

8 *Richard Pringle et al.*

goose-bumps, shivers of excitement), socio-cultural context and mindset provide a challenge with respect to how to theorize sporting pleasures. In **Chapter 4** Richard examines this by discussing the difficulties and benefits of interdisciplinary approaches with respect to the possibilities of producing a rapprochement between sociology and psychology and/or a more body-aware sociology. The chapter then selectively examines theories of sporting pleasure that have been used within sociology (e.g. affect theories, body-reflexive practices, edge theory), biology (i.e. runners high) and psychology (flow theory). Richard illustrates that although there are advantages through studying sport pleasures 'in the round' (Elias and Dunning, 1986), interdisciplinary approaches are difficult to undertake in light of the problems of epistemological boundary crossings. He nevertheless concludes that there is value in theorizing and examining pleasure from multiple perspectives and in reading across the disciplines.

Jayne extends discussion concerning theorizing in **Chapter 5** by illustrating that one productive way of examining sporting pleasures is via feminist theorizing, particularly in relation to the French feminists Hélène Cixous, Luce Irigaray and Julia Kristeva. Feminist critiques of sport have become somewhat *de rigueur* within the sociology of sport, yet a less flattering view of feminism pervades mainstream society where feminists are regarded, by some, as a 'killjoys' (e.g. see Sara Ahmed's blog http://feministkilljoys.com). Yet sport feminism, in our view, is distinctly tied to pleasure/happiness, as it aims to enrich the lives of females through challenging unjust practices, policies (e.g. the IOC's sex testing regime) and disrespectful representations and, of course, promoting equitable opportunities to enjoy sport participation. Within this chapter Jayne excavates the complex links between sport, pleasure, femininity, beauty, sex and sexuality.

Chapter 6 turns from feminist pleasures to examine the pleasures of aging bodies. There are times in life when most youth look forward to being older; aging at these times is equated with increased ability, responsibility and freedom. The desire of a 13 year-old basketballer to be 18 might equate with a yearning to be taller, increased ability to shoot three-pointers, to play in the 'seniors' or to travel independently to games. Yet for most adults, perhaps more so for keen sport participants, the idea of aging into one's 30s, 50s or even 90s, is not typically looked upon with relish. In this chapter, Robert's literary approach uniquely explores differing worldviews on aging by drawing from poetry to compare Western and Eastern (Japanese and Korean) philosophies toward the (dis)pleasures of aging. He contends that the masculine ethos of the Western sporting world, which exemplifies competition and a fighting spirit, underpins attitudes towards the aging athletic body. Correspondingly, the aging body must 'fight the good fight' and not 'go gently' with respect to aging. His interpretations of select poems from the East, in contrast, reveal a more optimistic view of aging and an acceptance, even celebration, of imperfect bodies and the natural processes of getting older.

Proem 9

The following three chapters provide more empirical studies of the plea-sures associated with performing and consuming sport. In **Chapter 7**, Jayne co-opts scholarly literature, sporting narratives and her own experiences to provide a highly personal and moving account of the pleasures of running—a form of autoethnography. She illustrates the socio-cultural connections between running, class, gender, sexuality and the disciplined pleasures of performance, measurement and efficiency. She then raises concern about these achievement-based pleasures and, in following Margaret Wetherell's (2012: 75) recognition of the importance of providing more 'dynamic, sen-sual and lively accounts of social life', vividly reveals running as an affec-tual practice. Jayne's aim, in part, is to blur the emotional and physical to emphasize the visceral, sensual, emotional and ludic aspects of running.

The exploration of affectual practices is continued in **Chapter 8** with a focus on the embodied pleasures of watching the Olympics. Critical stud-ies of media representations of sport have tended to focus on discursive/political messages rather than the affective/corporeal dimensions. Yet by bypassing these dimensions there is a risk that these critical studies produce limited insight for understanding how sport media productions garner such popularity. In this chapter, Richard introduces and undertakes an analysis of the role of affect associated with the production of viewing pleasures of the Olympics. He confesses that although he was highly critical of the expenditure and politics associated with the staging of the 2012 Olympics he nevertheless found himself to be an embodied fan. To explain this appar-ent contradiction he draws on Brian Ott's (2010) multi-modal analytical approach for examining cinematic rhetoric and analyzes two video clips of the London 2012 Olympics. The results reveal how the mediated techniques employed in broadcasting the Games can work to encourage uncritical cel-ebrations of the Olympics and thus allow the Games to be staged with con-tinued expense and little political protest. Richard concludes by discussing the importance of the politics of affect.

In **Chapter 9**, Jayne extends the analysis of the pleasures of being a sport fan through recognition that the majority of fandom studies have focused on so-called traditional fans, and traditional aspects—such as chanting, drink-ing, group solidarity, hooliganism and issues of class and resistance, with a particular focus on white, heterosexual able-bodied males. Yet these studies have tended to omit 'pleasure', which is undoubtedly a central experience to being a fan. She reveals the significance and complexities of the pleasures of being a fan through an in-depth interview study with 'Paula', a fan of Nor-wich City Football Club (UK) who self-identifies as transgender, transsexual and queer. Jayne provides an intriguing analysis that reveals how Paula first became a football fan, her experiences of transitioning and the resulting impact her new identity has had on her fandom. Although Paula experiences moments of discomfort in relation to the sexist, homophobic and racist cul-tures that exist on the terraces, for the most part she experiences a freedom

10 *Richard Pringle et al.*

from her identity when she vanishes or blends into the crowd and shares the same diverse emotional—almost uncontrollable—experiences of pleasure. Throughout this chapter the politics of pleasure, identities and sexualities are scrutinized.

In **Chapter 10**, Robert examines *Love + Guts*, an art exhibition themed around skateboarding, with respect to the pleasures it affords to skaters, the viewing public and the artists. Drawing from Foucault, Baudrillard, Baumann, Benjamin and others, he introduces the theoretical framework that underpins his 'snapshot ethnographic' examination by discussing the links between aesthetics, hyper-reality, consumer life and the judgment of tastes. Robert's subsequent examination of the artworks reveals, in part, the tensions between skateboarding and art and an art show that is seemingly anti-establishment but is sponsored by Oakley sunglasses. His analysis of the three prime motifs that dominate the exhibition (skateboarding nostalgia, pain and suffering, and the absence and place of girls and women) reveals that the potential of the aesthetic to trump the culture of skateboarding fails. He concludes that the skateboarding artworks provide a pedagogy of the hyper-masculine.

In **Chapter 11**, Robert examines the pleasure or, more aptly, displeasure effects of extreme or thrill sports. He links the neoliberal turn, the subsequent commodification of alternative sports and the flattening of affect to suggest that the extreme sport participant, as akin to a consumer within capitalism, is never completely satisfied. He provocatively argues that extreme sport participants live a paradoxical life in that they experience a vague sense of inability to experience pleasure yet are still urged to experience intense forms of pleasure, seize the moment and push the envelope. Robert concludes that this contemporary pleasure paradox is difficult to escape from.

In **Chapter 12**, we turn from pleasure shaped by commerce to pleasure as regulated via the state in Richard's exploration of the connections between sport participation, subjective wellbeing and governmentality. He notes that Western governments have realized the significance of a population's level of happiness and have begun designing social policy for the associated biopolitical management of citizens. This shift in policy, he suggests, is now shaping the aims of national sporting organizations. The global encouragement of mass participation in sport has correspondingly become an important public policy issue, with claims that sport participation can enhance public health, reduce anxiety and depression and enhance a population's sense of wellbeing and levels of happiness. But Richard questions whether the promotion of sport participation can really achieve such aims. In following Valerie Harwood (2008), who encouraged critical exploration of how truths and knowledges about the body and life are circulated via techniques of biopower, he questions why sport is prioritized as a governance strategy to promote wellbeing and happiness. Through reviewing the limited literature that has specifically examined the connections between sport (not exercise) and subjective wellbeing, he argues that governmental attempts to enhance a population's wellbeing via promotion of sport are currently unfounded, potentially futile and, at worst, problematic. Richard concludes by discussing more prudent public policy strategies that can be employed to enhance a population's state of happiness.

As might be expected of a 'messy' text (see Law, 2004) we eschew the opportunity to provide a tidy conclusion or a set of definitive last words but hope that the text works as an 'opening rather than a closing' (Law, 2004: 2).

2 Pleasures Small and Large

Robert E. Rinehart

What is this thing—or rather, are these things—we call 'pleasure'? Is it whimsy, as Katie Gosset (2014) posits about The Inconvenience Store in Christchurch, Aotearoa New Zealand? In this store, according to one of the rotating shop keepers, 'you can't buy [items] with money, we only want your time . . . the catch is that you have to spend the whole time in the shop, while it is being made for you. . . .' The very idea of 'inconvenience' creates a *frisson* with normative Western capitalistic expectations of shops. It is 'part shop, part art installation, part joke, and part flight of fancy'. It is a contemporary 'pleasure' project, meant for an earthquake-traumatized Christchurch. But through it, according to the Inconvenience Store's 'creator', Ryan Reynolds, runs not simply whimsy, but also perhaps social commentary: '[it can be] a kind of comment on our fast pace of contemporary life, to be able to walk into a shop and buy and often without thinking about how it's made, where it's come from. . . .'

Outside-of-the-box thinking, creative processes, spontaneity—these are some of the components of what makes The Inconvenience Store pleasurable. These kinds of surprises also grant some insight in to how sportspeople 'pleasure' themselves through their own and others' physical movement.

It is clear that the allure of pleasure itself runs a broad spectrum, meandering from the satisfaction of a job well done to physical release within a sport action; from the pleasure of the company of good mates simultaneously accomplishing a team sport task to a surfer's sublime, tacit recognition of the vastness of the sea, the horizon, the sunrise; from sharing dangerous (or aesthetic) experiences to a dazzled, deep engagement with a 'beautiful' work of art (as seen in the aesthetic appeal of human form and accomplished movement). And just as surely, pleasure is a multifaceted, complex construct, rarely appearing (even in sport!) by itself. Oftentimes, 'pleasure' is mixed with other affects—it is mitigated by competing feelings—and the combination can at once be overwhelming and powerful.

'Pleasure', then, can take place within many realms: emotional, intellectual, visceral, social, physical—the list goes on. Pleasure itself is a very complex set of overlapping ideas about what it means to enjoy aspects of life. As with 'definitions' of play (or games or sport), attempts at defining pleasure—at describing each instance of it in sport—are problematic. To attempt to pin down what

Pleasures Small and Large 13

'pleasure' constitutes is like having a debate about who was the best boxer, Muhammad Ali or Mike Tyson. Rather, illustrations of what pleasure might *mean* (in this case in a sporting context) may more readily sketch out its complex characteristics and begin an examination of how we might identify pleasure in sport, take notice of it and increase opportunities for an appreciation of deep and genuine sporting pleasures.

One of the points of the extremely variable examples above is that pleasure as a concept is not easily quantified or even agreed-upon by its common characteristics or facets: pleasure is a complex, multi-directional and -dimensional concept that, situationally, may demonstrate the subjectivities of a pleasured subject's response. But one person's pleasure (and joy, fun, enjoyment, jouissance, and other stand-ins that do not quite match *pleasure*) may make no sense to another: how can a man (or woman) experience pleasure in the juxtaposed midst of violent fear, agony and pain—even psychic pain—for example? How might young men become seduced into believing, as Isabel Allende (2008[1991]) reminds us, that the camaraderie of war, the pleasures of brotherhood amid terror and fear, is the peak experience of pleasure in their lives? In short, how might pleasure co-exist with the reality of pain, loss, negative affect—and, in fact, be enhanced by that very tensioned and conflictual co-existence?

In this book, we seek to examine the intersections of pleasure (and its antecedents and synonyms) with contemporary sporting practices and cultures. Because this is an initial venture into this particular topic, we shall trace the historical, philosophical and academic threads regarding pleasure—both in a global, non-sporting sense and in a specifically sport-related sense.

In discussing Epicurus (341–270 BC), Julia Annas (1993) points out several historical anomalies: 1) the way Epicurus (and other Hellenites) viewed 'pleasure' as the ultimate goal in life was more thoughtful than presently conceived; 2) 'pleasure', in ancient Epicurean texts (most of which have been lost), is framed quite differently than modern and contemporary definitions; 3) in the Epicurean philosophy, pleasure consists of absence of pain and of living a virtuous life. More specifically, 'happiness applies to the agent's life as a whole' (Annas, 1993: 46); this happiness is shaped by daily actions, but those actions are shaped by 'intelligence or *phronēsis*' (Annas, 1993: 85) that is, in turn, directed by virtue.

Furthermore, Epicurus divided 'pleasure' into 'kinetic' and 'static' pleasures ('. . . *ataraxia*, the state of being untroubled, unhindered in one's activities') (Annas, 1993: 85), consisting of three types of desires: 'some are natural and necessary, some are natural but not necessary, and some are neither natural nor necessary' (cited from Epicurus' *Vaticanae Sententiae* in Annas, 1993: 190). As Annas puts it,

> Pleasure understood as an untroubled overall state is not the kinds of things that we can produce units of; nor does it even allow of quantitative comparison of an ordinal kind in any obvious way. (1993: 85–86)

14   Robert E. Rinehart

The virtuous subject would assess individual acts of pleasure/pain, determine if they were in alignment with her Epicurean philosophy and if they would, on the whole, lead to more overall pleasure, then act. In thus accommodating the painful with the pleasant, Epicurus wrote:

> . . . we do not choose every pleasure, but sometimes we pass over many pleasures, when greater annoyance follows for us from them, and we judge many pains superior to pleasures, when greater pleasure follows along for us when we endure the pains for a long time. Every pleasure, therefore, because of having a nature which is familiar to us [*oikeian*] is a good, but not every pleasure is to be chosen, just as every pain is a bad thing, but not every pain is always naturally to be avoided. . . . we make use of the good on some occasions as a bad thing, and the bad, conversely, as a good. (*Epistuala ad Menaeceum* in Annas, 1993: 85)

I would suggest that sporting pleasures often are of the latter kind: 'when we judge many pains superior to pleasures, when greater pleasure follows along for us when we endure the pains for a long time' (ibid.).

Finally, Annas (1993: 236) points out how Epicurus was grounded in the everyday virtuous as well as the trajectory of one's life: 'Epicurus . . . has no idea how to conceive of the end [pleasure] . . . if he removes pleasures such as those of taste and hearing, the pleasures of sex and of seeing beautiful objects'. The sensory apprehension—the linkage to the proprioceptive and tactile, to sight and sound—is fundamental to ultimate pleasure within a lived life.

Sporting struggle, success and participation, as best I can imagine, would likely fall into the 'natural but not necessary' realm of kinetic pleasures on the way to a pleasant life. In the realm of sporting pleasure, it is evident that kinetic pleasure is enhanced by the successful struggle, which may be natural but not necessary or not natural and not necessary, depending upon one's subjective outlook. As Orwell puts it,

> Serious sport has nothing to do with fair play. It is bound up with hatred, jealousy, boastfulness, disregard of all rules and sadistic pleasure in witnessing violence: in other words it is war minus the shooting. (1970: 63)

Often, however—paradoxically—the harder the struggle, the sweeter the success. So, pleasures may derive from such seemingly antipathetic contexts, as Orwell suggests. This parallel/dual/multiple nature of pleasure and pain is present in ancient Indian stories of 'the well-known god Siva who is, at one and the same time, both creator and destroyer' (Maffesoli, 1993: 32). The tension that exists between two competing impulses often creates more, not less, pleasure when it is resolved.[1]

According to some scholars, the enactment of these social performances is not always a learned, socially constructed effort (cf. Berger and Luckmann, 1966), but may be hard-wired into human consciousness. It is likely, of

Pleasures Small and Large 15

course, that the striving for—or avoidance of—pleasure is both a biological imperative and a socially constructed warning: in many historical examples, pleasure has been stultified, muted, tamped down in the name of increased civility, surveillance and control. And, just as historically, the backlash against such attempts at control results, at least for a while, in heightened attempts at pleasure (cf. Bakhtin, 1984; Gillette, 2005).

Nevertheless, pleasure as a motivator, as a perversity, as a driving force (among, admittedly, many other forces) seems to be ubiquitous. While pleasure—both broadly as a concept and specifically as an individual goal—remains a basic tenet of what it means to be human, the academic study of pleasure in Western popular culture,[2] and more certainly in sport, has been comparatively ignored.

There are twin postulations underpinning this dearth of study: one assumption regarding pleasure is that, because of its historical ubiquity and hegemony within human cultures and societies, most of us already 'know' what dimensions it takes, what limits it may have, what characteristics it embodies. A second assumption derives from a guilt regarding things pleasurable that runs through Western Judeo-Christian thought (cf. Bakhtin, 1984). Though related, these postulations regarding pleasure, especially within the contemporary study of sport, are only just beginning to be investigated, and their very invisibility highlights the lack of interest in the study of pleasure within sport and sporting practices.

The first assumption posits that we need not talk about that which we already tacitly know (and presumably agree upon). In the case of 'pleasure', this stance is age-old, leads to structural strictures that create barriers to pleasure, works as an ephemeral panopticon and serves to delimit discussion (cf. Foucault, 1990a, 1990b). (It also works to reinforce strong conservative rhetorics of scientific knowledge within the 'social sciences'.) By confronting our own surroundings, however, we in fact often learn more about that with which we already may be intimately familiar: in order to better understand a process or concept or value, we need to make it strange, or see it with a new lens (cf. Kuhn, 1996).

In the case of the study of pleasure in sport, I suggest that there exists a need for scholars to become mindful of *examples, types* and *degrees* of pleasure. In short, if pleasure is a prime mover within life activity, we must begin to take notice of the very existence of pleasure, both explicit and tacit, within sporting culture, and make it visible. We should strive to proactively create a world where pleasure stands as the default setting, and where quality of pleasure(s) becomes the object of serious examination and one of the goals of community policy.

As an example of this first assumption, sport itself is tacitly assumed to be pleasurable; otherwise, why would an individual participate in it? Like play (and pleasure), sport is something we all seem to *know* about, but something that is quite difficult to pin down. *We*, many of us say, *know it when we see it.* And the pleasure in sport—though there are many examples

16 Robert E. Rinehart

of displeasure or unpleasurable occurrences within sport, many distasteful aspects to its very unfolding—seems to be a part of that unexamined mix. To begin to unravel 'problems' in sport, it may be enlightening to get back to understanding basic joy in movement, to celebrating the pleasure that physically active bodies may give us—and to understand why and for whom this pleasure works.

There may be a way through the second assumption—that a sense of shame and guilt pervades (particularly) Western, Judeo-Christian ethics to such an extent that it disallows not only the enjoyment of things pleasurable, but the very recognition, study and discussion of such matters. Pleasure, in this sense, remains a bit of an untouched taboo. Threaded throughout sport discourse—and much of physical education—is this rhetoric that that which is not pleasurable 'will make us stronger'.[3] Though substantially imbricated within the fabric of Western society, this—for want of a more elegant term—'cultural baggage' is nevertheless socially constructed, and so it can be dismantled. But it requires study. It requires lifting the veils from 'pleasure' so that we all, at our core, take on the 'given' nature of our own and our community's (however characterized) conceptions of 'pleasures'.

Currently, pleasure of and in the body is often—especially in many Western cultures—seen as 'shameful'. Enjoying pleasure, pleasure in the workplace, pleasuring oneself—all these forms of pleasure are often seen as deviant. Even 'performing' pleasure, in some contexts (like professional sports) is restricted and sanctioned. One only has to note the preponderance of recent rulings banning celebrations after scores as an example of this institutionalized repression of the overt displays of pleasure. Pleasure, in this sense, is the absence of shame, and shame cuts deeply through contemporary Western society. Mikhail Bakhtin (1984), Elspeth Probyn (2005) and Michael Warner (1999) all separately describe shame within 'non-mainstream' culture. Their discussions work to inform an identification of the extent of the problems—and suggest possible solutions as well.

Bakhtin (1984), looking at medieval folk feasts, discusses performative pleasures that individuals take when they disrupt hegemonic roles. His specific writings about the grotesque, degradation, shame and 'laughter' explain the dynamical relationships between dark and light, and between 'the unchanging established order and ideology . . . [and] change and renewal' (Bakhtin, 1984: 81). Probyn (2005: 46) systematically unpacks shame, fear, guilt and humiliation, and writes: 'shame can revisit you long after the particular moment of shaming has passed'. Her categorizations—ancestral shame, intergenerational shame, white shame and bodily shame—establish and examine precise contexts in which shame can be understood.

One possible way of understanding, and a possible way out of the downward spiral of shame (and its companions) may be through the use of a queer 'theoretical' lens, specifically what Michael Warner (1999) terms an 'ethical vision' of queer. In his manifesto, Warner challenges basic assumptions about the genealogy and politics of shame.

Pleasures Small and Large   17

In so doing, Warner lays out some precepts for an ethical vision of queer, in which he suggests:

> In those circles where queerness has been most cultivated, the ground rule is that one doesn't pretend to be *above* the indignity of sex. And although this usually isn't announced as an ethical vision, that's what it perversely is. . . . sex is understood to be as various as the people who have it. It is not required to be tidy, normal, uniform, or authorized by the government. This kind of culture is often denounced as relativist, self-indulgent, or merely libertine. In fact, it has its own norms, its own way of keeping people in line. . . . A relation to others, in these contexts, begins in an acknowledgement of all that is most abject and least reputable in oneself. Shame is bedrock. (Warner, 1999: 35)

In Warner's view, rejecting the norms of larger society (the 'normal') becomes a freeing move towards 'a moving and unexpected form of generosity' (ibid.). This bridge between what Bakhtin (1984) calls the 'upper stratum' and the 'lower stratum' has a place within sport culture, which has become stultified, bureaucratic and, as many 'drop-out' children tell us, not *fun*. One of the reasons is the incipient shame in and of our own bodies.

What Bakhtin terms 'laughter' is what I see as an overall pleasure, but in this case surrounding sport:

> The serious aspects of class culture are official and authoritarian; they are combined with violence, prohibitions, limitations and always contain an element of fear and of intimidation. These elements prevailed in the Middle Ages. Laughter, on the contrary, overcomes fear, for it knows no inhibitions, no limitations. Its idiom is never used by violence and authority. (1984: 90).

The Middle Ages that Bakhtin describes could easily describe contemporary sporting culture, laden heavily with bureaucratic and institutionalized guilt and shame.

Contemporary capitalist advertising culture is driven by desire, which feeds on shame and guilt. While Bakhtin lays out descriptives of the problem, Warner goes a bit further: he rejects the normative view of sexuality (and pleasure of the body) as 'shameful', and by so doing, proposes a way forward that sports scholars as well as general publics might heed. Fundamentally, if Western sports cultures are grounded in a deep sense of shame (and, as an institution of a society grounded in shame, the logics would have that they are), admitting to it, leveling the playing field (reducing hierarchical 'positions') and seeing everyone as equally capable of discovering their own 'pleasures' is a possible way for sportspeople to (re)learn to enjoy bodily pleasures—but also, perhaps, a way for society to de-stigmatize such a perspective.

18　*Robert E. Rinehart*

PLEASURE WITHIN CONTEMPORARY SPORT

As varied as the forms of sport have become, in the late 20th and early 21st Centuries, particularly at the 'top' levels, they are more and more commodified, rigid, restrictive, formulaic, fraught with surveillance (cf. Foucault, 1995; Markula and Pringle, 2006) and predictable: their 'spectacle' value has increased while participation is ever more elite and exclusive (cf. Debord, 1995[1967]). But where is the fun? Where is the joy? Where is the pleasure? One of the ambiguities of contemporary elite sport is that it has taken something that children enter into willingly and joyfully and made it into work (with all accompanying conservative and rigid restrictions).

In asking such questions about fun, joy and pleasure, I acknowledge that there are qualitative differences between such constructs as jouissance, hedonism, joy, fun, affect, happiness and pleasure. Many of these terms—and their synonyms—overlap both in the public consciousness and in real life, and it is often only in specific situations that they are fully understood. I do not intend to delimit these terms to 'variables', because such a reductionistic approach essentially kills what makes the terms vibrant and animated. As Huizinga wrote, 'the *fun* of playing . . . resists all analysis, all logical interpretation' (1955: 3). In this book, then, 'pleasure' comes to mean something that gives positive meaning to an individual or collective life.

Pleasure as a construct is often noted after the act that created it. Pleasure itself can be non-productive, similar to how Huizinga defined 'play':

> Summing up the formal characteristic of play, we might call it a free activity standing quite consciously outside 'ordinary' life as being 'not serious' but at the same time absorbing the player intensely and utterly. It is an activity connected with no material interest, and no profit can be gained by it. It proceeds within its own proper boundaries of time and space according to fixed rules and in an orderly manner. (Huizinga 1955: 13)

It is quite true that many Western theorists have viewed pleasure as 'non-productive', yet I suggest that play itself can be thought of as productive. It is not simply productive in the sense that we as humans enjoy pleasure, instrumentally rated on a one to five Likert Scale; it is productive in that it produces both cultural and symbolic capital (cf. Bourdieu, 1984). It shapes and forms bodies in ways that lack of exposure to the pleasures of physical bodies cannot.

While pleasure in sport or physical activity seems so obvious that it is not even verbalized, it must be spoken. The ranges of pleasure (from, on one hand, displeasure to pleasure, on a unidimensional track (cf. Schimmack, 2001); from lack of pleasure—anhedonia—to exultation in the jouissance of hedonism) also must be noted. If, in the sociology of sport (physical culture), we lack a vocabulary for measures of pleasure, that speaks volumes to our Western, hegemonic Judeo-Christian approach to the subject.

Before we delve deeper into what I mean by pleasure, it might be necessary to place the authors a bit more directly and overtly into our text. When discussing pleasure—and in co-writing this book—we found that we were all coming from at least slightly different philosophical worldviews regarding what pleasure might constitute in individual's living spaces.

While this is typically a question that first-year university students might explore, I think it is critical to the study of pleasure: what is the meaning (or meanings) of life? Do we exist to somehow perpetuate the species (biological determinism)? to gain the most individual pleasure we can (hedonism)? to provide the greatest good for the greatest number (*summum bonum* principle)? There are multitudes of nuanced worldviews that might construct one's values regarding what a good life is.

What then, essentially, might be major determinants for existence, keys to well-lived lives? Answering these fundamental questions may provide windows to how we understand such a concept as pleasure. To wit: pleasure could be re-conceptualized as a combined 'primordial blood lust', relief, joy, excitement, camaraderie, risk; perhaps there can even be, to cite an extreme example, depending upon one's point of view and experiences, a sociopathic joy/thrill in symbolically killing another human being in Laser Tag or Paintball (and yet in war that thrill/agony is 'normalized'). Of course, these extremes only serve to contextualize normative versions of sporting pleasure.

How we experience pleasure, in some ways, indicates how we accept current sporting practices. For example—and we must admit this—if there is pleasure in teasing and making fun of fellow players, it comes out in bullying behaviors in normative sporting practices. When young people learn that intimidation is something to be celebrated, it is no wonder that powerful coaches (who have grown up through that system) perpetuate that particular pleasure upon their charges. As another example, pleasure can reflect the dimensions of bliss that a conscious relationship to nature and the sublime vastness of the universe may instantiate in surfers, trekkers, tri-athletes, climbers and the like.

Not all may agree with Allende that there might be pleasure in war. Or, poignantly, that it should even be noted. Noticing violence, suffering and war (which, incidentally, many team-sport, 'land-acquisition' games are modeled after) as activities tinged with pleasure might seem anathema to a project discussing pleasure in sports.

But, just as hedonism can be described as a subjective response—a matter of one's attitude toward the accrued pleasure, or one's stance toward certain relatively objective situations or actions—so too can pleasure be seen as reflective of one's stance toward the types of pain (inflicting pain, bullying, dominating and so on) that can be found in sport and sport contexts. The kinds of sensory pleasures that accrue from taking part in sport certainly are pleasures that have not been discussed in any large degree, but there are more complex pleasures, sometimes-malevolent pleasures, that come to dominate certain sport forms. It is not coincidental that these pleasures *at the expense of others* are highly regarded in what Hughes and Coakley (1991)

20 *Robert E. Rinehart*

termed 'the sport ethic', particularly in those sports that are power and performance sports as opposed to pleasure and participation sports (e.g. Coakley, 2008).

In utilizing critical theoretical stances, many sports scholars have characterized public issues as at the far end of a pleasure spectrum. That is to say, they typically look at problems within sport rather than pleasures within sport. But, as we've seen, pleasure is often mixed with pain, joy with frustration or sorrow. But—and space does not allow for a larger discussion—the very nature of 'critical' work sometimes precludes the very things that we, as human beings living in the world, perhaps should celebrate.

US *VIS A VIS* PLEASURE

The broader project regarding pleasure and sport, then, may be understood as primarily existential, detailing an organizing principle of social life, and examining a key productive force in the constitution of identities, moral codes, governmental strategies and the development of cultures(s) and associated relations of power. If we are to see pleasure as one of the major *raison d'etre* of a well-lived life, then it follows that pleasure is a defining principle—and purpose—for that life-project. Philosophers term this *hedonism*, though the term itself is contestable.

Fred Feldman (2004, 2007), a philosopher, points out two differing forms of hedonism: 'sensory hedonism', in which he 'indicate[s] views according to which pleasurable *sensations* or *feelings* make for a good life' and various forms of 'attitudinal hedonism', in which a 'person takes intrinsic attitudinal pleasure in some state of affairs' (2007: 405). The distinction between what is popularly thought of as hedonism—self-centered, superficial and momentary titillations—and attitudinal hedonism is critical. Among other nuanced subjectivities concerning hedonism, Feldman proposes 'Intrinsic Attitudinal Hedonism', which 'is based on the idea that the ultimate sources of a person's welfare are episodes in which the person takes intrinsic attitudinal pleasure in various propositional objects' (Feldman, 2007: 406).

Somewhat conversely, Ulrich Schimmack (2001: 81), a psychologist, posits the pleasure dimensions this way:

> Some researchers consider pleasure and displeasure—that is, feeling good versus bad, positive versus negative, happy versus sad—as semantic opposite labels for different regions of a single dimension. . . . Other researchers consider pleasure and displeasure as two distinct feeling qualities—just as hunger and thirst are two distinct feelings—that are sometimes experienced concurrently. . . . (2001: 81)

Margaret Wetherell (2012), in her accessible book *Affect and Emotion: A New Social Science Understanding*, aims to bridge some of the debates surrounding *affect* writ large. She discusses the nature debate for social scientists, but her stance regarding the nature-nurture dynamic appears to be one of moderation, where both genetics and experience impact on one's affective range:

> An affective practice is a figuration where body possibilities and routines become recruited or entangled together with meaning-making and with other social and material figurations. It is an organic complex in which all the parts relationally constitute each other. (Wetherell, 2012: 19)

Thus, for Wetherell, 'nature' ('body possibilities and routines') and 'nurture' ('meaning-making') come together in interrelated practices that characterize as human performances.

Zakaria (2012), discussing Abu Ali al-Husain Ibn Abdallah Ibn Sina's categorizations of three forms of pleasure within gnostic thinking, writes:

> Ibn Sina divides pleasure into three types: (i) sensual pleasure (*al-ladhdha al-hissiya*) such as sex and eating, (ii) inward pleasure (*al-ladhdha al-batina*) such as preserving one's dignity and self-respect, and (iii) intellectual pleasure (*al-ladhdha al-aqliyya*). (Zakaria, 2012: 1284)

As intellectual pleasure is viewed by Ibn Sina as the highest form of pleasure, it is no wonder than he views the body as a barrier to true happiness:

> . . . the soul, while in the body, must purify itself all kinds of attachments to corporal things that are opposed to the means for happiness. By practicing this, the soul is then able to become a pure being and perhaps free itself from being affected by the bodily states, and accordingly prepares for the true happiness. (Zakaria, 2012: 1284)

A continual question perhaps worthy of reflection for sport philosophers is: can bodily pleasure co-exist with 'true' pleasure, however characterized? Postmodern, non-essentialist, poststructuralist sport scholars would likely question what is meant by the word 'true' and be concerned by the subjective bias in such a truth claim.

But even more than these distinctions about the basic sources of a desire for hedonism and/or pleasure, there are at least three categories/degrees of pleasure. These include a) pleasure itself, b) *ur*-pleasure—a prototypical, originary pleasure (cf. Frijda and Parrott, 2011)—and c) *dis*pleasure, which work together to circumscribe one's body. If a lived body has experienced (and can remember) pleasure, the pleasure itself becomes embodied. We hold pleasure in our minds, but we carry it in our movement.

So a *sensation* aspect of hedonism is in our lived experience, if not in our cognitive apperception of it: we are embodied, fluid in our responses and simultaneously constitute our genetics and our experiences. In other words, try as we might, we, like Huizinga, may be unable to wrestle a clear 'analysis, [and] all logical interpretation' (1955: 3) from that which we name as

22   Robert E. Rinehart

pleasure. But, as with Epicurus, the sense of pleasure runs across the trajectory of one's life. Pleasure is complicated and, at least for our purposes, untangleable.

With an overview that may include some of the world's most influential thinkers (from Epicurus to Bentham to Johan Huizinga), writers (from Shakespeare to Mary Wollstonecraft to Hunter S. Thompson) and academics (Freud, Deleuze, Lacan, Bakhtin, Lyotard, Kristeva, Irigaray, Foucault, Derrida, Huyssen)—those who have all been fascinated by human experiences of pleasure and the importance of developing an ethical approach to developing virtuous but pleasurable lives—we provide a context for sporting practices that both elicit, accompany and produce pleasure. In highlighting the broad social importance of pleasure, we then illustrate, through drawing on various examples, the social significance of sporting pleasure.

The pleasures experienced by both audiences and performers, by creators and viewers, may or may not be similar to those pleasures experienced in enacting artistic and sporting performance (cf. Rinehart, 1998a; Lowe, 1977). What we do know is that, in this particular historical moment (cf. Wetherell, 2012), there are dominant ways that both performers and audiences see their efforts, *vis a vis* work, play, joy and pleasure. According to Wendy Steiner (1995), and, I suggest, concomitant with sport, there is a contemporary

> . . . crisis in aesthetics as such. Neither the expert nor the layperson can say what makes art art [or sport sport], and though aesthetics has always been an area of opinionated speculation rather than scientific truth, there have been times of greater consensus than today. . . . (Steiner, 1995: 10)

This 'consensus', or contemporary lack of consensus, reflecting, respectively, modernist and postmodernist stances, holds true for the aesthetics—and thus, pleasurable, often unmeasurable enjoyment—of sport. One participant's joy in physical contact with another body flying through space is distasteful to someone else, who, in turn, enjoys the nuanced moment of pleasure, the thrill of precision when a 30-foot putt drops into the hole, despite the terrain and speed of the green. This is pleasure in the doing. Spectators derive pleasure from sport in many ways. They may enjoy and take pleasure in banter over impossible arguments: both in their prime, would Ali defeat Joe Louis? Would Helen Willis, in her prime, be victorious over Martina Navratilova? This is pleasure in imagining. There is pleasure in seeing in-person a graceful Michael Jordan lift to the basket for a slam dunk. This is pleasure in appreciating.

Examples of unusual pleasures abound, but two should suffice. The ranges of pleasure—all pleasure, not simply dominant forms of 'acceptable' pleasure—within life are almost unimaginable, so why would they not be within sport and re-creative leisure practices?

Pleasures Small and Large   23

For example, the Quiché Maya played a ballgame, which was described and mythologized in the Popol Vuh as a game played by the gods with two mortal brothers, Hun-Hunahpú and Vicub-Hunahpú, who 'lost their lives in the Underworld' (Salter, 1996: 127). While the potential outcome/penalty for losing the game (death) was known to the two brothers, the challenge and potential pleasure of possibly defeating Lords of the Underworld proved to be too enticing for them.

Following this, might the Taliban, who came to epitomize the '. . . landscape littered with the remains of vilified artworks and discredited orthodoxies' (Steiner, 1995: 209), still celebrate, enjoy, take pleasure in, a simple game of [male] soccer football? Or is there a religious repression of that *joie de vivre* stemming from physical movement (much as there presumably was for the early Puritans in 17th century America (cf. Daniels, 1991)) that becomes embodied in everyday lived life for the strict, fundamentalist Taliban? Within this culture, does the pleasure only instantiate from instrumental enthusiasms—that is, activities that are goal-oriented, in which pleasure comes to signify itself as a gratuitous add-on—or might pleasure also remain hedonistic—for its own sake? Questions such as these, while located in a specific time (the present), place (Afghanistan, Pakistan) and people, also locate more broadly throughout the ranges of the human condition.

Pleasure, then, more broadly, is what Annas (1993: 35) sees as 'the agent's final end [which] is generally taken to be happiness'. One of the satisfactions of a so-called well-lived life is that the agent's life is '. . . unified by that fact that all [the] projects and attitudes hang together and tend in a certain way' (ibid.). This 'life's *oeuvre*' kind of harmony demands a cognitive inspection of hypocrisies and balances. While pleasure may exist across all cultures, in every time period known to humankind, and likely in every possible context, the ways that people anticipate, enjoy and reflect on what is pleasurable—in Epicurus' terms, kinetic pleasure—vary greatly.

CULTURAL FORMS OF PLEASURE

> Then let fall
> Your horrible pleasure. . . .
> William Shakespeare, *King Lear*, Act III, Scene 2

The oxymoronic 'horrible pleasure' that King Lear speaks of evidences a wide range of possibilities toward the apperception of this thing called pleasure: one person might enjoy deeply, for example, the physical interplay within an American football game, Argentinian rugby match or intensely physical netball contest, while someone else may be horrified by such performances of violence. The Romans' much-celebrated decadence, perhaps stemming from Greek Bacchanalian feasts, and the Marquis de Sade's infamous sexual exploits (Gillette, 2005): these pleasures, often quite class-based, came at

24 Robert E. Rinehart

the expense of a concomitant sorrow or pain. Without dazzling sunlight, there can be no sharpened shadow, and pleasure and horror or revulsion or sorrow come to exist simultaneously.

On the other hand—and this is only demonstrating two points on a continuum, not describing a simplistic binary—the concept of a *'delightful pleasure'* may seem redundant and hyperbolic. But clearly, the very idea of positive and negative aesthetics comes into play within this discussion, for, while majorities within a given society may come to consensus regarding that which is pleasurable—or, for that matter, that which is painful—the existence of both threads within a given cultural performance is a co-dependent relationship which, though it may be intensified (e.g. 'delightful pleasure', 'horrible pain'), still requires its obverse for appreciation of its own existence.

And what has this to do with sport, and sporting pastimes and 'pleasures'? The most obvious reason for the interest in the intersections of sport and pleasure is that, while pleasure, joy and fun have all been *assumed* as integral parts of sport participation (and I mean this in the broadest sense: primary, secondary, tertiary 'performers' of sport, ancillary support members and spectators are all 'sport participants'), they have been relegated to just that: prior assumptions. Perhaps it is time the sport studies community of scholars reinvestigated such residuals of discourses within our areas, both questioning our fundamental assumptions and bringing renewed force and focus to current and future problematics.

These 'problematics' might include studies of how people of many stripes bring meaning to their sport and exercise and body regimes; how the very concept of pleasure is dulled or sharpened through various lenses, such as feminist/queer discourse, ascetic and/or hedonist journeys, instrumentalist or pragmatic relativism or even an aesthetic viewpoint. We might look at how bodies are shamed and guilt-ridden within Western contemporary society, and how these shamings play out on sporting fields and in sporting arenas. Each of these ways of looking at pleasure, of course, is both limiting and freeing in its own way. But on more useful and everyday levels, these kinds of standpoints provide an opportunity to examine questions about youth and child, and middle-aged and elderly participation in sport; about equity issues, particularly those surrounding movement, sport and dance; about discourses regarding pain and injury, in power and performance sport and in pleasure and participation sport; about professionalism and professionalized attitudes regarding the very place of pleasure; about media representations of various bodies, including the ascetic body, the satiated body, the 'disabled' body, the mortified body and the 'perfect' body and how those discourses resonate with pleasures of control, abjection and self-efficacy; and about risk, self-realization and selfishness within sport and movement—and how these naturalized stances influence and are influenced by contextualized notions of pleasure and hedonism in 21st century sporting practice.

Pleasures Small and Large   25

As one example, Miller (1994: 137) discusses 4th- and 5th-century ascetics, particularly pointing out Palladius' views of 'emaciated and mutilated bodies . . . as angelic bodies'. Discussing the worldview of these ascetics, Miller goes on to say:

> It may be that such conventional descriptions of ascetic persons as leading 'heavenly' or 'angelic' or 'resurrected' lives were not mere metaphors of pious behavior but rather real indicators of a perceptual construct embedded within ascetic discourse. This perceptual construct enabled observers to 'see' ascetic persons as performance artists, enacting the spiritual body in the here-and-now. This perceptual construct, moreover, was immensely satisfying . . . (Miller, 1994: 137)

Deriving pleasure—in this case spiritual or intellectual pleasure—from emaciated bodies at the very least demonstrates how subjective perceptions can impinge upon objective realities.

In another (related) case, Joanna Frueh, a contemporary performance artist and academic, writes about a 20th-century fascination with 'feminine perfection and women's fear of being undesirable and worse unloved' (1991: 70). Characterizing this as a 'fear of flesh that moves', she writes:

> Because structures of power, such as the art world, gender or erotic behavior, close in on themselves by providing habitual and proper ways for a human being to exist, writing that dislocates the reader or that names her 'unfittingness' in ways that she herself does, lets the reader know that people needn't remain stuck in societal constraints. (1991: 70)

In other words—and returning to a point made previously about revealing that which is somehow made invisible—Frueh is suggesting that the very discussion of issues creates an opening for insight and discussion—and change. In addition, the very abjectification of the body reproduces a mantra of 20th- and 21st-century advertising that relies upon mortification of the self to create desire. These two examples also pinpoint the fluid nature of societal views of 1) the body and 2) various incarnations of pleasure.

Examining pleasure from multiple standpoints also allows us to look at new questions within sport and movement studies. For example: drawing from Coveney and Bunton (2003), these questions might include issues concerning the possibility of a well-lived and satisfying life, through and with pleasurable movement; the introduction of affect—in particular, passion—to the study of sport; carnality and bodily pleasures, disciplined or rationalized pleasure, ascetic or self-control/denial pleasures, ecstatic or passionate thrills, deviant pleasures, cognitive pleasures, political pleasures and identification/display kinds of pleasures. There are deep and shallow pleasures; there are transitory and lasting pleasures; there are nostalgic and imagined pleasures.

26 Robert E. Rinehart

Going on a roller coaster ride entails the pleasure of anticipation while standing in line, and also includes the actual experience of what Caillois (1961) has termed 'vertigo'. But this pleasure is, relatively speaking, rather short-lived, and even recalling the experience of pleasure is sometimes difficult. On the other hand, the first enervating slice into a pool of cold water, perhaps because it is repeated so easily (and frequently), can be both 'vertiginous' and a lasting pleasure, both replicated and recollected throughout the trajectory of a life.

Life pleasures, to be sure, can be deeper, less transitory and often more satisfying than momentary ones—but, like 'epiphanies' (cf. Denzin, 2001[1989]), deep, life-altering pleasures can be made up of minor or gradual or momentary pleasures.

'PLEASURE' AS A HUMAN RIGHT

> The only position that leaves me with no cognitive dissonance is atheism. It is not a creed. Death is certain, replacing both the siren-song of Paradise and the dread of Hell. Life on this earth, with all its mystery and beauty and pain, is then to be lived far more intensely: we stumble and get up, we are sad, confident, insecure, feel loneliness and *joy and love*. There is nothing more; but I want nothing more.
>
> —Christopher Hitchens, *The Portable Atheist: Essential Readings for the Non-believer* (emphasis added)

As Hitchens points out, despite outcries to the contrary, there is no codified rulebook for life. To essentialize such a code, a one-size-fits-all prescription, might be in the realm of belief, faith, religion or the like. Each individual, then, finds her/his own way through the traceries of a well-lived life, often fumbling along, sometimes sure of the way. For our purposes, we have engaged with the facts of both pleasure and sport with the assumption that *there is no stated purpose for life*. As humans, we are not given a universal instruction sheet telling us each what our life's purpose might be. It might be noteworthy to remember that the United Nations' Declaration of Human Rights guarantees essential human freedoms, but is not directive: that is, even its essentialisms do not prescribe what constitutes a valuable, or even well-lived, life. So we're on our own. We have the capacity to determine to what extent we privilege a concept like *pleasure*—or ignore it. We also have the agency to determine to what extent we will accept pleasure into our general lives and our sporting lives. We also, finally, have the wherewithal to determine the very direction our pleasures can take: do we pleasure ourselves at the expense of others, or pleasure ourselves through the edification of others?

It is important, then, to trace the social constructions of dampened forms of pleasure—particularly in the Western world, both within the larger societies and in relation to sport—as well as those of heightened pleasure. Pleasure has not only been tamped down and packed into a commodified, commercialized, convenient package meant for mass consumption, it has often taken on a sense of experiential flatness. As George Ritzer (2005) has rightly pointed out, the disenchantment of many things both cultural and personal has gradually eroded even our *recognition* of pleasure, especially in a consumerist society. But it is more than this erosion of recognition because of course there is pleasure in both delivering and producing.

TRACINGS OF PLEASURE

This section is not meant to nostalgically hearken back to a 'golden age' of innocent pleasure within sporting practice, but rather to note the ways that our apperceptions of pleasure may have changed over time. The following cultures spanned hundreds, if not thousands, of years. In broad strokes, some populist notions have remained, and suffice for our purposes of teasing out some genealogies of current views on pleasure.

Epicureanism, based on the teachings of Epicurus, stresses pleasure as the primary good (hedonism): happiness would not be achieved by sensual and material overindulgence, but rather by avoidance of pain, or *aponia*, and '. . . *ataraxia*, or tranquility . . .' (Annas, 1987: 5). In essence, this form of Epicureanism—unlike the way the term has been spirited away in contemporary times—and many other Greek philosophies, seeks a virtuous life. Yet Epicureanism (and hedonism) is seen by many in contemporary society as pleasure-seeking at the expense of individual responsibility.

The Gnostics, mentioned previously, eschewed bodily pleasures for spiritual or intellectual ones, celebrating transcendence in their worldview (Hoeller, 2014). Most people, according to contemporary gnostic summative statements, are not meant for transcendence through 'interior, intuitive means':

> Not all humans are spiritual (pneumatics) and thus ready for Gnosis and liberation. Some are earthbound and materialistic beings (hyletics), who recognize only the physical reality. Others live largely in their psyche (psychics). (Hoeller, 2014, ¶14)

Gnostics regarded the body as a physical prison from which, through ascetic behaviors, they sought to escape. Pleasure through the senses was largely regarded as a temptation to be avoided.

Gnosticism has its traces in 'the role of an ascetic morality in the first formation of capitalism' (Foucault, 1990: 141). As these anti-pleasure ethe were hegemonic, bio-life emerged where 'methods of power and knowledge assumed responsibility for the life processes and undertook to control and modify them' (Foucault, 1990: 142). Thus, according to Foucault, the relative inevitability of the 'randomness of death' became mitigated, and social controls—and the dance of power and knowledge—began to take form.

Well before the gnostics or the late European Middle Ages, when the sensible fracturing of human subjects' lower and upper strata began to coalesce into

28   Robert E. Rinehart

body-mind forms of dualisms, the ancient Chinese likewise explored a heightened privileging of the mind: according to Van Dalen and Bennett (1971),

> . . . in the earlier eras, bodily conditioning play a more important role in Chinese society than it did in later times. The development of a bookish, classical type of education and the spread of Taoism, Buddhism, Confucianism, all of which emphasized the contemplative life, reduced interest in the physical development of the child. (Van Dalen and Bennett, 1971: 13)

'The earlier eras' of which Van Dalen and Bennett (1971: 12) write 'predate . . . Christianity by approximately 2500 years'. We can infer from Van Dalen and Bennett that, accompanied by a reverence for the wisdom of aging, the ancient Chinese saw ultimate happiness as stemming from a balanced, tranquil, contemplative life, free of disease but also free of conflict. In addition, Diener and Suh (2000: 3) write that the 'Confucian school in ancient China described the good life in terms of an orderly society in which individuals correctly performed their roles and responsibilities'.

Foucault (1990[1978]), as he often does, has the last word on this principle of pleasure traced from before the 17th century. He is writing about the '*scientia sexualis* versus *ars erotica*' (Foucault, 1990: 70), but similar musings might easily apply to pleasure within sport, pleasure in engagement, and pleasure in apprehension:

> It is often said that we have been incapable of imagining any new pleasures. We have at least invented a different kind of pleasure: pleasure in the truth of pleasure, the pleasure of knowing that truth, of discovering and exposing it, the fascination of seeing it and telling it, of captivating and capturing others by it, of confiding it in secret, of luring it out in the open—the specific pleasure of the true discourse on pleasure. (Foucault, 1990: 70)

Simply put, that is what this book is about: 'luring [pleasure regarding sport] out in[to] the open'.

NOTES

1. It is worth noting that these simple binaries can be conceived of as end points on a continuum, suggestive and instructive for understanding the limits of the concepts.
2. Notable exceptions from the west include Rabelais (1984); Foucault (1990[1978]), (1990[1985]). In the east, of course, the classic Kama Sutra (Vātsyāyana, 2009).
3. Apologies to Friedrich Nietzsche, 1998.

3 A Short History of Pleasure

Richard Pringle

The interconnected topics of pleasure, happiness, joy and life satisfaction have long been of interest to a diverse range of eminent scholars, including: philosophers, historians, politicians, psychologists, theologians, biologists and evolutionary and socio-cultural theorists. Attempting to understand how one can gain a state of happiness, what makes life desirable or which pleasures are worth seeking has long been discussed, examined and debated. The results of these debates have had profound influences on the societies we have created, what we value, the development of laws and moral codes, how we understand ourselves, interact with each other and lead our lives and, of course, the games and sports we play. In this chapter, I provide a *selective* examination of the diverse works on this subject to trace and illustrate the place of pleasure and happiness within the historical development of Western culture.

Writing the history of pleasure/happiness/satisfaction is a somewhat complex task given, in part, that the meanings of these words (and other such synonyms) have changed over time, have been subject to the faults of translation and are, at times, used interchangeably in popular discourse (Kretchmar, 1994; Maguire, 2008). 'Happiness' as typically used in daily discourse, for example, is very different from how Aristotle used the term '*eudaimonia*' (which is typically translated as happiness). Aristotle did not use the term '*eudaimonia*' to refer to a subjective state of mind or emotion, as we might do today, but more broadly to the goal of living a good or quality life.

Given the multiple meanings and blurred understandings of terms such as happiness and pleasure, I do not provide tight definitions but, where appropriate, define how others have used them. I do, however, tend to use the term 'pleasure' in a broad, inclusive, positive-affect sense, so that it overlaps with understandings of joy, fun and delight. My preference for a loose definition of pleasure follows Chris Shilling (2002: 12) who asserted, somewhat boldly, that it is not 'useful or even possible to provide a precise definition of emotions'. Moreover, attempts to precisely define and examine various 'pleasures' (e.g. eudaimonic or hedonic happiness) have proved difficult, as empirical evidence suggests considerable overlap amongst differing terms (Kashdan, Biswas-Diener and King, 2008). An additional advantage of using

30   *Richard Pringle*

a definition with porous boundaries is that wider aspects of the phenomena, which might be beneficial for understanding complex social processes, are not eliminated from consideration (Izard, Kagan and Zajonc, 1984).

In this chapter I aim to reveal the enduring social significance of pleasure and some of its seemingly nebulous characteristics. I highlight that pleasures have been understood as diverse, socially constructed, productive, political and tied to existential issues, the body and the arts of living a 'good life'. In other words, I highlight that there are multiple and, at times, competing conceptualizations of pleasure. Throughout this abridged chronological examination I make links between understandings of pleasure and contemporary sport.

AN ABRIDGED HISTORY OF PLEASURE

Before human civilizations had arisen, even before our ancient ancestors had evolved into human-like creatures, animals played. So contended Johan Huizinga (1970: 19), who asserted in his classical study of *Homo Ludens* (or *Man the Player*) that 'play is older than culture, for culture, however, inadequately defined, always presupposes human society, and animals have not waited for man to teach them their playing'. Indeed, lion cubs play fight, dogs chase their tails and dolphins ride waves. Although we can only speculate as to why animals play, Huizinga claimed that the prime reason why humans play was to experience 'fun'. He further characterized play as distinct from 'ordinary life' and suggested that it was undertaken freely and without desire for a material outcome or profit. In this respect, Huizinga regarded play as an autotelic activity undertaken for 'its own intoxicating momentum' (Kretchmar, 1994: 211). He stressed that the 'fun' element of play has always been of social significance. Indeed, Huizinga (1970: 23) argued that 'culture arises in the form of play' and 'pure play is one of the main bases of civilization'. In this manner, he considered play as paradoxically *unproductive* and *productive* in that it not only produces pleasure and other emotions, but is also related to the production of drama, dance, sporting contests, games of love and, at a much broader level, human culture. Huizinga accordingly theorized, in an undoubtedly grand and romantic manner, that play and the *pursuit of fun* have underpinned the development of human civilizations.

To explain the significance and constitutive abilities of play, Huizinga emphasized the importance of lived experiences of fun. Fun, in accordance with Huizinga's logic, can be understood as the motivational force that is integral to the development of human culture. Drawing from Huizinga, I suggest that sporting pleasures can be similarly understood as productive. The ubiquity and social pervasiveness of contemporary sport can, correspondingly, be explained as the outcome of the pursuit of multiple and diverse sporting pleasures such as the joy of winning, the pleasure of becoming a respected sportsperson, the thrill of ilinx or the satisfaction of being fit. The subsequent production of the sporting world and associated cultures, via pursuit of sporting pleasures, is also tied to the production of a range of social issues and problems, as evidenced via the numerous critical studies concerning sport. Thus, the unintended consequences of the pursuit of sport pleasures are associated with the production of both positive and negative outcomes.

Huizinga's (1970: 21) least defensible claim (according to some) was that the 'fun element' of play, the element that makes 'play' desirable, 'resists all analysis, all logical interpretation'. Yet fun and its synonyms have been the focus of analysis for thousands of years. Aristotle (384–322 BCE) (1962/350 BCE), for example, defended the social importance of examining happiness and provided qualitative examinations of various 'goods', such as the nature of virtue, self-care and friendship. He argued that every activity, whether it be playing the harp or building a house, has a 'good' that is its own particular end: the good of playing the harp is the production of pleasing music and the good in building is the production of a functional house. To develop his treatise on *eudaimonia* (generally translated as 'happiness' but perhaps more accurately defined as 'human flourishing', 'living well' or to a lesser extent 'wellbeing'), Aristotle asked, 'Why seek any particular good?' His answer was that the 'good' could produce happiness and that happiness is the only good that is always chosen as an end in itself. Thus, he proclaimed eudaimonia the highest good. Cumulative evidence over time has indicated that there is general agreement with this sentiment (i.e. that 'happiness' is the ultimate state that humans strive for). The Dalai Lama and Howard Cutler (1998), for example, clearly articulate within their text, *The Art of Happiness: A Handbook for Living*, that the prime purpose of life is to be happy. Aristotle, however, illustrated that debate is rife with respect to how best to attain happiness. The (shallow) hedonist, for example, seemingly seeks a life of repeated but nevertheless ephemeral pleasures while others might live for honor, fame, wealth or virtue.

To help clarify this existential debate, Aristotle made distinctions between pleasure and happiness. He suggested that animals were a lower form of life that were governed by a desire to satisfy physical urges, thus gaining 'pleasure' through eating, sleeping and reproducing. He claimed that humans have a capacity to reason and correspondingly suggested that a life governed by the uncritical and unreflexive pursuit of pleasures would not necessarily constitute a virtuous or 'happy' life. To resolve this dilemma, he emphasized the importance of critical reflection (or rationality) and suggested that virtue, happiness and rationality were all intimately connected in the production of a 'good life'. This interconnection is revealed in his understandings of the happiness gained through playing the harp:

> . . . the function of the harpist is to play the harp; the function of the harpist who has high standards is to play well. On these assumptions, if

32   *Richard Pringle*

we take the proper function of man to be a certain kind of life, and if the kind of life is an activity of the soul and consists in actions performed in conjunction with the rational element, and if a man of high standards is he who performs these actions well and properly, and if a function is well performed when it is performed in accordance with the excellence appropriate to it; we reach the conclusion that the good of man is an activity of the soul in conformity with the excellence of virtue, and if there are several virtues, in conformity with the best and most complete. (Aristotle, 1962: 6)

Influenced by his spiritual beliefs, Aristotle appeared to conclude that the highest good is that which most resembles the life of a divine being, a life that revolves around contemplation and pure thought (which, perhaps not surprisingly, appears to resemble how Aristotle attempted to live). Aristotle's ethics subsequently influenced Christian beliefs and have contemporary resonance in the axiom that a good life consists in developing one's talents to the fullest. His views on happiness and the good life have also been the subject of critique. Bertrand Russell (1945: 173), for example, suggested that Aristotle's views on the highest good would likely appeal to the 'respectable middle-aged', as he appears to defend bourgeois values (i.e. work hard, do your best, respect mainstream customs). Cynthia Freeland (1988) further critiqued Aristotle as a misogynist, despite his recognition that a society can only function smoothly if women are also provided with opportunity to lead a good life and obtain happiness.

Drawing from Aristotle's ethics, one could potentially live a 'good life' through participation in sport, but only if the participation has been rationally considered and if the sport is performed at a high standard and in accordance with the excellence appropriate to it. Yet this is no easy task. There is a risk, for example, that the pursuit of sporting excellence (or virtue) could turn into an obsession (i.e. an uncontrolled desire) or that the sportsperson becomes seduced by a desire for wealth or fame rather than seeing happiness as an end unto itself. Concomitantly, a 'life well lived' would not likely be obtained via an unreflexive pursuit of various sporting pleasures, such as the perfunctory consumption of televised sport, the seemingly thoughtless antics of football hooligans, the pursuit of sporting success via doping or, more typically, mundane participation in sport.

Foucault's (1985) examination of ancient Greek ethics similarly revealed that individuals (or more specifically 'free men') were encouraged to reflect on their pursuit of pleasures in order to live an ethical (and in relation pleasurable) life. Foucault claimed that although the ancient Greeks acknowledged that respecting custom and laws was important for the constitution of an ethical self, certain attitudes towards pleasure were more important:

The accent was placed on the relationship with the self that enabled a person to keep from being carried away by the appetites and pleasures,

A Short History of Pleasure   33

to maintain a mastery and superiority over them, to keep his (sic) senses in a state of tranquility, to remain free from interior bondage to passions, and to achieve a mode of being that could be defined as full enjoyment of oneself, or the perfect supremacy of oneself over oneself. (Foucault, 1985: 31)

The 'appropriate' use of pleasure by the ancient Greeks accordingly played a significant role within the tradition of *caring for oneself*, which Foucault considered as a primary organizing principle of the classical art of existence. Foucault, however, recognized that this reflexive project of self, which centered on controlling desires and the use of pleasures, was not necessarily easy to achieve. Indeed, he intimated that the temptations of specific pleasures (e.g. alcohol, food, sex) could be so strong that individuals had to actively work, via techniques of the self, to control their desires. The intimation from Foucault is that the draw of select embodied pleasures, such as the desire to eat calorie-dense foods, could be difficult to control by mere rational thought.

In a comparable manner, Huizinga (1970) suggested that the social significance of play/fun highlights that humans are constituted, in part, as irrational beings. He claimed: 'We play and know that we play, so we must be more than merely rational beings, for play is irrational' (Huizinga, 1970: 22). Yet the rationality of play is a debatable point. Friedrich Nietzsche (1999[1872]) was similarly concerned with how the place of pleasure in social life was both a potential source of inner tension and an apparent reflection of irrationality. In *The Birth of Tragedy* he drew on Greek mythology to examine the dualistic forces of Apollo (god of sunlight, order and harmony) and Dionysius (god of wine, parties and disorder). He declared that the Apollonian force manifests itself in the desire to craft the self as a well-balanced work of art, whereas the Dionysian celebrates the 'immorality' of sexuality and natural desires. More to the point, Nietzsche suggested that forces of Dionysius could induce narcotic states of complete self-forgetfulness—which could be a great source of pleasure for some. He further argued that the Greeks averted the supposed dangers posed by Dionysian forces by their invention of the Olympian gods, who were of prominence within their various sporting festivals. Yet this social invention came at a cost, as it restricted certain creative life forces and these restrictions, Nietzsche claimed, still haunt modern existence. More specifically, he lamented that the Greek ethic of caring for oneself (which also demanded the need to care for others) was subsequently marginalized within the West via the human 'invention' of Christianity and its subsequent focus on the unrealistic salvation of the soul rather than the practical arts of everyday earthly life.

Foucault (1986), directly influenced by Nietzsche, was also critical of the advent of Christianity and the associated impact on human pleasures/ethics. He argued that although there were clear links between the Ancient Greek,

34 Richard Pringle

Roman and Christian practices of ethics, the antique ethic of 'caring for thy self' was surpassed by a Christian moral system, which was:

> . . . based on finitude, the Fall, and evil; a mode of subjection in the form of obedience to a general law that is at the same time the will of a personal god; a type of work on oneself that implies a decipherment of the soul and a purificatory hermeneutics of the desires; and a mode of ethical fulfillment that tends toward self-renunciation. (Foucault, 1986: 239–240)

Certain pleasures, under the subsequent influence of a Christian moral code, became linked to the body (as opposed to the mind or spirit) and regarded as sinful. Although Christianity did not invent mind-body dualism, the pleasures that have been regarded as tied to the body (eating, drinking, dancing, sex and sport) were consequently degraded in value and/or repressed. The marginalization of sport and physical education within contemporary education curriculums can be understood as a latent effect of this dualistic thinking. Indeed, sport is typically regarded as an 'extra-curricular' activity within schools, as its educational value is still questioned by some educational authorities. Nevertheless, the pleasures associated with sport have ensured that sport is still of significance within schooling processes.

The mind-body dualism encouraged by Christian philosophies did, however, encourage the growth of *ascetic pleasures* or pleasures gained 'from the acknowledgement of total control of the body's natural urges . . . a total *conquering* and *domination* of the body' (Coveney and Bunton, 2003: 172). Ascetic pleasures, somewhat oxymoronically, are the pleasures experienced through the act of denying pleasure. The pursuit of ascetic pleasure reached its pinnacle, according to John Coveney and Robin Bunton (2003: 171), in the practices of early Christians such as St Benedict and Catherine of Assisi, who 'all reached heights of ecstasy through severe fasting and other ascetic rituals'. I suggest that some contemporary individuals may achieve similar forms of 'ecstasy' through various ascetic practices, such as restricting caloric intake, undertaking painful fitness regimes, or practicing various forms of abstinence and teetotalism. The growth of asceticism illustrates that pleasures are socially constructed in diverse ways while still tied to the body.

In an apparent opposition to the Christian moral code and its tendency towards self-renunciation and condemnation of the so-called animal side of life, Mikhail Bakhtin (1984) wrote about the importance of the pleasures of the carnival in the medieval-cultural consciousness (see also Chapters 2 and 5). Bakhtin (1984: 7) drew from the literary works of Rabelais to suggest that medieval people lived in two worlds: one dominated by the church and state and the other that freed 'them completely from all religious and ecclesiastical dogmatism, from all mysticism and piety'. The carnival, he suggested, did not simply take place at a certain time but could be regarded

A Short History of Pleasure   35

as another space for living or even as a 'country' that had to endure occasional border skirmishes with officialdom. The carnival was a temporal and spatial place where the rules, restrictions and regulations of everyday life were turned upside down: it was characterized by laughter, offensiveness and excessiveness. Bakhtin explained that a carnivalistic sense of the world takes place when: 1) social hierarchies are disbanded, 2) eccentric or 'unacceptable' behaviors are legitimated, 3) boundaries that normally separate are blurred (e.g. the profane with the sacred) and 4) acceptance and even celebration of the sacrilegious occurs.

Bakhtin lamented that the central and potentially therapeutic role of the carnival started to disappear during the 1800s but suggested that the regenerating aspect of the carnival still has holds in modern life via literature. Moreover, he argued that it is in these literary forms that a form of resistance to authority could legitimately be expressed, as these literary works seemingly stand apart from the 'real world' but nevertheless offer opportunities for thinking new ideas that allow for possibilities of resistance.

John Fiske (2005: 79) more recently suggested that elements of the carnivalesque survive within select television programs such as '*Rock n Wrestling*' and various sporting practices. With respect to sport, he stated:

> Carnival is an exaggeration of sport, the space for freedom and control that games offer is opened up even further by the weakening of the rules that contain it. Like sport, carnival abides by certain rules that give it a pattern, but unlike sport (whose rules tend to replicate the social), carnival inverts those rules and builds a world upside down . . . (Fiske, 2005: 78).

Yet sport can also provide opportunities to invert social rules. Rugby union, for example, requires participants to normalize and even celebrate pain and violence (Pringle and Hickey, 2010). Laura Chase (2006: 229), more pointedly, stated that rugby participation requires 'women to get dirty and bloody, and to hit other women'. She correspondingly argued, 'the image of the bruised and battered female rugby player exists in opposition to images of ideal female bodies and to notions of normative femininity' (Chase, 2006: 229–230). The rules of femininity, according to Chase, are inverted when women play rugby, which offers a form of resistance (and pleasure) to the existing social order. The carnivalesque within women's rugby potentially allows opportunities for existing hierarchies and social privileges to be subverted.

Roland Barthes (1975) writings on the pleasure of the text resonated with Bakhtin's carnivalesque thesis by arguing that jouissance is an embodied pleasure that occurs at the point of breakdown between the cultural and the natural, such that the social self is lost in moments of ecstasy. He argued that given that subjectivity is constituted via ideology, jouissance allows for the evasion of ideology. In this light, Barthes considered that certain texts

36   Richard Pringle

legitimate embodied pleasures that remove the reader from the constraints of the existing social order. Similar arguments could be made in relation to the embodied viewing pleasures of sporting contests. Indeed, many fans appear to lose their 'selves' in moments of sporting celebrations, yet how these transitory pleasures relate to the broader social order is a topic under-examined (see Chapter 8 for further discussion of this topic).

During the enlightenment, with the rise of humanism, liberalism and nation states, the idea of happiness grew more secular and there was 'an increased emphasis in Western cultures on pleasure as a path to, and even a synonym for, happiness' (Kesebir and Diener, 2009: 61). Indeed, John Locke (1823: 245) stated: 'Happiness then in its full extent is the utmost Pleasure we are capable of, and Misery the utmost pain'. Pleasure and the governmental control of populations became an issue of increased philosophical and political concern. Subsequently, the utilitarian philosophers (e.g. Jeremy Bentham, John Stuart Mill) influenced ideas of governing populations in relation to how pleasure/pain was conceptualized. In 1879, Jeremy Bentham boldly asserted that:

> Nature has placed mankind under the governance of two sovereign masters, *pain* and *pleasure*. It is for them alone to point out what we ought to do, as well as to determine what we shall do. On the one hand the standard of right and wrong, on the other the chain of causes and effects, are fastened to their throne. They govern us in all we do, in all we say, in all we think . . . (Bentham, 1879: 1).

Bentham highlighted the social significance of happiness (which he conceived as a predominance of pleasure over pain), yet he was concerned with the related chain of unintended consequences. He therefore encouraged government intervention to control the 'sovereign masters' of pleasure and pain. To help provide a pragmatic approach for governing pleasure, Bentham formulated the 'greatest happiness principle', which asserted that one must act so as to produce the greatest happiness for the greatest number of people. He even provided a series of questions, called the *hedonic calculus*, which he designed to determine the utility of an action. These questions related to the various elements of pleasure, including: its intensity, duration and certainty (i.e. how likely is it that pleasure will occur?), propinquity (i.e. how soon will the pleasure occur?), fecundity (i.e. will similar pleasures likely follow?), purity (i.e. what chances are there that displeasures will follow?) and the extent of actions (i.e. to what extent will the experiencing of these pleasures affect other people?).

Modern gladiators, who run onto the football fields and risk injury and pain for the delight of fans, could possibly be justified via Bentham's utilitarianism. Indeed, critics of Bentham have been concerned that his hedonic calculus, at its extreme, could potentially justify the torture of an individual if it created more happiness than pain. Yet Bentham's calculus was more

A Short History of Pleasure   37

sophisticated than this critique, as he was aware that the sacrifice of a few could not be morally justified even if the overall pleasure balance within a society was increased (Kelly, 1990). Moreover, he was concerned about the individual pursuit of happiness, as he recognized that 'selfish' actions could create less pleasure more broadly. In this manner, he advocated for government legislation as a strategy to ensure the maximum pleasure and minimum pain for a population. Utilitarian thought, which John Stuart Mill contributed to, subsequently shaped governance strategies.

Thomas Jefferson, notably, believed that the ability to protect an individual's pursuit of happiness was a central justification for maintaining a system of governance. Although he regarded the pursuit of happiness as an 'inalienable right', it has proven difficult for governments to develop appropriate legislation to ensure that all can pursue their own forms of happiness, as evidenced by ongoing political debates related to, as examples, the consumption of drugs, various sexual acts, abortion and censorship.

Debates concerning the governance of sporting competitions are similarly rife. Ongoing disputes surround sporting rules in relation to determining who might participate in particular sports or events (e.g. as related to age, sex, race, religion, ability and size), the rules of competition (e.g. there seems to be more action off the water than on in America's Cup yachting events) and the prohibition of performance enhancement aids, for example. John Hoberman (2005) illustrates that the so-called war on drugs in sport shows no signs of victory or armistice. Individual experiences and interpretations of sporting pleasure are undoubtedly shaped by public policy and broader systems of governance.

One set of governing rules that has shaped the opportunities to attain sporting pleasures relates to women and the historical and ongoing struggle for the right to participate in sport. Contemporary sport feminists owe a debt to Mary Wollstonecraft's (1992) revolutionary work *A Vindication of the Rights of Women*, published in 1792. Wollstonecraft is regarded as one of the founding feminist philosophers, and her text advocates equal opportunities for women. Her discussion concerning equal educational opportunities was crafted partly in response to Jean-Jacques Rousseau's sexist belief, as expressed in *Emile*, that women should be educated primarily for the benefit of men. Wollstonecraft's advocacy for equal rights for women can also be read as a response to Thomas Jefferson's 1776 declaration 'that all men are created equal' and that 'men' are 'endowed with certain inalienable rights'. Wollstonecraft's text encouraged recognition that women should also be considered 'equal' and undoubtedly also have inalienable rights. Her advocacy has encouraged more recent acceptance that women should have the right to pursue diverse sporting pleasures. For example, the adoption of the International Charter of Physical Education and Sport (UNESCO, 1978) promoted participation in sport as a *human* right. Yet this charter has had little impact in some societies. Within Saudi Arabia, for example, it was illegal for women to participate in the Olympics until recent times.

38 *Richard Pringle*

In the early 20th century, Sigmund Freud (2010[1930]) was similarly concerned by the rules that regulate social relations and the production of a civilization that can undermine human happiness. He theorized that the unconscious mind or id was governed by the *pleasure principle* and the associated innate drive to satisfy desires with urgency. The id, he claimed, runs supreme in the infant but as socialization processes occur and contribute to the development of the ego (or consciousness) the unrefined drive for pleasure is tempered by the *reality principle*. The reality principle acknowledges that there is still a fundamental human urge to satisfy the desires of the id, but this process is now tempered by social understandings. From these (essentialized) psychological propositions, Freud drew sociological insights. He proposed in his classic text, *Civilization and its Discontents*, that civilization is based on the subjugation of the pleasure principle (Freud, 2010[1930]). Freud (2010[1930]: 14), a devout atheist, argued that there is no god-given purpose to life, but if one examines 'what human beings themselves reveal, through their behavior, about the aim and purpose of their lives . . . the answer can scarcely be in doubt: they strive for happiness, they want to become happy and remain so'. Freud (2010[1930]: 24) acknowledged three primary threats to achieving sustained periods of happiness: 'the superior power of nature, the frailty of our bodies, and the inadequacy of the institutions that regulate people's relations with one another in the family, the state and society'. He recognized that humans have little control over the first two threats but, given that humans create the rules that regulate social relations, the third threat could be ameliorated. However, Freud argued that the social relations constructed by humans prove to be the greatest source of displeasure. In this respect, Freud highlighted an apparent paradox: humans strive for happiness, but the civilizations that they have created (presumably to increase chances of happiness) are also the prime source of human unhappiness. In similar respect, sport can be understood as having developed primarily for the purpose of promoting pleasure (although it is politically appropriated for other purposes), yet for many ex-participants, sport involvement eventually becomes a prime source of displeasure and many 'retire' injured, disappointed, frustrated. A question of some import arises: how can sporting/broader culture be changed to allow for greater opportunities to attain happiness?

Herbert Marcuse (1961), of Frankfurt School fame, built on Freud's proposition concerning civilization and the suppression of 'innate drives' and blended his insight with Marxist thought to produce a critique of capitalist society. He restated Freud's thesis to suggest that pleasure is:

> . . . subordinated to the discipline of work as fulltime occupation, to the discipline of monogamic reproduction, to the established system of law and order. The methodical sacrifice of libido, its rigidly enforced deflection to socially useful activities and expressions, is culture. (Marcuse, 1961: 3)

A Short History of Pleasure   39

Marcuse (1961: 3) was concerned that this sacrifice of pleasure, for the progress of Western civilization and increased productivity, was bound up with 'mechanization and standardization of life . . . mental impoverishment . . . growing destructiveness (and). . . . intensified unfreedom'. His broad aim, accordingly, was to extend the sociological analysis of Freud to diagnose the general disorder of contemporary life and to encourage, at a fundamental level, social change to produce greater freedoms (primarily from the demands of capitalism and associated bureaucracy) and a happier society.

And at this point I end my short and selective history of Western pleasures to suggest, somewhat boldly, that Marcuse's fundamental aim is similar to what all critical scholars desire, that is, to promote change in the social world so as to enable humans to have greater opportunities to experience various pleasures (without harming the pleasures of others) that can contribute to the constitution of lives of self-perceived value, equity and quality.

CONTEMPORARY LESSONS LEARNT FROM DIVERSE SCHOLARLY WRITINGS ON PLEASURES

Jim Holt (2006) suggested in his insightful review of Darrin McMahon's (2006) book, *Happiness: A History*, that:

> The history of the idea of happiness can be neatly summarized in a series of bumper sticker equations: Happiness=Luck (Homeric), Happiness=Virtue (classical), Happiness=Heaven (medieval), Happiness= Pleasure (Enlightenment) and Happiness=A Warm Puppy (contemporary). (Holt, 2006: 20)

Holt's satiric summary of the history of happiness suggests that humans have made little progress over the years in attempting to gain happiness or live lives of quality. In similar respects, the result of this condensed and selective tour of historical treatises of 'pleasure' could be summarized in relation to what is sometimes called the paradox of happiness: the more one searches for happiness the more elusive it proves. Nevertheless, my examination has illustrated the enduring social significance of pleasure/happiness and some of its associated issues and malleable characteristics. Pleasure can be understood as a primary existential project and as an organizing principle of social life. The significance of pleasure is further illustrated by its productive abilities. Pleasure has been assumed by diverse scholars to lie at the constitutive core of identities, moral codes, governmental strategies and, more grandly, the development of human cultures. Pleasure can even produce 'hyperreality' or an experience that seems 'more real than the circumstances of day-to-day existence' (Lyng, 1990: 861). A skydiver told Stephen Lyng (1990), for example, that free-falling 'is much more real than everyday existence' (Lyng, 1990: 861).

40   *Richard Pringle*

Yet pleasure has also been recognized as a productive force in eroding identity, removing consciousness and constituting a sense of disembodiment. Indeed, some aim to 'get lost in pleasure' or 'get out of it' through pleasure. The pursuit of pleasure has also been linked with death, moral decline and the destruction of civilizations. The complex and seemingly contradictory qualities of pleasure can be understood as peculiarly constitutive and destructive, embodied and disembodied, natural and socially constructed, political and personal, inconsequential and significant, good and evil, and serious and playful. Pleasure, accordingly, is experienced through multiple subjective lenses as linked to specific discursive contexts. Despite its amorphous characteristics, pleasure is worthy of continued sociological examination, particularly within the field of sport, which is intimately linked to participant desire to experience some form of pleasure.

More broadly, the critical aims of the selective scholars reviewed in this chapter (e.g. Wollstonecraft, Foucault, Nietzsche, Bentham, Bakhtin, Marcuse, Freud) can be conceptualized as broadly similar to what most contemporary critical researchers strive for; that is, the desire to offer critique and advocacy to improve quality of life, particularly for those who have less ability to exercise power. Within critical sport studies, for example, numerous researchers have problematized various understandings and practices within sport (e.g. as related to gender, sexuality, violence, racism, disability and injury) with the aim, we presume, to enhance the quality of life for sportswomen, sportsmen and youth. Despite this broad aim, relatively few critical sport scholars have explicitly examined sporting pleasures or how participants conceptualize a quality life. This seems somewhat remiss, as participation and consumption of sport is closely tied to the desire to experience pleasure (in one of its various forms). Indeed, in drawing from Aristotle, I suggest that happiness can be understood as the only 'good' that is always chosen as an end in itself and, correspondingly, the prime 'good' that comes from sport can be conceptualized as some form of pleasure. Yet we ask a more ethical question: can the cumulative experiences of sporting pleasures and pains constitute a life well-lived?

The following chapter takes heed of the advice that it is important to examine pleasure, but in recognition of the somewhat amorphous nature of pleasure asks: how best should pleasure be theorized?

4 Theorizing Sporting Pleasures across the Disciplines

Richard Pringle

'Detested sport,
that owes its pleasures to another's pain'
—(William Cowper, 1785)

'I adore simple pleasures.
They are the last refuge of the complex'
—(Oscar Wilde, 1891)

It is not Wimbledon, far from it, yet this second grade men's interclub match has got me a little on edge. My opponent for the evening, the 'robot', has been mechanically returning my shots and, in moments of frustration, I've been making an increased number of unforced errors. I am breathing hard and deliberately walk slowly to retrieve the ball. The pain in my Achilles has returned and my palms are sweaty, making it difficult to grip the racket. The heat of the summer night is relentless and I wipe my hands once again on my shorts and use my sleeve to soak up the sweat on my brow. I'm only vaguely aware that I'm breaking social taboos by using my clothes in this manner. I move into position to return his serve and momentarily dance on my feet. The ball ricochets off of the top of the net and goes long. I'm pleased and move in a little closer for his second serve. I return it deep onto his backhand. He methodically plays it back down the line. I hit it harder this time and watch it arc onto his forehand with a pleasing top-spin bounce. Yet the ball returns with equal speed. I decide to play it onto his backhand once again but at the last moment resolve to drop it short. The indecision results in the ball hitting the net and falling on my side. The game's lost, but I have a smile on my face; it's a simple pleasure to be out on a summer's evening having a hit.

This vignette of a fairly mundane sporting pleasure lacks the excitement of narratives of extreme sports, grand victories or elite competition. I am not surfing the hole in a slab, getting big air while snowboarding or playing in the grand final in front of a stadium of rapturous fans. Yet the pleasures

42   *Richard Pringle*

gained on the court have lead me to play tennis once or twice a week, most weeks of the year, for the last decade. I contend that these seemingly simple (but often under-examined) pleasures can be understood as *productive*, as they are related to my desire to keep participating. My brief tennis vignette also subtly reveals the interplay of the body (e.g. sweat/pain/skill), psychology (e.g. frustration, focus) and the socio-cultural context (e.g. *men's* competitive tennis), in the production and experiencing of sporting pleasures (and displeasures). Yet the complex nature of pleasure, as already illustrated in Chapters 2 and 3, creates an issue with respect to how to theorize pleasure in order to examine it. Should embodied sporting pleasures be examined via sociological, psychological or biological lenses, or perhaps via some form of interdisciplinary theorizing? This chapter examines this issue, via analysis of sociological, psychological and biological theorizing and the problem of how to read pleasure across the disciplines.

THE CASE FOR INTERDISCIPLINARY READINGS OF SPORTING PLEASURE

Norbert Elias and Eric Dunning (1986) argued that an understanding of sporting emotions could not be adequately examined within only one of the academic disciplines. In their study of sport and the quest for excitement they highlighted the interconnectedness of the socio-cultural, psychological and bodily dimensions of social life and argued for the benefits of interdisciplinary analyses of sporting pleasures. Their promotion of interdisciplinarity was not new, as the advantages of examining a topic from multiple perspectives had been recognized much earlier. In the 1920s and 30s Marcel Mauss (Emile Durkheim's nephew) discussed the 'tripartite integration of the physiological-psychological-sociological' (cited in Probyn, 2004: 234) in order to promote a rapprochement between psychology and sociology and with desire to produce 'a more holistic and body-aware sociology' (Ignatow, 2012: 4). Gabriel Ignatow (2012: 5) contended that it is only in recent years, however, that sociologists have returned to Mauss's advocation for a 'holistic position regarding the interactions of the bodily and mental dimensions of social life'.

Elspeth Probyn (2005), for example, argued for the benefits of incorporating interdisciplinary research with respect to her innovative examination of shame (which is a more specific emotion than the multifarious concept of pleasure). She advised that, instead of ignoring knowledge constructed within different disciplines, such knowledge could be critically appropriated and used:

> Rather than dismissing or ignoring ideas about biology, psychology, and the innate nature of shame, let's see what these ideas do. This is not to say that arguments about the physiology are any truer than those about its cultural expressions; it is to ask how very different ideas might mutually inflect and extend what we know. (p. xiii)

Theorizing Sporting Pleasures 43

The increased interest in interdisciplinarity has been fueled, in part, by the assumption that 'disciplinary research has become too narrowly specialized', parochial and is now providing 'diminishing returns' (Krishnan, 2009: 2). Michael Atkinson (2011) appears to concur with Krishnan's assumption, as he recently asserted that the sociology of sport is in danger of becoming too focused on a small range of topics and that the critical messages emanating from the field tend to circulate too narrowly. The broader academic growth in interdisciplinary research has also occurred in relation to the increased recognition of the complexity of social life, such as the recognition that the 'nature versus nurture debate is a false dichotomy' (Maguire et al., 2002: 184). John Evans and Brian Davies (2011: 263) even boldly asserted that all dualisms, once deconstructed, have 'been found wanting, incapable of adequately addressing the complexity of embodied subjectivity . . .'. The increased recognition of the complexity of human lives has encouraged some critical scholars to promote boundary crossing among disciplines as a pragmatic strategy for enacting social change. Mary Fonow and Judith Cook (2005: 2225), for example, argued that: 'It will take interdisciplinary teams of feminist researchers in different locations to carry out the types of research that our new conceptions of agency and activism demand'.

Despite the alleged advantages of interdisciplinary research, it has not generated significant attention within the sociology of sport (for exceptions see the report by the Tucker Center for Research on Girls and Women in Sport, 2007; Avner et al., 2013; Thorpe, 2012a; Vertinsky, 2009). I assume that this is primarily because interdisciplinary research is difficult to do: as each discipline (and its underpinning paradigm) has its own language, epistemological beliefs and rules of legitimation. Theoretical understandings and concepts, accordingly, 'cannot be simply borrowed across disciplines without mobilizing disciplinary boundary struggles' (Papoulias and Callard, 2010: 50). The issue of how to negotiate competing, or perhaps incommensurable, theoretical perspectives has accordingly made the task of developing a rapprochement between sociology and psychology, or the production of a more body-aware sociology, difficult.

Boundary struggles are also evident within the broad study of pleasure. Deborah Lupton (1998) noted, for example, that two prime *discursive* understandings of pleasure tend to circulate in the literature and complicate analysis: one discourse positions pleasure as primarily an inherent human phenomenon and the other as broadly socially constructed. The view of pleasure as an inherent phenomenon typically regards pleasures as tied to the biological workings of the body, whereas the socially constructed view tends to suggest that pleasures *materialize* via discursive practices of diverse descent. Lupton cogently argued that any discussion or analysis of pleasure can be understood as a subjective practice that draws upon select discourses (and/or theories) that are themselves contingent on specific sociohistoric contexts. The subjective use of discourses/theories of pleasures, more

44   Richard Pringle

pointedly, works to focus attention on specific ways of understanding pleasures while simultaneously obscuring other ways. Lupton thus intimates that an interdisciplinary analysis of pleasure is a fraught task, given the tensions that exist between theoretical/discursive perspectives.

Despite such a discouraging intimation, Robert Donmoyer (2006) suggests that it is still of pragmatic sense to at least read the work stemming from other disciplines that concern the same topic. He explained that in socio-cultural 'fields, one must consider issues from a range of paradigmatic perspectives precisely because . . . what can be seen by examining the world through one perspective or paradigm may not be visible from the vantage point provided by another' (Donmoyer, 2006: 23).

In this chapter, with particular respect to recognizing the alleged advantages (and challenges) of *reading* across the disciplines, I critically review diverse theories of sporting pleasures. I selectively focus on theories linked to sociology, biology and psychology. In doing this, I follow Norbert Elias and Eric Dunning's (1986) call to study people 'in the round' with an interest in knowing what different understandings of pleasure (and sport) can be gained via the employment of different theoretical lenses.

I begin this chapter by reviewing sociological research that has specifically theorized sporting pleasure. Next, I turn my attention to biological understandings of sporting pleasures. I turn to biology, in part, because of recent claims about the biological dimensions of emotional life. For example, Mary Immordino-Yang and Antonio Damasio (2011: 116) assert that 'modern biology reveals humans to be fundamentally emotional and social creatures'. They correspondingly claim that: 'the study of emotions, creativity, and culture is ripe for interdisciplinary collaborations among neuroscientists, psychologists and educators' (Yang and Damasio, 2011: 128). Having examined the influence of the social and biological on sporting pleasures, I turn to psychology to examine what is known about human ability to manage pleasures via training the mind. I specifically examine Csíkszentmihályi's concept of flow, given his contention that people who have a higher frequency of 'flow' experiences are happier and have an enhanced quality of life. In the final section, I offer insight about the benefits and weaknesses of reading theories of pleasures across the disciplines.

SOCIO-CULTURAL THEORIES OF SPORTING PLEASURE

With a few exemplary exceptions (e.g. Duncan and Brummett, 1989; Elias and Dunning, 1986; Wright and Dewar, 1997), the topic of pleasure lurked in the background of the sociology of sport throughout the 1980/90s, somewhat 'like a ghostly shadow; neither fully present nor fully absent' (Coveney and Bunton, 2003: 162). As in the wider discipline of sociology, analyses of social problems typically took precedence over the study of pleasure (O'Malley and Valverde, 2004).[1] The topic of pleasure was seemingly treated as 'a taken-for-granted concept that need(ed) no further exploration'

Theorizing Sporting Pleasures 45

(O'Connor and Klaus, 2000: 370). This was remiss, as the politics of pleasure have real consequences. Lionel Tiger (1992: 6) acknowledged, for example, that: 'there is a fierce endemic contest in many communities about who gets pleasure, which pleasure, when, with whom, and with what cost or tax'. The absent presence of sporting pleasures was, however, noted by some researchers. Jim McKay, Jennifer Gore and David Kirk (1990: 60) lamented that the sporting or physically educated body was 'seldom portrayed as a pleasurable site for ecstatic, aesthetic, vertiginous, autotelic, sensuous and holistic experiences'. Joseph Maguire (1992: 118) similarly asserted, with respect to socio-cultural analyses of lived experiences of sporting pleasure, that: '(w)e are dealing here with a relatively unexplored landscape'.

In the last decade, with respect to the broader turn to the cultural and emotional/affective dimensions of social life, socio-cultural analyses of sport pleasure have gained increased attention. The growth in scholarly interest in sport pleasure has spurred examinations via a now-diverse range of social theories. Researchers, for example, have examined the socio-cultural articulations between sport and pleasure via: affect theory (e.g. Booth, 2008; Evers, 2006), Bourdiuean (e.g. Flectcher, 2008; Thorpe, 2012) and Deleuzean theorizing (Pronger, 1999; Roy, 2013), edge theory (e.g. Laurendeau, 2006; Lyng, 1990, 2005a; Olstead, 2011), figurational sociology (Elias & Dunning, 1986), poststructuralism (e.g. Bridel, 2010; Fiske, 1991; Pringle, 2009; Smith, 2000; Maguire, 2008; Thorpe, 2011) and postmodernism (Stranger, 1999). Richard Giulianotti (2005: 116) has further reported that interpretive and phenomenological approaches are 'particularly germane for assessing intense corporeal experiences as lived, embodied practices, rather than in Cartesian terms that separate the mind and body analytically'.

Although a diverse range of sporting pleasures have now been examined, the pleasures of seemingly dangerous, deviant or extreme sports have gained specific attention (e.g., Booth, 2008; Bridel, 2010; Donnelly, 2004; Evers, 2006; Finn, 1994; Fletcher, 2008; Laurendeau, 2006; Le Breton, 2000; McNamee, 2007; Møller, 2007; Olivier, 2006; Olstead, 2011; Pringle, 2009; Rinehart and Sydnor, 2003; Stranger, 1999; Thorpe, 2012b). These pleasures have often been examined in an attempt to understand why a growing number of individuals purposefully seek risk and how the postmodern condition relates to this growth (e.g. Celsi et al., 1993; Le Breton, 2000; Møller, 2007; Stranger, 1999). The online description for Jason Laurendeau's (2012) book on BASE jumping, for example, begins by asking: 'How does a human being get to the point where he or she considers jumping from deadly heights, simply for the thrill of it?' John Smallwood, in commenting on the recent death of Caleb Moore during the 2013 Winter X Games (after Moore crashed his snowmobile while attempting a backflip), raised a similar concern with why sport participants would voluntarily risk serious injury or death:

> So I say it's insane when I see some teenager shoot 30 feet into the air
> out of a halfpipe to do twists and flips on a skateboard or a snowboard;

46   *Richard Pringle*

or when I see some free climber risk a fatal drop just to reach a summit; or when I see a young man trying to do a backflip on a snowmobile or a motocross bike. (¶ 1)

Yet the athletes who take seemingly 'extreme' but no doubt calculated risks expect to gain something in return, whether it is experiences of thrill, prestige, social capital or money (all of which are tied to pleasures).

Mark Stranger (2011) argued that to understand extreme sport participation it is necessary to examine how participants construct meanings about the sporting activity and social context that they are embedded within. In the following section I follow this advice by examining three socio-cultural theories that have been specifically, and somewhat uniquely, developed to understand the pleasures of sport. I first examine Stephen Lyng's edge theory, then Norbert Elias and Eric Dunning's quest for excitement thesis and, lastly, Mark Stranger's postmodern theorizing on extreme surfing.

Edgework, Figurational Sociology and the Postmodern Sublime

Stephen Lyng (2005a: 5) synthesized 'Marxian and Median ideas relating to the dialectic between spontaneity and constraint in social action . . . that give rise to "alienation" (Marx) and "oversocialization" (Mead)' to inform the study of risk takers in late modernity. His challenge was to 'explain how life-threatening experiences come to acquire a seductively appealing character in the contemporary social context' (Lyng, 2005a: 5). Lyng argued that the tension and alienation felt by workers in increasingly bureaucratized and disciplined workplaces results in few opportunities for spur-of-the-moment, innovative, self-realizing actions. To compensate for this predicament, Lyng (2005a: 4) speculated that some people are encouraged into 'edgework' activities, such as BASE jumping, free climbing and high-speed motorbike racing, where individuals negotiate the edges between 'sanity and insanity, consciousness and unconsciousness, and . . . the line separating life and death'. The negotiation of the fine line between such boundaries is assumed by Lyng to produce the thrill of edgework. Successful negotiation of risk activities, according to Lyng (1990), demands high levels of skill, control and concentration. Moreover, the greatest potential pleasure demands the greatest skill as it rests on the notion of 'being able to *control the seemingly uncontrollable*' (Lyng, 1990: 872). The experiences of pleasure, control and personal authorship, Lyng theorized, are alluring as they compensate for the dehumanizing conditions of post-industrial capitalism and allow possibilities for discovering new forms of embodied existence.

Jason Laurendeau's (2006, 2008, 2012) research on perceptions of risk/control, gender and social interactions within skydiving/BASE jumping has drawn from edgework theorizing. His intriguing research reveals a depth of understanding about the culture of skydivers. Yet his research

Theorizing Sporting Pleasures   47

does not directly support Lyng's underpinning assumptions about *how* the social conditions of late modernity are linked with the voluntary pursuit of risk (although I note that Laurendeau does not specifically interrogate the skydiver's motivations for risk taking). I suggest that Laurendeau's work *indirectly* illustrates shortcomings in Lyng's thesis, as he reveals how playing at the 'edge' does not constitute escape from the suspected problems of late modernity. More pointedly, he reveals how skydivers are still subject to numerous forms of external and internal controls and various relations of power (e.g. gender relations). In this manner, Laurendeau does not portray skydiving as a context that necessarily allows for spur-of-the-moment, innovative and self-realizing actions.

Norbert Elias and Eric Dunning's (1986) *quest for excitement* thesis has similarities to Lyng's notion of compensatory edgework while also drawing indirectly on Freud's argument that civilization is based on the subjugation of the pleasure principle. They argued that the smooth functioning of advanced societies is dependent on people being 'able to maintain a fairly even and stable control over their more spontaneous libidinal, affective and emotional impulses as well as over fluctuating moods' (Elias, 1986: 41). However, the costs associated with life in so-called civilized societies produce stress and, correspondingly, modern societies have developed a compensatory range of leisure activities, including sport and television, that allow for mimetic expression of excitement and emotions that induce a cathartic response. The 'well-tempered excitement' (Elias, 1986: 48) experienced in sport, they argued, is produced by the creation of balanced tensions that do not have the same risks associated with other life situations yet can still evoke anxiety, pain, despair and euphoria. Thus, the pleasures of sport revolve around feeling alive through experiencing various emotions within relatively safe and controlled contexts.

Although Lyng's (2005a) and Elias and Dunning's (1986) theories offer valuable insight into the peculiar pleasures of sport, their attempts to construct a 'single, all-embracing theory' (O'Connor and Klaus, 2000: 371) capable of accommodating the fluidity and multiple subjective experiences of pleasure has several weaknesses. Frith (1982: 503) had earlier argued that the possibility of a single theory of pleasure was flawed because 'the concept refers to too disparate a set of events, individual and collective, active and passive, defined against different situations of displeasure/pain/reality'. More specifically, Lyng (2005a) and Elias and Dunning's (1986) theses fundamentally treat sport pleasure as a 'response to circumstances—a reaction, a compensation, a transcendence' (Donnelly, 2004: 43). Although some individuals may participate in edgework activities or sport as a form of reaction to life stresses, such explanations are not universally tenable. Many adults, for example, begin and *enjoy* participation in sport as children, before one could convincingly argue that they are dehumanized, alienated or stressed via the pressures of civilized/modern life. In addition, as Peter Donnelly (2004) argued in relation to Lyng's work, it appears a simplistic

48 Richard Pringle

generalization to suggest that people take voluntary risks in edgework leisure activities due to poor job or life satisfaction. Mark Stranger (1999), with more sting, argued that Lyng and Elias and Dunning undermine the pleasures experienced within sport and edgework activities, as these pleasures are not deemed significant enough to account for the direct involvement in the activity. That is, the pleasures of BASE-jumping or sport participation are supposedly not sufficient enough to motivate participation.

To explain the current popularity of high-risk sport, specifically big wave surfing (which is currently dominated by male participants), Mark Stranger (1999) extended the work of Lyng (1990) and Elias and Dunning (1986) through drawing on Huizinga's (1970) call to examine the aesthetic elements of play in combination with the postmodern recognition of the increased aestheticization and stylization of life. Stranger rejected the notion that sportspeople in search of thrill operate rationally in response to the social conditions. Through an extensive 'surf safari' ethnography he argued that 'the allocation of "meaning" to risk-taking behavior is not so much an intellectual process as an affectual one that is based on desire rather than the ego; images rather than words . . . "Kantian intuition" rather than a "Kantian logic"' (p. 270). This seemingly irrational response allows surfers to construct a belief system that positions surfing, irrespective of the risk, as 'good in itself' (p. 270).

To explain this irrationality, Stranger drew on Kant and Lyotard's writings on sublime judgment. Sublime judgment in Kantian terms is associated with the blurring of emotions linked to an understanding of the power, horror and beauty of nature. The mountain climber, for example, supposedly experiences the awe and terror of the mountain as sublime. Jean-François Lyotard (1994: 92) suggested that the contradictory and sublime feelings of 'pleasure and pain, joy and anxiety, exaltation and depression' mediate a dedifferentiation between sign and signifier and reality and image. Stranger concludes that the aestheticization of surfing is driven by a sublime appreciation of the ocean and surf action so that the surfer, as blinded by emotion in pursuit of ecstasy and transcendence, operates with a distorted interpretation of risk:

> The postmodern nature of surfing's sublime is such that the distinction between the appreciation and the experiences become blurred. This dedifferentiation between the sign and signifier distorts any rational assessment of risk. Images of the sublime act upon the surfer's 'faculty of desire', and in combination with the aestheticized perception of risk, override or circumvent the fear of personal harm. (Stranger, 1999: 273)

Although I am intrigued by Stranger's turn to postmodern theorizing, it does not fully resonate with my own experiences. As a fair-weather surfer of limited ability I do not seek large waves to maximize thrill nor do I have overt concern about my image while surfing my longboard (or 'log' as keen surfers might refer to it). In this respect, I suspect that I am not blinded by emotion when surfing. But I still enjoy the 'rush' of dropping in on a wave and the challenge of attempting to ride the face. The 'rush', or what surf aficionados call 'stoke' (Booth, 2011: 50), is vaguely similar to catching a wave when body surfing or boogie boarding, but standing on the water when surfing literally changes one's perspective and appreciation. In my view, the rush—which is apparently the aspect of surfing that can encourage addictive behaviors—is tied to the thrill of accelerating the body while attempting to maintain balance. Yet Stranger does not adequately unpack the embodied experiences of stoke.

Surfing is undoubtedly linked to other pleasures such as the joy of being in the water, the social connections and identities formed via surfing and the possibilities for attaining a 'flow' state (which is one important form of pleasure). Yet the embodied sensations and rush of catching the wave seem paramount. Thus, Stranger's (1999) somewhat disembodied account seems remiss. His final sentence, a quote from a professional surfer (cited in Booth, 1995a: 205) appears to contradict his prime argument, as it suggests that surfing simply 'feels good'. The pro-surfer crudely exclaimed: 'I surf for the same reasons I perpetually flog myself to the heights of orgasmic pleasure—because it feels good' (Stranger, 1999: 274). Such a comment works to dismiss the postmodern theorizing purported by Stranger. Conversely, I doubt whether Stranger would analyze masturbation and subsequently theorize that it involves a 'postmodern incarnation of the sublime that distorts rational risk assessment' (Stranger, 1999: 265). Nevertheless, it is also remiss to simply accept that a sporting experience simply 'feels good'.

There are many social theories that can be used to examine the 'feel good' aspect of sport and movement (e.g. phenomenology, interpretivism, etc.), but in recent years affect theorizing has gained attention. My concern with Stranger's postmodern thesis has resonance, correspondingly, with why a number of researchers have turned to affect theorizing. That is, the increased interest in affect theorizing has been purported as a reaction to the *alleged* limitations of postmodern/poststructural thought and its apparent neglect of 'matter, biology and energetic forces' (Liljeström and Paasonen, 2010: 1). Marianne Liljeström and Susanna Paasonen argued:

> . . . that there has been an overuse of textual metaphors in cultural theory since the 1990s (as in the readings of bodies, landscapes or artifacts as texts to be interpreted or 'decoded' without accounting for their materiality): a broad range of intellectual concerns are bypassed or even lost if focusing solely on the semantic and the symbolic. (Liljeström and Paasonen, 2010: 1)

This argument asserts that poststructural/postmodern theorizing neglects the 'biological or material' in favor of reading the body as a text. Although such an argument is subject to debate (e.g. see Larsson, 2012; Wetherell, 2012),

50   *Richard Pringle*

in the following section I examine what is known about sporting pleasures from studies emanating from the biological sciences.

BIOLOGY AND SPORTING/MOVEMENT PLEASURES

> *The 'fear fall' or the 'big drop' or whatever it was called dominated the skyline of the local amusement park. I'd often seen it from the motorway, but it looked more ominous closer up. My two boys had coerced me into taking them to the theme park in order to celebrate a recent birthday and they were now attempting to coerce me into riding this 'tower of pointless risk'. I had no real qualms about riding the tower— at least I think I thought not—but nevertheless wasn't all that keen. I told them: 'well . . . we will need to see if you are both tall enough to take the ride'. I was confident that my youngest son would be too short but added another proviso: 'and have a look at the length of the queue. If it's too long, we'll leave it'. They both raced to the bottom of the tower and my younger son soon yelled back: 'we're in luck Dad, we're both tall enough and there are only two people in the line'. His excitement was palpable. 'What?' I thought to myself. 'Why are there only two people in the line?' Without further time to think, we were strapped into the ride, with our bodies rising into the blue sky and our legs kicking free. As the ride paused for effect at the tower's pinnacle, I had time to check my loose restraint safety system and find a button. I wondered if I pushed it whether the seatbelt would un-buckle? I then had a moment of panic, as I thought that my younger son would undoubtedly find this button and push it. I leaned over to check his restraint system and the plummet began. 'Jeeeesus', I unexpectedly yelled. And with the momentary weightlessness my sons and I hollered with excitement. Soon we were back on the ground and I was surprised to find myself laughing with genuine animation, talking at great volume and seemingly unaware that others were looking at me a little strangely. I didn't care, I was experiencing a distinct body rush, it was tangibly electric and I loved it.*

The vignette above refers to an incident from several years ago. Its occurrence encouraged me to reflect further about the complexity of sporting/movement/ body pleasures. I had not been expecting much of a thrill from the amusement ride—a ride that took place in a controlled consumer environment, free from *real* risk—so the distinctly tangible and electrifying body rush was unexpected. It was, however, similar to experiences I've had at the end of a fast ski run or catching a wave. At times I have even laughed excitedly— perhaps hooted is a more apt adjective—while experiencing these movement thrills. I speculate that the amusement park 'rush' was likely related to

Theorizing Sporting Pleasures   51

some physiological or neurological response, possibly the release of massive amounts of 'fright and flight' hormones, as my surprisingly pleasurable reaction appeared to transcend the social.

In a previous study on rugby pleasures (Pringle, 2009), my adopted theoretical position drew from Foucault and revolved around skepticism that pleasure was 'the simple product of biological, psychological, or personal appetites' (Pringle, 2009: 214), as I accepted:

> . . . that human experiences of pleasure are constituted, negotiated, and organized through available discourses and are simultaneously the product of certain forms of training or disciplining. Different systems of thought and mechanisms of power in different epistemes, therefore, shape how humans experience, understand, manage, and use pleasure. Pleasure, in this manner, can be understood as a multifaceted, complex, subjective, and, at times, seemingly contradictory emotional experience. (Pringle, 2009: 214)

My electrifying response to the thrill ride, however, encouraged me to think more about the *unconscious* workings of my body. I surmised that the socio-cultural context and my body played a complex role in how I experienced and made sense of the amusement park ride. Yet I was uneasy to suggest that biological responses played an *active* role in this complex process. Such a suggestion, I believed, would counter my anti-essentialist and social-constructionist positions. I was also aware that within the sociology of sport, understandings of the body were dominated by social-constructionist views and, conversely, biological knowledge was seldom considered. Perhaps this was simply because biological dimensions were taken for granted by sociologists of sport or, more likely, deemed irrelevant to socio-cultural concerns, given 'our' social focus. Alternatively, biological knowledge was perhaps marginalized because it has been linked with the problems of genetic determinism and was, therefore, viewed as a potentially dangerous topic (e.g. *The New York Times Magazine* dropped plans to print an adaption of Jon Entine's 2008 text, *Taboo: Why Black Athletes Dominate Sports and Why We're afraid to Talk About It*, due to editorial concerns of a public backlash).

Despite such risks, a number of prominent critical researchers from diverse disciplines (e.g. Connell, 1995; Massumi, 2002; Probyn, 2005; Sedgwick and Frank, 1995; Thrift, 2004; Wetherell, 2012) have advocated the importance of re-considering the relevance of biology for understanding socio-cultural issues. Andrew Sparkes and Brett Smith (2012: 168) have highlighted how a growing number of researchers are now exploring and undertaking 'more sensuous forms of scholarship in sport and physical culture'. This increased interest in the senses and embodied pleasures reflects a concern that previous research about the moving body 'ignored the fleshy,

52   Richard Pringle

messy, material (biological) and sentient body along with the lived practical experiences of those who inhabit . . . "real" bodies' (Sparkes and Smith, 2012: 168). In this section, I follow this lead and examine the role of the biological in relation to movement pleasures. I begin by providing a case history of scientific examinations of 'runner's high' and then consider how such knowledge might be theorized to enrich socio-cultural understandings.

SCIENTIFIC UNDERSTANDINGS OF RUNNER'S HIGH

I have not experienced runner's high, but it has been variously described as a sense of euphoria experienced at the end of an endurance run, of peace or relaxation while running, alleviation of pain or boundless energy. The phenomenon is well known by runners and many I have talked to report that they have experienced it, but that it is a somewhat elusive state. Most of these runners assumed that it was related to a release of endorphins and/ or associated with the development of a transcendental state due to a profound connection between the running 'body' and mind. These assumptions perhaps stem from related biological and psychological research. So what is the biological knowledge of getting 'high' from running?

Michael Sachs (1980) first examined runner's high in an attempt to connect its occurrence to various psychological factors (e.g. relaxation, distraction, alleviation of personal problems, hypnotic susceptibility, transcendence). Sachs subsequently examined running as a potential source of therapy or of addiction. By 1985, vigorous exercise had been correlated with reductions in anxiety and the development of a sense of wellbeing; hypothesized causes included endorphin release and monoamine metabolism (Morgan, 1985). Researchers had already found that plasma levels of ß-endorphin, a morphine-like substance originating in the body, were significantly elevated after aerobic exercise (Carr et al., 1981; Pierce et al., 1993). These endorphins have also been found to be produced in times of pain, excitement, sexual activity and through consumption of spicy food. Concerns were raised, however, that ß-endorphins could not be source of runner's high due to the blood-brain barrier, which was assumed to prevent the endorphin from affecting the mental state. Sforzo and colleagues (1986) subsequently found that circulating ß-endorphin levels could not cross the barrier, as the molecules were too big. In addition, the usage of ß-endorphin blockers did not appear to prevent the occurrence of runner's high. The notion of endorphins and runners high was subsequently assumed by some to be a 'myth perpetuated by pop culture' (cited in Dietrich and McDaniel, 2004: 536).

Attention turned to examination of other neurotransmitters, including other endorphins, dopamine, ACTH, serotonin and endocannabinoids. Dietrich and McDaniel (2004), for example, found that exercise increases blood serum levels of endocannabinoids and that these naturally occurring neurotransmitters produce psychological states that closely parallel several experiences described as similar to the runner's high. They claimed:

> Activation of the Endocannabinoids and exercise endocannabinoid system also produces sedation, anxiolysis, a sense of wellbeing, reduced attentional capacity, impaired working memory ability, and difficulty in time estimation. This behavioural profile is similar to the psychological experiences reported by long distance runners. (Dietrich and McDaniel, 2004: 539–540)

Although different researchers examined the influence of different neurotransmitters, interest in endorphins was rekindled by the research of Henning Boecker and colleagues (2008), who found evidence that brain endorphins were influenced by exercise and connected with states of euphoria. Their study involved brain scans of ten experienced distance runners who had all previously experienced runners' highs. The scans were able to map the workings of the endorphins after strenuous running. Findings revealed reductions occurred to opioid receptor sites in the frontolimbic region of the brains of the runners, a region known to play a key role in emotional processing and the generation of affective states. More specifically, these reductions were closely correlated with the runner's self-reported accounts of euphoria. Boecker and colleagues concluded that the endogenous opioid system played a specific role in the generation of the runner's high. In a more general view, they suggested:

> . . . it might also be assumed that opioidergic effects in frontolimbic brain structures mediate not only some of the therapeutically beneficial consequences of endurance exercise on depression and anxiety in patients (Morgan 1985) but also the addictive aspects of excessive sports, where injured athletes continue their training in spite of detrimental consequences to their health . . . (Boecker et al., 2008: 2530)

In this manner, Boecker and colleagues (2008) connected the results of their neurological study to social issues (e.g. running addiction, depression, anxiety).

Rod Dishman and Patrick O'Connor (2009) cautioned that, although the study by Boecker et al. was innovative, it should *not* be assumed that the 'truths' about the runner's high are now known. In contrast, they suggested that no single neurotransmitter could explain mood states, as they depend on complex interactions between numerous other physiologic and neurologic factors. Dishman and O'Connor neglected, however, to comment on the various social and psychological dimensions that interact with endogenous factors.

So how should a critical sociologist make sense of these biological findings? On the one hand, I suggest it seems reasonable to conclude that biological

54   Richard Pringle

factors (i.e. brain endorphins) potentially play a role in shaping *some* runners' experiences of pleasure. Yet, if this is the case, then can it also be assumed that 'biology' plays a productive role in shaping running desires, motivations, identities and relations of power? Such a contention, for some, might be dangerously close to biological determinism, whereas for others, it might underestimate what they believe is a closer link between culture and biology. Biocultural synergy theorists, for example, 'argue that biology and culture are mutually dependent and continually transform each other throughout the organism's lifetime' (Levenson, Soto and Pole, 2007: 782). Lisa Blackman's (2008) interpretation of embodiment similarly rests on the notion that 'nature' and 'culture' are not separate entities that interact but that 'they produce each other in such a way that it is impossible to disentagle one from the other' (Blackman, 2008: 35).

Regardless of one's position, the pragmatics of how to represent biological and sociological knowledge within accounts of sporting pleasures are under-examined. If sociology of sport researchers are to produce such accounts, at the least, we need to draw on theories that acknowledge the possibilities of the interweaving of biology and the socio-cultural. In the following section, I examine Raewyn Connell's concept of body-reflexive practices as one such theoretical possibility.

Body-Reflexive Pleasures

In her critical analysis of masculinities and gender relations, Raewyn Connell (1995: 60) provocatively argued that bodies share in 'social agency, in generating and shaping courses of social conduct'. She acknowledged that the materiality of bodies matters, as bodies can do certain things and not others and are, therefore, 'substantively in play in social practices such as sport, labour and sex' (Connell, 1995: 58). She argued further that bodies could also be recalcitrant as they 'disrupt and subvert the social arrangements into which they are invited' (Connell, 1995: 58). She illustrated this point, somewhat explicitly, by drawing from the reflections of one of her interviewees, Don Meredith (a pseudonym). Meredith told Connell of a surprising sexual experience and his pleasant reaction to it. Meredith stated: 'She really touched a spot well and truly' (Connell, 1995: 60). This embodied experience subsequently encouraged his recalcitrant desires to eventually partake in a homosexual relationship.

Connell referred to Don Meredith's experience as a 'body-reflexive practice' (Connell, 1995: 61) and suggested that Meredith's experience was 'not simply a matter of social meanings or categories being imposed on Don's body, though these meanings and categories are vital to what happens' (Connell, 1995: 62). Instead, she asserted, body-reflexive practices call or interpolate these meanings and categories 'into play, while the body experience—a startling joy—energizes the circuit' (Connell, 1995: 62). In this seemingly iconoclastic manner, Connell suggested that: 'agency does not

Theorizing Sporting Pleasures   55

seem too strong a word for what Don's sphincter, prostate gland and erectile tissues . . . managed between them' (Connell, 1995: 61).

Connell's (1995) thesis rested on the assumption that the anatomical structures of the body, in relation to their neurology and physiology, play an *active* role in shaping social performances, interactions and contexts. The body's 'agency' was therefore assumed to shape how humans make meanings of certain pleasurable experiences:

> Through body-reflexive practices, bodies are addressed by social processes and drawn into history, without ceasing to be bodies. They do not turn into symbols, signs or positions in discourse. Their materiality (including material capacities to engender, to give birth, to menstruate, to open, to penetrate, to ejaculate) is not erased, it continues to matter. The social process of gender includes childbirth and child care, youth and aging, the pleasures of sport and sex, labour, death from AIDS. (Connell, 1995: 64–65)

Connell's reassertion of the biological influence of social life appeared to run counter to the then-dominant theoretical position within sociological studies that centered on what Papoulias and Callard (2010: 32) called 'the "social construction" of whatever object or phenomenon was under analysis'. Connell's thesis, accordingly, encourages further consideration about how biology is enmeshed with the socio-cultural.

Bryan Turner (1984: 1) argued that the body was initially neglected by social theorists because: 'Any reference to the corporeal nature of human existence raises in the mind of the sociologist the spectre of social Darwinism, biological reductionism or sociobiology'. Anti-essentialists, as an example, have long been concerned about attempts to naturalize behaviors and/or abilities in relation to the apparent functioning of particular bodies (e.g. 'sexed' or 'raced' bodies), as such attempts can be used to justify social injustices and stall possibilities for social transformation.

Connell, however, was not guilty of biological determinism in promoting her theory of body-reflexive practices. Although she suggested that it is necessary for bodies to be seen 'as sharing in social agency, in generating and shaping courses of social conduct' (Connell, 1995: 60), she did not suggest that bodies determine behavior. More pointedly, Connell gave preference to the 'social', as she understood bodily experience as a form of 'proprioceptive consciousness'. Yet this prioritizing of the social body over the physiological body has also generated critique.

Peter Douglas (1996), for example, suggested that Connell positioned the body as 'nothing more than the awareness of physiological excitations by consciousness' (Douglas, 1996: 112) and, therefore, was ultimately concerned with how individuals' construct meanings about bodily sensations. Douglas lamented that Connell did not fully bring the fleshed body into social theory, but indirectly reproduced 'the culture/nature dichotomy in

56 Richard Pringle

the guise of a conscious subject/material body (or mind/body) dichotomy' (Douglas, 1996: 112).[2] Douglas argued further that Connell's prioritization of consciousness meant that her theoretical position subsequently ignored the workings of genes, hormones and brain structures and closed 'off any dialogue with the insights provided by fields such as genetics, neurophysiology, embryology, endocrinology, primatology and evolutionary theory' (Douglas, 1996: 112). He added: 'To assert that these fields have no contribution to make towards an understanding of the social "agency" of bodies is both dogmatic and unhelpful if the body is to become a meaningful presence in social theory' (Douglas, 1996: 112).[3]

Yet for many years, socio-cultural researchers have been reluctant to draw from the biological sciences. Eve Sedgwick and Adam Frank (1995), for example, noted in a somewhat tongue-in-cheek manner that one of the key assumptions that constituted 'good' socio-cultural theory from the 1980s to the mid-1990s was that: 'The distance of any such account from a biological basis is assumed to correlate near-precisely with its potential for doing justice to difference (individual, historical and cross-cultural), to contingency, to performative force and to the possibility of change' (Sedgwick and Frank, 1995: 1). In more recent years the apparent need for socio-cultural theorists to distance themselves from biological sciences has been questioned. Indeed, nine years after Sedgwick and Frank's (1995) observations, Nigel Thrift (2004) offered a new set of assumptions about what constituted good socio-cultural theory. He asserted provocatively that: 'Distance from biology is no longer seen as a prime marker of social and cultural theory . . .' (p. 59) and that 'naturalism and scientism are no longer seen as terrible sins' (Thrift, 2004: 59).

Although Thrift's (2004) claims about what constituted good theory may have contemporary currency in some fields of socio-cultural study (e.g. affect theorizing), his assumptions would likely be debated within sport sociology at present time. Relatively few sociologists of sport appear to have reduced their distance from biology or embedded science within their research (see as exceptions Booth, 2011; Thorpe, 2012). Douglas Booth (2011: 54) commented that the interface between the biological and social is 'currently little understood' and 'we know very little about the neurobiology and psychophysiology of pleasure induced by movement' (Booth, 2011: 154).[4] At a broader level, affect theorists who have allegedly 'recalibrated the relationship between (cultural) theory and science' (Papoulias and Callard, 2010: 30), such as Brian Massumi (2002) and Nigel Thrift (2004), have generated significant research interest but have also been subject to stern critique. Concern has been raised that Massumi and Thrift cherry-picked psychobiological findings in order to primarily support their underpinning political arguments (Papoulias and Callard, 2010; Wetherell, 2012) (see Chapter 8 for discussion of affect theorizing in relation to the pleasures of viewing the Olympics).

Theorizing Sporting Pleasures 57

Although I am supportive of attempts to blend the biological and the sociological to enhance understandings of sporting pleasures, my provisional exploration suggests it is clearly a difficult task to do well. Margaret Wetherell explained this difficulty by drawing from Donna Harraway's string analogy: 'it is like holding two pieces of string and discovering that they are just the ends of the most enormous, chaotic, knotted ball that needs to be unraveled' (cited in Wetherell, 2012: 50). Indeed, there are difficulties with 1) selecting (and understanding) alternative disciplinary knowledges, 2) working within competing theoretical frameworks and 3) limited exemplars of what constitutes good boundary crossing. There is still value, however, in reading across the disciplines and in conceptualizing that the relationship between the social/discursive and bodies/physiology can operate in a reciprocal manner.

In this chapter thus far, I have considered the place of social context (e.g. as related to extreme sport pleasures and the postmodern condition) and biology (e.g. endorphins) in the shaping of sporting pleasures; these are factors that individuals have seemingly little ability to control. In contrast, individuals have some ability to control their own 'thinking'. In the following section, accordingly, I turn to psychology and examine Mihály Csíkszentmihályi's notion that an individual can enhance his/her feelings of happiness through controlling consciousness, and, that sport is a prime context within which this can occur.

PSYCHOLOGY: FLOW, HAPPINESS AND SPORT

Mihály Csíkszentmihályi's (1990) seminal work on the psychology of optimal experience has had considerable influence within happiness studies, positive psychology and to a lesser extent sport and exercise psychology, yet it is rarely drawn upon within the sociology of sport. In this section, I examine his concept of flow to consider the possibilities of a rapprochement between psychology and sociology and to gain a rounder comprehension of sporting pleasures.

Csíkszentmihályi (1990) proposed that individuals are *happiest* when they are in the flow state: a state of consciousness that produces a feeling of involvement, concentration and absorption; a state without ego, where one becomes lost in the activity so that there is little awareness of time or effort. Flow, he reported, produces a sense of transcendence and is so enjoyable that individuals desire to repeat the activity. From this brief definition of flow, it might be assumed that flow is akin to an 'out of it' experience, perhaps similar to the pleasurable and potentially habit forming effects of drugs or alcohol, where one's identity and anxieties can be momentarily lost in a state of intoxication. Yet Csíkszentmihályi (1997) clearly differentiated the flow state from intemperance by emphasizing that flow occurs

58   Richard Pringle

when challenges are high and skills are used to the utmost. He was critical of passive leisure, as he believed it required little skill or challenge (e.g. watching sport).

To help justify his particular claims about optimum experiences, Csíkszentmihályi differentiated pleasure from happiness. He defined pleasure as 'a feeling of contentment that one achieves whenever information in consciousness says that expectations set by biological programs or social conditioning have been met' (Csíkszentmihályi, 1990: 45). Sleep, rest, food and sex, he suggested (as similar to Aristotle, see Chapter 3), can all be pleasurable activities but they may not make an individual happy. He claimed that happiness, in contrast, is similarly linked to meeting a prior expectation or desire, but also conveys a sense of achievement and of moving forward. The self, he claimed, grows in complexity as a consequence of performing enjoyable activities and of being in the flow state. Yet being in the flow state does not mean that individuals also feel happy, as to feel happiness an individual must focus on her/his internal state and this would disrupt the flow experience. Csíkszentmihályi suggested, accordingly, that it is only after immersion in the flow state that an individual can reflect and recognize that the experience was enjoyable and, thus, recognize retrospectively the feelings of happiness.

Csíkszentmihályi argued that flow is the key to a quality life. His research findings suggested, for example, that individuals who often experience the flow state have higher self-esteem, tend to be happier and are less prone to stress-related illness. In apparent agreement with some Eastern philosophies, Csíkszentmihályi concluded that it is the ability to be totally absorbed in the challenge of an activity that is the prime ingredient in the constitution of a satisfied life. Similar sentiments have been expressed by the French philosopher Alain (1868–1951), who stated: 'A man is occupied by that from which he expects to gain happiness, but his greatest happiness is the fact that he is occupied' (in Holt, 2006: 20). Alain's point is that it does not matter what one is absorbed in, as it is the process of absorption that creates happiness. But if this is the point, I start to question Csíkszentmihályi's devotion to flow, as I wonder whether the idea of total absorption in a challenge, irrespective of what the challenge is, is something that humans should strive for to achieve happiness.

Csíkszentmihályi (1990: 2) reported that his major discovery was that happiness 'is a condition that must be prepared for, cultivated and defended privately by each person'. Although he recognized that happiness was an elusive goal, he nevertheless claimed that an individual could work at controlling her/his consciousness and have greater opportunity for experiencing flow states and achieving happiness.[5] He noted that participation in a sport could provide a good opportunity to experience flow and gain happiness.

Csíkszentmihályi (1990: 51) claimed that games and sports have been 'developed over the centuries for the express purpose of enriching life with enjoyable experiences'. Yet, as many ex-sport participants know, sport

Theorizing Sporting Pleasures   59

participation does not come with a guaranteed outcome. Sport psychologist Susan Jackson (2000: 135) stated that, 'although sport begins as an activity viewed as fun, it can yield a mix of positive and negative emotion'. This recognition has underpinned her examinations of the connections between flow and sporting experiences with a particular desire to know how to enhance the positive experiences of sport participation. The results from Jackson's studies suggest that athletes who perform at their best (i.e. peak performances) tend to describe their experiences in a manner that matches the characteristics of flow (e.g. see Jackson and Kimiecik, 2008). That is, athletes talk of a narrow focus of attention, calmness, feelings of control and confidence and positive affects. Yet athletes can also experience the flow state and perform below their best. Thus, they can be totally absorbed in the sporting activity, participate with confidence and feelings of enjoyment but also perform relatively poorly. Irrespective of an athlete's performance levels, the experiencing of flow is recognized as 'a motivating factor to participate in sport on a regular basis' (Jackson and Kimiecik, 2008: 385), yet evidence also suggests that athletes experience flow relatively infrequently.

Somewhat ironically, in my view, a key element of sport—*competition*—has been postulated as a prime factor that decreases the likelihood of experiencing flow, as competition encourages athletes to focus on the outcome or the extrinsic aspects of the experience, and such a focus can disrupt the feeling of being totally absorbed in the activity. Surfers, for example, report greater experiences of flow while free surfing in comparison to participating in surf competitions (Jackson, 2000).

In an attempt to understand how to induce flow states in sport competitors, sport psychologists have examined the psychosocial mechanisms that correlate with flow experiences. Findings suggest that athletes who are confident, intrinsically motivated, optimally aroused and who use precompetitive plans are more likely to experience flow during sport competitions (Partington, Partington and Olivier, 2009). Yet such knowledge does not necessarily help athletes experience flow, as such psychosocial variables are difficult to control in the extrinsically focused and dynamic context of competitive sport. An athlete can only feel confident, for example, if she/he believes that they can perform to a certain level and have a good chance of winning.

Csíkszentmihályi's concept of flow is typically recognized as a valuable contribution to understandings of sporting pleasure and many readers may resonate with the concept. Yet, as with any theory, it has also been the subject of critique. Karen Fox and Gordon Walker (2002: 17) suggested that: 'Csíkszentmihályi presents people's experiences as if they were self-evident and in no need of explanation regarding race, class, culture, ethnicity, ability, sexual orientation, cultural forces, power situatedness, and so forth'. In other words, they argued that experiences of flow within sport can be understood as constituted/mediated by a host of socio-cultural factors, but these factors have not been typically subject to interpretation or critique.

60 Richard Pringle

For example, flow has been typically represented as a positive and desirable state to strive for, yet there has been little analysis of the power relations associated with experiencing flow in a sporting context. It is possible, for example, that one athlete's ability to achieve a flow state might be to the detriment of another player's enjoyment and, over time, his/her continued participation in that sporting activity. In this sense, the flow state could potentially promote and suppress levels of happiness simultaneously. Analysis of flow, accordingly, demands a broader socio-cultural critique of the sporting environment and the associated workings of power to determine, in part, whether the flow state—beyond the individual athlete—is a key aspect for promoting happiness more broadly.

Karen Fox and Gordon Walker (2002) have also raised concern that Csíkszentmihályi's focus on the balance between challenge and ability works to marginalize many other sporting pleasures. For example, there is little challenge associated with watching televised sport, yet many sport fans gain immensely from viewing *their* teams and athletes (see Klugman, 2013). In contrast, Csíkszentmihályi would likely regard this form of sporting activity as passive and, accordingly, as a leisure activity that does not improve the quality of life. Sport fans would disagree with such biased assertions. Csíkszentmihályi's dismissal of so-called passive sporting pleasures is accordingly akin to ignoring the complexity, nuances and subtleties of sport as a socio-cultural phenomenon.

Leonard Wankel (1997) raised a similar issue in discussing the limitations of the concept of flow. Wankel suggested that sport participants do not make distinctions between enjoyment and pleasure, as Csíkszentmihályi does, and that their reports on what they enjoy goes far beyond the 'matching of perceived skills and challenges' (Wankel, 1997: 103). Although Wankel acknowledged the importance of Csíkszentmihályi's work, he argued that the flow experience is just one of many enjoyable aspects associated with sport and that these diverse aspects need to be considered to fully understand pleasurable sporting experiences.

As a further cautionary note on the concept of flow, it is also apparent that the experiencing of flow can be detrimental to an individual. As Csíkszentmihályi (1990) acknowledged, flow can have a negative aspect when one becomes addicted to the experience, 'at which point the self becomes captive of a certain kind of order, and is then unwilling to cope with the ambiguities of life' (Csíkszentmihályi, 1990: 62). Sarah Partington and colleagues' (2009) examination of the dark side of flow in association with addiction to the thrill of big wave surfing is enlightening. Their interview study revealed that surfers often experienced flow and were subsequently seduced to attempt to surf bigger, faster and correspondingly more dangerous waves. They concluded: 'Surfers talked of being addicted to the euphoric feelings experienced, and were willing to continue to surf despite family commitments, injury or potential death, to replicate these sensations' (Partington, Partington and Olivier, 2009: 183). In this manner, they illustrated

Theorizing Sporting Pleasures   61

that the experiencing of flow does not necessarily lead to growth and a quality of life, but at times to a problematic dependence on feelings of euphoria and total absorption.

Like Wankel (1997), I recognize flow as a particular form of pleasure that can be gained while playing sport. Yet I am aware that Csíkszentmihályi's theorizing acts to position alternative sporting pleasures as inferior, flawed and/or socially insignificant. For example, the ecstatic pleasures of fans celebrating a victory on the buzzer, the mundane pleasures of jogging (see Chapter 7), the ascetic pleasures of body-building or the social pleasures of feeling part of a team are all marginalized via the concept of flow. The everyday lives of numerous sport participants and fans revolve around a range of these pleasures and, as such, have considerable social significance and deserve greater examination.

FINAL WORDS: ON THE MERITS OF INTERDISCIPLINARY ANALYSIS

In this chapter I examined the possibilities of gaining a more holistic or rounder understanding of sporting pleasures through reading across the disciplines. I also aimed to promote thinking outside the boundaries, encourage a more 'body-aware sociology' and challenge dualistic thinking that proposes pleasure as either biologically or socially constructed. Through undertaking this endeavor I now accept that our psychologies, social contexts, experiences and biologies all play a role in shaping our diverse understandings of what is pleasurable in sport. I even accept the possibility that the biological and socio-cultural work in an entangled and reciprocal manner in the production of pleasures. Yet, given the difficulties associated with undertaking interdisciplinary research, I am not advocating that sociologists of sport should undertake such research. Nor do I think that this review will promote a rapprochement between psychology and sociology.

Moreover, I suggest it would be problematic to attempt to assimilate sociological, biological and psychological theories into one explanatory narrative of sporting pleasure. Firstly, such a grand theory would be destined for failure given the malleable, multiple and contradictory characteristics of pleasure. Secondly, it would be a very difficult task given the competing epistemologies and research approaches. Indeed, I could not bracket out my own paradigmatic biases in the writing of this chapter and, as such, they are evident in relation to my critiques of Lyng's edgework theorizing and Csíkszentmihályi's concept of flow.

More broadly, I suggest that all researchers have paradigmatic biases (including those who study the biological dimensions of pleasure via the scientific method) and tend to gravitate towards using particular theories that resonate with their paradigmatic views. Within this book we do not promote a particular theoretical lens for the examination of sporting pleasures.

62 Richard Pringle

Although we find attempts to offer singular, all-embracing theories of pleasure somewhat problematic, we recognize that all theories have strengths and weaknesses and that there is value in examining pleasure from multiple perspectives. We, accordingly, draw on diverse theories (e.g. affect theorizing, queer theories, Foucauldian), concepts (e.g. subjective wellbeing, eudaimonia) and research approaches (e.g. autoethnography, poetic sensibilities, in-depth interviews, textual analysis) to examine and reveal the complex, diverse and fluctuating character of sporting pleasures.

Although there were clear contrasts and contradictions between the sociological, biological and psychological theories reviewed, there was also a degree of overlap: all of the theories suggest that experiences of pleasure (e.g. flow, thrill, runner's high) can motivate ongoing sporting involvement. Pleasures, as such, can be habit forming and shape routines, interactions, identities and risks of injury. In this respect, adults should think carefully about the sporting activities that they encourage youth to experience.

NOTES

1. A cursory scan of articles published in journals concerned with the sociocultural analysis of sport throughout the 1980s and 1990s could affirm O'Malley and Valverde's (2004) broad thesis. Indeed, the overwhelming focus on sporting issues would create the impression that sport is deeply problematic: a social institution that is overtly sexist, racist, homophobic, violent, nationalistic, discriminatory, ageist, disableist, highly commodified and corrupt. The sporting world, accordingly, was not primarily portrayed as a context that has capacity to generate excitement, inspiration, passion, love and pleasure. Yet the sporting world can simultaneously be understood as a social problem and as a source of pleasure.
2. Similar criticisms have been directed at Foucault's ideas on the production of docile and disciplined bodies. Lisa Blackman (2008) contended that although Foucault was concerned about how 'bodies' become disciplined, his ideas illustrated that the workings of disciplinary power primarily work on minds rather than bodies; thus, she alleged that Foucault privileged the social and subsequently propped up a mind/body dualism. Chris Shilling (1997: 79) similarly argued that, 'Foucault's epistemological view of the body means that it virtually *disappears* as a material phenomenon'. He added: 'the body tends to become an inert mass controlled by discourses centered on the mind (which is treated as if abstracted from an active human body)' (Shilling, 1997: 79). Shilling's concern of the dominance of the social over the body is reflected in the following observation of patriotic sport fans 'moved' by hearing a national anthem: 'If tears well up in their eyes, this discourse of nation has become powerful enough to produce involuntary physiological responses in those subject to it' (Miller et al., 2004: 86). The 'physiological' is thus deemed by Toby Miller and colleagues to be subject to social discourse, but the reciprocal notion that biology can impact discursive understandings is rarely considered.

   Håkan Larsson (2012) suggested that such critiques of Foucault misunderstand his prime arguments. Larsson argued that Foucault's understanding of the materiality of bodies, offers a viable 'alternative to the conventional and dualist understanding of the relationship between mind/subject and body/

object' (Larsson, 2012: 7). Larsson drew from Foucault's detailing of his genealogical approach to illustrate that bodies (which breath, reproduce, digest etc.) do not exist in some alternative reality prior to social understanding but 'materialize' simultaneously with the social. Thus bodies are always biological and social entanglements. Judith Butler (1990) clarified this contention by stating:

> The body gains meaning within discourse only in the context of power relations. Sexuality is an historically specific organization of power, discourse, bodies, and affectivity. As such, sexuality is understood by Foucault to produce 'sex' as an artificial concept which effectively extends and disguises the power relations responsible for its genesis. (Butler, 1990: 92)

Foucauldian analysis does not, however, embed scientific understandings of bodies within its theorizing but encourages researchers to critically analyze how such knowledge is enmeshed with the workings of power in the production of particular bodies. Thus, Foucauldian analysis primarily encourages critique of the discursive effect of scientific knowledge.

3. In opposition to Douglas's criticisms concerning the perpetuation of a mind/body dualism, Ian Wellard (2012) drew from Connell's concept of bodily reflexive practices to examine how bodies, and associated pleasurable capacities, influence understandings of self within physical education. He argued that Connell's theorizing encourages examination of the dialectical relationship between the social, the embodied and bodily practices. Such examination, he illustrated, is of importance within physical education as it can be used as a framework to help students develop reflexive understandings of movement pleasures.

4. However, a small number of socio-cultural scholars of sport have drawn on the concept of 'affect' (which can have linkages to biology) to examine embodied pleasures (e.g. Booth, 2008; Evers, 2006; Humberstone, 2011; Pavlidis and Fullager, 2013; Thorpe and Rinehart, 2010a).

5. In contrast to Csíkszentmihályi's conclusion, David Lykken and Auke Tellegen (1996: 189) fatalistically suggested from their study of over 3000 fraternal and identical twins that: 'it may be that trying to be happier is as futile as trying to be taller and therefore is counterproductive'.

5 Studying Sport, Feminism and Pleasure

Jayne Caudwell

The title of this chapter conjures up lists of potential topics for discussion, most of which remain significant to the study of sport. Here are a few exemplars I offer for consideration, and the imagination, in terms of their individual and collective connections with sport and feminism:

> . . . aesthetics and pleasure, beauty and pleasure, carnivalesque and pleasure, femininity and pleasure, pleasure and danger, pleasure and patriarchy, pleasure and pornography, the politics of pleasure, fatness and pleasure, spectator pleasure, queerness and pleasure, discipline and pleasure, guilty pleasure . . .

As a has-been lesbian feminist as well as a radical feminist; a current queer feminist, poststructuralist feminist and sport feminist; and at times a wannabe non-feminist (I return to this in the conclusion), it is difficult to know where and how to start this chapter. Perhaps one easy place, for me, is to re-work the claim: 'The pleasure of the rich is the labour of the poor' (Elias, cited in Tester, 1989); in other words, to focus on gender relations within sporting contexts and the idea that 'the pleasure of men is the labour of women'. Or, as stated by Paul Willis (1994: 35): 'the female athlete is rendered a sex object—a body which may excel in sport, but which is primarily an object of pleasure for man'. Such a focus would be easy to achieve and a recent public event (at least in the UK)—Wimbledon tennis—provides a somewhat ridiculous reminder of how women athletes are expected to serve as 'beauties' for the pleasures of the traditional hetero-patriarchal male gaze:

> I just wonder if her dad [Marion Bartoli], because he has obviously been the most influential person in her life, did say to her when she was 12, 13, 14 maybe, 'listen, you are never going to be, you know, a looker. You are never going to be somebody like a Sharapova, you're never going to be 5ft 11 [*sic*], you're never going to be somebody with long legs, so you have to compensate for that. You are going to have to be the most dogged, determined fighter that anyone has ever seen on the

Studying Sport, Feminism and Pleasure 65

tennis court if you are going to make it . . .' (John Inverdale, BBC Radio 5 Live, commentating on the winner of the women's singles, 2013)

To concentrate on this and similar incidents certainly addresses some of the items on the list of possible pleasure-related topics for feminist scrutiny. Also, it allows a critical exploration of long-standing feminist debates; for example, discussions within key texts such as Naomi Wolf's *The Beauty Myth* (1991). And yet, we know gender relations are a complicated set of lived social and cultural schemas. Another troublesome—for me anyway— example of how complicated gender relations are for some people in some societies is reflected in the recent public debates, again in the UK, concerning the launch of a new journal: *Porn Studies*.

> The editors, Feona Attwood (Middlesex University) and Clarissa Smith (University of Sunderland), and Routledge are pleased to announce the launch of a new journal devoted to the study of pornography.
> *Porn Studies* invites submissions for publication, commencing with its first issue in Spring 2014. Articles should be between 5000 and 8000 words. Forum submissions should be 500–1500 words. Book reviews should be between 800 and 1500 words. Submissions will be refereed anonymously by at least two referees. (http://www.tandf.co.uk/journals/cfp/rprncfp.pdf)

One of my points here is how topics concerning women, gender and aspects of pleasure—aesthetics and pleasure, beauty and pleasure, femininity and pleasure, pleasure and patriarchy, pleasure and pornography, the politics of pleasure, spectator pleasure, guilty pleasure—are re-presented through UK institutions such as the BBC and Routledge Publishers. In other words, the feminist politics of pleasure appear to be largely ignored in public, institutionalized forums. Public discourses, reflected by the ease with which John Inverdale presents his highly hetero-patriarchal gender logic and the mundanity of a new *Porn* journal alert, appear to conceal the depth and range of tensions surrounding gender relations and pleasure.

For the purpose of this chapter, I trace two pleasure-related themes pertinent to sport from the list above. By doing so, I aim to offer a particular view of the feminist study of sport and pleasure, albeit merely a slice of the fuller picture. The two themes selected have been somewhat artificially separated out for the purpose of writing. First, I discuss sport, femininity and pleasure. Within this discussion, the emphasis is on women and Western practices of beautification. For a long time, feminists have problematized the naturalizing and normalizing of feminine beauty: 'Taught from their infancy that beauty is woman's scepter, the mind shapes itself to the body, and roaming round its gilt cage, only seeks to adorn its prison'(Wollstonecraft, 1992: 132). Patriarchy, heteronormativity and neoliberal capitalism—to name

66 Jayne Caudwell

a few structural systems—co-operate in processes and practices of beautification. However, the politics of beauty and the politics of gender are not straightforward. As Colebrook (2006: 132) suggests, it is not simply a question of '. . . is beauty good or bad for women?' Instead, beauty relates to embodiment, sensual enjoyment and pleasure as well as to ideologies of the aesthetic.

Second—and as I have suggested not wholly independent of the first theme—I consider sport, sexuality and pleasure. More specifically, I explore the concept of *jouissance*, which has been used variously to refer to joyousness, enjoyment, deep pleasure and sexual orgasm (the latter is the case within French language and meaning). I turn to the French feminists Hélène Cixous, Luce Irigaray and Julia Kristeva to offer a new way to consider sport and the social significance of pleasure.

SPORT, FEMININITY AND PLEASURE

If we follow the line of thought laid down by feminist Mary Wollstonecraft and later by feminists Germaine Greer (1970), Simone de Beauvoir (1976[1949]), Naomi Wolf (1991) and Sheila Jeffreys (2005), we can conclude that female beauty—manifest through traditional embodiments of femininity—ultimately functions to oppress women. For many feminists, feminine beauty becomes a 'beauty myth' (Wolf, 1991), because any pleasure and power women might believe beauty grants them is false. As Colebrook (2006: 131) highlights:

> . . . the real effect and intent of the beauty myth was the maintenance of women in a subordinate position: as long as women's only means of power and persuasion was through the body, there could be no genuine liberation.

Within this kind of feminist theorizing, feminine beauty serves to lure, manipulate and debase women. Women, through the embodiment of femininity, become passive objects of a patriarchal cultural construct, namely feminine beauty. However, in terms of the pleasure project, perhaps an interesting question to ask is: to what degree might there be productive potential in femininity and feminine beauty? In addressing this question, Colebrook (2006: 132) goes some way to providing a response for us when she considers if '. . . the concept of the beautiful and its associations with pleasure, non-cognition and the particular, might itself form a counter tradition'. She explores the idea of how feminine beauty can provide counter tradition by turning to philosophies of the aesthetic and making a challenge to current philosophies of aesthetics. In particular, she argues that: 'Prior to the establishment of a discourse on aesthetics, the concept of beauty had always involved considerations of pleasure, judgment, value, life, social esteem and ethics' (Colebrook, 2006: 135–136).

Studying Sport, Feminism and Pleasure 67

By re-considering these aspects of beauty, she argues we are able to engage with beauty in a more nuanced way, a way that takes us further than the sentiments of the 'beauty myth'.

Before we can view feminine beauty as pleasurable, it is worth noting Colebrook's general approach to a feminist politics of beauty. For instance, she advocates a framing that positions the pragmatic over the moral, that is: '. . . how is beauty defined, deployed, defended, subordinated, marketed or manipulated, and how do these tactics intersect with gender and value?' (Colebrook, 2006: 132). Moving from this starting point, her overall aim is to redeem aesthetics (as well as a philosophy of aesthetics) and to retrieve female beauty/beautification from contemporary commercial industries and markets of spectatorship. Thus, she makes concerted attempts to liberate the pleasures of the feminine and beautiful from the manufactured.

For the purpose of discussion in this chapter, Colebrook offers a way forward. She does this by first acknowledging that gendered, misogynist and sexist assumptions work to define beauty, which we witness in John Iverdale's commentary about Marion Bartoli, and second, by suggesting that '. . . the experience of the beautiful *as feeling* can be neither explained away nor reduced to its political uses and abuses' (Colebrook, 2006: 134). From the point of view of the latter, it is clear that women, specifically sportswomen, are so much more than passive, one-dimensional objects for the male gaze. In other words, Bartoli's feminine and sporting subjectivities are far more intricate and complicated than Iverdale is able to impose.

With the aim of furthering the feminist analysis of femininity and pleasure in physical activity contexts, I turn to three areas in which women participants claim enjoyment via the feminine. These are Burlesque, Roller Derby and the figure of the Lesbian Femme (cf. Caudwell 2006).

Although burlesque is not viewed a sport, it undoubtedly provides an interesting starting place for a discussion of femininity and pleasure in physical activity contexts. In burlesque, feminine subjectivities are re-shaped and re-cast via caricature and extravaganza. These aspects—caricature and extravaganza—intend to subvert the structures of traditional forms of femininity and challenge configurations of gendered being. Similar to Bakhtin's (1984) take on carnival and the carnivalesque (see Chapters 2 and 3 for discussions on Bakhtin), the event (burlesque) suspends familiar rules and regulations surrounding the feminine, and therefore provides opportunity for pleasurable, albeit ritualistic, acts of femininity.

Following a Bakhtinian line of thought, carnivalesque, and by extension burlesque, mess with the usual hierarchies of power and subordination apparent in societies and cultures. This messing and messiness of normative hierarchies functions to rupture the norms. However, according to Bakhtin, individuals are never entirely free of tradition and the orthodox, but, importantly, in these moments of rupture they are free to indulge in fun, enjoyment and the sensual. It is these dimensions of pleasure that are significant to this study of sport.

68 *Jayne Caudwell*

Burlesque has a long history, within which there have been shifts in genre and popularity. Past and present subcultures of burlesque are fertile ground for feminist analysis, especially the seemingly pleasurable attachment women participants—both women performers and women spectators—have to the feminine. These pleasures relate to adapting and re-creating the feminine, which can include the embodiment of excessive forms of femininity. In her article on 'Showing the Girl', Debra Ferreday (2008) scrutinizes the 'new' burlesque—as opposed to burlesque of the 16th, 17th, 18th and 19th centuries—for its feminist and queer potential. She does not disregard the long histories of burlesque, and in summing up her argument references the broader subcultures of burlesque in their capacity to:

> . . . powerfully dramatize the fact that femininity is not reducible to a single object or practice: that feminine identities are multiple, and may be experienced as pleasurable. However, it is not enough simply to claim that femininity is always a source of parodic pleasure. Like drag, burlesque also works to destabilize the ways in which dominant feminine identities become normalized (2008: 49).

Ferreday's research consistently engages with the tensions between the feminine, the pleasurable and a feminist politics of feminine beauty. Through a focus on burlesque websites and online fan communities, she charts the ways the subcultures appropriate feminist sensibilities. However, similarly to Colebrook, she remains mindful of broader feminist debates surrounding women's beauty, processes of beautification and consumer cultures. In a lengthy discussion of *Red Lipstick* (52) she makes the important, and perhaps overlooked, point that it is too simplistic to assume women are duped into femininity, and that women's feminine embodiments are merely a matter of adding on 'whatever society is selling' (Ferreday, 2008: 52–53). Borrowing from Sabina Sawhney (2006), Ferreday posits:

> Feminism seems to be relying on the notion that the authentic identity of woman would be revealed once the drag is removed. That is to say, when her various 'clothes'—racial, ethnic, hetero/homosexual, class textured—are removed, the real, genuine woman would appear whose identity would pose no puzzles. (Sawhney, 2006: 5 in Ferreday, 2008: 52)

This is a significant insight, and it is at this juncture, with these feminist arguments in mind, that I move to consider the reemergence of roller derby and its relationship with femininity and pleasure.

The historical and contemporary analyses of roller derby often document the juxtaposition of this full contact sport with notions of Western [white] femininity (Carlson, 2010; Finley, 2010; Pavlidis, 2012; Storms, 2008). Much of the research captures the productive links between women participants' various embodiments of the feminine and womanhood, and the apparent

Studying Sport, Feminism and Pleasure   69

aggressive nature of the activity. Ethnographic research (see Carlson, 2010; Finley, 2010; Pavlidis, 2012) of roller derby subcultures reveals the potential for women and girls to take a Do-It-Yourself (DIY) approach to defining their own femininities and feminine subjectivities during roller derby participation.

> Her hair is in child-like pigtails, her tattoos glare through strategically placed holes in fishnet stockings, and a short skirt reveals the pink panties that match the tight T-shirt altered to provide the most potent view of breast cleavage. The image portrays the outlandish, extravagant conventions of sexuality associated with the tawdriness of "pin-up girls." And yet the salience of knee pads, shin pads, elbow pads, and helmets resist simple assessments of sexualized femininity, as do facial scowls and the brutish postures through which she powers her way around the skating rink. (Finley, 2010: 359–360)

The contrasts and seeming incongruities evidenced in the above description demonstrate the scope of roller derby—as well as other 'aggressive' sports—for providing women the opportunity to make messy traditional notions of femininity, especially in competitive sporting contexts. Like the hyperbole in burlesque, the DIY femininity in roller derby might seem a smack in the face to some forms of feminism. And yet, many women participants testify to how much they enjoy the embodiment of the feminine.

Various studies (Carlson, 2010; Finley, 2010; Pavlidis, 2012) highlight the role of satire, parody and mockery within roller derby subcultures and the ways these aspects undermine traditional notions of femininity, especially the idea of emphasized femininity. This turn to humor, the amusing and comical suggests laughter and fun. At this level of the humorous, roller derby provides women an enjoyable sport/leisure opportunity to be both competitive and playful. Pleasure is gained through exaggeration and the dramatic, theatrical, creative and expressive. For example, Carlson (2010) shows how skaters develop enjoyable derby personas and derby bodies through names and clothing, and Finley (2010) analyzes how these strategies serve to positively reclaim pariah femininities such as 'bitch', 'slut' and 'witch'.

Within sport studies literature, much has been made of the gender apologetic as well as the gender unapologetic (cf. Broad, 2001). Emphasized femininity sits within the idea that women are complicit in the production of traditional gender relations through the passive reproduction of extolled heterosexual femininity. Carlson, (2010), Finley (2010) and Pavlidis (2012) document the ways roller derby women disrupt and alter these familiar meanings of sporting emphasized femininity. For instance, Finley (2010) argues that, via anachronistic imagery, roller derby women reveal the absurdity of the social construction of traditional gender relations and concomitant femininity. Carlson (2010) and Pavlidis (2012) focus on the productive

70 *Jayne Caudwell*

potential of subcultural style as a means to contest the lineage between femininity, gender relations and legitimized heterosexual desirability. Drawing from connections with punk rock, subcultural style and the work of Dick Hebdige (Carlson, 2010), they show how music and gender politics (Pavlidis, 2012), and chaos and appearance (Carlson, 2010) function to generate pleasurable feminine subjectivities for roller derby women.

In the introduction to his book *Subculture: The Meaning of Style*, Hebdige (1979) tells of the sparse conditions facing Genet's (1966[1949]) imprisoned thief. Of significance, to this prisoner, is a tube of Vaseline: 'This "dirty, wretched object", proclaiming his homosexuality to the world, becomes for Genet a kind of guarantee—"the sign of a secret grace which was soon to save me from contempt"'(Hebdige, 1979: 1). For Hebdige, objects such as a tube of Vaseline carry remarkable significance in terms of subversion ('secret grace'), refusal and revolt ('to save me from contempt'). They are implicit to breaking the so-called natural order and they reflect the power of subordinate groups to triumph within such obdurate order and ordering (e.g. prison).

I think we can assume that subordinate groups gain pleasure during these moments of expression (via objects and style), and successful rebellion. This is why scholars of roller derby have turned to Hebdige's work. Perhaps of greater significance, however, is the scope for exploring the sensual, pleasurable meanings attached to the object: a tube of Vaseline. In this instance, Hebdige falls short of such an explicit analysis, and I wonder how a queer lens might interpret the following passage: '. . . I turn the back of the regulation sheet towards me. Smiles and sneers, alike inexorable, enter me by all the holes I offer . . . ' (Genet, 1966[1949] in Hebdige, 1979: 1). Although pleasure is not Hebdige's main project in his treatise of style, is it worth wondering how Genet's prisoner gains pleasure in such harsh, bleak and presumably brutal homophobic conditions. The symbolic value of a tube of Vaseline, the images conjured by the references to turning the regulations away, holes and entry, might suggest that this prisoner's sexuality provides some pleasures in spite of the palpable institutionalized and omnipresent hostility.

By no means directly related, but nevertheless a return to how roller derby women experience their embodied sexuality, Carlson (2010: 433) writes: 'Importantly, skaters are not simply women-turned-Amazons; their mini-skirts, bras, and panties suggest a sexually availability that is belied by the aggression implied by their weaponry and injuries'. It is apparent, in the roller derby literature to date, that women are maneuvering within traditional femininity and producing feminine subjectivities that behold pleasure through asserted feminine style. Finley (2010) argues that this maneuvering extends beyond individual women and can be described as intragender. In other words, she studies the relations between femininities and between women and demonstrates how this might help us identify emerging expressions of pleasurable femininity in sport. A specific example, provided by Finley (2010: 375), is 'derby crushes'. This is when women, regardless of their sexuality, '. . . love to watch another woman skate'.

Studying Sport, Feminism and Pleasure 71

The potential pleasures within intragender relations in sporting contexts might be further explored through a consideration of the figure of the lesbian femme. As a way to pick up this discussion, I start with Erica Rand's declaration:

> . . . I love spectating consensual gender, just as I love participating in it. Skating suits my strong identity as femme, and while I don't want figure skating to require femininity, I experience it, as I've said, as an expression of mine. (2012: 98)

In her book *Red Nails, Black Skates* (2012), Rand offers an eloquent and fascinating account of her experiences of skating. In the text, she identifies as a '. . . queer femme dyke' (p. 52); '. . . yep, a femme jock' (p. 98), and explores the many aspects of femme (p. 5, 52, 115), superfemme (p. 165) and her '. . . own pleasures in gender' (p. 98). Related to contexts both on the ice and off the ice, Rand provides insights into the pleasures of the queer erotic: 'Personally, I love being the object of someone's taste for queer femmes, which makes me feel recognized and possibly in for a great time . . .' (Rand, 2012: 233). She goes on to claim that figuring skating, especially at the Gay Games, was not the 'event for spectators in search of butch eye candy' (Rand, 2012: 5).

At the same time as celebrating the femme (and butch), Rand is careful to highlight the ways femininity remains unfixed and how slippages occur when moving between athletic and non-athletic subjectivities. Clearly, sport and physical activity have a significant bearing on feminine subjectivity and the relationships go beyond the sentiments captured by John Inverdale in his commentary on Wimbledon Champion Marion Bartoli. Insights such as Rand's from women who identify as lesbian femme and/or queer femme provide wealthy testimonies to challenge stagnant and traditional notions of femininity.

Femme and butch are coherent terms within non-heterosexual cultures. But, as many have warned, these subjectivities are not simply replicas of normative heterosexual genders (Caudwell, 2006), they are not always erotically inflected (Rand, 2012) and there are misconceptions of both within sexual stereotypes (Walker et al., 2012). With these warnings in mind, the femme-butch aesthetic does offer scope for the exploration of pleasure as it relates to sport. As with burlesque and roller derby, lesbian femme subjectivity is replete with pleasures of the feminine for the women involved.

And yet, we have been slow to acknowledge physically active women's agented relationship to femme. My first realization of the productive potential of the feminine, as opposed to the feminine as a duped subjectivity, was during fieldwork within a lesbian-identified football team (2006, 2007). Despite the appearance that femininity was often dismissed as a non-viable footballing body, the femme players were active in their pleasures of participation. These pleasures ranged from the ways they adorned their playing

72 Jayne Caudwell

attire to embodied displays of the curvatures of hips and breasts and talk of make-up. There was also the tacit recognition by femme players of the importance of the so-called butch back line, which is the last line of defenders positioned in front of the goal and goalkeeper. Rand (2012: 115), borrowing from Patrick Califia, makes an interesting point, and one which I now find relevant to an analysis of the lesbian-femme footballer:

> He (Califia) was warning butches not to let their own display of chivalry and masculine prowess fool them into having a misogynist sense of superiority over femmes. When you're out in the rain dealing with a dead battery, Califia wrote, there's a good chance that those femmes waiting in the warm coffee shop know as much about jump cables as you do. You can chose to view them as helpless, or you can appreciate their participation in the gendering that animates butch/femme erotics and prize the way they honor your masculinity with a respect too scarce for butches in a society with rigid sex and gender norms.

This discussion of femme-butch relations and erotics serves to highlight the nuanced operations that subvert prevailing and traditional notions of gendered subjectivity. It comes after discussion of the potential for assumed heterosexual femininity—in burlesque and roller derby—to reconfigure women's relationships with the pleasures of the feminine (and butch). Moreover, it provides an appropriate preamble for discussions of sexuality and women's pleasure.

SPORT, SEXUALITY AND PLEASURE

Jouissance

> *"I finally had an orgasm and my doctor told me it was the wrong kind"*
> —Polly, in Woody Allen's film *Manhattan* (1979)

> '. . . what is most strictly forbidden to women today is that they should attempt to express their own pleasure'
> —(Irigaray, 1985: 77)

Few scholars within sport and leisure studies have explored the concept of jouissance. Even fewer have engaged with the so-called French feminists Hélène Cixous, Luce Irigaray and Julia Kristeva. Notable exceptions include Montserrat Martin's (2011) Irigarian framing of female rugby subjectivities and Simone Fullagar's (2002) use of Cixous' 'feminine jouissance' to explain women's travel and tourist subjectivities.

Studying Sport, Feminism and Pleasure 73

Prior to the contributions of Cixous, Irigaray and Kristeva, the concept of jouissance was embedded in a Freudian-Lacanian model, with emphases on psychoanalysis and the phallus. Sigmund Freud's notion of *The Pleasure Principle* (1895) and later his work on *Beyond the Pleasure Principle* (1921) helped establish pleasure as an always-present instinctive drive linked to the male libido. Initially, Freud viewed pleasure-seeking as relatively unproblematic; however, later he began to document the relationships between pleasure and pain, pleasure and death (death-drive) and immortality (see also chapter 3). Jacques Lacan continued (in the late 1930s-1970s) some of Freud's focus through an exploration of the possible boundaries between pleasure and pain, and Lacan's concept of jouissance seems to exist at, and beyond, the thresholds of pleasure and within zones of pain.

As with Freud, Lacan's treatise considered pleasure in the development of phallo-centric sexuality, relating it to the moment of male orgasm (pre-ejaculation), the death-drive, castration-complex and lack/loss (Freudian terms). Put simply, the Freudian-Lacanian model presented a male-centric view of sexuality (male orgasm) 'where sex is always related to death' (Ives, 2010: 73). That said, Lacan also drew on the works of Karl Marx and his idea of surplus-value and, as a consequence, Lacan coined the term *plus-de-jouir* (surplus-jouissance). In this way, he initiated different questions about the value of some pleasures. By highlighting the rampant insatiability and dissatisfaction implicit in desire (sexuality) he moved beyond Freud's notions of death-drive and castration-complex.

The coming together of psychoanalysis and Marxism, according to Kingsbury (2008), is apparent in the Frankfurt School of Critical Theory (1930s) and more recently in the work of Slavoj Žižek (late 1980s-present). The theoretical fusion of psychoanalysis and Marxism has encouraged analysis away from a wholly psychic domain—with its emphasis on the phallic economy of pleasure—and instead has prompted a turn to pleasure and society, history and subjectivity. More specifically, Žižek demonstrated how pleasure functions alongside ideology, alienation, exploitation and commodity-fetishism (Kingsbury, 2008). Clearly, these are important broader developments and they signal the expansion of the Freudian-Lacanian model of pleasure/jouissance.

Although Lacan (1972–3) and Žižek (1994) acknowledge a specifically female jouissance, of greater significance to the feminist project of pleasure are the developments of the concept of jouissance by Roland Barthes and the poststructuralist movement. Specifically, Barthes' work on *The Pleasures of the Text* (1973) helped inform Kristeva's ideas, in particular her thoughts on the jouissance of the text and the text as jouissance (Ives, 2010). For Barthes, the pleasure of the text has two dimensions: *plaisir* (pleasure) and *jouissance* (bliss). The former is described by Barthes (1975[1973]) as *texte lisible* (readerly/readable text). In this version, pleasure (plaisir) reflects the enjoyment of passivity and recognition. The text presents homogeneity and unity, and the reader is not challenged; their subject position remains unmoved

74 *Jayne Caudwell*

and traditional literary codes remain intact. The *texte scriptible* (writerly/ writable text) presents an open, exploded, indeterminate text. Such a composition allows for fractured subject positions, re-interpretations, slippages and a re-establishing; it can be written anew and this aspect is viewed as blissful (jouissance). It is the latter, specifically the scope for rupture and the possibilities to re-interpret language and re-invent meaning, that underpinned the work on pleasure by French feminists Cixious, Kristeva and Irigaray.

Feminism in France has a long history, and can be mapped back to women's liberation and the fight for women's rights during the years of the French Revolution (1789–1799). However, the idea of a distinctive French feminism emerged more recently, during the 1970s, 1980s and 1990s. Reflecting the developments in feminist theory and activism in other parts of the so-called Western world, French feminism appears to have taken a more philosophical and literary turn. Perhaps influenced by Simone de Beauvoir's (1976[1949]) work on Woman as socially constructed as the Other, Cixous, Irigaray and Kristeva are known for their individual and collective feminist contributions to debates surrounding philosophy, literary critique and psychoanalysis. Through a focus on women and the feminine, they have challenged existing male models of thought and the phallocracy of reason, which operate at a fundamental level to silence and exclude women. More specifically, French feminists developed the term phallogocentrism to denote the focus on men and the masculine in the production of meaning and the exclusion of women from social existence.

Through the feminist lens of the 2010s, the work of Cixous, Irigaray and Kristeva might be viewed as essentialist, given their critique of maleness, emphasis on sexual difference and advocacy of women's ways of knowing and being. In defense of Irigaray, Martin (2003: 2) argues that she '. . . is a philosopher of change who cannot be reduced to some essentialist position'. On reflection, the now-familiar term 'strategic essentialism' seems more apt. Clearly, the contributions of the French feminists must be considered in the context of historical developments of theory and philosophies of change. As a consequence, their works have relevance to the study of sport and pleasure.

Refusing to repress female sexuality, and connecting it both literally and metaphorically to pleasure, Cixous asked 'What is feminine jouissance?' (1986: 151). In her questioning she explores the embodiment of pleasure and how pleasure can be put into words, language and written text. Phallogocentrism, according to the French feminists, operates to construct a monolithic, singular and unitary model within which women become the silent, negative image of male sexuality. Cixous, Irigaray and Kristeva argued for a deconstruction of this established one-sided view—which they identified as informing broader epistemological projects—and for recognition of the multiple, limitless, diffuse, abundant and infinite nature of being. Therefore, their various projects aim to avoid the assimilation of female sexuality, pleasure and subjectivity into existing male-centric ontologies, and they offer new ways to create new meanings and knowledge.

Studying Sport, Feminism and Pleasure 75

Irigaray's project of rewriting Freud and Lacan disrupts the isomorphic unity and replaces it with a series of dense, poetic, parodic discourses, in which female repression is unleashed and the female unconscious is allowed to explode into academic patriarchy. Irigaray's specular project disrupts the insistence in phallic, patriarchal sexuality on one organ (penis), one orgasm or pleasure (male), one identity (male), one model of representation (masculine). (Ives, 2010: 47)

The focus on female libidinal economy and female bodily rhythms by Cixious, Kristeva and Irigaray is subject to critique; however, their works opened up the synesthetic of sexuality by introducing the morphology of the female genitalia[1]; by emphasizing the multiplicity of female sex organs and by advocating an all-over eroticism and embodied multi-sensuality. Through explorations of the previously private spheres of the sexual and embodied, and the sharing of these thoughts (referred to as extrimacy in Lacanian terms), they help multiply and diversify notions of pleasure.

Cixous, Irigaray and Kristeva made significant contributions to the development of feminist poststructuralism via their emphases on deconstructing existing models of jouissance, the diversity present in emerging models of [sexual] pleasure and the impossibilities of fixing down a stable sexual subjectivity. They also advocated new ways of writing the sensual, spiritual and effervescent aspects of sexuality and pleasure. Through fiction, dramatic writing and poetry, they provided linguistic and literary challenges to the rigidity of existing representations of pleasure. At times, they captured the mystic, magical and cosmic, and highlighted 'unnameable jouissance' (Kristeva, 1981: 16).

Throughout their works, there are acknowledgements of the difficulties in re-writing meanings, especially in relation to jouissance. This is because jouissance—despite its legacies of male power—functions beyond language and culture. Perhaps this is also the case for pleasure, so that once jouissance is incorporated in to expressions of pleasure something is lost. Similarly, in their works, any attempt to define female sexuality is recognized as prescriptive. These points might make the feminist pleasure project un-representable. And yet, for me, Cixous, Irigaray and Kristeva provoke important feminist critique, of which I offer an example below.

During the men's football World Cup in South Africa (2010), the British media posed the question: 'Is scoring a goal better than sex?' thus alluding to the synergies between sport, sexuality (sexual acts) and pleasure. Scientized responses followed (e.g. references to testosterone, etc.) and these onto-epistemological models gave reason and meaning to this seemingly male metanarrative of sport and pleasure.

Starting with a Barthesian approach, this simple question—is scoring a goal better than sex?—might appear as *texte lisible*. As such, the question is a readable text in which there is passive recognition of the unity between men's football, goal scoring, sexuality and pleasure (plaisir). The striker, the ball, the goalkeeper and the goal provide easy analogy with the act of

76 Jayne Caudwell

male-penetrative sex (for a similar analysis of competitive male team sport and penetrative sexual references see Brian Pronger, 1999). The analogy sits easy within the popular cultural contexts of football and the sport media. This act of successful penetration (scoring a goal) symbolizes pleasure at the level of the normative and monolithic. The question and the act of scoring might be understood through Irigaray's insight in to the singular '. . . one organ (penis), one orgasm or pleasure (male), one identity (male), one model of representation (masculine)' (cited in Ives, 2010: 47). For example, taking a shot followed by the passage of the football into the goal is, symbolically, a very linear, progressive and one-dimensional form of pleasure. Within this reading, traditional subjectivities (of male footballer) and codes of sporting pleasure (scoring) remain unbroken.

But what of *texte scriptable* and a Barthesian turn to re-interpretations of the blissful in sport? Perhaps, for a deeper discussion of this to happen, we have to ask new, more sophisticated, questions. Cixous, Irigaray and Kristeva went some way towards posing new questions and their works concerned with *l'ecriture feminine*[2] helped change theories of sexualities and embodiment within both feminism and psychoanalysis. However, within the study of sport, too few new questions regarding sport and pleasure exist. That said, Heather Sykes (2011: 98), in her invaluable text *Queer Bodies*, considers 'the theft of enjoyment'. She introduces the idea of queer pleasures through a turn to the game of dodgeball in physical education lessons, and the assumption that it offers a playful alternative to traditional curricula activities.

Before considering Syke's contribution, I take a moment to introduce enjoyment since this and the work of Žižek feature in her analysis. Enjoyment, according to Kingsbury (2008: 50), is '. . . one of Žižek's most enduring theses'. Žižek considers enjoyment a political issue, arguing that it both upholds and disturbs the emotional dimensions and mechanisms of class and racialized ideologies and relations, nationalistic movements and the capitalist production and consumption of commodities. By linking enjoyment with a broader politics and the political economy, Žižek moves from the extrimacy of pleasures evident in the works of Lacan, Cixous, Irigaray and Kristeva to the material worlds of the politico-socio-cultural. In this way, enjoyment does not only take place in the minds and bodies of individual subjects (their private worlds); it plays a role in broader social, cultural, political and economic power relations.

Sykes (2011) situates her analysis of 'the theft of enjoyment' within a broader politics of physical education and sexualities, genders and fatness. She considers dodgeball, played during school time, as one form of physical activity that continues the traditional sporting processes of idealizing some bodies and marginalizing other [queer] bodies:

> Dodgeball, it seems, is the archetypical space within PE in which normatively bodied students repeatedly confront their own annihilation,

Studying Sport, Feminism and Pleasure   77

their own abject relation to queerness, while emerging with the illusion of being unscarred and unscathed. (Sykes, 2011: 100)

Fun—for those with normative, able and athletic bodies—is premised on the presence of queer bodies. Success in dodgeball, unlike scoring a goal in football, is based on the explicit exclusion of others. The game, sporting success and pleasure, according to Sykes, entails both excitement and horror. The idea of the horrific connects discomfort and pain to pleasure, and Sykes refers to 'the awfulness of fun' (2011: 99). In this way, she poses new questions about pleasure that relate to fractured subject positions, slippages and the re-establishing of meaning by normative physically active bodies (*texte script-able*). However, at this moment in time, there is little by way of the ruptures and re-inventions of meaning, and/or writing anew, queer pleasures. Perhaps queer pleasures are implicit in 'the theft of enjoyment'. In other words, there might be some pleasure in the illicit nature of the incongruities between the overriding cultures of competitive sport and the messiness of queer bodies. Here we might return to Genet's prisoner and his tube of Vaseline, and begin to imagine how the aberrant and abhorrent are peppered with pleasure. And so, for example, there might be pleasures in conceding a goal in competitive sport. Yet we know little of these pleasures; this is because in rendering them, mistakenly, as insignificant, they have not been subject to sustained critical analysis.

Working from the basis that French feminists have challenged existing models of pleasure, especially the concept of jouissance, and that *Queer Bodies* offer potential for re-interpretations of enjoyment in sporting contexts, I wonder how pleasure might be registered within a feminist-queer framework. Can we queer the apparent jouissance within the scoring goals-sex analogue, which, currently, appears male-dominated? Can we re-queer the horrible fun of excluding queer bodies during dodgeball?

One way—there are many more—might be to pay more attention to transitioning bodies and how transgender subjectivity opens new ways to experience body parts and embodied sensuality (see Davy, 2012), especially during moments of physical activity. In a similar way to how the French feminists questioned the phallogocentrism of Freudian-Lacanian model of pleasure/jouissance, can queer scholars and transgender bodies challenge existing assumptions related to pleasure and embodiment? Perhaps interesting questions might be: do new sensual, erogenous and erotic body zones appear and develop for transgender athletes? If so, how do these new sensations shape sporting pleasures at different levels, such as the personal, interpersonal and cultural?

CONCLUSIONS

In the end, I return to my wannabe non-feminist statement made in the introduction to this chapter. I do this through a consideration of Sara Ahmed's

78 Jayne Caudwell

recent turn to the idea of *Feminist Killjoys*. In several on-line commentaries (e.g. http://feministkilljoys.com and http://sfonline.barnard.edu/polyphonic/ahmed_02.htm), Ahmed (2010) asks important questions about happiness. For example, 'does the feminist kill other people's joy by pointing out moments of sexism? Or does she expose the bad feelings that get hidden, displaced, or negated under public signs of joy?' (¶12). As feminists, many of us develop advanced and well-informed responses to incidents of abuse, injustice, oppression, prejudice and subjugation. As activist and academic feminists, we are often willful—as Ahmed points out—in our communication of these responses. We are also skillful in providing rational, coherent and convincing arguments; these treatises are serious declarations, which are made in earnest and accompanied by intensity. Many feminists are angry.

Clearly, I do want to be a feminist, and the idea of a wannabe non-feminist is a fantasy moment in which I imagine I will no longer be a killjoy, no longer be intense, serious and rational. And I will no longer be angry. In other words, I will be free to be happy and free to—perhaps irrationally—'laugh out loud'. Or, will I?

In terms of pleasure and living a meaningful life (I think this was one of Richard's initial questions at the beginning of this book project), maybe one way forward for feminists and other political and social activists is to acknowledge pleasures regardless of their size and impact (Bob makes this point when he refers to pleasures small and large, see Chapter 2). In many ways, Genet's homosexual prisoner and the harsh reality of how lives are structured, fortified and regulated both haunt and horrify me. At the same time, I recognize individual agency and I am inspired by the work of feminist writers, and other social activists, who document humor, satire, subversion and the generative dimensions of social existence, compassion and humanity. And yet I'm still unsure, sometimes, of when to laugh.

In an article entitled 'Laughing within reason: on pleasure, women, and academic performance', Erica McWilliam (1999) examines modes of pleasure and rationality. She discusses, among other things, how carnival and fun might offer women in the academy the potential for pleasure. Starting with a moment in a university committee meeting, when a woman laughed the wrong way—too loud and therefore irrationally—for the likes of a male colleague, she unravels the importance of feminists' laugher to a broader feminist politics. Drawing on Foucault's (1985: 2–3) work, she interrogates 'feelings such as pleasure and rationality' and argues that pleasure-as-fun has been produced 'outside bourgeois traditions of conduct', in other words, beyond the walls of universities.

McWilliams' discussions have left me with some lingering thoughts and questions. For instance, does fun ever escape rationality? Do structures of feminist politics inform an ethics of pleasure? And must feminists laugh within reason? Some of the answers lie within this chapter. For some women who are participants in burlesque and roller derby, fun does escape the conventions of heteronormative-gendered rationality and femininity is

Studying Sport, Feminism and Pleasure   79

re-created for self-pleasure. Similarly, feminist theoreticians such as Cixous, Irigaray and Kristeva have re-written philosophies, and arguably ethics, of pleasure through a challenge to male-dominated models, which are steeped in male-centric ontologies, thus providing women with epistemologies of pleasures that are related to sexuality and acts of sex.

Finally, must feminists laugh—experience pleasure—within reason? Well, of course not, and of course we must. Pleasure is a complicated political issue for feminists, and this chapter has sidestepped the contentious topic of sexuality, pleasure and pornography, which was hinted at in the introduction. Perhaps it is easier, and therefore more satisfying, for me not to address this issue at this moment in time.

NOTES

1. Luce Irigaray, through her focus on 'This sex which is not one', introduced the idea of women's two lips (labia) as a means to diverse and self-sustained pleasures for women.
2. This term was introduced by Cixous in 1976 and can be interpreted simply as 'feminine writing'. Her intent was to challenge the marginalization of women and the feminine in structures of language and the symbolic order of representation. The term functions to disrupt phallogocentric rationalism and provide a perspective from the female body.

6 Aging Bod(ies) and Pleasure
Poetic Orientations

Robert E. Rinehart

The aging sportsperson: is this term an oxymoron, despite contemporary pleas that older folks can compete, can challenge and forestall physical deterioration (cf. Grant, 2001; Grant and Kluge, 2007; Iso-Ahola, Jackson and Dunn, 1994)? Despite exceptions like George Foreman,[1] Bernard Hopkins,[2] Al Oerter,[3] Libby Callahan,[4] Dara Torres,[5] David Tua[6] and 71-year-old Japanese dressage rider Hiroshi Hoketsu,[7] who were still internationally competitive into their fifth decade (and beyond), it is undeniable that each individual older body is capable of less than when it was a younger body. The age of Olympians varies widely, however, depending upon country and type of activity: for example, at the London 2012 Olympics, the average age 'for the equestrian events [is] 38' (Hughes and Rogers, 2012), while female gymnasts at the Beijing (2008) Olympics averaged 18.6 years of age (Gymbit, 2008). A website even has video footage of a 63-year old Japanese gymnast named Wakamatsu (Gymbit, 2008) swinging on the high bars and attempting an iron cross.

Interestingly, when we think of aging sportspersons—whether male, female, transexed, transgendered, straight, gay or bisexual—Western audiences typically think of Western examples, so that a reinforced and naturalized ethnocentrism exists within even sport studies. But remarkable (albeit singular) examples of Eastern athletes makes one wonder if there are different attitudes toward aging (and thus, perhaps, differing social, political, symbolic support systems) that are exemplified in older, pleasurable participation within sport practices.

In this chapter, I provide a series of exemplars examining pleasure within and through sport for older individuals: by example, I hope to tease out some of the discussed themes of pleasure, demonstrating both the ubiquity of pleasure as it attaches to sport and physical activity and a specific series of illustrations of both *Western* and *Eastern* popular cultural artifacts regarding attitudes toward the aging body. In order to do this, I draw upon a comparative, dominant Western set of attitudes toward aging.[8] With singular examples, I hope at least to demonstrate a wide variety of human responses to aging—and thereby disrupt taken-for-granted Western (hegemonic) views

Aging Bod(ies) and Pleasure 81

and ideologies that tend to re-create salient aspects of Western postmodernist societies.

It is enough to know that aging, while deemed to be a rather solitary project, is 'performed' by most human beings in widely variable manifestations. In addition, the experience of aging is located within the senses: humans infer aging through sight (for example, age spots, and wrinkles), texture (skin thickness, toughness, moisture, pliability, elasticity), smell (odiferousness), hearing (acuity, texture of voice, volume, clarity), sharpness (of mind, of verbal wit, of physical response), fluidity (of joints, impingements, acceptance) and other bodily senses, such as responses to demands of pressure, balance, power or stamina (respiratory, muscular, perseverance). But, as astute humans age, they also infer their own 'aging' through—typically—awareness of declines in such sensual abilities.

There are, of course, different ethos—and different worldviews—extant within larger societies regarding aging, even characterizing such a seemingly clear-cut concept as 'decay'. Infirmity, for some societies, is a marker of a life well-lived, or an outward indication of inner wisdom. Additionally, some attitudes within societies tacitly promote either a celebration or an avoidance of aging through interventionist and pro-active measures such as body modification, various types of aromatics (such as perfume and cologne (cf. Weston, 2004)) or an increase in vigorous physical activity.

These types of interventions are thus not only contemporary; they are also historical, and of course attitudes toward such interventions may vary by geographical location, locale, mores and practices, and many other societal factors. As celebratory of 'aging' (or 'youth'), for example, the Māori *moko* (facial tattoo) recounts one's history, ancestry, life journey—and of course the moko is intended to adorn one who has had an extensive, rich and remarkable life (Nikora, Rua and Awekotuku, 2003; Simmons, 1997; Te Rangikāheke, Grey and Simmons, 2007). As Ngahuia Te Awekotuku says: '[moko] is a symbol of integrity, Māori identity and prestige, as well as a reflection of whakapapa [genealogy] and history' (in 'Māori culture', 2013).

Beauty and its pleasures are not universal. To assure subjective forms of 'beauty'—albeit through relatively long processes of 'shaping'—ancient Chinese girls 'receive[d] a foot massage followed by every single toe being manually broken then bound tightly in cloth. The foot would be unwrapped and re-wrapped tighter until her feet reached 4 inches long' (Catalano, 2013: ¶5). (This is a contemporary practice as well, though not so universally applauded.) Such body modifications assured the recipients a culturally positive response, based on specific subjectivities regarding beauty—and were also attempts to mitigate the inevitability of aging: a beautiful moko or gracefully trained feet assured their owners of respect and admiration throughout their lifespans.

The presence of perfumes, cosmetics and deodorants not coincidentally implies a societal legislation (often reflecting class bias) against 'decay' in all

82   Robert E. Rinehart

of its forms or suggestions. Perfumes and cosmetics in ancient Egypt were, according to Chaudhri and Jain (2009), utilized to mask and modify natural processes of life (and, by inference, aging and death processes):

> In Egypt, as early as 10,000 BC, men and women used scented oils and ointments to clean and soften their skin and *mask body odor*. Dyes and paints were used to color the skin, body and hair. They rouged their lips and cheeks, stained their nails with henna and lined their eyes and eyebrows heavily with kohl. (¶1, emphasis added)

Throughout ancient India, Rome and Egypt—as well as the Middle Ages in Europe—the use of perfume was intended to provide a means of sexual attraction and an approximation of spirituality. In other words, aromas— stemming from oils, incense and unguents—were used to create alternate pleasurable scents in the presence of malodorous aromas: 'The deceased who were not naturally sweet-smelling might be made so. . . . corpses were washed and anointed with sandalwood oil and turmeric' (Aftel, 2001: 192). Scent was a means to mask and overwhelm unpleasant odors, contagion smells and the rot of decay. Historically, where there was distaste for the signs of aging (admittedly, one among many sources of odors), individuals and groups intervened to mitigate it, to create a pleasance from an abhorrence.

Of course, in many contemporary Western nation-states, this *contestation* with aging has become an even more creative, if naturalized, stance: breast modification and firming, liposuction, injections of potent drugs like Botox (Botulinum toxin), not to mention athletically relevant surgical interventions to stave off physical deterioration, have become relatively normalized procedures in Western society. As Gergen and Gergen (2000: 289) put it, 'Fighting body fat, graying hair and balding pates, age spots, varicose veins, yellowing teeth, and facial wrinkles [is] pervasive even among those in their 30s and 40s'.

In the following sections, I examine some popular cultural reflections of cultural attitudes toward aging, primarily through an examination of poetry dealing with aging. By looking at a written form that often signifies deep cultural understandings and attitudes, we may discover societal and cultural attitudes toward a well-lived life, physical enjoyment and pleasure, and even towards sport-like activities. This strategy parallels Denzin's (1991a) look at societal attitudes toward alcohol use through examination of popular films of different historical eras.

In slight contrast with a dominant Western model that privileges competition, and, in some cases, capitalist ethos and tenets, there exist in the world societies where a relative acceptance of aging occurs. There is a whole range of practices regarding dying, ranging from senilicide among Inuit during times of famine (cf. Kjellström 1974) to artificially-elongated periods of sickness, weakening and dying, with medical interventions often altering

Aging Bod(ies) and Pleasure   83

drastically the time period of decay and eventual death. These practices marking the processes and end points of life mirror many of the attitudes toward aging populations in a variety of societies, and even within each society there may be radically different practices and attitudes.

METONYMIC POETICS

Since many readers will be familiar with dominant Western practices toward aging and so-called declines of the lifespan, I use poetic exemplars from Western and Eastern cultures alike to explore some of the ranges of 'serious' attitudes people have toward aging—sometimes explicitly, sometimes by inference—and the aging body. This discussion is not meant to imply global truth, but rather to open up examination of alternative ways of being in the world.

The *pleasure* of a 'good death'—except in a combative, and glorified, sense during battle—is something unspoken in much of Western contemporary society. Can one die pleasantly? Can one wither away happily? Is it a part of pleasance to accept the inevitability of death? This possibility of a 'good death' becomes a vital touchstone for how we subjectively experience the 'pleasures' of the aging body, in anticipation of its certain biological death. Thus, looking at some the pleasures to be found in aging bodies and in the actual process of aging, I explore the populist concept of Wabi Sabi and apply it to terms of selected historic poetic writings, specifically drawn from works by Lu Yu (701–762) and three Korean sijo poets.[9]

The Western aging body has been (and I use the passive voice deliberately) measured, scientized, medicalized and viewed as a 'health and wellbeing' object of discourse (e.g. Huber, 1997). In some ways, this has produced a body that is imbricated with a certain narrow type of 'self-knowledge'. This aging, self- and other-policed body has the ability to comprehend itself in ways formerly unheard of, if only through just this deliberate emphasis on measurement, scientization and medicalization.

If we look at the inevitable process of aging, however, as both a public and a private concern—in terms of its aspects of pleasure—we see that the rough generalities of scientific discourse (the 'one size fits all' mentality) fail to achieve accurate resonance regarding many of the actual lived and embodied experiences of aging adults. The scientific framing doesn't fit the lived reality.

In addition, this very scientization fails to engage with questions regarding quality of life and subjectively lived realities resulting in responses that may be framed as pleasurable. For example: *what might be the pleasurable moments that aging individuals can identify in their daily lived lives? How are they differentially constructed through intersecting forms of discourse? And: what might poetic rhetorics and logics tell us about those stereotypes of popular culture that scientific rhetorics and logics do not?*

84   *Robert E. Rinehart*

Of course we can only truly speak with any authority about our own experience. Or rather, we can only do that with any *embodied* authority, for, cognitively, we can aspire to 'put ourselves in the other's place', to empathize. And our own experience is contextualized based on how we 'wear' our bodies, how we *produce* our bodies through pain and injury; ailment, both traumatic and gradual; types of usage; care, wear and tear (cf. Alon, 1996; Dawson-Cook, 2007; Feldenkrais, 1972, 1981); and our reactions to aging, use and violence: how we simultaneously produce, experience and conceive our bodies.

One's standpoint matters a great deal: as American poet Arthur Guiterman writes,

'Youth' is the ailment that hindereth thee;
'Age' is the sickness that conquereth me. (1921)

In this brief couplet, Guiterman reflects (later, Dylan Thomas, in 'Do Not Go Gentle Into That Good Night' will portray it similarly) that the natural process of aging is a contest, an agonistic pursuit, where there are 'good fights' that ennoble the individual in her/his accommodation to age.

Aging 'successfully' is judged against culturally perceived standards, and of course this 'competitive' model is gendered (cf. Kohn, 1992). The poets who generally view aging as a struggle or contest have generally been deeply immersed in male culture. In addition, as Gilligan (1992) has pointed out, an 'ethics of care' has become a *gendered* logic, but it doesn't have to be. 'Care of the aging self' is something that Western, patriarchal, competitive societies simply do not teach their male citizens, and this hegemonic view carries over to the whole fabric of the societies. Similar to an appreciation of the arts, aesthetics and beauty in sport (cf. Lowe, 1977; Rinehart, 1998b), both denial and appreciation of aging and the pleasures of aging are simply complex social constructions (cf. Boxill, 1988) that, created, can be un-created.

REFLECTIONS OF THE WEST

Some examples of Western poems that touch on key attitudes towards aging and/or decay follow. These poems reveal the motifs of 'fighting the good fight', resistance to bodily decay and degradation and a desperate striving for control over time. Taken together, it is safe to say that the poems reflect societal attitudes toward aging and death that show a general sense of competitiveness, capitalist striving and anticipation of a rhetoric of improvement (cf. Sutton-Smith 1997).

Dylan Thomas' 'Do Not Go Gentle Into That Good Night', though a complex and quite brilliant poem, reflects a stereotypical Western agonistic and combative bias—resulting in personal anger—at his own father's

Aging Bod(ies) and Pleasure 85

impending death. But, as poems do, it locates itself in a societal angst—as a masculine sense of solitary agency:

Do not go gentle into that good night,
Old age should burn and rage at close of day;
Rage, rage against the dying of the light.

On one level, this stanza suggests that not only the physical body, but also the spiritual self, should retain control over all life processes, including the process of dying. This 'rage' against the unfairness of death, this continuation of activity despite any contraindications, seems to be a highly Westernized stance. Upon deeper reflection, however, 'Do not go gentle into that good night' could signal a recognition of balance within life, and a desire to hold onto the physical 'other' for just a while longer: the conditional word 'should' ('old age should burn and rage') implies this paradoxical sense of impotence within the sense of inevitability.

Dylan Thomas' 'The Force That Through the Green Fuse Drives the Flower' works with powerful natural images to liken a human lifespan to the inevitable forces of nature: Thomas, while celebrating life forces, simultaneously laments the coming death of an individual: 'the hand that whirls the water in the pool/Stirs the quicksand; that ropes the blowing wind/Hauls my shroud sail' evidences the inevitable tensions between selected points within life, decay and death.

In expressing the sublime nature of natural processes with the finite nature of human existence, however, Thomas also demonstrates a resistance to the inevitability of aging. It is a less demonstrable resistance than that in 'Do not go gentle'—perhaps because the narrator of 'The force' is speaking for himself, and the narrator of 'Do not go gentle' is railing on behalf of his father—but it is still a deep unwillingness to accept things as they inevitably are. I see these two poems as exemplars of a Western stance toward aging that is both resistant and agonistic, reflecting a worldview that believes in its ability to *control* nature, physical forces and, symbolically, time itself.

Perhaps one of the key concepts that bears discussion regarding pleasure and apprehension of pleasure—particularly within the institution of sport— is the idea of competition. In terms of pleasure, Western sports(men)—for even now, in an age of relative equivalence in sporting realms, sports is still a pleasurably patriarchal endeavor—have been driven to learn about the satisfactions of competition within capitalist societies. This socializing has become a hegemonic imperative for what it means to be(come) a man. Alfie Kohn (1992) has detailed the sometimes-destructive forces of competition that result in, paradoxically, less pleasure and happiness for individuals than outright acceptance and joy, and less actual productivity and overall 'fun' for those deriving from a society that drives and stresses competition.

In Western societies, older adults have, rather than rejecting competition in favor of more sedentary and reflective lives, embraced the ethos of

86 *Robert E. Rinehart*

competition even up to their moment of death (usually figurative, though exceptions abound[10]). This failure to reject the competitive spirit of youth is relatively novel and unique to contemporary Western society, abetted by a constellation of forces, including a heightened sense of the salience of individualization, medical practices and attitudes toward dying (and institutionalized for-profit medicine), mediated discourses that nudge attitudes stressing a societal preference for youth culture and of course a(n) (extreme) valorization of the exceptional physical body.

Boy babies are given professional sports teams uniforms to wear. University females are taught to fear playing paintball. Former cricketers ask to have their ashes scattered over the cricket grounds, or their bodies buried within the pitch itself ('Carisbrook', 2010). Competition has colored our beings, sometimes from our first to our last breath—and it often overpowers many of the aesthetic, processual and actual pleasures that are generally not derived from the simplistic binaries of winning or losing a game.

Gardening, however, a relatively low impact activity (though, just as it can be shaded as 'gendered', anything can be made competitive: one only has to look at televised reality shows—for example, 'cooking shows'—as an example), is more often practiced by older than younger people. One of the reasons given is that it is a more sedate physical activity than exercise or sports (cf. DiPietro, 2001; Grant, 2001).

But there may be more to it: gardening, planting seeds in the ground, is a life-affirming gesture. (The acts of tilling previous plantings, re-planting, managing—all forward-looking endeavors deeply-felt within the psyche of gardeners—overtly fulfill the first premise of Dylan Thomas' 'The force through the green fuse drives the flower'.) To garden is to hope for the future, for generations to come, for continuity. Perhaps after seeing so much pain, hurt and deliberate violence in the world, aging people are convinced that competition as it is enacted—that is, zero-sum competition, not competition with oneself to test one's own limits—can be anti-life in many ways, or, at the least, comprises activities for younger, more hot-blooded youth.

The turn from generic, dominant, often macho, forms of sport to alternative, communal, cooperative physical activity—certainly not comprising a hegemonic critical mass, but for some youth—is a similar gesture, and bodes well for the future. Just as communal gardens are flourishing in Western cities, and front-yard gardens challenge dominant ways of existing in a neighborhood, so too do more performative, artistic, self-actualizing forms of sport and physical activity indicate that there is, indeed, a resistant minority still challenging some of the status quo norms of sporting culture. This too can be seen as a turn towards 'sporting pleasure', just as recognizing joy in mundane motion, happiness in the interconnectedness of the whole body (being mindful of the quick fix, for example), and celebrating the more usual types of pleasures—scoring a try, coming from behind to win, knowing one's physical limits and somehow exceeding them—are delightful forms of bodily hedonism.

Aging Bod(ies) and Pleasure   87

While many of the readers of this book will live in the Western world—with its own imbedded worldviews—many of us also know about and celebrate some Eastern sensibilities regarding fate and inevitability. The interpenetration of Eastern-oriented martial arts and other body practices into Western leisure pursuits and lifestyles has helped create interest in non-hegemonic (Western) ways of living in the world.

WABI SABI AND MORE

If we were to apply a traditionally Eastern angle (possibly stemming from Japanese/Buddhist traditions) to a non-integrative view of the body,[11] perhaps we might use the philosophical concept of Wabi Sabi—a sense of perfection within the inevitability of imperfection (cf. Gold, 2004). In this worldview,[12] for example,

> Appreciation—emotional appreciation, artistic appreciation, appreciation on every level—is an important part of living Wabi Sabi. . . . Appreciation manifests joy. We don't need to live by some impossible standard to have a joyful contributive, 'enlightened' existence. (Gold, 2004: 29)

In Wabi Sabi, the very appreciation of one's own body—its limitations, imperfections, abilities and so forth—becomes a source of joy, of pleasure.

As Wabi Sabi frames the discussion, putting everyday concerns and disappointments in perspective, it is important to remember how many of us may relate to our aging bodies. In terms of how our bodies and selves relate to the physicality of intentional bodily movement, we may both cognitively and affectively recall how our gut bubbled in anticipation of the first pitch, the starter's pistol or the first contact of any sort in a combative sport. Or how we sat, amazed, realizing that stretching something as basic as the quadriceps is now a very tight stretch. We may feel a palpable amazement at our lessened flexibility and reduced capacity: a sense of wonder at the basic deterioration of control over our own bodies. We may stem the 'advancing tide' by engaging in yoga, or Pilates or self-rendered programs.[13] Many of us involved in sports studies may, in fact, view our own bodies more as sites of loss and diminished relevance simply because we were previously at such an apex of physical capability.

For that is what it really comes down to: aging—especially for bodily active people—is the recognition of a simple lack of *perceived* (and, eventually, real) control over our own bodies. Rarely, except in imaginative anticipation, do we pre-'recollect' our aged selves while we are younger. But of course it can be done, at least cognitively.[14]

For example, Lennon and McCartney's 'When I'm Sixty-Four' was a light-hearted look at how two people might age together, how they might adjust each to the other's changing bodies—but the *caveat* for that song was

88 *Robert E. Rinehart*

that it was about loyalty: the aging process ('you'll be older too') was, as in all relationships, reciprocal. It's an idealistic song, a song that relies upon the concept of everlasting love, in this case. It is joyful, pleasurable, and cognitively anticipates the solace of grandchildren: 'Grandchildren on your knee/Vera, Chuck, and Dave'.[15] It is not embodied, or sensory, but rather reflects a future without aches, pains, infirmities or limitations.

Clearly, there are both objective and subjective/interpretive dimensions to the aging body, and sometimes these two dimensions blend. An objective aging reality—looking at the lines on one's face in the mirror, for example—is often mitigated by the philosophical stance of having 'good days and bad days'. Gubrium and Holstein (2003) discuss Kathy Charmaz's (1991) work, which focuses on the everyday lived lives of adults with illness, either chronic or acute:

> Assuming that one recovers from an acute illness, the illness runs its course fairly quickly and those affected return to their "normal" lives, once again taking their now relatively transparent bodies for granted. In contrast, those suffering from serious chronic illness live in relation to their illnesses for long periods. . . . individuals can construct their illnesses in distinctly different fashions. (Gubrium and Holstein, 2003: 220)

The objective reality of the illness, then, affects the subjective or interpretive focus of the actual person—their attitude, the 'pleasure' they derive from day-to-day living. But it goes the other way as well. Limits, if there are such, are within *parameters* of limitations, based more on perceptions than on a static and objective reality: 'Neither the subjective contours of embodiment nor the objective status of the body determines the other' (Gubrium and Holstein, 2003: 219). Pleasure, then, is a concept and affect that is created by its negative capability—in its absence of pain, illness, fear; but it can also become a self-celebration in and for its own right.

Attitudes toward aging may percolate to the surface, presenting as frustrated anger, reluctant acceptance or even more dedicated and strenuous training. However, the bemusement that older humans may feel towards this aging process is one that, if we live long enough, we all will face. Haruki Murakami, the novelist of *Norwegian Wood*, states this existential truth this way:

> My peak as a runner came in my late forties. . . . Things continued at [a] stable plateau for a while, but before long they started to change. I'd train as much as before but found it increasingly hard to break three hours and forty minutes. . . . What was going on here? I didn't think it was because I was aging. In everyday life I never felt like I was getting physically weaker. But no matter how much I might deny it or try to ignore it, the numbers were retreating, step by step. (2008: 11–12)

Aging Bod(ies) and Pleasure 89

Murakami characterizes his physical 'peak' in terms of an objective time, which of course in running a marathon is never objective, consistent or comparable: the courses change and the conditions (weather, competition, attitude) always change. And yet this reliance on 'measuring' aging through objective measures—fundamentally a Western trope—discounts people's individual experience of physical aging.[16]

So: we experience this process of living—this process of aging, of simultaneous growth and decline—idiosyncratically, uniquely. Fit and 'trained' bodies may experience their bodies more acutely than those who are not absorbed in recording and assessing their own capabilities and limitations, so the peaks and valleys, gains and losses, of physical pleasure might be more pronounced for those who are more in tune with their bodies.

While there are shared experiences with others (e.g. gaining of perspective through a series of imbricated experiences), there are also perceptions, functions, abilities, senses that are specifically locked in to one individual's experience and that are fluid, context-specific and contingent. Murakami, writing in the existentialist style that has come to define his greater works, seems fascinated by his own aging—and his attitude reflects a certain kind of bemused pleasure at watching himself age (and simultaneously diminish).[17]

Murakami's looking to his own self as a solitary exemplar for the aging process is a part of a larger project dealing with the third space where public issues meet private concerns. But, as Sotirin (2010) points out, drawing from Deleuze and working within a poststructuralist frame, we can privilege 'an implicit yet critical dimension of autoethnographic work as the basis for the distinction [between personal and public] . . . [that will] grasp the specificity of any particular time, place, or thing' (Section 6, ¶1). Using the concept of 'radical specificity', Sotirin argues for autoethnographies that simultaneously celebrate uniqueness and the singularity of any given experience—along with its concomitant ineffability—as forms of research that are 'distinctively critical, creative, and affirming' (Section 7, ¶5).

Seen in this way, aging is both a profoundly private and a selectively public issue—witness the acceptance of it by graceful individuals, and the policy puzzles over public health care for seniors—but the embodied aspect of aging, the physicality of it, the pleasurable and not-so-pleasant aspects of it, remain *largely* private and idiosyncratic (cf. Sotirin, 2010). That is why I now turn to poetic expressions of these private 'troubles': the poetic form, done well, manages simultaneously to convey general truths and individual specificities.

Poetry—and a poetic sensibility towards prose (cf. Rinehart, 2010)—serves as one type of marker of societal attitudes toward issues like aging. How does a society see its aging populations, how might it negotiate aging and how would one be expected to age (e.g. gracefully, with honor and respect; a threat to dwindling food supplies; a necessary evil to be tolerated; a burden dismissed)? Through the lens of poetry—though it is artistic—parameters of possible attitudes towards aging may emerge. These poetic

90 *Robert E. Rinehart*

expressions, already hinted at within Dylan Thomas' poems and Beatles' lyrics from 'the West', signify somewhat different attitudes toward aging in 'the East'.

REFLECTIONS OF 'THE EAST' PRE-MCLUHAN

Lu Yu (701–762), living twelve hundred years previous to Dylan Thomas (and the Beatles),[18] wrote a poem about aging that puts a positive spin on the physicality of aging.

> Written in a Carefree Mood
>
> Old man pushing seventy,
> in truth he acts like a little boy,
> whooping with delight when he spies some mountain fruits,
> laughing with joy, tagging after village mummers;
> with the others having fun stacking tiles to make a pagoda,
> standing alone staring at his image in the jardiniere pool.
> Tucked under his arm, a battered book to read,
> just like the time he first set off for school. (Lu Yu, 2012)

Such a stance, where a seventy-year-old man 'acts like a little boy', indicates Lu Yu's belief in the power of mind and mindset to shape and flavor one's approach to aging. It is remarkable that, in the 21st century, an everyday (that is to say, non-athletic) aging person who would frolic in such a way as this 8th-century poem describes would generally be seen as frivolous, or as behaving inappropriately. The specifics of 'spy[ing] some mountain fruits', 'tagging . . . mummers', and 'stacking tiles' convey 'universal' and empathic moments of joy, *because* of their presence within aging. Lu Yu's poem, however, does not deal with the process of physical death, but rather celebrates key pleasurable moments of life.

In Lu Yu's poem, the aging body—and the aging athletic body—works in contraindication to such societal strictures as assigning utilitarian values to everything the body does. I don't view the poem as uncritically celebratory of youth; rather, I see it reflecting a holistic worldview that does not fall into Western-based Cartesian duality (indeed, is unaware of Rene Descartes!) and that merges the best of different lived ages together: the paired 'old'/'young' statements are not only fond remembrances of physical capability, but also cognitive markers of different ways of enjoying the various things that the 'old man's' body could do.

While the term 'frivolity' connotes uselessness in some aging bodies, in this poem it appears to be a key link to pleasure: the old man enjoys 'act[ing]', 'whooping', 'sp[ying]', 'laughing', 'tagging', 'stacking', 'standing' (implying a transition to a more thoughtful way of being in the world) and

Aging Bod(ies) and Pleasure   91

'staring' at the pool, deep in thought. In the Western world, the image of the *irascible* aging body is dominant: Clint Eastwood's performance at the recent Republican National Convention is one example.[19] The (ironic) basis for the textual rhetoric that was Eastwood's performance stems from an Eastern philosophy, where age is equated with wisdom, so that when an aging adult speaks there is a reverential hush due to an expected insight and perspective.

As it is for the aging mind, so too for the aging body. When 20 (as my son is), there is no question whether one will jump down from a four-foot ledge: it is seen as a challenge, a test of one's plyometric fitness. When in one's 60s—even in a physically active body—there is at least a slight reticence to 'take the chance' based on the possibility of injury.

These various attitudes reflect aspects of both disengagement theory and activity theory. Disengagement theory was first developed in 1961 by Cumming and Henry; it attempts to explain why some individuals initiated a slow and gradual dwindling of activity and of their engagement with 'life' that reflected their own recognition of the inevitability of death. Activity theory, stemming from 1940s work by Russian psychologist Alexei Leont'ev, essentially suggests that people remain active in their 'continuation of role performances' (Harris, 2007: 84), replacing one activity with another. Either theory potentially synchronizes with acts and perceptions of pleasure during aging, as it is the articulation between (hegemonic, idealized) societal ideologies and the individual's matching to them that often creates satisfaction. But the sense of continuity—of energy forming into different outward actions—is synchronous with Wabi Sabi.

WABI SABI, POETRY AND PLEASURE

Wabi Sabi, as a philosophical stance, requires reflection. In a consumer culture, where 'more recent' is somehow linked to 'better', and where 'faster' is perceived as 'more hip', slow, reflective thought has often been replaced by near-constant stimulation. For example, those with terminal illnesses become subjects of their own documentaries—remain busy, up to the very end—and often haven't time for reflection, for appreciation of the trajectories of their lives. Wabi Sabi reminds us to seek 'pure freedom, joy and creativity', as they are the 'intentions of the Universe' (Gold, 2004: 83). I take that as the beginning of understanding a simultaneously individual and group reaction to (and with) aging, to what pleasure in the physically aging body means both privately and publicly.

The Korean *sijo* is exemplary of a tradition of pastoral, metaphysical poetry, older than haiku, but stemming from an ancient Chinese tradition. Traditionally, it is a three-line poem, with 14–16 syllables in each line. Important facets of the sijo, according to Gross (2012, citing Elizabeth

92 Robert E. Rinehart

St. Jacques): '. . . never lose sight of the three characteristics that make sijo unique: basic structure, musical/rhythmic elements, and the twist' (¶8).

With these elements in mind, we can look at four sijo for their literal and/ or metaphorical reflections on physical aging (I briefly give *an* interpretation of these sijo—as with all interpretations, these reflections are meant for discussion and debate.) In these four tone poems, we glimpse the ephemeral nature of joy and pleasure within an aging person—indeed, within all ages.

> The spring breeze melted snow on the hills then quickly disappeared.
> I wish I could borrow it briefly to blow over my hair
> And melt away the aging frost forming now about my ears.
> —U T'ak (1262–1342) (in Gross, 2012)

This sijo asserts the inevitability of the physical aging process, yet also calls for moments of youthfulness. It is gentle in its remonstrance toward aging, using words like 'melt' (as opposed to 'fight' in 'Do not go gentle') to ask for a bit more time—it is a celebration of the imperfection of shortened time, a request to work with aging, not to oppose it.

The second sijo returns the poet back to a natural, natured state.

> You ask how many friends I have? Water and stone, bamboo and pine.
> The moon rising over the eastern hill is a joyful comrade.
> Besides these five companions, what other pleasure should I ask?
> —Yon Son-do (1587–1671) (in Gross, 2012)

Yon Son-do's narrator, in an aging that is implied rather than explicit, comes to realize the fundamental connectedness of life elements—including the human body—and is satisfied with his place in the scheme of things. In this sijo, Yon Son-do relates the natural, enduring world to the steadfastness of friendship, posing the celebration of loyalty and inter-reliance together.

The third sijo is more explicit, less metaphorical. While still celebrating the processes of aging, the poet ironically points out that his mind grows sharper while his outward body (Wabi Sabi) grows ever more imperfect ('the years pile up on my body'). The obvious juxtaposition of the two elements exemplifies a wisdom of acceptance that is subtle, gentle and sublime.

> Mind, I have a question for you—How is it you stay so young?
> As the years pile up on my body, you too should grow old.
> Oh, if I followed your lead, Mind, I would be run out of town.
> —Anonymous (in Gross, 2012)

Aging Bod(ies) and Pleasure 93

While this sijo is more whimsical than the others, it gently reminds us that the balance between mind/spirit and body is more complex than Rene Descartes may have posited and than Western populist culture assumes.

The fourth sijo expresses a hope for a transformative act—for the poet's body to 'become a lovely swallow'—and for this act to create a new pleasance:

> My body, in its withering, may become a lovely swallow.
> Under the eaves of my loved one's home I'll build my nest of twigs.
> After dusk I'll fly aloft and glide gently to his side.
>
> —Anonymous (in Gross, 2012)

It is difficult to resist a Judeo-Christian interpretation of this poem, but if we might, we see that the wish for mobility, for having done 'good deeds', for preparing for the future (and generations of the future) is packed within this simple sijo.

While these sijo each demonstrate Korean attitudes toward aging—where scientism and explicit discourse is seen as somewhat crass (to what degree this is a result of the poetic form, to what degree agrarian attitude, is unclear)—they also exemplify precepts of Japanese Wabi Sabi: they are 'perfect moment[s] in a most imperfect place—a sublime experience engraved as a treasure. . .' (Gold, 2004: 117–118). They importune the reader to seek quiet moments of joy, to savor the pleasure derived from such moments as gentle and sublime facets of the process of aging. As such, they serve as islands of celebration, as archipelagos leading to a mainland filled with new perspectives.

FINAL TOUCHES

My contention in this chapter was to demonstrate differing possibilities for worldviews toward the aging body, to disrupt the hegemony of Western views. This discussion has been deliberately counter-scientific, counter-Western-hegemonic, and as a result it has also over-simplified and generalized very complex societies and worldviews. The West's dominant discourse has naturalized such attitudes toward the aging athletic body as one that 'fights the good fight', that continues to exemplify a dominant, masculine ideal of the sporting body. In short, the dominant Western attitude towards aging, decay and death sees a body as one that 'loses a battle' with disease; that never backs down or gives up; that sees cancer as the enemy. This is not surprising in a context of science, where prediction and control are two major rationales for study.

Contrariwise, some of the examples I have shown from the East's dominant discourses have presented an aging athletic body as one that may try to blend in with natural processes of aging, that may gracefully exemplify the aging process itself, and celebrate it within a worldview that accepts imperfection and decay as beautiful, aesthetic ways of performing one's life.

94 *Robert E. Rinehart*

In this worldview—increasingly homogenized (as we see with Murakami)—death, decay, decline and dying are all seen as natural processes, inevitabilities that we may accept, embrace and welcome. Which view may give more pleasure?

NOTES

1. Foreman, an Olympic gold medalist, won the heavyweight boxing title from Michael Moorer at age 45 in 1994 (cf. Anthony, 2008).
2. Hopkins was 46 when he won the WBC, IPO, and The Ring titles in May of 2011 ('Golden oldie', 2011).
3. Oerter won gold in four consecutive Olympics in the discus, finishing in 1968. However, 'In 1980, at age 43, he threw 227–11, a career best and the second longest in the world that year' (Litsky, 2007).
4. Callahan was 56 years old in 2008 when she competed in the 25-meter pistol at the Beijing Olympics ('American shooter', 2008).
5. Torres made the US Olympic swimming team at age 41 (Michaelis, 2008).
6. Age 40, Tua fought Alexander Ustinov in his last professional bout (Lewis, 2013)
7. While Hoketsu was the oldest athlete at the London Olympics, 'there are 187 athletes over 40 at this year's [2012] games' (Hughes and Rogers, 2012).
8. Of course, this strategy is problematic, not least because, as a series of broad strokes, it denies individual exceptionalities. As the focus on this type of study may possibly increase, such generalities (racist, sexist and ageist) may be more deeply examined, but for now, opening up the discussion about different forms of pleasure and aging bodies will have to suffice.
9. As the contemporary world is more and more a homogenized, globalized one, it seems reasonable to explore the fundamental (and yet somewhat stereotypical) ethical groundings of attitudes towards aging. Thus, I have not looked at contemporary poetry from either Western or Eastern (and that bifurcation itself is problematic) cultures, but at poetry that seems to stand as somewhat emblematic of those cultural broad strokes regarding the aging body. While it is certainly not my aim to provide a cause-effect relationship, or to gloss over many of the subtle differences, broad strokes will have to suffice as an opening gambit. The basis for this piece is that 'competition', in the way it presents in contemporary physical life, however, is a social construction (cf. Berger and Luckmann, 1966), and, as such, it can be deconstructed—or at least interrogated.
10. As one example, Phillips points out the rarity of 'death by competition', this from the New Zealand Masters Games:

    > A death at Masters Games is a rarity and it was unfortunate that a 51-year-old local ridge runner died last week. This is only the fourth death in 11 Games in Wanganui since 1989, the others coming in swimming (an elderly visiting woman), squash (a local male player) and touch football (a Palmerston North man). A minutes silence was observed in the main marquee in memory of the ridge runner with event organizer Allan Caird and Games chairman Leigh Grant offering their condolences to the man's family. Since the inaugural Games in Wanganui 20 years ago more than 72,500 competitors, some of them in their 90's, have competed. (2009)

11. Throughout, I use mediating terms like 'traditionally' and 'hegemonic'. This is deliberate: it is reductionistic, racist and simplistic to characterize one culture

Aging Bod(ies) and Pleasure   95

a certain way. But, in 'doing' research of the 'other', broad strokes are ways of beginning the conversation. To date, there has been very little discussion of things 'Eastern' in Western sport scholars' discussions. Some exceptions, of course, apply, but—again, dominantly—the discourse surrounds (typically unexamined) Western worldviews.

12. Arguably, the aspects of pragmatic acceptance of *what is* are not simply confined to Eastern traditions, but also find expression in Dewey's American pragmatism, Blumer's 'Symbolic Interactionism' and in traces of other worldviews—the modernist notions of constant progress and achievement, however, are somewhat antithetical to these stances, partially because of a lack of tacit acceptance of the *now*.

13. Note how, for example, then-49-year-old Courtney Cox (Hollywood star of '*Friends*' and '*Cougar Town*') has been so characterized in a magazine article title: 'Courteney Cox: Fighting my age is "a constant daily vicious battle"' (Patel, 2013).

14. And actors, putting themselves in roles where they have not actually experienced bodily the 'feel' of aging, or grief, learn to 'embody' accurately the feel of something outside their ken. See, for example, Brad Pitt's enactment of Benjamin Button (Fincher, 2008) in *The Curious Case of Benjamin Button*, Dustin Hoffman's role of Jack Crabb in *Little Big Man* (Penn, 1970), and the actors communicating deep grief in the play *Rabbit Hole* (Lindsay-Abaire, 2006; see also Poole, 2012). Actors put on these affective states often having not experienced them in their own lives; rarely do we, though, except as children, *enact* future possible states of feeling.

15. With thanks to Jay Coakley for mentioning this song as an example of legitimized popular culture views of aging in the West.

16. There are other forms of aging, as well, which implies that there may be different 'ages' for different kinds of 'peaks': intellectual, physical, emotional, spiritual peaks may all, to some degree, be conceived similarly to this sense of a physical peaking. Again, this rationalization process—of an organism that doesn't simply keep growing (e.g. spiritually)—may be quite different culturally.

17. This relation of personal experience to shared societal ills is not unlike C. Wright Mills' (1959: 186) conception of public and private concerns:

> . . . [the social scientist's] public role has two goals: What he [sic] ought to do for the individual is to turn personal troubles and concerns into social issues and problems open to reason. . . . What he [sic] ought to do for the society is to combat all those forces which are destroying genuine publics and creating a mass society. . . . Only then might society be reasonable and free.

18. Again, I am aware of many difficulties with even discussing these concepts in such reductionistic terms, given the incomparability of time eras, geographical and political systems, and so forth—but since some of the same characterizations occur in depictions of both West and East (cf. Said, 1979), my characterizations fall under the rubric of 'idealized' notions of West and East. As Ibn Warraq points out of Said—implying him to be a cultural relativist: 'he has no interest in, much less capacity for, showing what the true Orient and Islam really are' (Warraq, 2007: 31). But Said got the discussion started, beginning with broad strokes (admittedly challengeable). Even Warraq himself struggles with the term 'the Other':

> . . . a phrase I am reluctant to use, for its use implies a certain attitude or acceptance of certain mental clichés, but the realiation that there is no

easy and succinct way to get around it has led to my temporary verbal surrender ... (12)

Clearly, reductionistic language is clumsy, over-simplification is awkward and language itself is sometimes halting and lame, but making the attempt to continue the dialogue is still important.

19. Eastwood, after having spoken for eleven minutes to the Republican National Convention, in a conceit addressed to President Obama, presumably sitting in a chair next to him, defended his speech partially on the basis of his age (he was 82 years old at the time of the speech):

'One advantage of being my age is that you know what can they do to ya?' Eastwood said in an interview with CNN. 'You just have fun and do what you think and then you can say what you think, you don't have to edit yourself'. ('Clint Eastwood', 2012, ¶2)

7 Running for Pleasures

Jayne Caudwell

> And I could hear the lords and ladies now from the grandstand,
> and could see them standing up to wave me in: 'Run!'
> —(Sillitoe, 1958: 46)

> People yelled, cheered, pressed in against me, radios blared,
> my tears were dry, so I yelled and cheered too
> and wind whipped leaves down the street
> as more runners came by, more and more thousands,
> until it seemed that they filled the whole city,
> and that all of us, all of us, were running.
> —(Levin, 1997: 296)

Colin, the young Borstal lad and runner in Alan Sillitoe's story 'The Loneliness of the Long-Distance Runner', ignoring the commands from the 'lords and ladies' to 'run', stood still before the finishing line. In Richardson's filmic version of the book, Colin smiles as he stands waiting to be beaten. He deliberately fails to finish in first place, blatantly breaking the rules of sporting competition as well as the expectations of his governors. The book's young character is anti-authority and anti-establishment, and Sillitoe's narrative is often viewed as an astute critique of post-WWII British class system, class privilege, ever-emerging capitalism and promulgated ideals surrounding competition and success.

In Jennifer Levin's story 'Her Marathon', Celía, struggling with a hangover and on her way to get breakfast, witnesses Alberto Salazar running the New York City Marathon. Impressed and inspired by the runners and the occasion, she decides to take up running. Levin writes how Celía, depicted as an overweight lesbian mother with a butch girlfriend who drinks a lot of beer, goes on to complete her first running event: the Women's Mini-Marathon in Central Park.

Both of the above short stories center personal experiences of running. At the same time, and not coincidentally, they capture important socio-cultural dimensions of class, gender and sexuality. They are dissimilar narratives,

98 *Jayne Caudwell*

but both protagonists are shown to relish the freedoms their running allows. In each text, Colin and Celía enjoy their early morning runs. Colin is let out like an owned racehorse to run the surrounding fields and woodlands. Under these circumstances, running provides a sense of liberty and independence. This is something he savors:

> . . . and as soon as I take that first flying leap out into the frosty grass of an early morning when even the birds haven't the heart to whistle, I get to thinking, and that's what I like. . . . It's a treat, being a long-distance runner, out in the world by yourself with not a soul to make you bad-tempered or tell you what to do. . . . (Sillitoe, 1958: 10)

Celía, after years of inactivity, decides to run regularly and frequently. She too takes pleasure from her moving body and the embodied feelings associated with the motion and rhythm of running:

> The mornings got darker, closer to winter, but every once in a while I'd wake up easier when the alarm hit, sometimes even with a feel of burning red excitement in my chest and throat, like running was something pleasurable, good, a gift. . . . Thighs move like water, arms pump rhythm. The feet did not want to stop. Those days I'd stay out longer—half an hour more—with happy buzzing like music in my head. (Levin, 1997: 301)

Capturing the pleasures of running—the seemingly intangible dimension of human movement—is not achieved easily via traditional academic approaches. Many sport scholars are prone to objectify and make scientific the body's motion. Referring to sport studies, Markula and Denison (2000) explore how it is possible to research and write about the motion of the body (running and dance) without turning human movement in to a disembodied practice. They highlight the potential of fiction to capture embodiment. Through reference to Rinehart's (1998c) work about skateboarding, they make an important turn to the aesthetic, sensate and visceral of moving bodies. More recently, Bairner—in his address of the '. . . main challenges that currently face the sociology of sport . . .' (2012: 102)— similarly explores the significance of fiction and semi-fiction, arguing that they 'provide valuable sociological insights into the world of sport' (p. 111).

In the two stories cited above, distance running, written through evocative prose, is presented as vividly and palpably pleasurable. Running is produced through these texts as embodied, and as a personal pleasure.

More broadly, it is apparent that distance running is contingent on socio-cultural location and there are valuable scholarly contributions that demonstrate the ways class, gender, sexuality, age and ability (Abbas, 2004; Allen-Collinson, 2011; Atkinson, 2008; Griffin, 2010; Leedy, 2009; Smith, 2000; Tulle, 2007; van Ingen, 2004) impact running, and are re-inscribed through running. Feelings of pleasure do feature in some of these studies. However, runners' pleasures are often connected to achievement: recording times and distances. These outcome-orientated principles of sporting competition (achieving, beating, placing and winning) are mimetic of capitalist ideologies (Brohm, 1978 and Sillitoe, 1958) and Bale (2004) successfully identifies the links between running and modernity, rationalization and standardization. More specifically, he compares the shifts in contemporary running cultures to the processes of production that underpin capitalist societies:

> Fordism has its analogies in running. Fordist foot-running involves production (of races) being geared to capital equipment (the standardized, synthetic 400-metre track), the optimization of processes (interval running), a growing division of labour and a standardization of outputs (a few Grand Prix spectacles). It is tightly organized with little, if no, space for deviations. (Bale, 2004: 71)

Bale's critique can be extended and applied to recent interventions governing human movement, especially distance running: the use of the Global Positioning Systems (GPS), for example. The advertising of these products and the meanings given to distance running through such advertising are steeped with notions of performance efficiency and productivity, echoing not only Fordism, but Taylorism too. Like Fordism, Taylorism involves rationality and standardization as well as empiricism, best practice, knowledge transfer and work ethic. The hyperbole is easy to see in this Nike advertisement:

More from your run

Train like you mean it

Map runs, track progress, and get the motivation you need to keep going. The Nike+Running app tracks distance, pace, time and calories burned with GPS, giving you audio feedback as you run. Automatically upload to nikeplau.com to see runs, including your route and elevation.

Extra Motivation

Activate a Powersong to help blast you toward a new record. The App also gives you positive feedback from some of Nike's top athletes.
Challenge yourself
Push for your longest, farthest, and fastest run yet. Take on yesterday, last Tuesday, or a personal best.
(nikeplus.nike.com/plus/products/gps_app/)

The advertisements for Global Positioning Systems for running carry all the hallmarks of efficiency and productivity. They provide stark reminders of how the capitalist principles of Fordism and Taylorism feature in contemporary running cultures. The moving body is subject to principles

100   *Jayne Caudwell*

of progress and progression. The exercise laboratory becomes mobile and individualized. Running becomes a highly sanitized form of physical activity. Pleasure, we can assume, is tied to quantifiable criteria, and it is about knowing and mastering.

In sport studies there is limited explicit engagement with running and pleasure. In this chapter, I draw on fictions and non-fictions, existing academic literatures and my own experiences (the personal and biographical)[1] to offer a socio-cultural analysis of running pleasures. This chapter, therefore, reflects a form of autoethnography and this approach, as Denzin posits, is a departure from traditional social science research. It requires different ways of writing, as well as of reading: 'The writer asks the reader to submit to the text's casual version of how and why something happened' (2010: 89).

Overall, my aim is to challenge running cultures of achievement (track progress, distance, pace, time and calories burned) and running discourses of success (push for your longest, farthest and fastest run yet. Take on yesterday, last Tuesday or a personal best). I seek to move beyond pleasure as fixed to work-ethic because too often, as Ahmed points out, 'Pleasure becomes an imperative only as an incentive and reward for good conduct, or as an 'appropriate outlet' for bodies that are busy being productive ('work hard play hard')' (2004: 163).

A BRIEF AUTOBIOGRAPHY

I look down at the several pairs of running shoes on the floor. 'No pink ones,' I tell him.

We look at each other and I get the feeling he submits to my steely-eyed stare. We are both in our mid-to-late-forties and this is an independent running shop tucked away from Brighton's main drag. 'Sam,' he shouts down the stairs to his mate 'No more pink ones.' I continue to look at him. He is dressed in loose jogging pants and a faded Beachy Head Marathon T-shirt. He stands—feet shoulder's width apart—poised and balanced. Despite his baggy clothes it is easy to see that his body is lean and taut. I enjoy looking at him.

'Well, would you run in pink trainers?' I ask. My voice is a little softer this time. He thinks for a split second.

'They don't make them for men.'

'Exactly,' I retort.

He looks down at the running shoes and then at me. He adds, grinning, 'I have worn orange ones'.

When school ended, I was 16 and I had passed three O'levels: maths, physics and art. In art I made a clay version of the torso of Michelangelo's David. It was green because the head of this male figure was a bulbous cabbage: his

Running for Pleasures 101

ribs, the veins of a cabbage leaf. I will never know why I made this sculpture, but looking back, rather conveniently and very simplistically, it suits my current belief systems—I'm critical of so-called male knowledge. Also, rather paradoxically, I was drawn to David's body.

Like many children born in the UK in the 60s, I spent much of my childhood playing outside. From the age of six to the age of 12, I lived with my family at a 'boys' school' for young offenders, ('naughty boys'), juvenile delinquents aged between 13 and 16 years. These boys were too young for the Borstal system, although some did end up there. My parents were residential social workers and for the last four years of our time at the school we lived in an apartment attached to a Unit. The Unit was home to 15 young men. Many of these young men were from nearby Birmingham and their ethnicities reflected both inner-city white working class and first generation Black British youth.

Despite latter-day media coverage of how such institutions housed abusive behaviors, it was a safe environment for my younger brother and me, although, I have three memories of feeling discomfort. The first was when one of the white boys pushed me underwater at the swimming pool and tried to hold me there. The second was when a small group of them encouraged me to smoke a cigarette. And the third was accompanying one of the white boys, because he had asked my dad if I could go along with them, to visit his dad in Long Lartin Prison (later in life, I learned Long Lartin was/is a Category A prison for inmates who are considered 'highly dangerous'). The rest of my memories are about playing outside, playing football, climbing trees, fences and walls, hanging and swinging from climbing frames, running across fields and through woodland, holidays in Wales and canoeing rivers and the sea. It all sounds very idyllic; the point is I was very active and my childhood was joyful because of it.

During some of these years, I played sport at Middle School (9–13yrs) and more formally in the school's teams. I was on the cross-country team, probably because I could run, but I disliked almost every run and certainly every race. At this age, the focus on achieving and success made me nervous, nervous beyond my young emotional capacity. 'Serious running', as Bale (2004: 18) argues, 'colonize[s] the bodies of youngsters'. I was very aware of my physical body, and the bodies of the boys I grew up with. I knew there was a link between physical activity and how we moved and what we looked like. However, at this age, I did not enjoy running in races.

As a young teenager, I was attracted to the torso of Michelangelo's David. It resembled the soft musculature of the boys' bodies I observed—and had playful physical contact with—in my childhood. I did not desire the bodies of the boys, or David; I was not drawn to their smooth, slightly muscled chests, arms and legs out of any childhood heterosexual attraction. These male bodies evoked a wish to be exactly the same as them. I wanted muscles and I wanted to be strong and fast. I wanted the same joys and pleasures I assumed some of them took from running, jumping, climbing and play fighting.

102 Jayne Caudwell

It seems remarkable now, but in my late teens and before I left home at 19 years old, I completed three half marathons. I was not a member of a running or athletics club; however, I was a member of the local hockey and rowing clubs. Running was part of the training for these sports. And, as Bale (2004: 16) makes the point, '[j]ogging and fitness running require getting people to run rather than taking pleasure in movement or simply enjoying themselves'. By my late teens I was conditioned in formal sporting competition. It was also the early 1980s, and organized marathons and half marathons were emerging as popular leisure activities in most UK towns and cities.

As a teenage girl, I participated in running for fitness (Bale, 2004) and not for pleasure. Also, I ran because I thought I could sculpt my body, not into a traditionally feminine-looking body, but into something more boy-like, which, I assumed would enable embodied pleasures.

GENDER, CLASS AND RUNNING

> 'ASICS has also created the Gender Specific Space Trusstic,
> as part of its aim to reinvent running shoes for women'
> Price: £105
> Colour: Hot Pink
> —(www.asics.co.uk, 2012)

> Freedom to run where they like may apply only to certain groups,
> often white, heterosexual males.
> —(Bale, 2004: 69)

In the literature, running for men (Murakami, 2008; Smith, 2000) and for both men and women (Abbas, 2004; Atkinson, 2008; Tulle, 2007) is strongly linked with middle class-ness. The relationships between class and running are evidenced in the ways runners' bodies hold and are given meaning. As Tulle (2007) argues, through her application of the ideas of Bourdieu, the runner's body is a source of habitus and as others highlight (Abbas, 2004; Atkinson, 2008), running cultures encourage and indulge middle-class cultural capital. In this way, many aspects of running are contingent on class privilege and the embodiment of this privilege. Buying expensive, specialized footwear might be one manifestation of this privilege.

Another class-based privilege I am personally aware of is running in extraordinary locations. Bale has also made this point: 'As a runner, one experiences many places at a variety of scales' (2004: 73).

Pleasures: Placing Litanies

Edinburgh, Newcastle, York, Lake Thirlmere, Manchester, Leeds, Bradford, Loughborough, Birmingham, Walsall, Bewdley, Stourport-on-Severn,

London, Shoreham-by-Sea, Brighton, Eastbourne, Oslo, Ishøj, Paris, Aix en Provence, Perpignan, La Manga, Zagreb, Skala Eressou, Nahariya, Masdar City, Bogor, Kimbe, Melbourne, Raglan, Napier, Wellington, Vancouver, Bangor, Denver, Chicago, Urbana-Champaign, New Orleans, Havana.

England, Norway, Denmark, France, Spain, Croatia, Greece, Israel, United Arab Emirates, Indonesia, Papua New Guinea, Australia, New Zealand, Canada, United States of America, Cuba.

And so, it is with some pleasure I tell people I have run in many different countries (places). I tell of the climates (tropical, sub-tropical, arid, dry, Mediterranean, temperate, cold) and runs through forests, woodlands, meadows, alongside lakes and on agricultural tracks, beaches and sometimes roads (spatial scales). I choose not to recount times and distances.

Talking about runs is not peculiar; other runners and writers of the subject (Bale, 2004; Murakami, 2008) often tell of their runs in what are for them faraway places. The stories of these runs often centralize the running environment—the climate, the terrain and the people. For me, these runs are about feeling place. The pleasures of being touched by a place are evoked, lived and re-lived through memories and narratives of these runs—what it felt like being there, running (cf. Hockey, 2005, 2006). These connections with place and their natural and human environments are sensual pleasures.

Out of all of these places, the only purpose-built facility I ran on was in Bogor, Indonesia (Figure 7.1). At 6 am, I joined local people and ran circuits of a very worn and uneven red-rumble oval track.

Running in tropical environments is a highly sensual as well as physical and energetic experience. The surface of the skin is wet within minutes, the entire body becomes saturated and sticky and fresh oxygen feels like it is in short supply. In Bogor, and on previous occasions in Kimbe, Papua New Guinea, my runs were hot, gasping, drenched affairs, and extremely visceral because of the humidity and what this does to my body and breathing. I ran alone in Papua New Guinea, but in Bogor I joined Indonesian people as we made our recurring, variously paced, but nevertheless anti-clockwise laps. I shared their running/walking space and our random and spontaneous mutual glances, smiles and nods were wonderfully simple human interactions. These moments of recognition are customary on my regular hometown running routes, but to make small, fleeting unions with people in places that are unfamiliar somehow reaffirms my beliefs in human kindness and compassion. I would end these runs with soaked clothing, beads of sweat streaming down my body, slippery skin, a heavy pulse in my head and a massive sense of fulfillment. Ahmed, in linking happiness to pleasure, suggests that '[t]he perfect end is the end of all ends . . .' (2010: 26). Like Celía in Levin's short story, I would finish '. . . with happy buzzing like music in my head' (Levin, 1997: 301). On occasions I would wonder if these sensual endings were my jouissance; a pleasure that is so complete and deeply embodied that, for me, it has sexual undertones.

104 *Jayne Caudwell*

Figure 7.1   Bogor, nr. Jakarta, Java, Indonesia (July 2010). Taken by Jayne Caudwell

The pleasures of running in unfamiliar places are not only cutaneous, sensual and about humankind and connectivity; they are not only about how air and skin interact, the feel of a sweaty, slippery, satiated body and how different people intermingle. Running in some hot places is also transgressive, and this can provide an exciting edge, which is pleasurable in a different way. I have visited Dhaka in Bangladesh, but failed to run in this city space (instead, I used a gym to exercise inside). I did not run in Bangladesh, partly because of the lack of appropriate space and the exaggerated clamor of this heavily populated country. However, the main reason I abstained from running was because of how public places in predominantly Muslim countries such as Bangladesh are populated entirely by men and boys only. I felt very ambivalent about breaking in to these very traditional cultural spaces. I wanted to be sensitive to religious imperatives (even though I identify as atheist). I did not want to be offensive and take the privileges of a white middle-class woman to brusquely infiltrate these obviously male domains. However, I did want to rebel against such absolute gendered spatial domination. Secretly, I wanted the pleasures of careering through—with my imagined-as strong, composed, woman's body—these men-only spaces.

I was able to run the dusty pavements of Masdar City, a purpose-built grid arrangement of gated communities on the outskirts of Abu Dhabi. This

Running for Pleasures 105

felt possible because of the huge imported population of white professional employees from Europe, the USA and Australia who appeared to dislocate some of the cultural traditions of the country. However, there were no other runners, let alone women runners. Instead, the streets, pavements and artificial embankments were occupied, very subtly, by work gangs; men who were most likely from Pakistan. Much of the United Arab Emirates has been converted, via cheap labor from the Asian continent, into what might best be described through Baudrillard's notion of hyper-reality. In what were desert lands and semi-permanent settlements, there are now facades of high rise buildings, manicured highways and large swathes of the greenest grass, old-world stores selling alcohol and fancy air-conditioned indoor shopping malls with the usual suspects (e.g. Starbucks and McDonalds). These Westernized trappings, absent in Bangladesh, somehow gave me license to run.

I would return from these runs with a dry mouth, a film of fine sand on my teeth and broken lines of salt-stains contouring my cotton T-shirt and shorts. Despite the harsh dry heat, running the newly built pavements felt good because my moving body provided a very rare sight: a woman running. Running in United Arab Emirates seemed like an act of gender-politico defiance; it might not have been all that, but challenging and possibly breaking some established gendered norms provided me with a willful sense of gratification.

Clearly, pleasure is a complicated concept. It can be considered under the remit of affect and in her work on affect and emotion, Wetherell asks: 'How can the relays and ricochets of the human body be grasped, and the visceral put in touch with the social?' (2012: 10). For her, the links between affect and the body involve an assembly of the relational (social) and the cultural. She argues: 'Power, then, is crucial to the agenda of affect studies' (p. 17). Running for pleasures—embodied pleasures, which are attached to the geographies of running in 'exotic' running locales, is undeniably linked to the relational (socio-cultural), namely class privilege.

My trips to Indonesia, Papua New Guinea, Bangladesh and the United Arab Emirates are very clearly enabled by my middle class-ness. That is, my ability to pay for regular and often expensive flights, my class-based self-confidence (in public spaces) as well as the many travel freedoms granted to UK passport-holders. These travel experiences are also dependent on the cultural capital of my family. Trips to the aforementioned four countries were to see and live with (for weeks at a time) my brother. He works in overseas agriculture development and without his privileged residency, I would never have been able to stay and move freely within these local communities. The extended list of places where I have run further reflects my class privilege, education, employment and opportunities to travel to conferences; moreover, working away from home and my largely unconstrained ability to take holidays and to visit friends, family and partners, for example, running through alpine forests on the outskirts of Oslo, running up remote dusty hills not far from Aix en Provence and running Raglan's beautiful Te Kopua and Ngarunui beaches.

106 *Jayne Caudwell*

Undeniably, some of my running pleasures are inextricably connected to broader structural social relations and individual cultural capital. My running-for-pleasures biography continues to reify the already known links between running and middle class-ness. Additionally, it introduces running pleasure as visceral and sensual as well as related to place and personal politics.

THE RUNNER'S BODY-MIND

> She has the most beautiful legs, hard, stripped down, with no wastage,
> and her Achilles tendons are like flexible rock. Running does that for her.
> And then I think, damn, damn, damn.
> I will not love her for those reasons . . .
> —(Maitland, 1997: 163)

> The farther I ran, the more weight I lost, too.
> In two and a half months I dropped about seven pounds,
> and the bit of flab I was starting to see around my stomach disappeared.
> —(Murakami, 2009, p. 15)

The physical body is central to many accounts of running. In Sara Maitland's story, entitled 'The Loveliness of the Long Distance Runner', Sally fights her desire to objectify her girlfriend's body. In the narrative, both women are cognizant of how competitive sporting ideals, in particular those apparent in marathon running, collide with their lesbian feminist points of view. Sally, the non-runner in the relationship, asks her girlfriend, repeatedly, why she must run marathons. The reply is a mixture of rationale, including: '"Call it sisterhood. You can't do it alone. You need—" at which Sally rasps: "You need the competition; you need people to beat . . ."' (Maitland, 1997: 162). The two women's differing opinions on marathon running remain unresolved throughout the short story. Yet Sally does find pleasure in looking at a woman-runner's body: the woman she loves. And her girlfriend continues to relish long-distance running.

Haruki Murakami, a famous Japanese writer of successful contemporary fiction, started running in 1982. He boasts at least one marathon a year (1982–2009) and a one-hour-a-day running regime. His book, *What I Talk About When I Talk about Running* (2008), is an allusion to Raymond Carver's (1981) collection and short story—*What We Talk about When We Talk about Love*, in which Carver articulates the multiple meanings and elusiveness of love. Murakami's title suggests intricate expressions of running. After enjoying his rather surreal and intriguing book *The Wind-Up Bird Chronicles*, I anticipated his writings on running to be similarly unconventional. However, I discovered that he writes of (talks about) his own running through

Running for Pleasures 107

his times, distances, body weight and disciplined routine. He expresses a progressive/competitive philosophy: 'In long-distance running the only opponent you have to beat is yourself, the way you used to be' (2008: 10). And, for me, some of his observations are mildly sexist: 'Most of these girls are small, slim, have on maroon Harvard-logo outfits, blond hair in a ponytail . . . it's pretty wonderful to watch these pretty girls run' (p. 93–94).

Although Maivorsdotter and Quennerstedt (2012) highlight the aesthetic content of Murakami's running through an analysis of his written text, I found the lack of an unusual and alternative embodied narrative of running disappointing. He admits he uses the physical disciplines and regimes of running to help manage his creativity as well as body weight. Despite echoing the instrumentality of running, these links begin to connect his running body with his creative mind. Still, I wonder what might have been the result of Murakami fusing the range of the 'real' of his marathon running and the diversity of the 'surreal' of his fiction writing. Would he write (talk) about his embodiment and the embodiment of other people (e.g. the Harvard women) differently? Would he write of pleasure differently?

Regular running, in most cases, does have an impact on the physical body. It makes some people's bodies change shape and weigh less than they previously weighed. This might make them appear more physically attractive—in the dominant Westernized sense of physical [sexual] attraction. The achievement of this sexualized embodied aesthetic most likely motivates many runners. In addition to competing against others/self and to achieving times and distances, runners often strive for visibly 'ideal' body morphology. Significantly, the ideal body cannot be bulging, excessive, overweight and slovenly. The ideal body is not a lazy body; it is the result of laboring, achieving and producing results, measured by time and distance, or even percentages of body fat. The runner's body serves to signify efficiency, productivity, the successes of individual toil, control and the ability to push through physical constraints and barriers. Running can become a physical fetish of achievement, and some running pleasures might best be described as painful and punishing. This is evident in Atkinson's study (2008) of the ways triathletes identify with agony, hurt and suffering. These feelings, when linked to endurance sport and in the context of Western capitalist lifestyles, are given meaning; they become pleasurable because they signify hard work (work ethic) and the ability to succeed, often against the odds. Such quantifiable pleasures are meaningful for many runners.

But what of the pleasures of running that do not valorize the objective dimensions of size, shape, time, distance, winning and defeating? Within achievement-orientated discourses of running pleasures, the physical body remains central and the corporeal is the focus of measurement. Clearly, there exist alternative ways to explore embodied pleasures, even the pleasurable agonies of running. There are, as I have mentioned above, the aesthetic, sensate, affectual and subjective feelings of running. Too few writers have made attempts to consider these. That said, Leedy (2009) does explore the connections between women's emotional landscapes and their running habits.

108　*Jayne Caudwell*

And Bale (2004) does raise slowness, playfulness and improvisation as significant dimensions of running. These emotional and playful aspects have often been forgotten and/or omitted from studies of long-distance running.

'I Can't Cry and Run at the Same Time' (Leedy, 2009)

Raw Emotion

At 17 weeks, I miscarried. The geneticist at Barts Hospital told me our genes—the father's and mine—were incompatible. I entered the Paris Marathon.

Ten years earlier, I took a job in Leeds. We'd been together for six years, including a previous move on my account. This time, she said she wouldn't go. I entered the London Marathon.

Last year, another heart-felt loss; my receipt number for the Jerusalem Marathon: 913799. I entered, but I didn't take part, this time.

Long distance running can provide an anesthetic and a pleasant way to forget adversity. It can displace emotions surrounding loss, unhappiness, sadness, misery and depression. In her qualitative research, Leedy (2009) considers the usefulness of women's narratives of running for broader agendas of social work practice, specifically the mental health of women. For the five women in Leedy's study, long distance running, usually competitive, offset current and past experiences of loss, bereavement, anger, addiction, stress and trauma. Running, for these women, provided sanctuary and solace; it permitted degrees of control and helped foster environments of accomplishment and self-worth.

Leedy's analysis of her research participants' testimonies slips easily into health promotion strategic frameworks, namely therapeutic functionality, stages of crisis and crisis resolution. Additionally, from the research, she advocates two specific types of long-distance running: self-efficacy and active coping. Clearly, physical activity, and in this case running, has been and continues to be viewed in functionalist and positivistic terms. Research from this perspective adopts epistemologies and methodologies that set out to uncover particular aspects of running—for example, women's empowerment and wellbeing. Running, then, is viewed as a form of medicine and/or therapy on the road to regaining 'normality'.

As I have argued from the onset, there are feelings of pleasure that exist outside of achieving normative outcomes, feelings and emotions that are much harder to analyze. For example, one of Leedy's research participants told of how her running was '. . . glorious! Glorious!' (2009: 85) and another spoke of her body's motion and/in her running environment:

I think [there was] something about the repetitive movements, the relaxing rhythm of feet—breathing. I looked around and breathed the air and looked up at the sky and at the changes on the trail. (p. 87)

Running for Pleasures 109

In his work on the body, nudity and the beach, Obrador-Pons focuses on the 'naked body itself, its movement and intensities as well as its interface with the environment' (2007: 125). He does this because he wishes to move away from existing socio-cultural explanations of the body as produced wholly through discourse and the body as an object of representation. Following Massumi, he argues that the body within socio-cultural thinking has been made sense of through 'ideas of objectification, resistance and inscription' (2002: 125). His challenge is to shift from the body that makes sense to '. . . an elusory and affectual body open to the world that feels and senses' (2007: 125).

Others have turned to the senses and affect to help understand the physically active body. For example, there is Seville's (2008) work on Parkour, and Straughan's (2012) research with scuba divers. For these writers, embodiment is in context; it involves a consideration of where the activity takes place and how spatial scales are implicated. Examples of spatial scales for divers are the sea, coral reefs, flows of water, air supply and pressure. Urban architecture, cityscape, brickwork, surface textures and clothing are relevant to those people who practice Parkour. Place and its spatialities are meaning-making in terms of affect and the body's senses. In this way, embodiment '. . . becomes an important facet for thinking through emotional geographies . . .' (Straughan, 2012: 20). Situatedness and sensation influence emotional effects and can help form what Straughan refers to as 'therapeutic landscapes'. It is place and space as well as embodiment that contribute to embodied sensation, for example, calmness (diving) and fear (Parkour).

Returning to Obrador-Pons' approach (to the body) and its relevance to running; he starts from the premise that it is not about seeing or showing nudity, but about how the body feels. For example, the sensation of the sun and wind on exposed skin. If we make an analogy between the naked body and the running body, then we can argue that running '. . . is something more than scripting upon the body or liberating it from social norms' (2007: 128). Running, for women, is not only about self-efficacy (empowerment) and active coping—it is an affectual practice. The research participants in Obrador-Pons' study considered lying on a beach naked as '. . . a pleasant and comfortable feeling . . .'; one of the women said: 'I like this feeling a lot' (p. 130).

Perhaps, some pleasures are not easily captured in words and text; they might be beyond conscious re-presentation, even cognition. However, tapping embodied sensation and holding in view the notion of therapeutic landscapes opens the way for the study of enjoyment, emotion and pleasures. It offers a lens of analysis that is not fixed on pre-coded cultural meanings that are attached to running (e.g. accomplishing times, distance and self-efficacy).

My participation in long-distance running, particularly marathon running, has in the past provided structure and an identifiable regime to counter hard times. My turn to running reflects learned behaviors, including a sporting stoicism, existing value-systems and the assumption that it will help

110   *Jayne Caudwell*

'improve' my emotional states. The shift to longer, more frequent runs was also possible because of an acquired physical capital (as well as acquired economic and cultural capital, as discussed earlier in this chapter). Over the last 40 years—since the age of five or six—my sporting 'habitus' (to borrow from Bourdieu) has developed to the extent that I experience almost constraint-free access to physical activity participation. As a consequence of this long-term involvement, my base-level fitness is sound. This sporting capital reflects a privileged ability-position, which means I can take up long-distance running relatively easily.

For several reasons, I did not participate in the Jerusalem marathon. Some of these reasons were logistical. One reason was because I discovered it would be impossible to run the streets of Jerusalem wearing a politically motivated T-shirt, one with a Palestinian flag on it, for example. What also happened—during the first few months when I extended my running routes—was that I began to think about running for pleasures. I started to feel my body's rhythms more keenly. Instead of being locked in to a deep-rooted achievement-orientated mind-set, I ran for the sheer fun of it.

The Pleasures of the Plod

It is affect's dramatic and turbulent qualities, along with the random, the chaotic and the spontaneous, which have marked it out as special for many.

This is misleading. Affect is about sense as well as sensibility. It is practical, communicative and organised. In affective practices, bits of the body get patterned together with feelings and thoughts, interaction patterns and relationships, narratives and interpretative repertoires, social relations, personal histories, and ways of life. (Wetherell, 2012: 13–14)

> . . . I skipped grocery shopping and just went home,
> changed into some sweaty old things,
> and I went outside into the wind and dark and I ran again,
> very sweet and happy and like music, the way I had that morning,
> running off and onto curbs,
> twisting around cars and garbage cans and people, I didn't care.
> (Levin, 1997: 302)

Running is an embodied mobile practice; it involves sustained and repetitive bodily motion, which is usually understood as monotonous, even boring. Long-distance running is not often associated with the dramatic, turbulent, random, chaotic and spontaneous. These characteristics, as Wetherell (2012) highlights above, are often linked with affect and work to produce affect's uniqueness. However, she goes on to argue that sense, sensibility, the practical and organized are significant to the ways affect becomes configured. In this argument, she alludes to the jumbling of body, feelings, thoughts,

Running for Pleasures 111

interactions, interpretations, relations and histories. I am arguing here for the insight that deliberate and slow pleasures can be just as affective as the sudden and dramatic.

In Levin's narrative of the woman runner—Celía—these patterns of affect Wetherell describes become apparent. Running, in the second quotation above, is no longer linear and monotonous. Instead, it is more akin with playfulness and improvisation. Combining how Celía moves her body, how she feels and thinks and how she interacts with the urban environment during nighttime provides an immediate and unusual narrative of the meaning of running. There is a rhythm in the narrative, a rhythm that reflects both mindfulness and physicality: sweet, happy, like music, skipped and twisting. The flow of movement is infectious and Celía's running sounds blissful. In this case, running is an affectual practice (Obrador-Pons, 2007) and/or affective practice (Wetherell, 2012).

Like other forms of embodied mobility, participation in long-distance running is, most likely, organized and routine. Murakami's one-hour-a-day running regime, as described in his book, is testimony to this. Some might imagine this apparent realm of repetition as banal and robotic, the quotidian of such a running routine inspiring nothing but ennui. Maybe; but, considered differently, this assumed monotony (of running) provides openings for [small] pleasures. These often-ephemeral pleasures can be related to running-rhythm. Running-rhythm can provide a backdrop for moments of joyful improvisations, playfulness, and even enjoyable melancholy.

Running is a relatively simple form of bodily locomotion. It does not involve complex and intricate movement patterns, but it does require synchronicity and the balancing of a dynamic asymmetry. It can take time to realize a comfortable embodied style of running. And yet, over time, running becomes automatic, seemingly natural for many people. Like other embodied mobile practices, affect and emotion are implicated and '. . . effloresce with particular rhythms' (Wetherell, 2012: 12). Like other forms of repetitive movements (e.g. rowing and swimming), running-rhythm, improvisation and playfulness have not been fully explored within sport studies. Having said that, rhythm, improvisation and playfulness are evident in Saville's observations of Parkour:

> . . . a certain level of maturity of the body to know a certain sequence of movements in relation to space leads to a type of immaturity, as the body in its excitement and playfulness finds new mobile relations with materialities. (2008: 900)

In his work, Saville acknowledges how 'mature' participants of Parkour complete endless practice and rehearsal. It might be odd to consider pleasure emanating from cycles of repetition, reiterations and the drilling of movement, and yet this is how, for example, great jazz musicians are able to create improvisation in their play; they practice and drill scales for hours on end. (The connections between running and music-making are not tenuous. Runners often have music in their heads, both imagined and pumped in via ear plugs).

Imagine preparing for a run. Standing, dressed, ready to run, and not having a pre-planned route. Instead, deciding directions—spontaneously—along the way. Running straight on, taking a right or left turn, up a hill or down a hill. Like Celía: off and onto curbs, twisting around cars and garbage cans and people. How many long-distance runners do this? Planned routes, involving pre-set distances, are staple parameters. Not knowing where and for how long is anathema to most runners. Running is so crudely bound up with a competitive sporting ethos. After all, it is a so-called endurance sport and consequently it appears to demand a hyper-disciplined regime (planning, measuring, recording). Unlike team games, there is small scope for creativity and playful moments.

Imagine running . . . changing direction, getting lost, sometimes walking, sitting on a bench to admire a view, staying out longer—or shorter. Is it possible to recreate running-time as spontaneous and non-linear?

Imagine running and performing small-embodied motions. These movements, like dance, are sometimes laced with fugitive emotions.

* * *

Today, the beach is empty. She decides to take off her T-shirt as she runs. A tricky maneuver and her head gets stuck inside the cocoon of white cotton. This amuses her and she runs for a while with her head gently trapped. A little later, she screws up the T-shirt and holds it in her hand. She smells the sea-salty air and takes a deep breath. She sucks in her stomach, expands her chest and squares her shoulders. This makes her laugh, loudly. Her body loosens; she feels cheerful and she runs with a grin on her face.

After running for some time, she wonders if her belly sticks out. She looks down: it does! She pushes it out as far as it'll go. She arches her lower back, tilts forward from the hips and lets her feet stay in contact with the ground for longer. Then, she becomes aware of her pelvis, her insides and the organs that define her as woman: her soft tissues, many tubes, secretions and red, red blood. The thought reminds her of Frida Kahlo's wonderfully grotesque artwork, the pictures of bleeding and injured women's bodies. Suddenly, she feels sad. She extends her thighs and raises her heels, irregularly. Tentatively, playfully, she changes her stride-pattern. Her running becomes messy and not running in a straight line, she leaves zig-zags of footprints in the sand. As she goes, she feels deep within her guts a skein of energy. She smiles.

* * *

Running for Pleasures 113

Running, as is implied in the above illustrative example, is an unfolding activity shaped by affective flows in which happiness, uncertainty and sadness effloresce and cause fleeting and condensed moments of pleasure. Long-distance running allows for the solitary cogitation hinted at in this scene. However, few writers have commented on how reflection, musing and upheavals of thought are lived through the rhythms of the runner's body. For the woman running on the beach, body and mind are entangled with meaning-making and this produces assemblages of affect. Running becomes a lively and sensual realm to explore these connections. She begins to improvise. She changes the speed of her heel lift, the reach of her thighs, the curvature of her spine and her running direction. She is not dancing *per se*, but her movements reflect a sensibility of small dance-like motions as she continues to run. Her emotions, thoughts and feelings are heavily woven with and into her body dynamics.

There are few socio-cultural studies of the moving sport body that pay attention to the interlacing and imbrication of the emotional and physical. However, as Wetherell affirms: 'Rightly, many of us are interested in developing more dynamic, sensual and lively accounts of social life' (2012: 75). Perhaps, considering these and similar embodied sensations opens the way for a broader view of pleasures derived from sporting and physical activities. Such a project works to de-normalize the powerful disciplinary regimes of running cultures and practices. It introduces the playful aesthetics of running and might help encourage a broader following, which could, dare I say it, increase participation levels.

CONCLUDING THOUGHTS

In this chapter I offer ideas on how running, and other similar repetitive movements, can be related to pleasure. I co-opt a range of literatures and personal experiences to show how running pleasures exist within the socio-cultural contexts of class and gender relations. For example, middle classness and running are known to be associated through cultural capital and habitus (Atkinson, 2008; Tulle, 2007) as well as the economic and material. I make visible my own location within class and gender relations and how, although my childhood was not scored by traditional middle-class values, it was highly institutionalized. Clearly, my current running-for-pleasures biography is underpinned by privileged positions: whiteness and middle classness. Because of this, class, ethnicity and gender remain central pillars to examining pleasures in this chapter.

However, my main argument is for a shift from understanding running pleasures as derived from producing and achieving times and distances—recording, measuring, competing, beating and winning. In running, these discourses and cultures of achievement (efficiency and success) are profound

114   Jayne Caudwell

and pernicious; they are underpinned by a work ethic which, arguably, has helped promote religious morality and capitalist wealth accumulation.

Instead, I explore the possibilities of an inclusion of the aesthetic, sensate and visceral (Rinehart, 1998c) to an understanding of running and pleasure. I disregard traditional notions of success and accomplishment in favor of embodied sensations, emotions and affect. Places and landscapes of running emerge as central to this developing point of view. Borrowing from cultural geography, I make visible the role of space, spatiality and spatial scales (e.g. temperature and humidity). In these discussions, integration, harmony and brushes with environments and peoples are more pleasurable than knowing, mastering and grasping these dimensions. Being touched by places, spaces and people provides a sense of wonderment as well as connectivity. This aspect is unusual, given that long-distance running is often viewed as individual, monotonous and highly regulated.

Many runners do gain pleasure from measuring time, distance, their body weight and percentage of body fat. These measurements can provide comfort and reassurance. They offer a tangible reminder (McLoughlin, 2010) of hard work, discipline, efficiency and a conditioned body. These characteristics are applauded in most Western societies and are therefore gratifying; running is an exemplar of modern virtue. Additionally, a focus on measuring and accomplishing can function to depose feelings associated with trauma such as loss, unhappiness, sadness, misery and depression. Returning to 'The Loneliness of the Long Distance Runner', we learn—through Colin's relationship to his running—of the recent gruesome death of his father. In the filmic version of the book, Colin's memories of his father are most vivid when he is running. Interestingly, in the academic literature there is some research (Leedy, 2009) on women's emotionality, mental health (un/happiness) and running habits, but little to date on men's (see Stone, 2009, for an exception).

Rhythm, playfulness and improvisation help produce running as a blissful activity, an affectual and affective physical practice not associated with objective measurement of the body. In running, playfulness and improvisation encourage a de-disciplining and de-regulating of the runner's body. They challenge the orthodoxies of running regimes by dislocating the rigidity of running ethos (planning, tracking, recording). In extreme cases, improvisation decimates the notion of pre-set running routes. It is hardly surprising that Global Positioning Systems (GPS), now available for runners to use, are completely void of metaphors of playfulness and improvisation.

Pleasures are evident in fictional and semi-fictionalized accounts as well as personal biographies of running. In these narratives of running-pleasures, the runner's body is not reproduced as a physical object for multi-measurement (how fast, how long, how efficient, and how productive). Instead, running becomes aesthetic, emotional, playful, sensual and visceral. Seeking out theses alternative explanations and interpretations is important if we want to realize the social significance of sport and pleasure.

NOTE

1. One of the ways I capture the personal and biographical is through Flash Fiction. Flash Fiction first appeared as a named style of writing in 1992 in Thomas' edited anthology entitled: Flash Fiction: Seventy-Two Very Short Stories. Flash Fiction is a form of short story writing. It is usually sudden and brief, although there are variations on how brief (wordage).

8 When the Pleasurable Is Political
An Affective Analysis of Viewing the Olympics

Richard Pringle

Regardless of one's passion or lack of interest in sport, the spectacle of the summer Olympics is difficult to ignore. They are the largest mega-sporting event globally and, as such, are a phenomenon of political, economic and social significance (Toohey and Veal, 2007). Coverage of the 2012 London Olympics saturated the global media for 17 days and viewer interest was readily apparent. The BBC1's television audience within the UK increased by 40% to secure more than a third of all viewers during their coverage (Plunkett, 2012). And within the US, NBC's coverage of the Games has been described as the most-watched event in US history, with a reported 219.4 million viewers (Collins, 2012). Although the Olympics are undeniably popular, concerns have been raised that 'sport serves as an economy of affect through which power, privilege, politics and positions are (re)produced' (Silk and Andrews, 2012: 5) and, more pointedly, that sports 'are commonly used to reaffirm national and global processes of neoliberalization' (Coakley, 2011: 67). Yet little is known about the (pleasurable) experiences of watching the Olympics and the (political) mobilization of its global audience. The recognition of this lack spurred me to write this chapter.

Initially, I became interested in this project as I became aware that my viewing response to the recent London Olympics seemed somewhat paradoxical. Let me explain: I am a stern social critic of the Games. I am critical of their exorbitant cost (Giulianotti and Klauser, 2010; Toohey, 2008), the bogus governmental justifications for this expenditure (Pringle, 2012), the disciplinary demands placed on athletes (Beamish and Ritchie, 2006) and the associated politics and history of corruption within the International Olympics Committee (IOC) (Booth, 2004; Hoberman 1995, 2011; Jennings, 2011; Lenskyj, 2010). Yet I confess that I enjoyed watching the 2012 London Olympic 'spectacle', the very spectacle that was the direct result of the excessive expenditure, bogus justifications and dodgy politics that I disparage and have publicly critiqued. I confess further that at times I found myself watching the sporting performances with fists clenched, mouth open and an uneasy feeling in my stomach. At other times, these embodied nerves gave way to feelings of awe and hoots of elation. Although a social critic of the Olympics, I was also an embodied fan: a somewhat awkward self-realization (see Chapter 9 for another analysis of sport fan pleasure).

My concern more broadly, however, is related to the assumption that the general viewing public (who potentially have not examined the critiques surrounding the Olympics) are possibly swayed by the pleasures gained through watching the Olympics and subsequently develop an apolitical stance or an *uncritical celebration of sport*.[1] Garry Whannel (1993) discussed, for example, how sporting performances could produce moments of jouissance (feelings of bliss that transcend the limits of subjectivity) that allow the 'temporary triumph of process over product' (Whannel, 1993: 348). He explained further that these are moments 'when the spontaneous inspiration of performance escapes, fleetingly, the tendency of capitalist commodity production to transform all such cultural processes into calculated packaged objects for consumption' (Whannel, 1993: 348). Whannel concluded that such moments of escapist pleasure '. . . symbolize a rare victory of people over the limitations that confine us' (1993: 348).

I agree with Whannel that moments of pleasure can work to obscure the workings of power and be uplifting. Yet I am concerned that the cumulative effect of such pleasures does not induce freedom from the workings of power but potentially allows power to operate in a more insidious manner. That is, in a more covert manner that might encourage sport fans to uncritically accept the political messages that are embedded within the sport media. These political messages are of concern, as critical scholars typically believe that they: 'emphasise images and narratives consistent with dominant ideologies in society as a whole' (Coakley et al., 2009: 377). Numerous critical commentators, for example, have raised concerns that sport-media representations tend to promote hyper-masculine ideals, sexualize or ignore sportswomen, promote win-at-all-costs attitudes, emphasize stereotypes of race and disability, promote nationalism and, more broadly, support neoliberal ideals (Berstein, 2002; Coakley, 2011; Wensing and Bruce, 2003). These problematic representations can be understood as sport media constructions that have been produced via various visual, verbal and auditory techniques with intentions to create *pleasurable* spectacles to hook viewers and make profits (Wenner, 1998).[2] Thus, televised sport, viewing pleasures and the workings of power appear intimately connected.

Yet despite the socio-cultural importance of the sport media, relatively few scholars have undertaken reception studies to understand how audiences interpret the political messages embedded within televised sport (for exceptions see Bruce, 1998; Gantz and Wenner, 1991; Millington and Wilson, 2010; O'Connor and Boyle, 1993; Wilson and Sparks, 1999). And although various scholars have analyzed the pleasures of viewing/reading sport representations (e.g. Booth, 2008; Duncan and Brummett, 1989; Rose and Friedman, 1997, Whannel, 1993), empirical examinations of how sport viewing pleasures impact a viewer's political understandings are rare (for an exception see Kennedy, Pussard and Thornton, 2006).

118 *Richard Pringle*

Garry Whannel (1992) suggests that the rarity of political/pleasure audience reception studies relates to misguided assumptions that pleasures are self-evident and do not require analysis, and to the difficulty of undertaking such studies, particularly via empirical examination. He astutely points out that the political outcome may not be a direct result of the pleasurable experience, but produced by other factors or forms of consumption. The political impact may even occur in a manner that the viewer has no conscious recollection of (Maguire et al., 2002).

Given these difficulties in examining the political impact of experiencing pleasure while viewing sport, Ellen Kennedy, Helen Pussard and Andrew Thornton (2006) turned to the concept of affect. In drawing from Lawrence Grossberg (1992: 16), they suggested that affect 'is perhaps the "missing term in an adequate account of ideology", because it gets at the way we individually invest in things in an embodied, passionate way, despite often cognitively knowing better'. In this chapter, following Kennedy, Pussard and Thonton (2006), I use my seemingly paradoxical viewing response of the Olympics as a case study to examine how mediated representations of the Olympics can induce viewing pleasures, as associated with the workings of affect, and in a manner that potentially shapes political concerns. Similarly to Lawrence Grossberg's (2010: 310) aim to understand the political significance of popular music in relation to a 'structure of feeling', I examine the pleasures of watching the Olympics to understand *how* the Games work *affectively* and *discursively*.

The chapter is structured via several intersecting sections. I firstly introduce my concerns with the Olympic Games and then examine why the Olympics remain vastly popular in the public imagination. I do so by paying particular attention to Roland Barthes' argument about sport and the production of myth. I then raise issue with this Barthesian argument by suggesting it rests primarily on a symbolic understanding and, accordingly, bypasses the affective/corporeal dimension of sport viewing pleasures. In relation to this concern, I introduce the concept of affect and discuss the social/political implications associated with the abstract workings of affect. Next, I draw on Brian Ott's (2010) multi-modal approach for examining cinematic rhetoric and analyze my viewing response to two video clips of the London 2012 Olympics. I conclude by discussing the importance of analyzing the workings of affect in relation to the politics of sporting spectacles.

CRITIQUING THE SPECTACLE OF THE GAMES

The hosting of the Olympics involves: the conspicuous construction of sporting arenas and upgrades to infrastructure (Broudehoux, 2007); urban regeneration and destruction (Lenskyj, 2010); the (mis)calculation of risk and security costs (Toohey, 2008); economic impact studies (Owen, 2005); global marketing campaigns (Maguire et al., 2010; Real, 2010); national and international politics (Booth, 1995b); media bidding wars and the expenditure of billions of pounds in relation to what Alan Tomlinson (2004) called the 'Disneyfication' of the Olympics. In times of austerity budgets and a global recession, the financial cost of hosting the Olympics is somewhat staggering (see Giulianotti and Klauser, 2010). Although it is difficult to ascertain the final cost of hosting the London Games (2012) it is likely that the official cost of £9.325 billion is a sizeable underestimation (Gibson, 2011).

The primary justifications used by governments to legitimize the spending of significant amounts of public money in order to host the Olympics typically relate to economics, health benefits, social cohesion and politics (Coakley et al., 2009), but numerous studies have systematically debunked each of these justifications (e.g. see Gieseck and Madden, 2007; Gold and Gold, 2010; Hogan and Norton, 2000; Kidd, 2010; Maguire et al., 2010; Owen, 2005). John Horne (2007: 92) concluded that the justifications for hosting the Olympics 'remain based on dubious, unethical and possibly illegal practices'. Despite academic recognition that the justifications for the expenditure of billions of pounds on hosting the Games are seemingly unfounded, there was little public outcry about the staging of the London Olympics. Although protests such as the *No London 2012* campaign and the *Counter Olympic Network* (with the apt acronym CON) formed, these groups gained only modest media coverage and little general public support. Counter to these minor protest groups, the Olympics saturated the global media and generated widespread celebration (Collins, 2012; Plunkett, 2012).

A seemingly simple question arises: how can the global popularity of the Olympics be explained? This question is of interest, not just with regards to understanding the economic and political significance of the Games, but also with respect to understanding the social processes that excite the public imagination and produce pleasures. There are numerous possible explanations that could account for the global popularity of the Olympics. The popularity could be explained in relation to the intrigue of the competition, the workings of nationalism, the practices/techniques of global media networks, the sheer spectacle and commodification of the Games and the aesthetics and thrills of viewing the athlete's embodied performances. Yet, in this chapter, I am more interested in examining *how* the image of the Olympics has been constructed, in part via media productions and the management of the IOC, to allow the Games to be globally celebrated in a seemingly uncritical manner. To examine this issue, I turn to Barthes' (1972) writings on myth.

THE CONSTRUCTION OF THE MYTHICAL STATUS OF THE OLYMPICS

Barthes' (1972) reading of the Tour de France cycling extravaganza revolved around his understanding of the perpetuation of myth, in the sense that myths do not falsify reality but blur historical and cultural narratives so that the

120   *Richard Pringle*

reality, under examination, appears as self-evidently natural. He stated that 'the Tour is the best example we have ever encountered of a total, hence an ambiguous myth; the Tour is at once a myth of expression and a myth of projection, realistic and utopian at the same time' (Barthes, 1972: 87). Barthes argued that myths work to enable one to uncritically enjoy the beauty of an object or phenomenon without having to wonder how it was produced. This mythical status accordingly allows fans of the Tour to gape unabashed with awe for the natural ability of the cyclists; in the process, the cyclists are positioned beyond mere mortals. Indeed, Barthes equated the athletes with Homer's heroic warriors from the Iliad. This mythical status, he argued, concomitantly prevents the fans from viewing the hidden workings or critical dimensions of the tour: 'What is vitiated in the Tour is the basis, the economic motives, the ultimate profit of the ordeal, generator of ideological alibis' (Barthes, 1972: 87–88). Barthes enjoyed the romance of the Tour's legend status and considered 'doping' inexcusable, as it destroyed the sublime myth.

Robert Beamish and Ian Ritchie (2006) drew on Barthes to argue that the Olympics are surrounded by a mythical aura so that they can be gazed upon as a spectacle of purity and of noble virtues. This mythical status, they argued, allows for the uncritical glorification of the Olympian's body while simultaneously obscuring the Olympic links with fascism, corruption, human rights abuses, transnational business deals, dictatorships and drug scandals. The myth also works to obscure that the IOC has deliberately crafted this idealistic image. So how has the IOC been able to help produce this mythical status?

The IOC has long positioned and advertised the Olympics as a humanitarian movement underpinned by a unique philosophy called Olympism, which purportedly 'seeks to create a way of life based on the joy found in effort, the educational value of good example and respect for universal fundamental ethical principles' (IOC, 1994: 10). The IOC has promoted the rhetorical virtues of Olympism primarily via educational programs and international marketing campaigns. Geoff Kohe argued that the Olympic education resources, which are distributed freely to schools in many countries, are based on uncritical and select interpretations of the past that idealistically endorse the Olympic 'movement' as valuable in 'promoting a better world through peace and understanding' (2010: 483). The IOC has also drawn on the services of international marketing agencies (e.g. Saatchi and Saatchi) to orchestrate global media campaigns that promote the Olympics as a humanitarian institution. The 'celebrate humanity' advertising campaign, as an example, has used the services of respected international spokespeople (e.g. Nelson Mandela, Kofi Annan, Christopher Reeve and Andrea Bocelli) to promote, in the words of the IOC (2004b: 3), the 'truth that the Olympic ideals—the values of hope, friendship and fair play, dreams and inspiration, joy in effort—are universal and shared by all'. This campaign, which promoted the summer and winter Olympics of 2000–2008, screened over 6500 times on CNN worldwide (Maguire et al., 2010).

When the Pleasurable Is Political 121

Integral to the IOC's promotion of a mythical reading of the Olympics has also been the requirement to promote or prove that the athletes are natural or pure, and that the sport domain is a level playing field (Cole, 2000; Magdalinski, 2009; McCullough, 2010). Sara McCullough (2010: 3) reported that the 'mythology of the "natural" athletic body—pure and untainted—remains crucial to the Olympic dream'.

The IOC has, accordingly, encouraged a regime of drug and sex testing to ensure that the Olympics are supposedly a fair competition. Media coverage of sports doping, as Andy Miah (2010: 170) contended, 'repeatedly demonise[s] drug-induced athletes' but implies that such actions are 'attributable to a flaw in the athlete's character'. This negative publicity does not typically extend to the broader sports world. In contrast, international sporting organizations such as the IOC and the World Anti Doping Association (which was instituted by the IOC) are portrayed in the media as moral vigilantes attempting to rid the sporting world of 'drug cheats' and 'sexual misfits' to ensure the integrity of sport (Miah, 2010). CL Cole (2000) refers to the disqualified athletes as *boundary creatures* to illustrate that they divide the normal from the abnormal and correspondingly buttress Olympic ideals/myths. In process, the sporting bodies that are allowed to compete are constructed as natural, ethical and hardworking: that is, they become bodies worthy of *glorification*.

In this section, I have argued that the construction of the mythical status of the Olympian champion, as propped up by the workings of the IOC, is integral to allowing uncritical celebration of the athletes' embodied performances. Although I believe there is merit in this discursive argument I nevertheless have two reservations about accepting it wholeheartedly. Firstly, I suggest that, given the number of drug scandals that have tainted the Olympics and international sports in recent decades, sport fans might now be complacent about athletic doping. The viewing public, accordingly, is perhaps more suspicious of Olympian athletes than they were when Barthes (1972) originally wrote about the mythical/sublime status of the Tour de France athletes. For example, two athletes who had already served two-year bans for doping, Asli Apltekin and Tatyana Lysenko, won gold at the London Olympics with little public concern. Perhaps many sports fans now accept Robert Beamish and Ian Ritchie's (2006: 115) observation that, 'for better or worse, the use of banned substances and performance enhancing practices in high performance sports is an integral component of the human activities that currently constitute the entire international, high performance sport system'. I wonder, accordingly, to what extent that the mythical status of the Olympian champion is still, if it ever was, intact?

Secondly, I am aware that the argument presented operates primarily at a cognitive level, through an analysis of the construction of symbolism and myth. As such, it indirectly positions the Olympic fan as akin to a discursive dupe, as it rests on the assumption that he/she has been manipulated in order to read the Olympians' performances in a mythical light. This

122   *Richard Pringle*

argument, however, does not resonate fully with my own response in viewing the Olympics; I was critical of the Olympic spectacle but still gained pleasure in watching the Games. Despite my critical views of the Games and my conscious awareness that the athletes were not heroes worthy of uncritical worship, I was *drawn* in to viewing the spectacle. In the following section, I draw on affect theory to offer another understanding concerning the uncritical celebration of the Games.

THE MEDIATED POLITICS OF AFFECT

Critical studies of media representations of sport have tended to focus on the links between the quality and quantity of representation and the production and interpretation of intended meaning/discourse/ideology and associated relations of power. They accordingly focus on the cognitive and political dimensions, rather than the affective and corporeal. Yet by bypassing the affective and corporeal dimension there is a risk that these studies produce limited insight for understanding the *popularity* of sport media productions and, by default, the mechanisms associated with *how* the political messages are potentially inculcated amongst viewers. An additional risk, as Douglas Booth (2008: 32) contended, is that this form of media analysis could perpetuate 'the theoretical determinism of structural analysis', and limit understanding of the relationship between 'publishers/editors/authors and readers'. In recent years, however, Brian Ott (2010: 41) reported that a growing body of scholars have begun to examine how 'cinema appeals directly to the senses, how it sways viewers somatically as well as symbolically'. This interest in the relationship between the somatic and the senses has been spurred by the turn to affect theorizing. In this section, I introduce affect theory and detail how I drew on the concept of affect to examine my embodied reaction to viewing the Olympics.

As a point of clarification, 'there is no single, generalizable theory of affect' (Seigworth and Gregg, 2010: 3). Not surprisingly, affect has been defined in multiple ways: DeChaine (2002: 86) defined affect as 'the intensity that allows us to feel', whereas Nathanson (1992: 49) drew from Silvan Tomkins to define affect as the 'biological portion of emotion'; Brian Massumi (2002: 28) similarly differentiated emotion and affect by suggesting that affect is autonomous but emotion is 'owned and recognized'; Sara Ahmed (2010a: 29) described affect as 'what sticks, or what sustains or preserves the connection between ideas, values, and objects'; and Clare Hemmings (2005: 551) suggested that affect 'broadly refers to states of being, rather than to their manifestation or interpretation as emotions'.

Affect, accordingly, is typically understood as stemming from the body and *unconsciously* influencing how humans act/think/feel by inducing a particular state of being or a 'non-conscious experience of intensity' (Shouse, 2005, ¶ 1). This intensity provides a motivation to act or prepares the body

When the Pleasurable Is Political 123

for action but it does not determine set actions. Seigworth and Gregg (2010) reported that the recent interest in affect stems primarily from the work of Eve Sedgwick and Adam Frank (1995), who were inspired by Silvan Tomkins' (1995) psychobiological study of affect, and Brian Massumi (1995), who drew from the work of Deleuze and Spinoza.

Affect can be linked to the thousands of sensations (e.g. sight, sound, smell, feelings of hunger) that continually impact and flow unconsciously through (and around) a body. An infant, who does not have the language skills or previous experience to cognitively interpret the ongoing flow of sensations, displays the influence of affect innately via facial expressions, vocalizations, skin color, breathing rate and posture (Shouse, 2005), for example. Over time, as the infant ages into an adult, she/he gains greater ability to make sense of the multiple affective sensations. Yet affects are notoriously dynamic and mobile in character (Wetherell, 2012); they continue to impact and flow through and around the adult body unconsciously and can subsequently act to produce a personal state of being, or intensity, that individuals have little control over (Tompkins, 1995).

Affect is not contained in the body but can be transmitted between bodies, so that a blurring occurs between the individual, the environment and others: one's affective state can unconsciously influence another's. Elspeth Probyn (2010) drew from Deleuze to explain there is no such thing as a unified person; rather, the subjective character can be regarded as an 'affective assemblage of bodies of different orders and elements' (Probyn, 2010: 78). Affect's social impact is not, however, consistent amongst various people, nor predictable; nevertheless, its capacity to shape a large number of people illustrates the political importance of examining the workings of affect (Massumi, 2002). Jean-Francois Lyotard (1984) discussed the affective/political interface within texts by suggesting:

> What is important in a text is not what it means, but what it does and incites to do. What it does: the charge of affect it contains and transmits. What it incites to do: the metamorphoses of this potential energy into other things—other texts, but also . . . political actions. (in Seidler, 2001: 133)

Eric Shouse (2005) similarly highlighted that 'the importance of affect rests upon the fact that in many cases the message consciously received may be of less import to the receiver of that message than his or her nonconscious affective resonance with the source of the message' (¶. 12). Music is an apt example, as the intended meaning of the music, as associated with the lyrics, is often of less importance than whether the music 'moves' somebody.[3]

Affective resonance, defined as the tendency to resonate with a display of an emotion from another person, is regarded as an important characteristic of affect (Tomkins, 1995). Daniel Stern's (1985) analysis of communication

124   Richard Pringle

between an infant and parent without the use of language is a prime example of affective resonance. His observations of an infant reaching for and successfully grasping a toy is telling:

> As she grabs it, she lets out an exuberant 'aaaah!' and looks at her mother. Her mother looks back, scrunches up her shoulders, and performs a terrific shimmy with her upper body, like a go-go dancer. The shimmy lasts only about as long as her daughter's 'aaah!' but is equally excited, joyful, and intense. (Stern, 1985: 140)

Affective resonance, or what Daniel Stern (1985) called 'attunement', does not mean that affects are flawlessly translatable between people. Nevertheless, the transmission of affect between bodies or within particular contexts, such as in protest marches or on the football terraces, is of undoubted social and political influence, as Eric Shouse (2005) explained: 'Given the ubiquity of affect, it is important to take note that the power of many forms of media lies not so much in their ideological effects, but in their ability to create affective resonances independent of content or meaning' (¶. 14). The 2011 Vancouver Stanley Cup riot is one example of the problematic effects of affective resonance within a crowd. The riot happened after the defeat of the Vancouver Canucks by the Boston Bruins, and resulted in over 100 arrests and 140 injuries (including several police officers). Although it is difficult to attribute a definitive explanation to complex social behaviour, there did not appear to be ideological grounds for the riots (as the riots were not linked to any overt ethnic or political tensions or the actions of disenchanted youth). Post-riot media discussion positioned blame on the actions of a few anarchists, the overconsumption of alcohol and inadequate crowd planning. Yet these 'explanations' miss the importance of affective resonance: the almost indescribable intensity associated with the domino effect of enthusiasm, passion, anger and energy that can form and spread when masses of bodies are tightly packed and produce a collective effervescence.

The social importance of affect is related, in part, to its abstract or unstructured quality. Yet these very qualities complicate how one can study the broader social/political influence of affect. Faced with this difficulty, Brian Ott (2010: 42) encouraged the use of an 'affective register' with respect to analyzing the politics of affect within the media. Brian Ott suggested that as affect refers to an *intensity* that allows *feeling*, that analysis of the media could take place via consideration of potential 'sensory experiences (of color, light, sound, movement, rhythm, and texture), along with the feelings, moods, emotions, and/or passions they elicit' (2010: 42). He drew from Lyotard to advocate a multi-modal approach for analyzing film/media productions that combined the analysis of discourse and the use of an affective register to enable consideration of the interactions of 'the aural with the visual, the sensory with the verbal, the narrative with the pictorial' (Ott, 2010: 43). In addition, Ott encouraged the consideration of what

When the Pleasurable Is Political 125

Marshall McLuhan (1988) termed 'ground', which refers to the context or environment created by the media: a context that an observer can be so drawn into that he/she loses touch with the immediate environment.

Brian Ott's (2010) approach for recognizing and analyzing the media as a fully embodied experience, accordingly, involved the analysis of discourse[4], affect (or what he termed 'figure') and ground (Ott defines ground as the media-constructed context through which viewers process their understandings) but with recognition that such an analysis is an art form and not a precise science. He acknowledged, for example, that his analysis 'will necessarily be selective and reductionistic' but his 'critical aim is not to account for every element and aspect of the film, but to suggest how its basic tenor and temperature function rhetorically' (Ott, 2010: 44). To help represent this 'tenor and temperature', Ott writes somewhat evocatively. In describing a dictatorial character from a film he states how he is shot in 'extreme close-up, making his worn, wrinkled face unnervingly immediate. . . . (so that) the audience can virtually touch the sweat oozing from his pores' (Ott, 2010: 45). In the following section I draw from Ott's quasi-artful analysis strategy to examine two of the most popular YouTube video clips of the 2012 Olympics. Given this analytical approach is more an art form than a science, I present my results with a degree of poetic sensibility (see Rinehart, 2010a) and a specific desire to highlight the visceral nature, sensations and intensities of viewing.

AFFECTIVE ANALYSIS OF THE OLYMPIC GAMES

Several days prior to the staging of the 2012 Olympics, I was in London on sabbatical. Although I had a socio-cultural interest in the Olympics, I had no desire to watch them live. In fact, I did not even want to be in London during the staging of the Olympics, as I was concerned about the crowds, cost and potential political unrest. Accordingly, I flew out of the UK before the Games started. I arrived home in New Zealand after a welcome few days in Hong Kong and found that the Olympics were on their third day of coverage. In a jet-lagged state, I lazily began watching TV and was drawn into the Games. It was at this stage that I realized I had a somewhat paradoxical relationship with the Olympics. Indeed, I felt like an alcoholic who had fallen off the wagon; I remained critical of the Games and the underpinning politics but was seduced by the spectacle.

Several months after the Olympics had finished, I was reading Brian Ott's (2010) paper on film analysis and the politics of affect and was reminded of my surprising viewing/affectual response to the Olympics. I was subsequently motivated to view YouTube clips of the Olympics, and found that I was still somewhat moved by them. It was at this point that I decided to analyze two of the clips in relation to Ott's idea of a fully embodied experience. The two video clips analyzed were produced by the IOC and released

126 *Richard Pringle*

on their 'official Olympic channel' via the internet. The first video, 'Best of London 2012', was prefixed these words:

> The London 2012 Olympic Games are now history, but their spirit will live on forever in the hearts of millions of people. Re-live some of the most exciting moments of these Games and watch the performances of the world's greatest athletes in our highlights video! (Olympic, 2012a)

The 4.06-minute video clip begins with a fly-over shot of the Thames River and the iconic Tower Bridge with the background sounds of a large cheering crowd. Then, as the Olympic Stadium comes into view, a bell tolls and inspiring music kicks in. There is no commentary—it is all image, sound, splendor, a kaleidoscope of moving colors: bright purples, oranges, yellows, greens and reds, that interweave a poetry between light and dark, the ephemeral and permanent, the primitive with high technology, the past and future. A jazz ensemble of staccato images populate the screen in short bursts: team uniforms blend with flashes of fireworks, cheering crowds meld under a river of flags, a clay target explodes in the hazy mysticism of dust to dust, interlocking rings become a molten waterfall, bursts of fire escape from a starter's gun. Nothing is solid, everything is moving, morphing, living, interacting, breathing. The roar of the crowd fades in and out. Moments of ecstasy punctuate the breathlessness of awe. The 'ground' is a space of celebration and excitement, a tribal-earthly pulsation, a ritual of belonging. I am drawn into this ground and embrace the carnivalesque atmosphere.

It is not until the 41st second that a sport image appears: a beach volleyball, launched from a jump serve, that is curving back toward earth. Then follows a cascade of spectacular sporting moments: a basketball shot from over half way, a reverse backhand water polo goal, an ace in tennis, a bullseye in archery, a sprinter first over the line. The technological aesthetic blends with the spectacular: a slow motion back flip, air bubbles escaping a swimmer underwater, a gymnast momentarily frozen in space before spiraling to the ground.

Yet what became patently obvious to me, admittedly after several views of the video clip, was that the purported Olympic highlights were *not* the actual sports performances but were vibrant displays of human emotions. These displays dominated the sporting performances and held the sports in place. At the end of each sporting performance was a visceral display of emotion: an embrace, a smile, a tear, an ignition of elation, a hug, a kiss, a shake of disappointment, a supportive touch. These displays allowed for moments of affective resonance: a sense of joy occurred when I watched others celebrating, and feelings of sadness upon the close-ups that intimated the dashing of dreams and the pain of loss. The display of emotions, more broadly, helped constitute the plot that enabled the story of the sporting performances to be told: the emotions were the glue that pulled the Olympic representations together and, as I will argue, offered an embodied justification for them.

Yet this was a highlights video, artfully produced to maximize audience delight. Perhaps, I thought, it would be very different from the screening of

When the Pleasurable Is Political   127

a 'live' sporting event. Although I had already viewed what many regard as the premier event of the Olympics—the 100m men's final—and was aware that Usain Bolt reclaimed his Olympic title, I decided to re-watch and analyze the race. The 13-minute clip was titled 'Athletics Men's 100m Final Full Replay—London 2012 Olympic Games—Usain Bolt' (Olympic, 2012b).[5]

The clip begins with an expansive view of the crowd and slowly focuses on the start of the 100m contenders. The accompanying soundtrack is the ubiquitous crowd roar: it is a sound that lasts the entire video clip, all except for the dramatic silence at the start of the race. The athletes' uniforms are bright red, yellow, green and orange, tight fitting, with musculature on display. Camera flashes are constant. As the athletes are introduced, to even louder crowd cheers, they momentarily perform for the global audience, they dance, salute, clown, wink, point, clap and nod with eyes wide. These introductory performances, however, are fleeting. After being introduced, their eyes quickly return to a glazed state and their bodies to their relentless movements: pacing, jumping, shaking, clapping, slapping. A raw intensity pervades this build up: it is a palpable display of nerves, concentration and anticipation. The commentator even encourages the viewers to pay attention to the 'more pensive look of the defending champion'. Usain Bolt, as if on cue, crosses his heart and looks toward the heavens.

The starting gun goes after five minutes of emotional build up. The race quickly proceeds and in subsequent replays the *discursive* status of the Olympic champion—as a hero, as a mythical being in a Barthesian sense—is then affirmed by the commentators. We are told that Usain Bolt:

> . . . emerged from the pack and powered his way to the line in the most emphatic way . . . that the King has retained his crown . . . that Bolt transcends the world of athletics once again . . . he is the superstar of world sport. (Olympic, 2012b)

In a slow motion replay, the commentator in a tone of ecstatic disbelief reports:

> But look at this! This is the point that he moves away, but how can you do this? This is the Olympic final, it is not a heat, this is not a semifinal, it is the Olympic final and that should not happen but he is so far ahead of the rest . . . that was incredible . . . these are moments to be treasured . . . it is a moment of history. (Olympic, 2012b)

Bolt's performance is presented as unbelievable, superhuman, sublime. The audience, as such, is discursively invited to uncritically celebrate this morally worthy/mythic Olympic champion.

The remaining eight minutes of the clip are primarily displays of emphatic celebration: crowd hugs, arm pumps, skipping, high fives, flag waving, clowning and smiles. I find it difficult to watch without a smile. There are, however, two interspersed and brief shots of Asafa Powell, who injured his

128 *Richard Pringle*

groin and finished last: his head is down, his Olympic dream destroyed. These brief displays of disappointment, perhaps symbolizing the fragility of the 'loser's' body, do not disrupt the celebration of the champion. In contrast, they contribute to the emotional significance of the event. The sadness crafts the Olympic tale/myth as much as the joy.

The interplay of discourse, affect (or figure) and ground (Ott, 2010) as presented in the live coverage of the Olympics 100m men's final and the IOC's highlight video of the 2012 Games worked to negate my critical concerns of the Olympics: I became an embodied fan and believed, at least while immersed in the pleasure of the moment, that the Olympics were, as the IOC has purported, a celebration of humanity. My idiosyncratic embodied viewing response, in apparent defiance of my critical views of the Olympics, may not be similar to how other viewers would react to or understand the Olympics. Indeed, the abstract and unpredictable nature of affect and emotion means that viewing responses to the two Olympic video clips will be considerably varied and is shaped, in part, by viewers' 'personal politics, background and previous (rhetorical) experience' (Ott, 2010: 48). Nevertheless, I support Brian Ott's (2010) contention that, to understand how televisual representations can 'move' an audience, it is advantageous to consider the interactions between discourse, affect and ground. Moreover, given the global popularity of the Games, I also recognize that my ability to affectively resonate with the displays of athletic emotion and sporting performances was likely an experience shared with many Olympic spectators. Indeed, 1150 people were so moved by the 'Best of London 2012' video clip (Olympic, 2012a) that they were compelled to contribute comments to the web site. The majority of comments were from emotional fans, who wrote, as examples: 'pure beautiful and inspiring moments' (MissVali9), 'I almost cried' (retroboydeccles), 'the best:)' (Tashokk), 'I loved the Olympics it was amazing' (SuperTegster), 'Goosebumps every time I watch this. London 2012 was simply amazing. I'll never forget it' (Salvador716) and 'I get shivers when i think back to all this!' (freestyle pigeon). Comments about embodied viewing reactions—such as goosebumps, shivers and crying—were relatively common. There were also a number of idealistic or politically naive comments about the social value of the Olympics. 'Amelia Dearie', for example, commented:

> this really only has 578,805 views?! this should be shown to every human being, its inspiring, put together really well! this just proves that the world can come together and compete and everyone enjoys it! no racism, no sexism, no nothing. at the end of the day, we are all human. (Olympic, 2012a)

And 'fraserrg' quixotically claimed:

> I've been thinking a lot about the games and this video captures some of those thoughts. Bottom line is that in a world of economic crisis, political

When the Pleasurable Is Political   129

incompetence, greed and secular intolerance the Games reminded us that they are not just an entertaining spectacle but that sport in general is a source of good, it teaches us tolerance and grace, it bridges cultures and above all it integrates us with our fellow human beings and shows us there is another way. Thank you London. (Olympic, 2012a)

In contrast to the idealism of these comments, a small number of comments revealed that the Olympics could also be a source of tension, nationalism, homophobia and racism. For example, 'xRyuBu' responded to comments on the monetary inequalities in Brazil and the prospects of the forthcoming 2016 Olympics:

What? I wasn't talking about the overall economy . . . about 70% of the country is poor by British standards, 30% of the country has ALL the money . . . Rio's going to have a shite Olympics . . . Face it, it's gonna be a bunch of tribesmen running around with spears stabbing hobo's . . . (Olympic, 2012a)

A number of comments concerned with the men's 100m final (Olympic, 2012b) revolved around the issue of race and sporting success (e.g. 'And not a white face was seen in that race: (') and the apparent 'misfortune' of Tyson Gay's surname (e.g. 'lol, GAY–USA..I'M SO GLAD I DON'T HAVE THAT LAST NAME!!'). Nevertheless, the overwhelming majority of comments revealed that the viewers of the video clips were affected/moved by the Olympics. Gerald Griggs, Kathryn Leflay and Mark Groves (2012: 99) recently concluded that 'viewing great sporting moments can take on an intense quality which' can produce intense memories: as such, the viewing pleasures of the Olympics could theoretically shape one's understandings of the Games and these romanticized meanings may not be ephemeral but have lasting impact.

I contend that the display of emotions within the Olympic videos helped craft the narratives surrounding the sport performances to provide coherence and *meaning* to the Olympic representations. Indeed, if the Olympics were represented *without* the displays of athletic emotion and the roar of the crowd, the sporting performances would seem somewhat inane, possibly even meaningless. The affective resonance associated with the display of emotions and viewing pleasures worked to justify the importance and spectacle of the Games. Athletic emotions, in this light, can be thought of as constituting an embodied defense or corporeal retort to critical concerns about the seemingly inane nature of sport, the extravagant cost of hosting the Olympics, the corruption within the IOC, the excessive training demands placed on athletes and the increased risk of terror attacks during the Games. The representations of athletic emotions, thus, can be understood as a key factor that allows for an uncritical celebration of the Games.

130 *Richard Pringle*

THE PLEASURES OF VIEWING SPORT: POLITICAL IMPLICATIONS?

This chapter was motivated, in part, by a desire to understand why the 2012 London Olympics induced such widespread public interest but little critical concern, despite their exorbitant cost and lack of defendable justifications. And, like Robert Rinehart in his (1998b) examination of ESPN's framing of *The eXtreme Games,* I was interested in understanding how the audience *participated* in the viewing experience. Through self-examination, I have illustrated that the display of athletic emotions prevalent in sporting broadcasts *can* operate in a manner that appeals directly to the senses and allows for the production of affective resonance and viewing pleasure. Further, I speculated that this resonance, in combination with the discursive (mythic) positioning of the Olympic champions by the commentators, can invite spectators to celebrate the Olympics in an uncritical manner. I contend that this uncritical celebration, induced in part by corporeal intensities, can divert attention away from the significant political and economic issues that surround the Olympics to leave the Games relatively unproblematized in the public imagination.

I recognize the speculative nature of this conclusion and encourage further critical examination of the links between affect, the sport/media complex and politics. Indeed, Steven Shaviro (1993: vii) argued that it is important to analyze how the media 'arouses corporeal reactions of desire and fear, pleasure and disgust, fascination and shame' as these affective experiences 'directly and urgently involve a politics'. Yet within sociological studies of sport, media analysis has tended to focus on the discursive and symbolic meanings of a text (for exceptions see Booth, 2008; Kennedy, Pussard and Thornton, 2006). These studies accordingly ignore or underestimate how sporting coverage, with its associated focus on athletic emotions, can draw viewers in at a visceral level and shape a viewer's (unconscious) understandings of sport. The meaning of a text, as Lyotard (1984) suggested, is perhaps not as important as understanding the affective change it can induce and what politics it mobilizes. In this case, I am concerned that the embodied experiences associated with viewing the Olympics could potentially mobilize a politics of apathy toward sport, a politics that resists the critical interrogation of sport (see also Chapter 11 with respect to discussion of consumerism and flattened affect).

Yet whether sport fandom mobilizes broader support for other political issues (e.g. neoliberalism, sexism, racism) is another question of relevance. Ava Rose and James Friedman (1997: 12) suggested: 'The very pleasures involved in sports spectatorship may involve some degree of taking up the dominant position offered by sports texts . . . (for example) identifying with normative masculine points of view'. They also noted, 'however, it would be simplistic to assume that any spectator who derives pleasure from TV sports spectatorship is unproblematically taking up the hegemonic values of television sports' (Friedman, 1997: 12). Conversely, as Lawrence Grossberg (1992) illustrated, many fans of political activist rock music, as associated

When the Pleasurable Is Political 131

with bands like U2, REM and Midnight Oil, can derive pleasures from such music without supporting the politics or even necessarily being aware of the group's political messages.

At the least, in paraphrasing Simon Frith and John Street (1992), the power of the Olympics comes from its mobilization of its audience: a series of individual choices (to buy tickets to the Olympics, to watch on television) 'becomes the means to a shared experience and identity. The question, though, is whether this identity has any political substance?' (Frith and Street, 1992: 80). My answer to Frith and Street's rhetorical question is 'yes'. But in making this claim I am not suggesting that fans of the Olympics are mobilized to any particular point on the political spectrum (left or right), but their uncritical fandom of sport allows billions of dollars/pounds to be 'sunk' into the building of stadiums, accommodating athletes/coaches and trainers and defending the Games from potential 'terrorists'.

Richard Giulianotti and Francisco Klauser (2010), for example, provided a financial backdrop to the escalating security costs since 9/11 and the so-called war on terror:

> . . . Olympic security bills in the pre-9/11 context rose steadily from the 1992 Barcelona Games (US\$66.2 million) through Atlanta 1996 (US \$108.2 million) and then Sydney 2000 (US\$179.6 million). The post-9/11 security costs subsequently ballooned, through Athens 2004 (US\$1.5 billion), the Turin Winter Olympics in 2006 (US\$1.4 billion), and the exceptional case of Beijing 2008 (US\$6.5 billion) . . . (Giulianotti and Klauser, 2010: 50)

Kristine Toohey (2008: 438) similarly reported that the Athens Olympics 'turned out to be the most guarded Olympic games in history and the "biggest— most expensive—peace time security operation ever"'. Toohey's claim about Athens is now undoubtedly superseded by the London Olympics.

I highlight the financial cost of the Olympics in order to argue that the 'identities' of the fans of the Olympics do have a political substance, as their uncritical support of the Olympics indirectly props up the sheer size and spectacularization of the Games. As such, *the pleasurable is political* and deserving of critical interrogation, particularly given that some pleasures are hard to resist.

NOTES

1. Eileen Kennedy, Helen Pussard and Andrew Thornton (2006: 19) have similarly raised concerns that the spectacle of major sporting events could shape sport fans' passions and structures of feelings so that they are drawn into 'potentially retrogressive political positions (like the embrace of nationalism) by altering the inflection of their investments in the world'.
2. These representational techniques involve the use of multiple cameras, slow motion replays, close-ups, colorful commentaries, sound effects, music,

132   *Richard Pringle*

biographical sketches, the hyping of rivalries and the production of soap-opera storylines (e.g. see Goldlust, 1987; Rowe, 2004; Wenner, 1998).

3. As an example, I am critical of the lyrics of Lynyrd Skynyrd's *Sweet Home Alabama* but years before I understood what I think the lyrics mean (they are often interpreted as a retort to Neil Young's critique of racism within Alabama) I had fallen in love with the riff, a moving riff that still hooks me in when I hear it.

4. Brian Ott (2010) uses the term 'discourse', in the case of cinema analysis, to refer to "those rule-governed movements or elements, namely narrative and language (i.e., shot selection, sequencing, and editing), that compose an orderly whole" (p. 41).

5. At the time of analysis of the clip, it had received 4,871,887 views (30 November, 2012).

9   'I Just Love Watching Football'

Jayne Caudwell

> . . . the vast majority of literature on sport fans focuses primarily upon what is deemed to be 'traditional' (often masculine) patterns of support, such as supporter chanting, group solidarity, aggression and 'resistance'.
>
> —(Crawford, 2004: 33)

> What's so thrilling is the sheer range of potential emotions, over which I have absolutely no control . . . These emotions are produced by the narratives of the games, and the League or Cup competitions—simple, but endlessly compelling.
>
> —(Paula, email correspondence)

INTRODUCTION

It is almost taken for granted that fans of men's professional football experience pleasure; otherwise, why would they attend live fixtures and/or watch games on various readily available media? And yet, contemporary discussions on football fandom from a socio-cultural perspective tend to omit pleasure as an integral aspect of fandom.

Early studies of football fans in the UK (1970s-80s) show how predominantly working-class men appear to enjoy the aggression and violence associated with fighting—for one's team, club and territory. In these studies, there is some suggestion that fans gain satisfaction from their symbolic resistance (via crowd disturbances at live games) to middle-class governance of the game, and, more broadly, resistance to middle-class governance of their un/employment, education opportunities and daily lives. In this way, these studies of so-called football hooliganism infer pleasure as significant to some football-fan [sub]cultures (Burford, 1992; Dunning et al., 1986; King, 1997).

In a more recent study of football-fan culture, Ruddock (2005) examines fan activity in the context of racism and West Ham FC's signing of Lee Bowyer in 2003[1]. This is one of a few football-related, socio-cultural

134   *Jayne Caudwell*

explorations to address pleasure (more specifically pleasure as problematic). Ruddock considers how the 'study of football fans can inform contemporary debates in critical audience research, particularly around issues of pleasure and cultural citizenship' (2005: 369). He goes on to show how rituals—including practices of racism—within fan cultures taint football as a sport in which '. . . pleasure and politics coexist but never meet . . .' (ibid., 373).

Another examination, which also implicates pleasure of football fandom, race and politics, is Farred's exploration of his own life-long (since the age of seven) love of Liverpool FC, '. . . the pain and pleasure of living and dying with every Liverpool result' (2002: 13). As a Black South African, he unpicks his enduring 'Long Distance Love' of the club, teams and players. His autobiographical account highlights his internal, complex anguish surrounding Liverpool's initial reluctance to sign a Black player and how his love of and passion for Liverpool and racial politics trouble his fandom.[2]

More generally, pleasure related to football fandom is noticeable in [sport] psychology and [sport] management literature. In other words, there is some mention of pleasure in attempts to make sense of supporters' (customers') behaviors, ticket-purchasing patterns and market trends (Tapp, 2004; Wilson and Gilbert, 2005).

In this chapter, I draw on small-scale qualitative research with a Norwich City Football Club (UK) fan: Paula. In itself, this seems unremarkable, but this fan and research participant self-identifies as transgender, transsexual and queer.[3] Many football-fan [sub]cultures are known to be hostile and abusive environments (Jones, 2008; Ruddock, 2005; Silk, 2008), especially for members of the lesbian, gay, bisexual, transgender, queer and intersex (LGBTQI) communities (Caudwell, 2011), and transgender, transsexual and queer subjectivities are profoundly stigmatized in most societies and cultures. This makes Paula's fandom interesting because her voice is from the far margins. From a critical socio-cultural point of view, there is value in reading about Paula's everyday experiences of football fandom.

I begin the chapter with a brief overview of sport-spectator pleasures, including mention of football fandom. This contextualization highlights the lack of research with same-sex attracted and gender-diverse individuals and communities. Following this, I interrogate the methodological issues surrounding small-scale qualitative research. Then, I focus on Paula's experiences of her transgender, transsexual and queer subjectivities and her football fandom. Specifically, I discuss her experiences of coming 'out' to the other—mostly male—football fans she knows and her on-going love of football. In the end, I aim to show football-fandom pleasures as complex, important and socially significant.

SPECTATOR PLEASURES, BRIEFLY

In 1989, Duncan and Brummett wrote of 'types and sources of spectating pleasure'. Their study 'explains the pleasures of televised sports viewing by

'*I Just Love Watching Football*' 135

building on the work of media theorists', and they claim '. . . three types of specular pleasure (fetishism, voyeurism, narcissism) are found in televised sports' (p. 195). Their research is underpinned by the following research question: what makes sport spectatorship appealing and pleasurable for the fan? They are careful not to homogenize either spectator groups or the concept of pleasure. And they go some way to differentiate, by highlighting that there are different types of sport events and different ways these events are observed, including interventions made by technological features that serve to enhance spectator satisfaction (e.g. 1970s/80s television technology such as 'super slo-mo').

Borrowing from film and cinema studies, Duncan and Brummett concentrate on the pleasures of looking (scopophilia). In other words, they focus on visual pleasures and visual medium. Elite, professional and competitive sports are now global phenomena, highly commodified mega-events and international and national spectacles. As such, in most Westernized/capitalist countries, it is difficult to escape looking at sport events and sportspeople. The viewing of mediated sport, according to Duncan and Brummet, can be classified in terms of pleasure derived from: invited/intended looking (fetishism); illicit looking (voyeurism); and looking that elicits identification (narcissism).

Acknowledging this line of inquiry, Merrill and Wann (2011) cite Duncan and Brummett (1989) as well as Guttmann (1996) and Madrigal (2006) to reiterate the relationships between sport spectatorship and voyeurism, the erotic and [heterosexual]physical attraction. They are not the first to consider this nexus. Miller (2002), in his aptly titled book *Sportsex*, pursues a similar project. Consumer cultures are relevant to these literatures. Miller (2002) tends to link athletes' bodies with notions of commodity, while Merrill and Wann (2011)—shifting to the realm of consumer behavior— view sport itself as visual commodity. In this vein, the latter concur with Stewart when he writes: 'In terms of sport spectatorship, the value of the sport experience is now seen for its immediate fun and pleasure rather than any strong and prolonged feeling of tribal identity' (2005: 287).

Immediacy suggests instant gratification and the consumption of sport, and sportspeople, as a form of consumer hedonism and hedonistic pleasures. In contrast, a large proportion of football fandom has been shown to be complex as well as sustained and incomplete. For instance, Jones (2000) and Giulianotti and Robertson (2004) emphasize football fandom as 'serious' and Crawford—drawing on existing literatures—spends time discussing the extent and depth of fan loyalty in his analysis of the 'career of a fan' (2004: 42–49). Additionally, Klugman (2009, 2013), Fleming and Sturm (2011) and Sturm (2012) make important turns to embodied passion, the visceral and affect within fandom. In this way, they provide significant critical readings of the often-contradictory nature of the deep devotion involved in supporting individual sportspeople, teams and clubs (usually professional sportsmen). For example, in Klugman's studies, Australian Rules Football fans display robust and rowdy dissatisfaction and displeasure through

136 *Jayne Caudwell*

'barracking' their own team's players, and yet they continue to attend matches and support the club and team.

Clearly, sport-spectatorship begets multiple and diverse pleasures and, as Crawford makes the point, '. . . fans can connect with, and experience, sport in many different ways and levels, and their actions can carry multiple meanings and readings' (2004: 31). Here I focus on the experiences of one Norwich City FC fan to provide a partial—nevertheless previously unheard—point of view.

SMALL-SCALE QUALITATIVE RESEARCH: A METHODOLOGY

> The number of participants in a qualitative interview study can range
> from 1 to 100
> (Markula and Silk, 2011: 93).

In many spheres, many of us no longer have to defend our qualitative stance. In some circles, qualitative methodologies are automatically assumed as creditable and legitimate, and debate has turned, instead, to the inner workings of qualitative research. For example, Markula and Silk highlight these interior mechanisms through their advocacy of the '7Ps: Purpose, Paradigms, Process, Practice, Politics of Interpretation, Presentation and The Promise of qualitative research' (2011: x). Although these constituent parts appear as distinct and separate entities within a neat, easy-to-grasp rubric ('7Ps'), they are worth bearing in mind, not least because they open ways to appreciate the value of small-scale qualitative research.

Simply put, this chapter is based on one semi-structured interview and follow-up emails with one Norwich City FC fan. In addition, however, it is also based on my on-going qualitative research involvement with football cultures, same-sex attraction and gender diversity, as well as getting to know Paula.

This chapter aims to offer '. . . purposeful research that is meaningful to a range of communities' (Markula and Silk, 2011: 11). The 'range of communities' might include those related to football, fandom, gender, sexualities, and those who are transgender, transsexual and queer. Such an aim is set within the bounds of interpretive constructions of meaning-making: in other words, how Paula and I understand, interpret, tell and re-tell her experiences of supporting Norwich City FC. Obviously, we are both implicated in how her football-fandom experiences are captured on the pages of this book. The representation is, of course, subjective, relativist and partial (cf. Denzin, 2010; Richardson, 2000); it provides a particular account of one person's love of watching football.

There is political matter in this small-scale research. Paula's fandom must be considered through an appreciation of her shifting and fluid sex-gender-desire subjectivities (queer, boy, gay, transgender, man, transsexual, woman, queer)[4] and the absence of a similar standpoint within sport spectator/

'I Just Love Watching Football' 137

fandom literatures. Only recently have we witnessed alternatives to the many male-dominated football-fandom studies by, for and with men (cf. Jones, 2008; Pope, 2010 and 2012). Here, I provide a further contribution.

I travelled, by train, to Paula's home in East London for the interview. The interview lasted one hour and ten minutes and was transcribed verbatim. On completion, the 13,000-word transcript was e-mailed (as an attachment) to Paula for her scrutiny. E-mail contact was maintained after the initial interview took place (on 29th May, 2012) and, as is likely with inductive qualitative research, I was able to ask further questions through this mode of communication. For example, here is a section of an e-mail I sent to Paula after I had transcribed the interview:

> You said in the interview: "The thing is . . . I like this queer counter-culture, but on the other hand I love football". Can you offer more on this? Do your queer counter-culture and love of football co-exist? Do they overlap/merge in any ways?

A re-visiting of interview transcript through an on-going interaction with research participants is not always possible. And yet maintaining strong bonds with the people and communities we share our research with is an obvious way to explore the details and contradictions of the everyday. It also helps develop and expand useful research agendas.

MEETING PAULA MCVEIGH[5]

At the beginning of 2011, I took on a voluntary role for a Brighton-based football campaign—The Justin Campaign. The campaign was initiated on May 2nd, 2008, ten years after the Black-British footballer Justin Fashanu took his own life. Justin Fashanu came 'out' as gay as well as bisexual during the early 1990s. During his teenage years—in the late 70s and early 80s—Justin showed incredible potential as a footballer, but his sexuality, ethnicity and lifestyle received severe criticism from various people within UK footballing institutions, including those in club management and sport media/journalism.

The main aim of The Justin Campaign, at its inception, was to make all football cultures safer for members of the LGBTQI communities and to help prevent others from feeling isolated and possibly taking their own lives because of abuse, hostility, prejudice and discrimination. During my 18 months with the campaign I worked on various education projects and through this work I met many local and national people, all of whom shared—in different ways—the concerns and aims of The Justin Campaign. One of these like-minded people was Paula; she was also a volunteer.

I met Paula for the first time at a Brighton Pride LGBT Football Tournament in August 2011. As with most of the campaign's volunteers, her

138 *Jayne Caudwell*

personal links to football and Justin Fashanu[6] are well-developed and weave through her own football biography, as is evident here:

P: Justin Fashanu was somebody, I mean, you can see it there [points]. I got a video, I think for my 13th birthday of highlights of Norwich City games over the years, and Justin Fashanu's famous goal against Liverpool was one of the real highlights of it. I remember the first time I watched it . . . being open-mouthed at how brilliant it [goal] was. Justin Fashanu was a name I kept hearing as I grew up in the 90s. My dad grew up just south of London, so Wimbledon was his team . . . John Fashanu[7] was there. We used to take family holidays in Torquay every summer, which is where Justin was playing. So, he kind of came on to my radar and I gradually twigged just through innuendo, I didn't really read the tabloids. I didn't really know about Justin's frequent tabloid appearances. But, through innuendo, I picked up that Justin was this gay player. His suicide in 1998 hit me really hard, you know, he was a hero of mine.

J: How old were you then?

P: I was 16. It hit me very, very hard. It just seemed like a horrible crushing turn of events at that age and it just made me think, you know, where is the place for me as a queer person who likes football and wants to be involved with it?

(From interview transcript)

On May 2nd and 3rd, 2012, Paula and I attended two events held at the University of Brighton. The first was a Justin Student Football Festival and the second a one-day Justin Campaign Symposium: Campaigning for Change. We were both active participants in the events. We shared the women's changing room space, played football alongside students and staff, posed for photographs holding placards inscribed with 'Football v Transphobia' and Paula contributed to a Football, Transgender and Transphobia panel. After these events, I wrote to Paula requesting an interview. She agreed. Since then, she has read and given verbal support to the accuracy of the interview transcript[8] as well as endorsing the content of the final version of this chapter.

THE INVISIBILITY OF PLEASURE

> Thus we should discard the question 'Did this researcher's feelings affect the study?' when we read fieldwork accounts and instead ask 'How did the researcher's emotions play a part in the data collection and analysis of this group or setting?' (Kleinman and Copp, 1993: 52)

For a long time now, many qualitative researchers have questioned the fallacy of remaining emotionally detached during the research process. Moreover, those advocating a distinctly feminist methodology have developed

'I Just Love Watching Football' 139

the concept of 'reflexivity' to make transparent the role of the researcher (Wilkinson, 1988) and challenge the scientific chimera of objectivity (Maynard and Purvis, 1994; Ramazanoglu and Holland, 2002). It is often acknowledged, and accepted, by a range of qualitative researchers—not only feminist researchers—that the researcher's presence is as significant as the research participants' (cf. Denzin, 2010).

After the interview with Paula I scanned the interview transcript for reference to 'pleasure'. Finding few references I actively sought the word 'pleasure' through a word finder. Paula had used the words 'enjoy', 'fun' and 'love' many times, but she had not uttered the word 'pleasure'. I, on the other hand, had said it several times. After making this observation, I wrote to Paula via e-mail and made this comment:

> In the interview you talked about liking the aesthetics and drama of football. You were clear about not enjoying the abusive cultures apparent in the game. You mentioned enjoying being part of a larger fan group both at the game and on the internet forum. Given how hypermacho fan environments can be and how transgender can be a marginalized subject position, I wonder if you could provide a bit more of the pleasures of being a Norwich fan?

Paula's responses to the direct question concerning '. . . the pleasures of being a football fan?' included a range of words that are synonyms for pleasure (e.g. 'love', 'enjoy' and 'happy'), but no direct reference to 'pleasure'. This becomes interesting for two reasons: first, because it demonstrates the invisibility of 'pleasure' in research on sport. For example, for those of us involved in sport, it might not be easy to articulate and/or describe the pleasures we experience. I suggest this is significant because it can be argued that the notion of pleasure *per se* has been squeezed out of contemporary, competitive sport practices and cultures. If this is the case, then such silences open avenues for critique and are, therefore, political. Second, the use of the word 'pleasure' reveals something about my role within this research process. Interestingly, in discussions of methodology, we rarely hear about the pleasures of conducting research.

Since the interview with Paula, during times of reflection, I have considered how I felt at various stages of the interview process. I recognize that I enjoyed interviewing Paula and hearing her stories of football and football fandom. I felt very happy in her company and delighted that she had mostly positive experiences to recount. In fact, getting to know Paula and completing the interview-research process was pleasurable. This pleasure is worth unpacking because it provides '. . . an idea of the life worlds, and indeed challenges, facing the qualitative researcher' (Silk, Andrews and Mason, 2005: 8). Perhaps, more specifically, my feelings of pleasure are useful in addressing an important question: 'What dreams am I having about the material presented?' (What issues am I pulling from my own biography and

140 Jayne Caudwell

what emphasis have I given these?) (Silk, Andrews and Mason, 2005: 9). Dreaming has many connotations. For example, there might be researcher fantasies about discovery, originality and innovation. There are also visions and hopes, which are more akin to Martin Luther King's eminent 'I have a dream' (August 27th 1963) speech.

My satisfactions during this research can be understood in the context of my previous qualitative work on football cultures and how lesbian (Caudwell, 1999, 2003) and gay male players (Caudwell, 2011), and one young transgender (Caudwell, 2012) player, experience a range of negative responses to their active involvement. Over the years, I have heard stories of abuse, bullying, discrimination, exclusion, hostility and prejudice. I anticipated similar testimonies from Paula, especially given her marginalized subjectivities of transgender, transsexual and queer. Instead, she told me of how she is—mostly—accepted within football-fan culture and how much she loves supporting Norwich City FC. Clearly, we must be careful not to idealize Paula's involvement; professional men's football in the UK is not, by any means, a utopia of joyful inclusion. But, for Paula, being on the 'terraces' watching her team has been relatively easy and comfortable. For many reasons, largely to do with my own interests in football, same-sex attraction and gender diversity, I was very keen to hear about Paula's pleasant experiences. As Rand puts it, I '. . . got to dwell on other people's enjoyment' which is '. . . a pleasure in itself' (2012: 57). In this way, I am emotionally involved in this research project.

> As Ahmed suggests, understanding what other people's lives are about—including their pains and their pleasures—is integral to making connections for social justice work that recognize people's histories, humanity, vision, and desires. Visceral pleasures, aesthetics interests, 'freedom dreams', and the ecstatic, as Robin D.G. Kelley argues, deserve honour and visibility in our past, our present, and our visions of possible futures. (Rand, 2012: 245)

Like many academic activists I have dreams of a better future, and because of this I know I have exulted in Paula's fandom. Clearly, my emotion-location shapes the contents of this chapter. It also highlights the gradations of pleasure that are present in sport-related—namely football—research.

PAULA: BECOMING A FOOTBALL FAN

I hated football until I was about eight years old and something suddenly switched in me, I'm not sure why. There were two things that piqued my interest. One of them was Crystal Palace getting to the FA cup final in 1990, although I didn't end up supporting them. The other was England making the

'I Just Love Watching Football' 141

World Cup semi-finals that summer and all the fervor around that. So, that was what drew me into football and I started playing at school and it was all I'd do any break time; any possibility of playing football I would do it. And then, when I was ten, I realized I was transgender. I hadn't really noticed this before and I hadn't been an especially feminine child. I was in some ways, but not in that kind of much-more recognized girly-boy kind of way and . . . I just suppressed this really. I was actually at a rugby playing school for two years. I left there and went to a State secondary, which was a football school. I'd been playing football for three years or so, and decided I wanted to have a go at playing competitively. And so, I joined Town FC and played half a season for the U12s. I just found that there was something about me that didn't fit. I was hiding my queerness, I guess. I already realized my sexuality was quite complicated. I didn't understand it. I didn't really think I was gay, but I didn't have a framework to understand my gender and my sexuality so I just kept it hidden and football was one of my means of doing that; if I played football, well, I intuitively knew that I'd get an easier ride from the guys at my school . . . the guys on the team. So I joined the team. I scored a couple of goals in the friendlies. But something about me didn't fit the team-culture, even then. There were a couple of guys I got on well with but lots of guys I didn't and, you know, this isn't just a matter of sexuality. I think actually at that point, I think it was more a matter of class and education. I went to a private school and I was quite obviously quite bookish and was very, very bourgeois, middle class and the guys on the team weren't. So I think the issues were actually more around class than anything else. But, I found I didn't really get on with the guys on the team. If they don't like you, they won't pass the ball to you. And so you don't impress, you lose confidence and it becomes a vicious circle. So, I quit the team after half a season and I wanted to go to City FC, but Town FC wouldn't let me break contract. So I ended up not joining them either and it kind of soured me on competitive football. I wasn't really good enough to make it worth fighting all these barriers. I ended up going to the local State school . . . but, I wasn't good enough for the first XI, so I'd play for the School B team. But, actually, the teachers in the school paid more attention to the first XI. The B side would play friendlies. I wouldn't always get in the team because I wasn't in with the kind of people I needed to be in with to get in. I think I had a couple of games at left back or something, which wasn't really where I was suited and I just gave up on it. By year ten, I just stopped playing, except once a week in PE lesson. I found that there wasn't really a place for me. I started exploring music more and started reading Oscar Wilde and started to discover this queer culture that suited me and so there was this weird tension. I would go with my dad—by this time I'd decided, for some reason, I was going to support Norwich, and my dad and I would go to three or four games a season together; a couple in London and maybe in Norwich once or twice a year. I just found there that my sexuality and gender weren't an issue.

J: At the ground do you mean?
P: At the ground, you know it didn't, it just didn't come up.

142 *Jayne Caudwell*

Paula's football-fan biography is not unusual. As Farred reveals, such initial commitment can be understood in terms of the 'arbitrariness of fandom' (2002: 6). It reflects patterns of childhood engagement, family and early affiliation with a particular team. Additionally, it suggests a so-called induction period (Crawford, 2004), which has been followed by her sustained support of Norwich City FC. This is despite living in various parts of the UK to study and work.

During the interview, Paula talked about her more recent fandom. Strong themes to emerge were her love of Norwich City FC, football, talks about football and other fans. However, the chanting she has witnessed at games complicates her love of all four. More generally, pleasure has a close relationship with disgust, and I explore this contradiction more fully below.

Given the literature on fandom and the pleasures of looking, and the case that there had been no reference to the love of looking at football players, I asked Paula (in a follow-up e-mail) about desire and her football fandom. She replied:

> I've never felt desire (or voyeurism) at football games. Not sure why—perhaps partly that's because desire is not what I'm looking for in that situation. I won't rule it out entirely though, but perhaps I just don't find footballers sexy.
>
> (Paula, e-mail correspondence)

As with many football fans, sexual (heterosexual, same-sex, queer) attraction appears low down on registers of pleasures.

'I GOT OUTED: SOMEONE POSTED IT ON THE FORUM'

> Even when the game is going badly, there's something about the camaraderie, the shared emotions that I really enjoy, and there's something strangely comforting in watching your team get hammered in a crowd full of fellow fans.
>
> (Paula, e-mail correspondence)

During the interview, Paula talked about coming out at different times in her life. At 16, she came out as 'gay and a cross dresser'. Reflecting on these identities, she said about 'gay': 'It just seemed the nearest and best understood'. 'Crossdresser' because transgender wasn't a term that was available to her at that time and transvestite had connotations she disliked. Together, gay and crossdresser allowed for 'all sorts of queer behaviour'. Later, I asked Paula if transgender was a good word for her. She was adamant: 'The idea of transgender saved my life, really.' When Paula began to identify as transgender she was working and therefore had money to go to Norwich City games more frequently:

> . . . my transgender identity and exploration didn't stop me going to games. I mean I would go to the games as male, which is how I was living at the time. I had long hair, but otherwise was male-identified and recognizable as male. I didn't tell my friends at the games that I had this parallel identity. (From interview transcript)

In 2009, Paula started to come out as transsexual. At this time, she contemplated how her friends and family would respond to her transitioning. She believed friends would be 'okay' and her family would find it 'challenging, but I think we will get there'. She thought her job and social life would require some 'managing'. Another important concern for her was 'well, can I still go to football?' She remembers transitioning on a Saturday: 'I think it was the 2nd of May; it was the day I emailed all my friends saying: I'm Paula now.' Her football-fan friends were not included in this e-mail. However, a couple of them were Facebook friends with her, and they noticed that she had changed her profile details. Changing Facebook information was actually a 'nice' way for Paula to come out. It meant she could 'come out to everybody without necessarily having to utter these loaded words: "I am transsexual"'.

Before Paula was able to explore her own ways of coming out to the rest of her football-fan friends she got outed by another fan on a football-fan forum. Paula was active on the forum and enjoyed the exchanges of information, football knowledge and the appropriately jovial nature of this Internet space. She thought the forum was a place where her 'transsexuality didn't stop me interacting with people'. At the same time, Paula was writing a column for a national newspaper. The column was about her experiences of transitioning. Another fan posted a link to this newspaper column on to the football forum. He also posted: 'look, this is that person's column'.

> P: A few people said 'ah you cruel bastard just because he looks like a girl' and a few other people said 'no, it really is his thing'. In the end I had to go on there and say 'yeah, I wrote that'. And, then there was this really weird thing because the forum hadn't had to deal with someone transitioning before.
>
> J: Did you feel exposed?
>
> P: Yeah, it was heart-in-mouth. Actually, it worked out really well, because I don't know how I would have handled coming out to all of my friends at the game . . . I ended up being really glad it had happened. (From interview transcript)

With time, Paula and some of the other fans used the forum less and less. Instead they switched to Facebook would see each other at games.

144 *Jayne Caudwell*

P: There is a big group of people I go with [to football]. One of them, my friend Luke . . . at Norwich they're all Luke's friends. Luke said, 'we all still want to see you and be your friend, if you want to have a chat, just drop me a line'. And I said, 'Luke that's really lovely, but it's quite simple, I'm known as Paula, she and her and other than that you don't have to do anything' . . . Next time I saw them, I went to a home game, October that year against Middlesborough. He said 'how do you want me to introduce you to everyone?' I said 'as Paula'. He said 'great'. I went to the game, I went to the pub with them afterwards, we went to dinner together. It was really easy, really simple.
J: Loads of blokes?
P: Yeah, they all treated me as female and that was that.

(From interview transcript)

"I LOVE GOING TO WATCH NORWICH [EVEN THOUGH I KNOW THEY HAVE BEEN ON A SUSTAINED RUN OF BAD FORM FOR ABOUT 4 YEARS]"[9]

In his piece on Long Distance Love, Farred describes—through a language of love—'growing up a Liverpool football club fan'. He refers to his '. . . beloved Liverpool . . .' (2002: 6) and describes his feelings as '. . . enduring love, blind, rock-solid faith, and abiding passion' (p. 10). He tells of his '. . . love affair with the central midfielders Graeme Souness and Steve McMahon' (p. 7), and stresses that '[a]s much as I loved Keegan . . .' (p. 8), 'I love Graeme Souness above all other players . . .' (p. 17). Perhaps unsurprisingly, he is unable to explain 'the moment that I first fell in love . . .' and he claims that his is '. . . a love that was consummated before it was understood, narrativized, or even articulated' (p. 11).

Verbalizing what it is, exactly, that conjures '. . . enduring love, blind, rock-solid faith, and abiding passion' (p. 10) is difficult, near impossible. As a researcher, accessing the logics of such love (and pleasure) is not easy. During the interview with Paula, I tried to probe for some kind of rationale:

J: . . . there's something about the game, watching the game, watching the team move the ball?
P: Yeah, very visceral, kind of aesthetic thing for me. I just love watching football. A really great team move or an individual run or [pause] there are so many things I love about football. That dynamic between the players and the crowd, just the sheer high drama of it. I don't like any of the culture that comes with it. But I just thought I love the sport so much I just have to try and [pause] at worst find my own space in that culture and at best try to change it.

(From interview transcript)

Paula finds the 'creative possibilities' of football endearing. In a recent discussion, Kreft (2013) recognizes the aesthetic appeal of football. He argues that the: 'Aesthetic attraction of football is not a sign of alienation, manipulation or ideology—it is just what it appears to be: a sign of rare pleasure' (p. 19). And yet Paula points out that '. . . loads of my friends hate football because the sport doesn't have the distinctive aesthetic appeal that it has for me.' She also acknowledges that there are times when football has made her 'very embarrassed to like it' and that certain chants and songs make her 'wince' and that she 'hates them'.

Love has a tricky, and perhaps turbulent, relationship with pleasure. Both are elusive. Describing what it is that people like and love about sport (football), what it is they find pleasurable, does seem to involve the visual and aesthetic as well as the sensate (e.g. felt atmosphere and felt drama). And yet, pleasure also collides with what is not pleasurable. In this way, it is not a pure concept.

In football-fan contexts, what is enjoyable sits within a broader culture that is often at odds with pleasure. For instance, Farred exclaims: 'In no other part of my life would I have been able to tolerate such incongruence between my cultural investment and my politics' (2002: 21). Such incongruence can be intense, and while it does not appear to contaminate feelings and expressions of pleasure, it does haunt and make uneven some fans' experiences of pleasure *vis à vis* the personal and political.

Paula has a friend, Ben ('who was doing a PhD in the works of Thomas Pynchon'). Ben is a Southampton FC supporter. Together they 'talk about football all night and literally, we'd have to go off on our own to sit in the football corner . . . it drove everybody crazy, but we really enjoyed it.' When I asked Paula if she liked having football knowledge and exchanging this knowledge with others, she said, 'absolutely, I love talking about football . . . I've always found—even in queer spaces or these kind of high-cultural spaces—people who like football as much as me . . . whether they're queer or not, Ben is a straight guy, he's always been in monogamous heterosexual relationships'.

Football, specifically 'fanspeak' (Ruddock, 2005) can help change the boundaries of [football] citizenship. Ruddock argues that some football fans might be '. . . willing to abandon certain elements of tradition to explore new ways of being' (2005: 372). For example, Ben and Paula appear to be abandoning their middle-class, high-culture context. Ben abandons a traditional male-heterosexual football-fan identity and Paula abandons explicitly queer subjectivities. Ruddock, focusing on this idea of a suspension of tradition, explores the possibilities for pleasures based on cultural inclusion (e.g. football cultural inclusion). More specifically, he draws from Barthes: '. . . Barthes' seminal text locates the political aspects of pleasure in the following dynamic: "Imagine someone who abolishes within himself [sic] all barriers, all classes. All exclusions . . ."' (p. 372). Pleasures in this sense and for some people are about willingness 'to desert what you are and what you

146 *Jayne Caudwell*

know' (p. 375). Ben and Paula appear to be doing this when they 'talk about football all night . . .'.

Paula and Ben's fanspeak and football-friendship provide one small example of how traditional boundaries and distinctions surrounding gender and sexuality can dissolve. During the hours they spend together, recounting stories of Southampton FC and Norwich City FC, they both enjoy a form of football-fan citizenship. Paula's sense of belonging and cultural inclusion is held together by their football knowledge, their respect of each other's knowledge, their joy in sharing, telling and listening to this wisdom. In this one-to-one situation, they have abolished traditional and exclusionary categories of sex, gender and sexuality.

However, as Ruddock goes on to discuss, these seemingly utopic moments can be fragile, especially when there are obdurate, unjust and unpleasant broader politics. Referring to football in Israel and the work of Sorek (2003), Ruddock suggests that despite Arab fans feeling a sense of belonging in football stadia, their football fandom (collective citizenship) can never change their minority, and inferior, status in Israel. Momentarily, football fandom does dislocate and rupture notions of Israeli citizenship; however, it never permanently alters the oppressive relations of power in the country. In this context, Ruddock concludes: '. . . pleasure is based on the ability to build and defend, not abolish categories' (2005: 375).

In one of the follow up e mails with Paula, I asked her about 'standing on the terraces':

> My favorite thing about standing on the terraces is the way I can vanish into the crowd. Everyone is focused on the match, so I can lose myself in conversation about the team and the tactics, the songs that people sing and the back-and-forth between the two sets of fans, incidents on and off the pitch . . . I like the way that my gender doesn't really matter . . . we're all fixated upon the match, and for this time, our individual and collective emotions are broadly the same.
>
> (Paula, e-mail correspondence)

The pleasures Paula experiences through fanspeak or in situ—at football stadia and on the terraces—are evident. However, from a critical perspective, some of these pleasures might conceal, through fantasies of liberal democracy (Ruddock, 2005), the socio-cultural and socio-political unpleasant (e.g. the subordination of Arabs in Israel and transphobia in sport generally) as well as warn us 'of pleasure's conservative potential' (p. 384). And yet Paula did not report experiences of abuse and harassment in terms of her own subjectivity. She did, however, find many aspects of football-fan culture unpalatable.

It might be useful to think about football-fandom pleasures as haunted by displeasures and the unpleasant. I am not promoting a binary model of pleasure; instead, I am suggesting sport-related pleasures are evanescent,

'*I Just Love Watching Football*' 147

fluid and in flux. Displeasures and the unpleasant are not only to do with broader regimes of social, cultural and political injustice (as in Israel), they are also about much smaller, intense moments of human indecency, which are often to do with racism and xenophobia. These moments—in football contexts—are frequently wrapped up as expressions of humour.

> . . . but, he [Ben] has this problem with football because he's an intellectual with a taste for modernist literature and how do you handle it when [pause] . . . one story he recounts . . . one of the Portsmouth players was a guy called Lomana LuaLua who was Congolese and he went to play in the Africa Nations Cup and got malaria, Ben said, the next Southampton game there'd be a big crowd singing 'Lualua has got malaria'.[10]
>
> (From interview transcript)

Paula also talked about her experiences of watching a League Cup game between Brighton and Hove Albion FC (BHAFC) and Gillingham FC. The game was at Brighton. It is common for away fans, in this case Gillingham, to sing homophobic songs at BHAFC home games, because the city of Brighton and Hove has the largest 'out' population of LGBTQI people in the UK. Paula recounts what happened after a popular song ('does your boyfriend know you're here?') was sung at Brighton fans: 'I heard someone yell, "oh fuck off, you bunch of pikeys", using this kind of regional stereotyping against Kent[11], and the Gypsy population there'. In other examples, when Norwich City FC plays Liverpool FC or Everton FC, songs about unemployment and theft are rife (the city of Liverpool is stereotyped in a way that exaggerates men's criminal activities) and away fans sing, to the tune of Sloop John B, 'I want to go home, Liverpool is a shithole'.[12]

The above incident surrounding the player Lualua led to further discomfort and disgust for Paula, and her friend Ben.

> . . . and how do you . . . the same player, he was playing for the Republic of Congo in the Africa Nations Cup and his son died during the tournament. Ben said he went to the next game and was really worried that people would sing songs . . . he was relieved to find that they didn't. This is the kind of dilemma . . . it's terrible, football culture is such that you can be a football fan and go to a game and feel a genuine sense of relief that nobody sings a song about somebody's infant son dying. The culture can be that abhorrent.
>
> (From interview transcript)

Many sport cultures, especially men's professional sport, are sites for discourses and displays of so-called banter. Football songs and chants—in the UK—are often aligned with, and framed through humor, the comical

148 *Jayne Caudwell*

and funny. However, in his analysis of microaggressions and microinsults in men's cricket in England, Burdsey argues: '. . . [J]okes can underpin divisive and exclusionary aspects of sporting subcultures, and they represent a powerful and symbolic means by which minorities are marginalized from dominant player collectives' (2011: 273). Such jokes and joking are exemplars of Ruddock's notion that '. . . pleasure is based on the ability to build and defend . . . categories' (2005: 375).

More broadly, and in relation to the comedy industry, there have been on-going debates over what counts as funny and why it counts as funny. For instance, Wagg (2011), in his critique of the British comedian Bernard Manning, demonstrates the unapologetic sexist, racist and homophobic nature of traditional British stand-up comedy. He claims there has been 'a negligible relationship between comedy and politics, and comedy was, by and large, seen as a separate and sanctioned universe of discourse in which things said did not matter outside that universe: facilitating the familiar comment "It's just a joke"'(p. 170). Comedy, jokes and laughing are fundamental to feelings of pleasure, but, as many see it, large parts of the comedy genre are problematic. As Burdsey (2011) concludes from his study with South Asian English male cricketers, 'that joke isn't funny anymore'.

In terms of gender and sexuality Paula does enjoy certain aspects of fan culture and being with other fans gives her a sense of belonging. For example she said: '. . . there's a woman called Beth who hangs out with us and I remember the first time I met her. I did feel this real kind of relief and happiness, like there's another woman. So, yeah, I love the guys to bits, but I would like a bit more female company'.

It is often difficult for the spheres of gender and sexuality and football to merge in productive ways for people who do not identify as heteronormative. Paula made this statement in the interview: '[t]he thing is . . . I like this queer counter-culture, but on the other hand I love football'. In a follow-up email (see above) I asked her to explain this further. She wrote back, making the point that queer and football do not co-exist because 'mainstream football isn't queer at all' and that most queer spaces do not include football. Despite these disparities, Paula suggests that the 'gulf is ideal' because at football her gender diversity and queer sexuality are, for the time being, forgotten about, suspended: 'I spend a lot of my time reading, writing and thinking about queer culture and politics, and football could not be a better release from that'. She also added: 'one of my favorite things about going to the games is not worrying about it [her body]—I take far less time over my appearance when going to the football then I do when going almost anywhere else, which is very liberating'. For Paula, there are pleasures in these freedoms, pleasure in forgetting, and unlike the rest of her daily life, Paula can, literally, 'vanish into the crowd'. She can become the observer of others and not the focus of often-judgmental observations and cruel banter, which has happened in other spheres of her life (e.g. walking home at night).

CONCLUDING COMMENTS

What is apparent from my communications with Paula is that she loves football, loves watching football, loves watching Norwich and loves talking about football. We can assume that this love produces a certain amount of pleasure. It is unusual to hear the voice of a transgender, transsexual, queer fan of Norwich City FC. Moreover, it is refreshing to hear how this fan has mostly positive experiences related to her sex-gender-sexuality subjectivities. This is significant, because as Rand claims: '. . . if an anti-oppression vision of a just and good world includes pleasure, then pleasure as an end, not just as a route to knowledge, matters, too' (2012: 10–11).

This chapter does present pleasure 'as an end'. It focuses on Paula's pleasures surrounding football and my pleasures in hearing about her positive experiences of a culture I have, for a long time, critiqued. However, her football pleasures are actually quite complicated and it is worth highlighting some of these complications.

For many football fans (cf. Farred, 2002; Ruddock, 2005) the pleasures obtained from following and supporting a men's professional football team are constantly plagued by displeasures and the unpleasant. For fans that adopt anti-homophobic, anti-sexist and anti-racist (and anti-capitalist) personal politics, the popular and dominant cultures of most football-fan groups engender discomfort. The aesthetic (style of play), visceral (sheer joy) and sensate (felt drama) pleasures of standing (or sitting down) on the terraces and watching your team are not fixed and enduring. Instead, these pleasures are affected by the soundscape within stadia and the idiosyncratic crowd chanting at UK football grounds (and, more broadly, the relentless commodification of the game). At live football fixtures, moments of pleasure are frequently punctuated. The boundaries between the pleasant and unpleasant are porous, and it is possible to feel both pleasure and displeasure simultaneously. For example, Paula talked about watching a good team or individual move on the field of play and, at the same time, hearing a terrible and abhorrent football chant. Clearly the sensate—the visual and auditory—do not always align, and there can be incongruence that might be unbearable for some. In these contexts, pleasure might be understood through notions of play-off and resolution. In other words, how do fans reconcile their love and passion for football when they know there are distressingly troublesome aspects? For Paula, and her friend Ben, it is not simply a matter of ignoring the unpleasant. It is more complicated, and their pleasures appear on an emotional (happy) landscape pockmarked with anguish and revulsion.

Some of Paula's pleasures stem from a suspension of her world outside of the football stadium. This is not in relation to her personal politics, but more in terms of her own sex-gender-sexualities subjectivities. The crowd, collectivism and sometimes-shared emotions mean that her presence is unremarkable and unobtrusive. For her, this is an enjoyable position to be in.

150   *Jayne Caudwell*

Finally, as Paula pointed out at the beginning of her story of becoming a fan, [middle] class plays a role in some of the pleasures she, and other football fans, are able to access and/or the unpleasants they are able to avoid. For instance, both Paula and Ben are postgraduates; the column that was posted on the fan forum is from a UK left-wing quality newspaper. This paper is usually read by the so-called middle classes. By inference I am not suggesting that the (male) working classes, which are significantly represented at live men's professional football in the UK, are not able to help include a football fan who identifies as transgender, transsexual and queer. However, some of Paula's pleasures (being part of a friendly and welcoming fan group) are, most likely, contingent on class and ethnicity, as well as other shared social locations.

NOTES

1. At the time, Lee Bowyer had a reputation for racist violence.
2. Pope's recent work (2012) on women fans of men's football (and rugby), 'The love of my life', continues this emphasis on 'love'. However, her work provides a broader analysis of types ('hot' and 'cold') of women's fandom in relation to women's gendered identities (masculine and feminine).
3. At the time of interview, Paula identified as a transgender-queer woman.
4. These shifting subjectivities must not be read as linear or chronological, despite appearing so through written words on a page.
5. 'Paula McVeigh' was selected by the research participant. It is a pseudonym and helps to achieve confidentiality and anonymity during the research process. The name was selected purposely because it carries particular meanings (related to Norwich City FC) and some readers might recognize its etymology.
6. Justin Fashanu started his professional football career at Norwich City FC in 1978. He was 17 years old and stayed with the club until 1981. During this time, he scored 35 goals in 90 appearances.
7. John Fashanu is Justin Fashanu's brother. In the media, John responded negatively to Justin's publicly self-declared sexuality.
8. Since the interview, Paula has been approached by others, including governing bodies of sport, for interviews. As a way to avoid repeating lengthy interviews, she asked me if she could send our interview transcript to those asking for interviews with her. I agreed to this.
9. Paula read the final version of this chapter. She made five comments. One of the comments was related to this quotation. It reads: 'This run covered 2005-summer 2009, when I started transitioning. They've been miraculously good ever since'.
10. Ben supports Southampton FC. Southampton FC and Portsmouth FC are long-standing local rivals.
11. In the UK, 'pikey' is slang and a pejorative term for Gypsies and travellers. It is also viewed as an ethnic slur. Kent is the county in the far South East corner of England. It is known as the 'Garden of England' because of the crops that are grown and harvested there. The region's population of workers is often transient (e.g. fruit pickers).
12. This song is sung by away fans at many clubs, not only at Liverpool FC.

10 Aesthetic Pleasure and Sport
The Case of *Love + Guts: Skateboarding Killed the Art Show*

Robert E. Rinehart

There are clear linkages between aesthetic pleasures and sport, physical engagement with the world and the exerting body (or embodied movement) in contemporary Western society. However, competition has often trumped the intrinsic pleasures of sporting—and even embodied movement—activities. The intrinsic pleasures of sport—including an appreciation of the beauty in/ of sport (cf. Lowe, 1977) and aesthetics—have been subsumed by extrinsic types of pleasures: more hyperbolic, yet more transitory, somewhat akin to the sudden flash mobs Kathleen Stewart (2007: 66) describes in *Ordinary Affects*. 'Such trajectories and metamorphoses are . . . forms of contagion, persuasion, and social worlding'. But the term *aesthetics* has also come to mean the relationship between values and the senses (cf. Bourdieu, 1984) and, in this regard, sport and aesthetics are inextricably connected.

The relationships between beauty and sport—this performative 'dance' of sport—are much more than just dynamics between how we comprehend the world and what we judge within that apprehension. As Barthes (2007: 9) writes about bullfighting:

> There is something else in the torero's style. What is style? Style makes a difficult action into a graceful gesture, introduces a rhythm into fatality. Style is to be courageous without disorder, to give necessity the appearance of freedom. Courage, knowledge, beauty, these are what man opposes to the strength of the animal, this is the human ordeal, of which the bull's death will be the prize.

For Barthes, beauty and style and the aesthetic of the bullfight are what create the limitations of 'what sport is'. But clearly, sport involves this sense of beauty, of grace, of almost unimaginable economy—so that sport, done well, nearly always touches on the sublime and ineffable aesthetic.[1]

Formally, the aesthetic is a branch of philosophy dealing with the nature of art, beauty, taste—put more broadly, the term aesthetics constitutes 'a kind of object, a kind of judgment, a kind of attitude, a kind of experience, and a kind of value' (Shelley, 2009: ¶ 1) based within a host of cultural and natural artifacts. Thus, what characterizes the aesthetic is situational,

152 Robert E. Rinehart

partial, open-ended, open to discussion, teased out by influences of culture, taste and preference. If there are any universal agreements on what has come to be known as aesthetic, they are quite rare.

Sport and things relating to the physical body—in contrast with the *strictly* cognitive, for physical activities include the cognitive—fit well with the study of aesthetics. For where else might we find bodies in full exertion, demonstrating the current limits, ranges and hopes of human effort, exemplified through such a complex array of sensory and emotional—and often silently pleasurable—positionings?

Historically, the study of emotions, for example, has been fraught with differing viewpoints regarding whether or not humans have *basic* and *universal* emotions, or whether human emotions are critically dependent upon interaction with social forces. To demonstrate the range of complex views on just what emotions *are*, it is helpful to remember that the 1st Century Li Chi counts seven basic emotions (joy, anger, sadness, fear, love, disliking and liking); the Stoics five (pleasure/delight, distress, appetite and fear). Spinoza emphasizes pleasure, pain and desire; Sylvan Tomkins counts eight pairs of similar 'basic emotions' (enjoyment/joy, interest/excitement, surprise/startle, anger/rage, contempt/disgust, distress/anguish, fear/terror, shame/humiliation), 16 in all; and Plutchik (1980) argues for eight basic emotions, which, like primary colors, constitute the 'stuff' of more complex emotions (joy, sadness, trust, disgust, fear, anger, surprise, anticipation) (cf. 'Emotion classification', 2012). My point is not to delve into the plausibility of any of these theories—as this example is a parallel to both the nature/nurture arguments of the study of pleasure as well as of an appreciation of aesthetics—but rather to point out the social-constructedness of humans' acknowledgement of such a seemingly-elemental issue as 'basic emotions'.

When a body is holistically involved, engaged in partial or full exertion, kinesthetic awareness, tactile sensoriness, pressure, hearing, smell, taste all occupy the self to varying degrees, along with the visual, which some would describe as the 'primary sense' in the 21st century (cf. Serres, 2008). In the matter of aesthetics of the body, these are matters for philosophers, not scientists,[2] for sport and exercise philosophers more than for sport and exercise physiologists. Questions relating to taste and aesthetics, which relate culturally to pleasure—for example: *how does one culture characterize beauty?*—so far have been most successfully discussed in the realm of the social sciences and humanities.

The term 'aesthetics' implies pleasure, primarily because of its links to 'beauty'.[3] But art can be disturbing, challenging and disruptive—often the antithesis of beautiful. Might the appreciation of such art—of such puzzles of art—be pleasurable too? When a new way of apprehending the world (Berger, 2009) gains purchase, a whole new set of pleasures may accrue.[4]

But perhaps we need to nuance this concept of the aesthetic, of aesthetics, more carefully. For example, is there a distinction between a 'disinterested' appraisal of art (be that visual art or, in the case of skateboarding

Aesthetic Pleasure and Sport 153

audiences, performance/performative art) and the actual 'doing' of something (cf. Sheppard, 1989: 72)? After all, in the case of *Love + Guts* and Bowl-a-Rama (skateboarding art show and worldwide skateboarding competition, respectively), consuming art has been deliberately conflated with actual skating by the skaters/artists and tour producers. The popular culture merging of skating with art works serves to advantage both, but doesn't provide much clarity of concept.

Unpacking such a term as *aesthetics* helps to provide a bit of distinction between skateboarding, doing art related to skateboarding and appreciating both skateboarding and skateboarding art. Potential for pleasure(s) exists at any point, within any subject position. Sheppard points out that aesthetics have been viewed, generally, in one of two ways: looking at the intrinsic commonalities of the objects of our gazes {'all works of art have something in common' (1987: 2); and 'examin[ing] . . . the interest we take in such objects' (ibid.)}. If we go back to Walter Pater's studies of aesthetics in the Renaissance, we find a degree of openness toward the very objects of aesthetics:

> The objects with which æsthetic criticism deals, music, poetry, artistic and accomplished forms of human life, are indeed receptacles of so many powers or forces; they possess, like natural elements, so many virtues or qualities.
> . . . The æsthetic critic, then, regards all the objects with which he [sic] has to do, all works of art, and the fairer forms of nature and human life, as powers or forces producing pleasurable sensations. . . .
> (1966: 259)

Certainly, these broad categories surrounding aesthetics and the aesthetic object serve to contextualize what we are about in regard to pleasure and beauty in sport. Not only is 'art' the object of aesthetic scrutiny, but also things natural—and even human life—are considered within the aesthetic realm. For example, American football, though arguably a 'macho' type of game/sport that became the site of National Football League (NFL)-produced videos normalizing war within a patriarchal culture, also celebrated the artistry and aesthetic pleasures of 'beautiful' catches by receivers (accompanied by classical music) during the 1970s and 1980s (cf. Archer, 2010). The interplay of natural with human-created objects of aesthetic gaze combines with a cognitive facility to gain greater or lesser pleasure from differing objects of that gaze.

But, more specifically, '. . . when we experience a very special kind of pleasure—namely, aesthetic pleasure—it is legitimate to issue a positive critical judgment about that pleasure's object' (Battin et al., 1989: 199). Thus judgment is included in our assessment of pleasures: more complex and fascinating objects tend to arrest our attentions—drive our aesthetic passions—before simplistic and boring objects. In Kantian terms, the judgment of taste,

154 *Robert E. Rinehart*

then, is negotiated by our own fascination and 'mental facilities . . . being stimulated' (Battin et al., 1989: 37).

In this regard, Foucault's overall project and specific work on Manet bears mentioning. According to Bourriaud (2009: 13):

> Foucault is less interested by what the image says than by what it produces—the behaviours that it generates, and what it leaves barely seen among the social machinery in which it distributes bodies, spaces and utterances. . . . Foucault tries hard to articulate the implicit and invisible strategies that confine painting, to render visible what it shows, but equally what it conceals.

A major part of Foucault's project was thus to excavate significant moments from social movements and mores: in institutions, in sexuality and in art. In assessing Manet, Foucault has created a judgment of taste: that is, Manet's various techniques and strategies only serve to enhance Foucault's— and presumably, all viewers'—appreciation of the artistic project, as evidenced by Manet creating a rupture in the ways viewers 'see' art.

In contemporary culture, the concepts of taste (cf. Bourdieu, 1984), beauty and aesthetic pleasure certainly rely upon a modernist sense of binaried elitism that is interpellated with the existence of a popular acceptance of such naturalized structures as mass and elite culture, high and low art (and food, dress, sporting practices) and the hierarchical distinctions between such cultural sedimentations. There is within contemporary culture, then, an acceptance from most members of a given group of what is both proper and natural for membership in the groups. Studying only key 'moments' in key actors' lives (e.g. Manet, for Foucault) is somewhat akin to historians studying only generals and nation-state leaders. And yet the heightened aesthetic appeal of an object that is more complex and therefore fascinating provides the major paradox of studying massive, populist movements. Nevertheless, the overriding hegemonic acceptance of such a paradox—as well as a bedrock sense of democratic egalitarianism—necessitates deeper examination of presumably 'less profound' events, key figures and movements (see also Chapter 7 on mundanity).

While, obviously, the 'object' of study within this chapter (e.g. the *Love + Guts* art show and Bowl-a-Rama) will no doubt be less notable and remarked-upon than the work of Manet, the significance of its 'implicit and invisible strategies', at the level of pleasure, is worth noting.

But, in the case of both Manet and skateboarding art, the very objects of study—the art of the visual and the art of the performative—serve as an exemplar of what they produce.[5] How then, do skate-art configurations work to produce certain kinds of skating subjects: how are they configured within the social production of skater as rebel, skater as aesthete, skater as hedonistic pleasure-seeker?

In addition, what kinds of pleasures might accrue from viewing such art and such skating performances?[6] If we follow Droney—and I suggest his take is both savvy and insightful—we should look at this skateboarding art not simply visually, but also contextually. Droney (2010: 99) examines the confluence of street art and corporate marketing in Los Angeles: while the artists insist on their resistance to mainstream culture, there are 'ironies inherent in this ostensible resistance, and . . . artists are aware of, enjoy, and seek to maximize the ironic qualities of street art [where they create] . . . irreverent and self-contradictory artwork'.

In some ways, this chapter extends previous work done by Atencio and Beal (2011), who explored the *Beautiful Losers* exhibition in terms of a re-colonization of (disinterested) symbolic capital by and for 'outsider' masculine identity formations. Atencio and Beal see *Beautiful Losers* as a populist art form that 'creates a social order that privileges "renegade" or "outsider" masculinity' within 'which the creative classes and their dispositions [simultaneously] are privileged in post-Fordist economies' (2011: 2). However, my aim is to examine the *Love + Guts* show in terms of its opportunities for skaters', public and artists' pleasures (sometimes, these bifurcated identities merge within individuals). On the way, I intend to discuss tensions within the show and skateboarding subculture itself that may lead to pleasure and to displeasure.

IMPORTANCE OF PERFORMANCES
TO AUDIENCE PLEASURE

The apprehension of art changed, according to Foucault, with the work of Manet: Manet, like Flaubert, signifies to Foucault one of the 'figures of rupture', one of the 'tipping points in the field of knowledge' (Bourriaud, 2009: 13–14); this sense of 'rupture' resonates with Denzin's (1989) discussion of four types of epiphanies: major, cumulative, illuminative and relived. Each of these, primarily based on time differences and degrees of *aha!* or *Eureka!* moments, nevertheless contributes to significant life-changes in the individual.

To Foucault, Manet changed how viewers perceive and apprehend (and thus experience pleasure in) visual art: '. . . at the heart of the great change wrought by Manet to painting . . . [is the] invention of the picture-object, this reinsertion of the materiality of the canvas in that which is represented . . .' (Foucault 2009: 31). Certainly, musings about viewer positionality, lighting external or internal to the painting itself and spatiality within the limitations of a tangible canvas represent critical, epochal changes in art, perhaps akin to the perception of dimensionality on a flat surface. These insights, and the discussion of them, lead to a depth of pleasure that derives—yet is also separate—from a holistic appreciation of the work.

The skating art in *Love + Guts,* though not nearly so profoundly influential (as we shall see), still signifies and represents several key, albeit

156   Robert E. Rinehart

superficial, moments of pleasure. There is the derivative, influential and/or incidental relationship between the actual act of skating and its representation in the art. Cutri (2009) has explored the relationships between surfers who are artists (and artists who are surfers). The creative aspects of skateboarding and doing art about skateboarding certainly include possibilities for improvisation (cf. Caudwell, 2010), self-direction, pursuit of vision—all potentially pleasurable activities. In addition, there is a certain playing out of masculine hedonism in the early 21st century; a less overt response to layers of corporatization, consumerism and the barrage of advertising; and a retroactive shift in gender relations, which may result in pleasures both for those who welcome a return to well-defined gender roles and to those who relish uncertainty and change.

Much of this work locates within a dominant, late-capitalist moment, where popular art, music, video and so forth, proliferate. In reacting to and situating within these dominant subcultural moments and artifacts, as an art show, *Love + Guts*—and the individual participants—must perform accommodations, derivations and oppositions to such invisible but insistent cultural forms.[7] The studying 'down' of less profound,[8] mass cultural moments such as the *Love + Guts* exhibition (as opposed to the oeuvre of Manet, for example) demonstrates an aesthetic that paradoxically strives for subtle and ironic resistance within consumer culture (cf. Droney, 2010). This kind of a show may, in fact, illustrate a series of ordinary pleasures that exhibit the *range* between both 'high' cultural, cognitive and aspirational pleasures and more bodily, sensory and fundamental pleasures.

And yet we live in a time where modernist worldviews still hold great currency, and simple binaries proliferate. Perhaps many contemporary sportspersons have been inculcated with the modernist notion of a Cartesian mind-body dualism for so long that it has become an entrenched 'truth' that any individual is either primarily cognitive or primarily action-oriented. Thus there is, even within some academic cultures, a strong functionalist sense that results in this type of anti-intellectualism. Dewey's pragmatism, for example, has been wrong-headedly conflated with an impatience for action—just the opposite of his call for experiential learning to ground us in the senses. Eschewing intellect—in this case, for aesthetic appreciation—is just as foolhardy as solely relying upon intellect in favour of the physical/ sensual.

CONTEMPORARY AESTHETICS AT PLAY

In somewhat sharp contrast to Walter Pater's positive enthusiasm for peak, 'gemlike' moments in life, Paul Simon, in 'Dangling Conversation', got it right, at least for this contemporary age of anomie: we live in a time where *renditions* of visual impressions have overwhelmed even the visual impressions themselves. His lyric, alluding to the virtual shadows of real people and the paucity of genuine contact between human beings, lets the listener knows that the disconnect humans feel with each other is palpable, present and unresolvable. In a sense, Simon's lyric might work to highlight a series of pictures of pictures of pictures, not unlike Baudrillard's sense of a simulacrum: '. . . abstraction . . . is the generation by models of a real without origin or reality: a hyperreal' (1994: 1)—there is no mirror, no map, no origination, just simulation. For the artists of *Love + Guts*, theirs is second-order simulacrum, a commodity with an originary which is, of course, the skating itself. Their statuses as skaters are highly visible, both within the exhibition and in the marketing materials regarding it. But for many audiences, absent of skating experience, the third-order simulacrum is what is portrayed: the art itself becomes its own originary, without a 'real' original or with an imagined original, an artifact of a land constructed by popular culture and longing. Much of contemporary culture revolves around this modernist/ postmodernist dance, with the third-order simulacra relying on the cultural 'knowledge'—or effervescent belief[9]—that there once was an original.

Simon's 'Dangling Conversation' points to a disconnectedness between two lovers, two human beings trying to (re?)capture significance with each other despite a lack of overt affect, despite an encroaching flatness of contemporary life (cf. Bauman, 2003), despite contemporary social alienation and personal feelings of ennui. Compare this sentiment with Pater's 'to burn always with this hard, gemlike flame, to maintain this ecstasy, is success in life' (1966: 267): clearly, though both are talking about the objects of aesthetic gaze, the worldviews are sharply in contrast.

But the disconnection I am talking about between the apprehension of the Bowl-a-Rama skateboarding competition and the *Love + Guts* art exhibition is one between the primacy of experience and a simulacra of that experience: in either case, the effects repeat each other like the mirrors in a funhouse. Or rather, like mirrors in a funhouse reflecting a holographic shadow: the unexperienced appreciation of actual skating.

However—and this caveat matters in what might be seen as 'pleasure' in contemporary life—both types of experience themselves may still remain embodied and sensual and, on their own merits, create some degree of aesthetic appreciation for the viewer. Also, both are, in some senses, simultaneously primary and secondary experiences.

BENJAMIN'S AESTHETIC OF REPRODUCTION

The obvious contemporary layering of primary experience by both secondary and tertiary re-creation and experience harkens back to Walter Benjamin's thoughts regarding mechanical reproduction, but it also touches on Denzin's characterizations of a cinematic society in an age where excluded groups 'are victims of anhedonia, they are unable to experience pleasure' (1991: viii). The scopophilic gaze that contemporary audiences take for granted—often without pleasure accruing—must enter into discussion of an art show about

158 *Robert E. Rinehart*

skateboarding. Pater's heightened principle of 'gemlike flame', in the contemporary moment, recedes into a flatlining aesthetic moderation.

How do viewers to the *Love + Guts 2012* art exhibition experience pleasure? The complexity, craft and genius of the artwork is likely not comparable to Manet's, but this question of experiencing pleasure entails more than that: do skateboarders, like surfers, find describing the act of skating to be practically impossible? Thus, is the art an attempt to recapture the so-called ineffable nature of skating (somewhat akin to the 'stoke' that surfers claim), or the 'flow state' of 'optimal experience' (cf. Csíkszentmihályi, 1990, 1996), using a visual medium to somehow replicate two seemingly inexpressible cultural texts? If the very concept of pleasure has migrated from appreciation of *symbolized* skating, for example, to only becoming representations of acts of the actual skating itself, we have lost something quite valuable: we have given up the effort at facilitating appreciation by non-participants of experiences that they do not necessarily share. We have somehow bought into the hierarchical and naturalized rhetorics of 'ineffability' or 'stoke'.

To many touched by modern technologies, Walter Benjamin's conception of exactitude between copies sings out as an obvious truth: as we reproduce actual lived experience, the reproduction—even if an exact copy in every way but one: for example, the temporal element—drops farther away from some of the affective devices of the actual lived experience. And it matters little whether the reproduction is visual, auditory, tactile or of any of the other dozens of ways humans apprehend and/or comprehend the world— the reproduction is still a reproduction.

The fact remains, however: though we eschew anything other than primary experience, in our paradoxically coterminous society, we mostly touch, smell see, and/or hear the world through the secondary, the tertiary and nearly endless echoes (cf. Battin et al., 1989). Contemporary humans increasingly experience the world at a second, third or fourth remove. And, in a lived experience that grows more technologically complex, virtual worlds rush to emulate the sensate, the sensuous, the primal. Thus, the actual playing of a sport or exerting ourselves in a physical activity conveys us back to the primacy of aesthetic, embodied enjoyment like little else in contemporary life. And yet, in contemporary society, we can also learn to appreciate non-direct experience. This is the stuff of pleasure at a second, third or fourth remove in the 21st century.

While Benjamin's essay concerns mechanical reproduction of art works, implying an exactitude from the original to the reproduction that is historically remarkable, current views of such 'reproduction' include accurate electronic, technologically seamless reproduction creating visual, auditory and frequently other sensual cultural 'memories'. The move to a humanly undetectable reproduction makes the 'authenticity' of primary or secondary 'experience'—at the level of human sensory reception and detection— a somewhat moot point, since secondary experience is, for all intents and

Aesthetic Pleasure and Sport 159

purposes, indistinguishable from its source (if in fact there is a detectable source or originary).

Furthermore, this move calls into question the rigid borders we have culturally drawn around what counts as the 'aesthetic'. The reproduction itself is an event, just as the *being thereness* of live attendance is an event—both fraught with value, pleasure and their own particular, idiosyncratic beauties and values (cf. Rinehart, 1998a). Still, as Bourdieu (1984) cautions us, we constantly compare experiences and rank their statuses accordingly. One of the concerns of this chapter is how we ascertain and rank various pleasures.

Witness, for example, the televisual experience of a 2012 London Olympics event. There is pleasure in a New Zealander being able to 'see'—albeit on taped delay—Usain Bolt winning the 100 meters (see Chapter 8), or Kiwi darling Valerie Adams' valiant effort putting the shot, since the reproduction of its 'happening' (again and again) is more real in many ways than actually having been a spectator at the event (cf. Baudrillard, 2002)—which is itself removed from actually being Adams, actually performing the event.

Some of the ways watching Valerie Adams on television[10] is more 'real' include: shared experiential memories with a majority of the New Zealand public (to be nostalgically recovered later); deeply imbedded 'epiphanic' (and later, epigramic/totemic) images from Adams' moments of glory; individual and group audience effects that result in emotions and affect such as collective disappointment, pride and joy at the Valerie Adams' 'story',[11] which was readily known, reproduced, consumed and re-reproduced (that is, gone into the pantheon of 'sport stories' a culturally literate Kiwi draws from) for and by a Kiwi viewing public, press and popular culture. Knowing the 'story' enhanced one's status, and thus, by extension, one's pleasure in being culturally competent. However, there is a limited audience for *Love + Guts 2012*: it lacks the massified reach of the London Olympics 2012 or, really, anything so televised.

BAUMAN'S AESTHETIC FLATNESS

> . . . Sound and sight seem to make equal parts of these impressions.
> . . . The next memory . . . was much more robust; it was highly sensual.
> . . . It still makes me feel warm; as if everything were ripe; humming;
> sunny; smelling so many smells at once. . . . The buzz, the croon, the smell, all seemed to press voluptuously against some membrane; not to burst it; but to hum round one such a complete rapture of pleasure that I stopped, smelt; looked.
> But again I cannot describe that rapture. It was rapture rather than ecstasy.
>
> —Virginia Woolf, from *Moments of Being*, 1985: 66.

160 *Robert E. Rinehart*

This layering of primary, secondary and tertiary experience—that is, the creation of hierarchies—also reflects what Zygmunt Bauman sees as a 'consumer life [that] favours lightness and speed' (2003: 49). This second connection between the produced, the reproduced and the consumer is less obvious than the simple reproduction of primary artifacts: Bauman speaks of a *homo consumens*, a contemporary being that doesn't just live to buy and accumulate, but that buys, uses, disposes and buys more, a being that gains pleasure from buying, using, disposing of and re-buying.

In this way, the accumulation of material culture within the social sciences has become a fast and rather flattened scape for the reproduction of that which is visual: photos, paintings, 'high' and 'low' art, video technology and so forth, proliferate within the visual. Similarly, Gillian Rose writes of DeBord's 'society of the spectacle', and of most contemporary culture becoming ensnared in an enhanced recognition—if not appreciation—of visual culture: 'the ways in which the visual is part of social life' (Rose 2012: 4). Yet without material 'distinction'—which runs counter to Bourdieu's thesis, in some key ways—the flattening of affective *response* remains the most salient feature in this onslaught of visual images.

Of course, Virginia Woolf's discussion of children's ability to recapture 'strong memories' (1985: 67) or 'exceptional moments' (1985: 71) runs counter to Bauman's thesis: Bauman is talking about a 21st-century 'aesthetic' for and by adults; Woolf harkens to a time of innocence and unfiltered experience, a time, perhaps, that is pre-self-conscious:

> . . . the peculiarity of these two strong memories is that each was very simple. I am hardly aware of myself, but only of the sensation. I am only the container of the feeling of ecstasy, of the feeling of rapture. Perhaps this is characteristic of all childhood memories; perhaps it accounts for their strength. Later we add to feelings much that makes them more complex; and therefore less strong; or if not less strong, less isolated, less complete. (1985: 67)

Woolf's layering adds the possibility that, as Bauman has intimated, the *homo consumens* is flattened by complexity, by too much 'stuff', which makes the experience of each set of 'stuff' less immediate, less powerful. This nuanced, contextualized reading of historical placement matters: it is, I think, what Rose means when she writes of 'the ways in which the visual is part of social life' (2012: 4), because of course the visual has *always* been a part of social life, just not in its current assemblage. In this regard, perhaps it is fruitful to examine sites of visual research more fully.

When Rose speaks about a critical visual methodology, she looks at three sites: the 'site of production . . . the image itself . . . and . . . its audiencing' (2012: 19). For *Love + Guts 2012*, the production, of course, is fundamentally the artist/skateboarders.[12] The image itself—examination of some of the dominant as well as recessive meanings—is, of course, a part of the

Aesthetic Pleasure and Sport   161

evidence of this study, though it seems a middle ground between production and consumption. However, the site of audiencing—in terms of the 'image encounter[ing] its spectators or users' (ibid.) in relation to *Love + Guts* and Bowl-a-Rama—is of primary interest for this case study. 'Audiencing' is a flattened space that celebrates an ephemeral engagement, snap judgement(s) and the alacrity of disposable experiences—or is it?

PATTERNS IN A SNAPSHOT ETHNOGRAPHY

Some of the photos[13] of the artwork at the travelling *Love + Guts* show in Wellington, New Zealand, on display at Manky Chops gallery from February 9–12, 2012—and, of course, the *being there* to take such photographs—comprise the bulk of the object of this case study. *Love + Guts* has been going on since 2005: it began in Southern California, said to be the child of founders Steve Olson, Lance Mountain and Pat Ngoho ('Pat Ngoho|What's your boggle?' 2012). The 2012 incarnation of this show, held at a temporary storefront sponsored by the Manky Chops gallery (the main gallery is on Cuba Street; this temporary gallery is across the street, roughly, from where the Bowl-a-Rama occurs), was juxtaposed rather seamlessly with a worldwide skateboarding tour (Bowl-a-Rama), and sponsored by sporting eyewear and apparel manufacturer Oakley: the show itself is an attempt to make more overt the artistic, improvisational skater-self blend with the embodiment and physicality of actual skating (cf. Cutri, 2009).

In the sense of writing an ethnography into existence, the 'stuff' of this piece is considered a 'snapshot' ethnography: that is, it is a non-traditional, non-exotic locale wherein compressed time is a major element of the object of the ethnography (Janzen, 2008; Jeffrey and Troman, 2004; Kupritz, 1998; Walford, 1991, 2001). Of course, there are differences between 'compressed', 'snapshot', 'blitzkrieg' (cf. Rist, 1980, cited in Jeffrey and Troman, 2004), 'zooming' and 'documentary' ethnographic approaches, as Jeffrey and Troman (2004) distinguish. But in the current snapshot examination, *Love + Guts* (the exhibition), already its own text, becomes a modified text, and I am the modifier. When you, an audience of readers, receive my modifications/interpretations, you further alter its makeup, values, ethos. In that sense, it could be argued, all ethnography is a form of 'snapshot' ethnography, as it always is co-created, by the object of the writing, the author(s) of the writing and the reader(s), all of whom bring to the work different sensibilities: but that discussion is for another time.

When contemporary sport forms trumpet their positions of opposition or sell themselves by announcing how they are uncommon, one should approach their rhetoric with a certain healthy dose of skepticism. Indeed, the louder they proclaim that they are anti-corporate (and yet are co-actors in the dance of *homo consumens)*, the more they may lead one to suspect that they protest too mightily. Usually, they are not only a part of what

162   *Robert E. Rinehart*

Becky Beal has termed 'endemic' advertising—'ad placement where it is native or natural to its market' (McFarlin, 2012)—but also a part of a symbiotic 'dance' (Beal, cited in Cutri, 2006) between endemic and non-endemic (or 'demographic') advertising. In this mutually-beneficial relationship, the endemics, coming from a position of 'insider' status in the market, use the non-endemics' financial capital to gain market share. The non-endemics gain new niche markets by their association with what is seen by insider consumers as more 'authentically' placed companies. They tend to use the mantle of 'authenticity' or 'originary' (as opposed to 'posers/poseurs' and 'pretenders'), which brings up the question of corporate 'authenticity': but skateboarders, though they have a history, reinvent that political history every generation.

What Beal has referred to as the 'dance' between endemics and non-endemics is played out in the *Love + Guts* world exhibition of skateboard art. This show 'in 2007 . . . formed a partnership with Oakley' ('Pat Ngoho', 2012), which resulted in a skateboarding competition that is accompanied by *Love + Guts*. While Oakley is associated loosely with an alternative sporting market through its primary sales item, sunglasses for sportspersons, it would probably be classified more toward the side of non-endemic *within* the niche of skateboarding: its Frogskins line of sunglasses, where they 'resurrected the original tooling from the early' 80s', begins at US$120 ('Oakley Men's Store', 2012), not above the line for middle- to upper-class skaters, but certainly also not a *de rigueur* status/identity marker. So Oakley's contribution certainly forms a certain portion of the contemporary skateboarder's sense of pleasure.

As well as the unstated yet assumed sensual linkages between sporting sunglasses—originally created for a Motocross (MX) niche market in the mid-1970s—and skateboarding,[14] there is an implicit assumption among these relatively new, action, extreme, alternative sport forms that they *naturally* link with both music and art. The explicit rendering of music with sporting contests could arguably be codified at least as far back as the 'modernist' age, as Pierre de Coubertin's 1906 'Consultative Conference on Art, Letters, and Sport' suggested that

> . . . the IOC should create 'five contests of architecture, sculpture, music, painting and literature for original works directly inspired by sport, such contests henceforth to become an integral part of the celebration of each Olympiad'. (de Coubertin, 2012)

In addition, Leni Reifenstahl's documentary use of Herbert Windt's stirring, militaristic accompaniment in the visually-stimulating and aesthetically-appealing 1936 Olympic and Third Reich tribute, *Olympia* (Riefenstahl, 1938) brought a nationalistic and patriotic pleasure to many of its viewers. So, while alternative sports sponsors—and some participants—have indicated that music and sport combinations are a new innovation for sport (linking back to 'music videos' perhaps), history shows it differently.

Aesthetic Pleasure and Sport   163

There is an interesting feel to *Love + Guts*, especially juxtaposed with the actual skating event. Borne by artistic sensibilities, skateboarding (and other so-called alternative sports) and skateboarders proclaim their connection to the spontaneous, to the avant-garde, to resistance to utilitarian instrumentality: in other words, the ethos of skateboarding and other extreme sports has historically stemmed from an anti-authoritarian stance where the process of doing the activity holds more weight than the end result. This stereotypical, populist view of skateboarding and skateboarders aligns with a populist, stereotypical view of art and artists (though, in both cases, Bauman's sense of an omniscient consumer culture is more the standard). As an aside, the populist and stereotypical views of both skateboarding and art are highly idealistic and romanticized notions, reinforced by the tales of 'starving artists' and 'street kids rising out of the ashes' which prevail in the Western world's media representations of creative endeavors.

But the rhetorical devices proliferate within skateboarding art, and, as, Wetherell has asserted, patterns exist: '. . . affect does display strong pushes for pattern as well as signaling trouble and disturbance in existing patterns' (2012: 13). This is a significant statement, if only to remind us that discerning patterns within what appears to be (perhaps deliberately) the chaotic may require a new sort of seeing.

Wetherell also points out that these

> . . . interweaving patterns often form affective ruts. . . . Swirling and dissolving emotion . . . precipitates in social formations, becoming distinct ways of doing things, familiar figurations repeated often *ad nauseam*. (2012: 14)

I suggest that the *Love + Guts* show has followed a pattern of collective affect (cf. Verkaaik, 2003) and a form of Durkheimian 'collective effervescence' (1976)—affect, emotion and identification with both skateboarding and art—that 'people experience . . . [which] make them do things they usually would not do' (Verkaaik, 2003: 17). Rather than totally decrying such postmodern sites as *Love + Guts*, however, Stjepan Meštrović suggests that Durkheim might embrace them, perhaps seeing them as 'sacred site[s]' that celebrate 'the genuinely human sentiments' surrounding them (1992: 134). Moreover, much like the discussion of skateboarding art in Southern California (Atencio and Beal, 2011), the *Love + Guts* version is calculated to produce this collective affect among a select group of male skaters. For while the art works are aesthetically marginal, the effects of them work to produce an insider knowledge and feeling that provides a close-knit (mostly) boys' club.

The 'patterns', then, emerging from this type of popular cultural exhibition (both Bowl-a-Rama and *Love + Guts 2012*) include membership in a boys' club that proclaims its anti-establishment status while embracing the rewards of establishment semi-membership. Viewers to the exhibition experience pleasure on one level at 'seeing behind the curtain', understanding

164   *Robert E. Rinehart*

the ambivalent dynamics that make a worldwide tour like this happen—and then by pretending to forget. Their pleasure is so transitory and superficial that it requires no real depth, no anguish at the hypocrisy, no self-reflexive angst: seeing the art is just another 'moment' within the pattern of flatness. But the insider status that accrues from having been to the competition, having seen the exhibition first-hand, generates a heightened form of capital for audiences.

Within the *Love + Guts* art show, as its audience may browse through it, there is an abiding overall sense of counter-hegemonic display and oppositional worldview while, simultaneously, the show is sponsored by Oakley and driven financially by the dollars of *non-edgy* wannabe pseudo-dropouts. Each piece itself displays multiple meanings and multiple readings. However, on the face of it, this show itself is a capable demonstration of Beal's point regarding endemic/non-endemic tensions, and much of the artwork appears satisfying because of its very predictability.

LOVE + GUTS 'TEXTS'

The work from *Love + Guts 2012* is created by—and primarily for—male skaters only. At some level, the artwork is intended for their shared pleasures. It is little surprise then, that the expected and predictable themes largely reflect a dominant male discourse, and adherence to what Hughes and Coakley (1991) termed the 'sport ethic'.[15] Paradoxically, though framed within a counter-hegemonic discourse (e.g. Atencio and Beal, 2011; Beal, 1996; Droney, 2010; Rinehart, 2005), these examples of skateboarding remain somewhat tame, contained, and consistent within larger discourses of hyper-masculinity. From a broader view, however, the malleability of the skateboarders/artists to align with such dominant themes reduces the quality of the art to a level that makes most, if not all, of the works non-critical 'commercial art'. There is nothing inherently wrong with 'commercial art', except when it is housed in a vehicle—like the *Love + Guts* show, aligned with Bowl-a-Rama—that protests its oppositionality to normative culture, to the very enterprise of commerce.

While the distinction between commercial art and 'message' art (art for social justice, as one example) itself is fraught with problems—not the least of which is a non-critical acceptance of an implied high/low art distinction—it also means that the art, while professing to be avant-garde and boundary pushing, merely works as a tool for self-promotion. Though some of the art is visually stimulating, as social commentary—and a formation to push social justice through a sport-art dynamic—little of it brings any new, oppositional or even reflexive stances to this new amalgam called 'skateboard art'.

I now look at selected representative photos of pieces of art from the *Love + Guts* exhibition in Wellington, 2012, in terms of three major motifs: *nostalgia*

Aesthetic Pleasure and Sport 165

in skateboarding, pain and suffering in the self-objectifying object, and *the place of girls and women.* I will briefly discuss these strains, with fairly superficial and dominant readings, using visual exemplars from the show.

NOSTALGIA IN SKATEBOARDING/PAEANS TO SKATEBOARDING

The brief introduction to the Manky Chops Gallery (see Figure 10.1), which exhibited *Love and Guts*, works to heighten the sense of nostalgia and respect for 1970s skateboarding culture. The title of the exhibition is 'Empty Culture: An Artistic Rendition of the Swimming Pool', so many of the art-works include some reference to backyard (California) swimming pools.

In an overt homage to the celebrated film *Dogtown and Z Boys*, the nostalgic trope of emptying a backyard pool and skating it becomes further reified. The occasional use of capitalization lends a quirky credence to the poster, which is meant to establish a worshipful tone towards these then-teenagers:

> . . . they would . . . drain the remaining water so they could skate it while the house owners were out. Hunting out new pools quickly became an obsession when a good pool would become too crowded, or the neighbours called the Cops . . . and so, vertical skateboarding was born, and influential hard core pool skaters transformed skateboarding into the minor religion that it is today.

This was a time that arguably has been recreated and self-valorized, often by males in their 40s or 50s, as a 'golden age' for skateboarding, and, since they run many of the companies with the financial clout to skew the message, their readings of several motifs from the past tend to become dominant.

Toby Jenkins' 'Solitude' (see Figure 10.2) is a painting of the wall of a drained-out backyard swimming pool, with the distorted glass housing for the light recalling the 1970s. The blue tiling below the pool coping also is from that decade—the aquamarine blue is a signifier of the 'California back-yard swimming pool lifestyle' in so many popular culture artifacts—and it cuts through the color choices of many of the other artists in the show. The heightened mirror-effect on the underwater light cover, with an idealized skateboarder dropping in, adds to the nostalgic mood of the piece. The viewer is meant to put himself (and, at *Love + Guts*, they are all *hims*) into the place of the skater dropping in—but, as in Manet's *Bar at the Folies-Bergere*, the perspective of an absented and/or reflected artist situates the viewer in a visual conundrum (cf. Foucault, 2009). This perspective use of an in-pool light fixture as the reflective device provides both nostalgia for skating and a postmodern sense of bricolage within the art itself. These are

Figure 10.1 Outside Manky Chops Gallery
Photo: R. Rinehart, February 2012

Aesthetic Pleasure and Sport 167

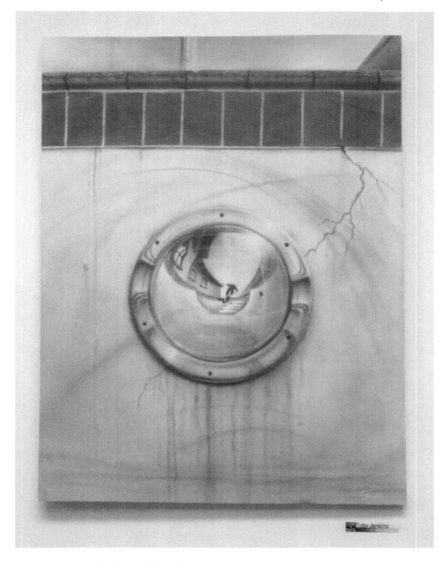

Figure 10.2 'Solitude', Toby Jenkins, artist
Source: http://manualmagazine.com/2012/02/09/2012-love-and-guts-exhibition-catalogue/
2012-loveandguts_20/ Accessed 10/09/12

sites for potential celebration of a pleasurable, satisfying sense of pleasure—
pleasure that seemingly will last into old age.

Mike Spittlehouse's 'Forever Rolling' (see Figure 10.3 top) and 'Mike's Will' (see Figure 10.3 bottom) could exemplify a Westernized stance toward aging—one where the skater resists aging by skating to the very end. The

Figure 10.3 'Forever Rolling' and 'Mike's Will', Mike Spittlehouse, artist
Source: http://manualmagazine.com/2012/02/09/2012-love-and-guts-exhibition-catalogue/2012-loveandguts_02/ Accessed 10/09/12

Aesthetic Pleasure and Sport   169

cartoon-like rendition of both the skater in the wheelchair and the distorted backyard swimming pool—and the perfect echoes of aquamarine with sky, pool, shirt, tiling—lend a whimsical, childlike feature to the work. In addition, the fact that the chaired man's eyes cannot be seen creates a universal mystique to his gesture, as if all aging male skaters will easily identify with his attitude of self-sacrifice in the name of skateboarding (though he is not really skateboarding).

In the second piece, the wall of a swimming pool is tagged with 'Take my ashes when I'm gone, mix with cement and make a coping block Mike'. The theme of nostalgia and an homage to the omniscience of skateboarding points to an idealist reading that insiders to skateboarding are, in Belinda Wheaton's (2000) term, 'lifestyle' sport participants who tend to exemplify the mainstream sport ethic, having incorporated many of the ethos into their everyday lived lives. For example, some (primarily male) loyalists to various cricket programs and football clubs (in Germany and Argentina) have requested that their remains be buried underneath or near the playing field.[16] The precept that this dedication to sport reflects is that 'Being an athlete involves refusing to accept limits in the pursuit of possibilities' (Hughes and Coakley, 1991: 363).

Clearly, the rhetorics of Spittlehouse's two works resonate with the nostalgic and single-minded logics that a committed member of the subculture of skateboarding might be expected to demonstrate. This ideological 'statement', housed within the _Love + Guts_ exhibition, prompts young skaters to idealize such nostalgic single-mindedness, but also to replicate narrow and constraining gendered identities (which resonates with _the place of girls and women_, below).

Chad Ford's series of duplicated photographs (see Figure 10.4), set in a sextych, attempts to recall parts of the decades of the 60s and perhaps 70s: there are girls in rather conservative bathing suits sitting on the edge of a drained (aquamarine) backyard pool, there are children in a blowup (aquamarine) wading pool (which really has nothing to do with skateboarding), there is what appears as a real-estate advertisement for a California-lifestyle home, featuring the requisite backyard pool and lolling sunbathing women—but the prominent feature is the sign that informs the viewer that there is a bomb shelter in the backyard. During the early 60s, it must be recalled, American children were witness to the Cuban missile crisis, and in California early 'survivalists' constructed underground bomb shelters in case of a nuclear attack.

The edge between a fond recollection of those childhood fears and the pleasure at surviving that time—indeed, hedonistically flourishing despite it!—resonates with older Americans, but also is a part of the cultural baggage that is repeated again and again in popular culture.

Ford's display and placement of the photos also recalls a nostalgic past: like the arranged photos of a family, these paralleled pieces (in their simple, rustic frames) subtly echo the decade of the 60s (skateboarding long past),

Figure 10.4 'Drain it, ride it'; 'Early Release'; 'Dive In'; 'Dive In'; 'Early Release'; 'Drain it, ride it', Chad Ford, artist
Source: http://manualmagazine.com/2012/02/09/2012-love-and-guts-exhibition-catalogue/2012-loveandguts_25/ Accessed 6/3/13

but with a difference: the photos are not artistic, presumably not staged as art. These are contextualizing photos, photos meant to elicit affect for the time, for the imagined and imaginary past (cf. Shaw, 1989).

PAIN AND SUFFERING IN THE SELF-OBJECTIFYING OBJECT

> The depersonalization that begins in sexual objectification is what makes violence possible; for once you have made a person out to be a thing, you can do anything to it you want.
> —John Stoltenberg, 1990, *Refusing to be a Man*: 54–55.

Figure 10.5 'Get rotten', Brydie Hall, artist
Source: http://manualmagazine.com/2012/02/09/2012-love-and-guts-exhibition-catalogue/2012-loveandguts_15/ Accessed 10/09/12

172 *Robert E. Rinehart*

'Get Rotten' (Figure 10.5), by Brydie Hall, is a depiction of an extracted tooth superimposed over a swirling mass of skulls. This work indicates a visual acceptance of pain and injury—which are seen as an inevitable part of the life of skaters. Presumably, this is an indication of the acceptance of pain and decay, all swirling down into a Styxian whirlpool filled with skeletons, bottles of poisons and gravestone markers with RIP written across them. This mass of decline is overseen by a large tooth with a single seeing eyeball and the words 'Get Rotten' in front of a cartoon skyline of a city. There are also bats flying above the city. All these elements combine to present the impression—when this art is aligned within the *Love + Guts 2012* show—of city street skaters who are risking their very bodies for skateboarding.

There is an alignment with the masculine motif of celebrating the tough, the stolid, the resolute, but there is more at play here: there is a singular moment of acceptance of self-violence. As Stoltenberg reminds us,

> . . . a man shuts off his capacity for ethical empathy—whatever capacity he may ever have had—in order to commit an act of depersonalization that is 'gratifying' essentially because it functions to fulfill his sense of a selfhood that is authentically male. (1990: 55)

But it doesn't stop there: the 'pleasure' that a man derives from harming others whom he has depersonalized ultimately results in grievous self-harm—which, like picking at a scab, is at some level 'pleasurable', but which, in the last instance, becomes an act of self-abnegation. Pleasure, as de Sade reminds us (Gillette, 2005) depends upon its obverse—pain—for its very existence.

It is not apparent that Brydie Hall intended these reflections upon his work, but when the work is coupled with other works that celebrate self-harming, the viewer of art must engage, as an act of aesthetic involvement.

Jake Mein's photo of a bleeding palm, titled 'Adro hand' (Figure 10.6) shows the hand thrust forward pridefully towards the camera, effectively covering the face of its owner. The hand itself becomes disembodied, as if the pain that is occurring can be somehow compartmentalized from the visual reds of the blood. Set within three other works, Mein's 'Adro hand' is perhaps the most arresting image.

This work again indicates a depersonalized objectivity that glorifies pain and suffering. This ethos aligns neatly with Hughes and Coakley's sport ethic that an athlete will accept risks and play through pain. This is doubly reinforced in a male sport culture where evidence of injury signifies alignment with the dominant ethos of how to become a 'proper' sportsperson. The disembodiment of body parts—the synechdochic representation of the bloody hand for the bloodied and resilient whole person, for example—works in this piece to form an afterimage of 'battle-hardened' male skater. This is, of course, both self-harmful and other-harmful (as it models hyper-stoicism), and is exclusionary of females (cf. Davis, 1997).

Figure 10.6 'Adro hand', Jake Mein, photographer
Source: http://manualmagazine.com/2012/02/09/2012-love-and-guts-exhibition-catalogue/2012-loveandguts_13/ Accessed 10/09/12

THE PLACE OF GIRLS AND WOMEN IN *LOVE + GUTS 2012*

Mostly, girls and women are absent. The aesthetic of *Love + Guts* is exclusionary of females. The artwork is generally of abstractions, male subjects or male subjects with female as object. As can be seen from some of these photos of selected artwork, women can loll around a pool, supplying audience for the males, or women can be completely absented. But women can also be the sexualized objects that work to demonstrate, reproduce and reify male supremacy (cf. Stoltenberg, 1990). There are several depictions of nude or semi-nude females, cartooned caricatures detached from the skateboarding sub-culture, as if the skating pool of the 1960s and 70s was a golden age for male supremacy, not the advent of a global women's liberation movement.

Shannon Rush's 'Untitled' (Figure 10.7) depicts a pointy-headed female, sitting, with sagging breasts drooping across her front, legs cut off at the ankles and a heart-shape settled into her crotch. It is a line drawing, and it passes as amusing and inoffensive in a grouping of four (three drawings: in addition to 'Untitled', one with 24 aligned cartoon faces; another featuring a stack of bodies in a pyramid; the fourth piece is a t-shirt with three nun-like—or monk-like—faces and a cross emblazoned across a black field). It is its very mundanity, its ordinariness, that perplexes: why must

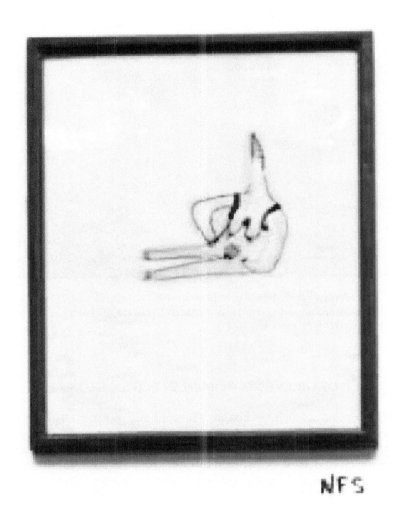

Figure 10.7 'Untitled', Shannon Rush, artist
Source: http://manualmagazine.com/2012/02/09/2012-love-and-guts-exhibition-catalogue/2012-loveandguts_17/ Accessed 18/03/13

the drawn person be naked, why the heart at the crotch? It is perhaps the taken-for-granted-ness of the objectification, the severed feet, the helplessness of the figure, that is most disturbing. This is not a female form that in any way demonstrates empowerment, or, for that matter, any life-affirming characteristics. This is a victim, an immobile object of the viewer's gaze.

Similarly, Wade Burkit's 'Drawings' (Figure 10.8) is carelessly rendered: the figure is a disembodied set of line-drawn breasts, partially nippled, with

Aesthetic Pleasure and Sport   175

Figure 10.8 'Drawings', Wade Burkit, artist
Source: http://manualmagazine.com/2012/02/09/2012-love-and-guts-exhibition-catalogue/2012-loveandguts_09/ Accessed 18/03/13

no abdomen or body behind—just a simple right edge that could be an arm, could be a torso. The woman, cigarette signifying a certain comfort or perhaps swagger, has raven hair, full thick lips (which, stereotypically, may signify a person of color), one heavily made-up right eye, and a black and closed left eye. It is disturbing, but not as social commentary: it disturbs in the utter repetition of the absence—again—of any females in the show who are empowered, strong, assertive, equal to males. This object of our gaze, apparently, *is* a bit 'sassy', and, in fact, may have been taught a lesson: she

Figure 10.9 'Non Compliance' and 'Six Fingers', Cam Ward, artist
Source: http://manualmagazine.com/2012/02/09/2012-love-and-guts-exhibition-catalogue/2012-loveandguts_08/ Accessed 10/09/12

has been punched in the left eye perhaps because of her attempts at swagger (a black eye is not a usual skateboarding 'injury').

Cam Ward's 'Non Compliance' (see Figure 10.9 left) and 'Six fingers' (see Figure 10.9 right) reflect a male-centered outlook sometimes seen elsewhere in prison art shows: an adolescent obsession with caricatures of females and the placement of females within their male-dominant worlds. It has antecedents in woodcuts from the Kama Sutra, but the connection to skateboarding is rather oblique, if present at all, and smacks of a consumerist cynicism that 'sex sells'. By using a caricatured naked female performing fellatio, and another of a male dominating a female, Ward performs an act of marginalization of girls and women—from everyday society and from skateboarding, except as sex objects.

ONE CONCLUSION: A MALE AESTHETICS OF PLEASURE

The alignment of sport and art via marketing is not a new innovation—yet Oakley and the other sponsors promote *Love + Guts* as a transgressive, hip, counter-culture art show that resists dominant sport formations and ethos. But when we look at the actual art, we can see that it reflects dominant, mainstream values—adherence to the sport ethic, patriarchal hegemony, and even misogynist stances—and that, at its core, it is yet another reproduction of a boy's club of sport formations. Are there, as in Dorney's fieldwork in urban Los Angeles' street art, ironic flashes that enhance and complicate the pleasure of viewing? Or has the realization of this sport/art/marketing matrix resulted in a cynical, lowest-common-denominator type of massified 'art' that reflects a modernist kitsch? Or—and more likely—is the result of *Love + Guts* more complicated, more fluid, more dynamic than the simple binaries detailed here?

This skateboarding art show gains and engenders pleasure for its participants—the skating artists, the competitive skaters—but it also reifies a subject-object dynamic that is very satisfying for adolescent males: if we can subjugate girls and women, they will help to reinforce the gender order. Housing this ethos within a dynamic of publicly accessible art provides a training ground for young misogynists, and it hegemonically reinforces a form of sexual and gendered stratification that proclaims the 'naturalness', the seamless commonsensical nature, of these power relations. Acceptance of such images—and it is hard to resist them—concomitantly means an acceptance of a stultifying and restrictive gender binary.

Moreover, many of the works reflect consumerist, televisual, second-level culture and produce, as a whole, the effects of alienation, elitism and anomie from others, but, fundamentally, from self. They hierarchize the skating over the art, rather than producing the declared intended effects of bringing art to the fore in skating circles—that is, rather than challenging the so-called hard masculinities with a softer vision of artistic and aesthetic masculinity, they accede to the dominant, stereotypical images of sporting male culture.

In addition, rather than contesting standard hegemonic forms of 'easy pleasure', this traveling skateboarding art is akin to a boy's club (like the barbershop of old) where what it is to be a man is highly dependent upon the suppression of everyone else. Small pleasures accrue to the winners; unsatisfactory hopes accrue for everyone else, and some (like girls and women) are stampeded—and lost—in the process.

NOTES

1. It is of interest, of course, that the example of bullfighting centers on an assumption of maleness in sport. Western 'sport', by definition almost, has been framed and claimed by and for men. Thus, the examination of an aesthetic or aesthetic beauty—stereotypically connoted as softer, subjective and 'female'—within a male-dominant sport like skateboarding works to disrupt naturalized expectations.
2. And yet Thrift (cf. 2008), Law (cf. 2004), Latour (cf. 2005) and others have attempted to classify and categorize such matters of aesthetics, taste and distinction.

178   *Robert E. Rinehart*

3. For an extended discussion of general aesthetics (and pleasure), see Sheppard 1989 and Battin et al., 1989; for a look at postmodern aesthetics, see, e.g. Foster 1983).
4. These new ways of apprehension may be due to technological advances, new ways of 'seeing' or, in many cases, both.
5. This chapter will only look at the appreciation of both skateboarding art and skateboarding, not at the *doing of* skateboarding and skateboarding art.
6. I have made the argument elsewhere (Rinehart, 1998) that sporting performance could be assessed in terms of its performative aspects: like performance art, it is embodied, practiced, choreographed, improvisational and requires audience for its display.
7. See Raymond Williams, *Marxism and Literature*, for classic delineations of dominant, residual and emergent categories of cultural formations.
8. Discussions of less or more profound, historical, significant, notable or 'classic' are fraught with political, cultural and virtual power relations, which are beyond the scope of this chapter. However, some sources might include: Fukuyama, 1989; Lowenthal, 1985; Stewart, 1993; Stewart, 2007.
9. The concept of effervescence, of course, stems from Durkheim's work on religion and the relationships of peoples to their totemic animal or vegetable. See Durkheim (1976). I am grateful to Oskar Verkaaik (2003) for triggering this connection while pointing to the fun that collectives experience while performing acts of 'collective aggression' and 'ethnocide'.
10. Clearly, the visual technologies—and their reception—create, promote and satisfy different elements of consumption. My intention is not to conflate two-dimensional recreations such as photographs, television, film, video and internet modalities, or to envision a template of compare/contrast between these offerings. Rather, I am simply attempting to describe, from an audience point of view, some of the elements of experiencing consumption of such popular culture that may result in identifiable pleasures. Thus, I draw from cinematic, television and other kinds of visual studies for a quite different purpose than description. The fact remains, however, that there are significant, noticeable and detectable differences in the quality of electronic production in presenting an Olympics for viewer consumption: witness some of the technical and logistical practices of broadcasts ranging from Melbourne 1956 to Sydney 2000 (cf. Wenn, 2000).
11. The story of Valerie Adams, already a household name in New Zealand before the 2012 Olympics, included her somewhat disappointing silver medal placement in the shotput, the Belarus competitor testing positive for drugs and Adams subsequently, belatedly (and contentiously), receiving the gold medal weeks later: 'The International Olympic Committee said Ostapchuk tested positive for the steroid metenolon' (Wilson, 2012). Many viewers in New Zealand were understandably moved to believe that Adams had been cheated of the moment on the victory stand and all that meant.
12. Though of course a case could be made that the various art galleries (Manky Chops in Wellington, e.g.) are 'producers' as well, but this is wandering rather far afield.
13. I took photos of the art on the wall, mostly as triggers for the feel, heft and ambience of the exhibition. For this chapter, I have used the photographs of the artwork from the Manual Magazine 'Love + Guts exhibition' website (http://manualmagazine.com/2012/02/09/2012-love-and-guts-exhibition-catalogue/2012-loveandguts), accessed between September 2012 and March 2013.
14. Oakley has expanded its market share to include 11 'action' sports; in addition, they have links to the London 2012 Olympics (including tennis, road

cycling (plus Tour de France), triathlon and track and field), motorsports and selected 'performance' sports ('Oakley Sports', 2012).

15. The 'themes' detailed within this chapter are, of course, debatable. This is one reading of the work—a different study, examining viewpoints of the audience, would undoubtedly find slight variances in interpretation.

16. Scattering of ashes at various cricket grounds is a not-unheard-of practice, but, for Old Trafford, 'Generally it is something they only do for people who have association with the club, e. g. former players, officials, Lancashire Members and supporters' ('Cricket grounds', 2013). In Germany, football club Borussia Dortmund offers cemetery sites 'just for football supporters' ('Dortmund fans', 2008).

11 Anhedonia and Alternative Sports[1]

Robert E. Rinehart

> Anhedonia (an′hē dō′nē ə), n. *Psychol.* lack of pleasure or of the capacity to experience it.
>
> —*The Random House Dictionary of the English Language, 1969: 58*

CONTEMPORARY AFFECTS

The 21st century: a millennial shift, with its requisite technologies that arguably separate us all from each other—we communicate with colleagues two doors down on the computer, by e-mail; we text on phones instead of meeting for a coffee; some of us even experience sexual gratification via our technological devices, eschewing the risk of rejection from another real person in favor of the instrumentality of efficient, disposable sex with . . . ourselves (cf. Bauman, 2003). But don't just take my word for it. Zygmunt Bauman points out a similar phenomenon: 'the advent of virtual proximity renders human connections simultaneously more frequent and more shallow, more intense and more brief' (2003: 62). Seeming—or apparent—pleasure isn't necessarily *actual* pleasure.

In short, in many areas, we have replaced human interaction with human-machine or human-material-object interaction.[2] But accompanying this social withdrawal is a concomitant explosion of often solitary, often narcissistic, frequently self-centered and selfish physically active behavior—termed, variously, lifestyle, action, extreme, outdoor challenge, 'whiz' and alternative sports. The names, of course, matter, but that is not my primary pursuit here; the fact that these activities have been counted, and numbers of participants estimated, with projections for profits deriving from such activities is what really matters.

The activities reflect an American—and in many ways, international—subcultural attitude, favoring what Roger Caillois (1961) termed *vertigo* pursuits: activities high on the scale of dizzying, disorienting, thrilling experiences. These experiences are, almost by definition, momentary, transitory and ephemeral: indeed, for participants, this is one of the pleasing effects. Their

Anhedonia and Alternative Sports   181

sensory experience is here and gone. They become memories almost as soon as they are enacted. From a psychological perspective, their allure is aligned with the 'intermittent rewards' that they grant participants, the momentary fractious frisson that pervades their very capture. Because of their very structure, you simply cannot hold onto these experiences long: that fact, paradoxically, makes them all the more coveted, all the more objects of desire.

Thus, the pleasure effect of thrill sports—the name itself gives away the sense of it—*is* the rush, the unwieldy loss of control, perhaps the seeming pushing of limits. But it is more than that: the pleasure effect, like most of these ilinx-prevalent activities—which have morphed into these kinds of sports and events—is in the re-narrativizing of them, the nostalgia effects that they produce. These nostalgic shadows, like the lingering traces of human bodies at Nagasaki and Hiroshima, imply the horrifying events of their participation, but the instance of their making is only momentary. And like the victims in Nagasaki and Hiroshima, the participants of these activities have been impacted by a global (really, grobal) tsunami of changed sensibilities and altered realities. The mixed metaphor—atomic bomb and tsunami—points to the real effects and lasting consequences of momentary disaster: the survivors of such unimaginable onslaught have a lifetime to re-remember them, to re-narrativize them. In addition, the instantaneousness flash of change forms an almost inverse relationship with its apprehension. All that remains is a dull, flattened, stunned affect, an unsettling recognition of the sublime power of the instant.

Thus, *samplers* of these alternative sport activities, recounting the momentary rush of excitement or terror, usually do not experience what Denzin terms 'a major epiphany' (2001: 145–46), but rather are closer to the 'relived epiphany', where one singular event casts new meaning on future events. For example, someone who decides, on a lark, to bungy jump into a river during holiday might relive that moment and see him or herself in a different light in the future: as a daring risk-taker. She can also purchase the video 'evidence' of that jump, which has been neatly packaged and marketed to sport tourists. (Strangely, this 'objective' evidence often—after time forgotten—doesn't match our recollection of the experience itself.) Or he can boast to his mates about his fear and courage. Conversely, of course, the experience of jumping may affect that person so that they seek more calm, mundane, 'safe' activities in the future. Clearly, the event has impacted them. Nonetheless, the reflection upon the experience is a key element in the experience of pleasure.

But in an age of almost constant messages, advertising and corporate branding—ever more creative and subtle, even subliminal—the question remains: to what degree does the experience affect and influence participants? To what degree do they experience, and embed, these depthless moments of pleasure? Or do they simply tick the experience off, running to the next thrill, forgetting or dismissing the current experience? A series of peak experiences, run one after another without pause, may become muddied experiences, and

182   Robert E. Rinehart

the pleasure that accrues quickly may become empty and average. In a very real sense, these blurred experiences represent postmodern angst.

Denzin's discussion of epiphanies is important for applying the sense of flattened affect to contemporary sport forms. He writes:

> In whatever form, bizarre, frightening, dramatic, or mundane, such contact [with the terror and repressive taken-for-grantedness of the postmodern] produces a shock of recognition in terms of lifestyle, and personal meaning. At the level of collective lived experiences, the epiphanic approach aims to identify how different social and cultural groupings. . . . attach themselves to and come to grips with those traces of postmodernism that invade and become part of their lives. (1991: 13)

Similarly, contemporary sport forms have sought to re-create the same experience, the same bodily experience, of participation in physically active sports or experiences by compressing the temporal element of the experience: the experiences are more efficient, more flash, more attention-getting—and, in a capitalist world, a more saleable commodity. But has the postmodern or contemporary body kept up with this onslaught of compressed time, which is becoming rather commonplace in all sports forms?

In mainstream sports, we have a media-influenced trend toward shorter events (e.g. 20–20 cricket, rugby sevens), presumably because the attention span of audiences has shortened, but also due to a greater choice for spectators. The quick shortened version of sports therefore gains a maximum audience. This version, while not endorsed by traditionalists of these sports, allows for a greater commoditization. It's about the money.

For alternative sports, similar trends have occurred. In fact, alternative sports may have begun this trend, with their method of MTV-style quick shots, rather than following the whole trick: this foreshortened version of the trajectory of sport *implies* the whole event, but certainly doesn't deliver the whole event. The satisfaction of what Jayne Caudwell (2014) terms 'mundane motion' in physical activity has been subsumed by Kroker, Kroker and Cook's (1989) postmodern implosion, as evidenced in their *Panic Encyclopedia*: the instant fix of culture through a series of 'panics'.

One moment can certainly become deeply felt and profound in one's life (cf. Denzin, 2001): the way that some extreme sport athletes experience the rush—that is, the sense of Stephen Lyng's 'risk' (Lyng, 2005a, 2005b)—may be 'an escape to a sensual universe of emotional intensity and self-determination' (Lyng, 2005b: 31). Lyng admits that '. . . edgework does not allow one to *transcend* the extant social reality of consumer culture; the experience merely represents an extension of that reality' (2005b: 33, emphasis in original). Yet a certain assumption of Lyng's thesis is that edgework—that is, the practice of risk taking in a variety of fields—'is a response to the over-determined character of *modern* social life . . .' (2005a: 5, emphasis added) that occurs more

Anhedonia and Alternative Sports 183

frequently and with greater intensity in the late 20th and early 21st century than ever before.

I suggest that Lyng's characterization of a risk factor in these 'life-threatening experiences [which] come to acquire a seductively appealing character in the contemporary social context' (Lyng, 2005a: 5) has been, like many mediated late-modern and poststructuralist realities, somewhat hyperbolic. To state that true 'edgework' motivates a surprising amount of individuals in their pursuit of 'life-threatening' endeavors is, I believe, overstating the case. Compared to such motivations as the sense of freedom from watchful adult supervision/surveillance, the sense of empowerment, the sense of camaraderie with mates and/or the sense of self-efficacy that she (or he)[3] can derive from participation in these alternative activities, true 'edgework' seems relatively rare. Surrounding oneself with fellow 'edgeworkers'—who are aggressively 'alternative' to the mainstream—does not mean that the world in general has followed along. (Similarly, to admit to a gnawing sense of anhedonism does not measure the degree of such flattened affect, only that it has increased in the contemporary moment.)

I do want to believe in Lyng's proposal, but I think he premises the ubiquity of edgework on an assumption of contemporary culture that parallels Gonzo journalism, as interpreted by Hunter S. Thompson. By his own admission, Thompson was an aberration to mass cultural values, not a standard of them; an alternative, not a mainstreamer; an exception, not a rule. There are those who are attracted to police work, extreme sports, even performance art, primarily because of these pursuits' so-called edginess, but as extreme, action, alternative and other kinds of sports and activities have grown in popularity, there is likely less and less relationship with the percentages of people who begin simply because of its self-promoting sense of 'edginess'. Studies simply haven't borne this out either way (see also Chapter 4 for a discussion of edgework).

Robert Putnam's[4] thesis regarding a decline in (specifically) American 'social capital' pushes this sense of contemporary malaise in different ways. He points out obvious trends towards civic disengagement in the United States, commenting that 'networks of civic engagement foster sturdy norms of generalized reciprocity and encourage the emergence of social trust' (1995: 67). Accounting for a heightened 'technological social-capital formation . . . [which is] "privatizing" or "individualizing" our use of leisure time and thus disrupting many opportunities for social-capital formation' (Putnam, 1995: 75), Putnam hints at how social capital reduces while the commodification of contemporary life rises. Some grass-roots sectors of the lucrative alternative, extreme, action and outdoor challenge sports might still be bucking this trend toward a lessened 'social-capital formation', but the commodification process works insistently to objectify and thus de-humanize participants. When athletes consciously seek to become 'models of consumption based on . . . fan identification' (Rinehart, 1998a: 407), they

184   *Robert E. Rinehart*

draw away from community concerns and have become seduced by greater self-centered and-individualized interests.

The caveat, of course, is the conditional nature of what one can gain from solely focusing on the end product, on the result, on the utilitarian. Just as in mainstream sports—where a good model can be attenuated and perverted by those who deliver it—so too can participation in adventure, action, outdoor challenge and other alternative-to-the-mainstream types of activities become commodified and, thus, altered by others with more power than the participants. Participants who seek commodification begin the process of loss of civic engagement (read: primary identification with mates, with peers) as soon as they decide to become a commodity. Interestingly, this aspect of commodification, at least in the early 21st century, seems to wash out any grounding, fundamental edginess and alternative nature of these sport activities themselves. In objectifying both the pursuit of 'more shallow, more intense and more brief' (Bauman, 2003: 62) physical interactions, the very process of commodification inculcates values that teach many participants how to evade and ignore long-lasting pleasures while ironically *feeling* they remain deeply embedded in highly pleasurable experience.

COMMODIFICATION: THE PROCESS

Much of the recent study of these types of activities (alternative sports) has based itself upon the 'representations and commodification of the sports within consumer culture' (Ormrod, 2009: vi). That is to say, there has been an insistence that these sports have become commodified through a process that is irrevocably linked to consumerism and consumer culture. But what is commodification?

Simply stated, commodification is the economic process by which something—some process, some previously unvalued object—becomes an economic object for commerce. Moor (2007: 132), however, points out some of the 'ubiquitous' ways that sports scholars have used the term 'commodification'—often resulting in less-than-nuanced ways of conceptualizing 'the ways markets and market logic are introduced into' football.[5] She also sees that many of the uses of the term by sport scholars 'to refer to any instance of commercial activity by clubs (and fans) blunts its usefulness . . .' (Moor, 2007: 132).

Andrews and Ritzer (2007), following Ritzer (1993, 1998, 2005, 2006), locate commodification within a dynamic relationship of global and local, with the effects of this relationship resulting in somewhat shared integration of global and local (glocal), or in the global influence effectively impacting and altering the local (grobal). Thus, in discussing anhedonia and alternative sports, the process of commodification has come to mean those objects or processes which, along the continuum of global and local, and along the pressure- and fault-lines of glocal and grobal, have gone from activities for their

Anhedonia and Alternative Sports 185

own sake to activities which are done with an instrumental eye to creating an economic object for commerce, where the local commodity (e.g. athlete) bends to the will of the global (e.g. trans- or multi-national corporation). Control has shifted.

In some ways, looking at branding, iconography and the cultural capital that sediments and accrues in these alternative sports objects and processes depends upon a recognition of the grobal; what Ritzer calls the 'imperialistic ambitions of . . . corporations, organizations' (2006: 338) always tinges and impacts even the local grass-roots participants. As a simple example, we only have to look to grass-roots skaters (skateboarders or inline skaters), those out skating in small groups, informally: it is important to remember that, as soon as their images hit the internet, they have become a functional part of the commoditizing machinery. Almost gone[6] are the days when they crafted their own boards out of wood, or somehow fabricated trucks or skates into a viable unit. In the 21st century, having the 'right' equipment—that is, the most functional, stylish and currently fashionable, within one's means—has become a fundamental (and naturalized) requirement of participation in action and extreme sports.

But the concept of the grobal and glocal also ranges beyond the mere commodification of tools and objects. Just as marketing for lifestyle in the 1970s and 80s changed the way consumerist culture operates, so too it changed what objects and processes could be commodified (cf. Goldman and Papson, 2000).

For example, Richard Tinning and Lindsay Fitzclarence (1992) discuss physical education students in secondary schools in Australia.[7] They determined that these postmodern subjects/consumers desired to become 'producers of their own biographies' (p. 299) wherein they became engaged in their own eclectic senses of what constituted physical activity, but not in the packaged forms of institutionalized programming.

In other words, these students 'are active in accepting or rejecting the messages that physical education (and the media) presents' (Tinning and Fitzclarence, 1992: 299), they self-choose activities and they look toward very pragmatic reasons for engaging in any activity. They are demonstrating some agency, but within (and against) narrow confines of institutional culture. Though Tinning and Fitzclarence did not use the terms 'glocal' and 'grobal', they were describing the influences of both—synthesized and 'colonizing' global and local cultural influences—within that emerging world of secondary physical education in Australia.

It is noteworthy that Tinning and Fitzclarence's study was published in 1992, just after the emergence of explicitly neoliberal agendas in both the UK and the USA. The uncanny and misguided senses of Reagonomics and Thatcherism, which effectively dismantled the essential Western governmental role of encouraging egalitarian opportunities for their citizens, is, of course, still in play 20-plus years later. We see the effects of neoliberalism in the privatization of sport, leisure and educational delivery systems, among many other de-centralized mechanisms (cf. Giroux, 2012).

186 *Robert E. Rinehart*

One of the purported goals of neoliberalism was to reverse the trends of liberal democracies as well as 'social democratic states (such as Scandanavia or Britain in the immediate post-war period)' (Harvey, 2005: 71). Previously, these states, according to Harvey,

> ... had long taken key sectors of the economy such as health care, education, and even housing out of the market on the grounds that access to basic human needs should not be mediated through market forces and access limited by ability to pay. (Harvey, 2005: 71)

Of course, the whole process of neoliberalism reduces the government's contribution, and increases pressures on individuals: this structural 'shaping' by neoliberal philosophies and actors thus returns us to the entrepreneurial statuses of would-be commodified action-sport participants.

We see the effects of neoliberalism in tertiary institutions that insist their employees use their 'branding'—for example, Microsoft Power Point presentations—to compete in an educational climate that is driven by market profits. Just as athletes become commodified, and sport formations become commodified, so too do large institutions—until commodification itself seems to be a natural thing. But its very ubiquity leads logically to forms of anhedonism.

The incentives for what X-Games Gold Medalist inline skater Arlo Eisenberg once—less than 20 years ago!—fondly termed 'lifestyle choices, in artistic presentations of the self as skater' (in Rinehart, 1998b: 404) have clearly been influenced heavily by a West-driven, and now grobal, neoliberal agenda. And the process of commodification—with its logics of the inverse relationships between becoming an object of the free market and the experience of joy and pleasure—just as clearly reduces the initial pleasures of participation for individuals. This is the slow slide from play to work, especially for successful activities, writ large on the now-commodified alternative, extreme, action, lifestyle, outdoor challenge scene.

But each of these categories has its own story. In the next section, I will attempt to sketch out how some of the similarities—and differences—between the commodification practices of these different physical activities may be playing out. This is, however, an initial effort, and I suggest that scholarly follow-up is necessary.

OBJECTIFYING LIFESTYLE, ALTERNATIVE, EXTREME, ACTION AND OUTDOOR CHALLENGE 'SPORT'

Why would someone want masses of people to essentially take over their preferred activity? If there is joy in the discovery, participants tend to go back to it—which means that they want equipment, sites, acceptance: but not too much. They don't want to have to struggle for finite waves, limited space or contentious territory. When participants grow older, some want to stay in the activity at any level: in addition to participating at senior levels, many alternative participants have tended to follow the mainstream model, where players become coaches and managers, but they also become writers for niche magazines, which allows them access to travel and the sport; they become entrepreneurs who fashion new types of equipment or ways to contest their sport; they, like Stacy Peralta[8], become filmmakers and control the historicizing of their own origination myth. But all of these activities work to nudge their sport towards deeper forms of mass acceptance and commodification.

The definitional terms of *lifestyle, extreme and action, alternative* and *outdoor challenge and outdoor education* all have varied places within the continuum of purely grass-roots to highly commodified forms of non-mainstream activities. The following comprises brief sketches regarding possibilities for study of these activities—and suggests how they may relate to overall possibilities for pleasure/anhedonia within such activities in the 21st century.

Arlo Eisenberg, back in the mid-1990s, pointed out some differences between inline skating and skateboarding. Skateboarding had a history, a committed core base and skateboarders *knew* who they were; but inline skating, at the time (and arguably still) was a loosely created formation (and identity) at the mercy of multi-national corporations, like ESPN, Disney and so on. Inline was considered a 'lifestyle' for many participants. In some cases—those 'sports' with a weakened 'core' of participants, for example—the *lifestyle 'sports'* (a term which, itself, seems oxymoronic), stemming from a genuine need to resolve the dissonance of the terms 'lifestyle' and 'sports', in many cases acceded to a neoliberal, self-centered capitalist commodification model. We only have to witness the way these sports/activities have been studied—with the researchers' own privilege dampened (one exception might be something like Joanne Kay and Suzanne Laberge's (2003) diatribe against Warren Miller skiing films) as they travel around the world. The simple act of (classed and privileged) reflexivity on the parts of researchers might go a long way toward exhuming the buried remains of Thorstein Veblen's 1899 classic, *Theory of the Leisure Class*, and creating research lines that examine class, privilege, Western privilege, subtle forms of imperialism and colonization within lifestyle sports (1979).

However, other *lifestyle sports*, given their aesthetic, financially and symbolically privileged positionalities and academic history (cf. Wheaton, 2004) have, at the level of practitioner, a very great chance of resisting such commodification. Activities like windsurfing, sky surfing, parasailing, paragliding, kitesurfing—and more—wall many people out of becoming core members simply because of their cost. For example, at the Raglan (NZ) KiteSurfing website, one may purchase a kitesurfing board ranging from $799–1399 (NZ); one kite (the Edge 2013 7M) lists at $1590 (NZ) ('Raglan KiteSurfing', 2013). Yet the core members who are adherents are relatively

188 Robert E. Rinehart

unaffected by the temptations of the marketplace. As in many of these activities, financial considerations may limit numerical 'core' membership to mere 'sampler' membership within the club. In some ways, this is a deliberate, albeit covert, strategy to enhance stratification practices—put simply, the wealthy covertly form exclusionary clubs. As a result, commodification of such activities, as signaled by media attention and massification of participation, is relatively low. Self-reported pleasure and self-gratification is, conversely, fairly high.

However, commodification of the actual lifestyle is quite another thing. Since at least the mid-1800s, there has been a capitalist move to incorporate the middle class into (high culture) taste cultures (Cross, 1990), which results in not only an effort towards incorporation of objects, accouterments and things surrounding these activities, but in the commodification of the actual lifestyle itself (cf. Bourdieu, 1984). While Wheaton (2007), following Redhead, posits a more fluid approach to the rigid markers of subculture, culture and the ilk, the identity issues she discusses also admit to an encroaching commodification process of the very idea of lifestyle (cf. Wheaton, 1998, 2007).

Somewhat in contrast to lifestyle sports, *extreme and action* sports have largely become commodified. Of course, this general statement can easily be challenged: many *participants* at the grass-roots levels have clearly not become commodified. But multi-national media corporations like ESPN and Sky TV have made it their mission to incorporate these kinds of sport activities so that the general public identifies with them as 'extreme' or 'action' sports forms (however, there is participant 'push-back': many participants choose intentionally to identify with any moniker other than 'extreme': as in all things, it remains contested ground). Yet the mere acceptance of the activities as 'sports' signifies that the move towards massified incorporation—objectifying both the participant and the activities—has already begun. The word 'extreme' itself has been a marketable entity (along with ESPN's 'X') for nearly twenty years (Rinehart, 1998b).

For example, the process of commodification for the same inline skaters that Eisenberg was hailing as lifestyle participants—kids who basically saw inline as a form of transportation, or a way of self-labeling themselves (as a skater), or as a form of active resistance to dominant youth models—back in the 1990s has gone quite a ways farther:

> . . . the processes of icon making and commodification are interdependent. In fact, many of the athletes *seek* to become commodities, finding lucrative careers through the process. This process is not unlike a symbiotic relationship, where companies, consumers, and individual athletes alike share (but not equally) in the profits. (Rinehart, 2003: 30)

And now, extreme and action sports (the terms are largely indistinguishable) are considered by most to be accepted mainstream sport activities.

Alternative sports, almost by definition, may remain resistant to the dominant. But it is important to remember that the activities that are loosely defined by the term 'alternative' keep changing (cf. 'avant garde' in Rinehart, 1998b). However, the compressed temporal element of contemporary life has impacted upon the time that something truly remains alternative: with both time and space compression, by dint of electronic technological advances and the naturalization of acceptance of such advances, hot 'alternative' activities quickly become recognized, commodified and mainstreamed. Sometimes this results in a cycle that resembles a quick fad; other times it means that that which has been alternative becomes mainstream very quickly, only to be replaced by something differentially alternative. The public appetite is voracious—almost like the span of a news cycle.

Outdoor challenge and outdoor education models, though often delivered from an institutional (educational) setting, have also fallen into the trap of a vaunted, and relatively unexamined, global neoliberal educational model where it is up to individual schools (or private enterprises), rather than government, to generate funding (cf. Giroux, 2011). Thus, we see the privatization of outdoor types of alternative physical activity just about everywhere, and we see schools entering into the marketplace, competing for 'customers' and skewing the fundamental democratic impulse that for so long defined public education.

Those within these fields can note some of the aggressive forms of commodification that have beset outdoor activities. Privatization, it seems, only serves to exacerbate the commodification of outdoor education (cf. Humberstone and Stan, 2012; Sandell, 2012). There is some resistance, however, which mostly comes from a reflexive type of delivery of such outdoor-oriented programs (cf. Martin and Leberman, 2004; Šebek, 2004; Wattchow and Brown, 2011).

TIME, TEMPORALITY AND COMMODIFICATION

The caveat that cuts across the commodification of lifestyle, extreme, alternative and outdoor challenge activities is time. If life has become, in a sense, a series of flattened affects for some, time and temporality—action speeded up—help to shape and even drive a creeping ennui towards their own sacred activity. Jean Baudrillard, writing from the vast empty stretches of Western deserts (both literal and figurative) in *America*, creates a classic temporal dimension for the apprehension of this collective flattened affect. He cautions the reader that, to really get at the feel and sense and heft of travel,

> We'd have to replay it all from end to end at home in a darkened room, rediscover the magic of the freeways and the distance and the ice-cold alcohol in the desert and the speed and live it all again on the video at home in real time, not simply for the pleasure of remembering but

190   Robert E. Rinehart

because the fascination of senseless repetition is already present in the abstraction of the journey. The unfolding of the desert is infinitely close to the timelessness of film . . . (1989: 1).

The initial, primary experience is unassailable, but of course it can be 'replayed' in so many ways.

A significant dimension of an appreciation for pleasure—at least as it has been 'taught' to the postmodern subject through how we are meant to classify acculturation, everyday experience, even sensory apprehension—relies upon anticipation or reflection. Despite the viral insistence on a contemporary cultural shift towards existentialism—in the products we are steered towards buying, the media we devoutly consume and so forth—there remains, in everyday lived life, a hope for the future, a desire for the past.

The dream of living existentially—this viral insistence—leads to a flattened affect. The only exception is within idealized art formations, within already flattened discourses, in novels and short stories and film and poetry and plastic art and sculpture, where Walter Pater's 'hard, gemlike flame . . . [that] maintain[s] this ecstasy' (1966: 267) may actually exist, unaffected by the patina of time. But these dreams of desire, ironically, lead to a postmodern subject position that is, like capitalism itself, never satisfied. And it is not coincidental that this lack of satisfaction occurs in a moment of late capitalism (cf. Andrews, 2004).

Pater suggests that we should live from existential moment to existential moment, 'burning always . . . [which will result in] success in life' (1966: 267). Pater's exhortation does not go so far as to assess a sense of existentialism, realism or idealism in his passionate subject, but a postmodern subject would: how do we, for example, assess the degree of 'burning' except by comparison with other experiences, past and future? The inbuilt competition of late capitalism flavors everything it touches.

Simone De Beauvoir, in an interview in 1965, reflected on thinking about lived life—as an existentialist:

When one has an existentialist view of the world, like mine, the paradox of human life is precisely that one tries to *be* and, in the long run, merely exists. It's because of this discrepancy that when you've laid your stake on being—and, in a way you always do when you make plans, even if you actually know that you can't succeed in being—when you turn around and look back on your life, you see that you've simply existed. In other words, life isn't behind you like a solid thing, like the life of a god (as it is conceived, that is, as something impossible). Your life is simply a human life. (in Gobeil, 1965)

In Jay Gatsby's world, created by F. Scott Fitzgerald, the reader is lead to believe that Gatsby is living a life of total satisfaction, his every need met, as admirers flock to his house nearly every weekend: we see him living from heightened moment to heightened moment. But Jay Gatsby is a fictional

Anhedonia and Alternative Sports 191

character. His universe is a created universe. We do not see Gatsby cleaning his teeth, sitting waiting for someone overdue to share a cup of coffee, being annoyed with trivia, enjoying the antics of an unselfconscious child at play or being uncertain as to others' meanings. We do not know Gatsby's reaction to these everyday moments because F. Scott Fitzgerald has *selected*—really, created—moments of Gatsby's life that tell us a certain story, a story of fallen triumph, a modernist tale that builds a dramatic irony within the reader, that portrays Gatsby as a singularly alone man. Any pleasures he might have are deliberately flattened—but is this a reflection of reality lived, or a produced effect?

The irony of Gatsby the man (within the novel) is that his *apparent* genuineness masks his actual biography. We find that Gatsby, as he invents himself, has a 'heart [that] was in a constant, turbulent riot', and that he comes to believe that 'the rock of the world was founded securely on a fairy's wing' (1953: 89). *The Great Gatsby* is a story= of appearance versus reality. Gatsby the man is a fiction. *Gatsby* the book is instructional for lived lives. No one—except in fictions, which may portray the world more truly than the kaleidoscope of life—lives from heightened moment to heightened moment in real time.

And extreme sport, or outdoor challenge, action, lifestyle, whiz or alternative sport athletes and participants do not either. Fitzgerald intimates that Gatsby had difficulties adjusting to mundane everyday life—except with Daisy. I suggest that these sport participants—to one extent by virtue of expectations of pleasure in part created by media, to another by the insistence upon commodification of themselves, their lifestyles and their sport—cannot really experience pleasure either, except by rejecting the available contemporary sport and capitalist models.

The very process of contemporary commodification relies on this sense of consumers living for the *now*, within a foreshortened world that, not coincidentally, demands they sanctify the present moment while they simultaneously look back nostalgically at former consumptive practices and anticipate future consumption patterns. A world framed this way becomes a flattened world, where ever-increasing possessions lead to ever-increasing desire. This emotional landscape, brought to consumers at least partially by purveyors of commodifications, results, at least emotionally, in a seemingly passionate, yet realistically bereft, life experience.

As Fitzgerald writes,

> . . . the expression of bewilderment had come back into Gatsby's face, as though a faint doubt had occurred to him as to the quality of his present happiness. . . . No amount of fire or freshness can challenge what a man will store up in his ghostly heart. (1953: 86–87)

Gatsby, a perceptive man, could only sense, but not know, how the process of object-acquisition had imprisoned him. Many contemporary alternative sport athletes follow a similar pattern.

192   *Robert E. Rinehart*

While film (and for that matter, mediated extreme sport) *can be* 'timeless' (Baudrillard, 1989: 1), a constant barrage of 'peak experiences' also reduces any actual lived moments that are mundane, boring, repetitive into the receding background. Mundane, day-to-day experiences have their own value, if only to provide relief to the peak moments (Caudwell, 2014). The result privileges major occurrences and major events but, in doing so, may flatten the pleasure and enjoyment of everyday experiences.

A CONCLUSION

One of the keys to the apparent paradox of participating in extraordinary events of physical skill and yet having a gnawing feeling of malaise is the presence or absence of a temporal element. With time to reflect, the experience itself may take on new pleasurable meaning. But where participants experience and privilege sudden rush over reflexive thinking about the experience; where one moment tumbles atop another, without pause for reflection; where there is a clamor for (a felt need to have) the latest experience to surmount others, without time passing to appreciate, enjoy, intensify and reflect on the experience is where anhedonism takes over in the postmodern subject's life.

It is up to those who commoditize to deliberately compress time, to reduce consumers' sense of historical perspective: in this way, of course, the strategy mirrors capitalism itself. Corporations need to demonstrate more and more profit, more and newer product, *ad infinitum*. Just as casinos in Las Vegas lack clocks in order to influence patrons' conception of time, so too do lifestyle entrepreneurs skew a sense of time to their advantage (cf. Cope and Kalantzis, 1999). This is decidedly an anti-sustainability strategy, meant for the momentary fix, but it does not come from nowhere (cf. Schumacher, 1975).

If we were to compare this current sense of compressed time (cf. Kroker, Kroker and Cook, 1989) for relationships to a WWII or pre-WWII generation, we would generally discover in the earlier generations a more linear, focused sense of relationships between people. There was a closer fit between the 'realism' of the novel and the 'realism' of lived life—but there has *never* been an exact fit. Episodic relationships still occurred, but there was more connection between individuals, families and communities (cf. Brokaw, 1998). Even with the sudden epiphanic moment (for a whole generation) of a profound traumatic invasion in global war—using tactics of storm troopers, the blitzkrieg and the atomic bomb (tactics which later devolved into the US military's use of 'shock and awe' (Ullman and Wade, 1996) and its justification)—there was time *after* to reassess, to mull over, to reflect.

Sometimes relationships happened quickly, but again there was a sense of potential lastingness as opposed to planned obsolescence. Relationships may have been based more on pragmatic, instrumental goals: courtly love was still a fantasy, not a goal; snap, instantaneous, immediate falling in love and Hollywood fantasies were only beginning to influence societal attitudes towards real, face-to-face relationships (cf. Denzin, 1991; Lyman, 1987); people dreamed that they could 'have it all', but didn't truly rely on that as a life trajectory. Hope was a reality, if only sometimes for survival (Wiesel, 1960). The paradox is that the more postmodern humans clamored for hedonistic pleasure, the more its actual realization receded, like Baudrillard's objects in the side-view mirror.

Yet the concept of anhedonia is not simply about time compression. As Stanford Lyman puts it in his study of fifty years of American film:

'Anhedonia' speaks to a deep and unresolved dilemma in the American *Lebenswelt*. In its penultimate form it expresses itself as a frenzied desire to escape coupled with a recognition that there is no place to go. Nothing is left but sudden, sharp, uncathartic aggressive displays, and then—ultimately—a grudging acquiescence to a life alternating between boredom and frustration. (1987: 264)

This vague sense of an inability to experience pleasure, and the concomitant panicked rush to experience it as quickly, episodically and deeply as possible, is what constitutes a major facet of the paradoxical nature of contemporarily lived life. It also parallels the strategies of modern and postmodern marketing and advertising campaigns to create uncertainty, need, want, desire in consumers. As this commodification process works its way through not just tangible product but also lifestyle, worldview and a gnawing sense of self as passive, there is an individual and collective backlash. But like the fly caught in the web, the more we struggle, the more we become enmeshed.

NOTES

1. A revised version of Chapter 11 (*Anhedonia and Alternative Sports*) by Robert Rinehart is due to be published in the French journal *STAPS* (*Revue international des sciences du sport et de l'education physique*), for which Rinehart has attained permission from the journal. Appreciation to *STAPS* for rights to reproduce this piece.
2. Our 'social science' observations of such phenomena as human-object, human-machine, human-nonhuman relationships have, to some extent kept pace with the actual interactions: see, e.g. Bruno Latour (2005), Nigel Thrift (2008) and John Law's (2004) works on Action Network and Non-Representational Theories.
3. The gendered nature of alternative sports, in any form, is well documented (see, for example, Beal 1996; Rinehart 1999, 2005; Thorpe 2005; Wheaton and Tomlinson 1998). Though there are hopeful pockets of breakthrough, for the most part these action/extreme sports have reflected the dominant mainstream sport models, which, in turn, have reflected the dominant patriarchal societal models extant in the 21st century world.
4. I am grateful to Jayne Caudwell for pointing out this piece.

5. The term 'commodification' has, until fairly recently, also been used by those in business as meaning the process wherein similar niched products become relatively indistinguishable from one another: thus their value drops, and they have become mere commodities. To distinguish between 'commodification' in the two senses, the term 'commoditization' has taken on the latter meaning.
6. 'Almost gone': of course, there are the rare exceptions, as Rinehart and Grenfell (2002) point out in their ethnography exploring the creation of a neighborhood BMX track.
7. I am grateful to Clive Pope for alerting me to this article.
8. Director of *Dogtown and Z Boys* (film, 2001).

12 Be Happy, Play Sport?
Governing Happiness via the Promotion of Sport

Richard Pringle

> . . . hedonic well-being refers to happiness, pleasure, and positive affect. In the sports domain, hedonic well-being can be viewed as an immediate consequence, and one that is easily reported and identified by athletes.
>
> (Blanchard et al., 2009: 546).

The above quote from Céline Blanchard and colleagues (2009) reflects a relatively common assumption that participation in sport leads to the experiencing of happiness, pleasure and positive affect. Limited research evidence from a variety of sources has also supported such contentions. For example, Paul Dalziel (2011), an economist within Aotearoa New Zealand, contends that the broader social value of sport to New Zealanders, calculated in relation to the opportunity cost of time spent in sport and recreational activities, is approximately $6.9 billion per year. In other words, Dalziel intimates by using monetary estimations that sport is 'good' for New Zealanders. Similar assumptions/findings about the alleged positive benefits of sport have subsequently shaped government policies worldwide. These policies are remarkably alike, as they typically desire to encourage more people to participate in *and enjoy* sport.

The national agency for sport in Scotland, for example, is driven by its primary aim to help more Scottish people *enjoy the benefits* of sport, whereas Sport New Zealand reports that it is 'dedicated to getting New Zealanders enjoying and excelling through sport and recreation' (Sport New Zealand, 2013a: ¶ 1). Sport England reports that it is committed to helping 'as many people as possible to find a sport that they enjoy and want to continue being involved in' (Sport England, 2013a: ¶ 1). In a similar manner, Australian ex-Prime Minister Kevin Rudd reported that his government would continue to fund the Active After-schools Communities program, as: 'It is extremely rewarding to see so many children participating in healthy activities but most importantly it is great to see children having so much fun participating in sport and physical activity' (Australian Sport Commission, 2013: ¶ 1). Governments are seemingly using sport as a technology to enhance a population's level of wellbeing and happiness. As a consequence, a new

196   Richard Pringle

social imperative appears to have emerged: all citizens should play sport *and* enjoy it.

Sara Ahmed (2010b: 14), in drawing from Nietzsche, argued that: 'what is apt to cause pleasure is already judged to be good'. In other words, she suggested that the various things that humans 'know' to cause pleasure—such as friendship and love—are already judged to be good. If this is the case, then the seemingly widespread belief that sport causes pleasure can be assumed to be underpinned by the equally widespread but *unquestioned* belief that sport is good for people. Indeed, the efforts of various governments to encourage their populations to enjoy participation in sports appear to be buttressed by such a belief. Sportscotland (2003), for example, alleges that:

> . . . participating in sport can improve the quality of life of individuals and communities, promote social inclusion, improve health, counter anti-social behaviour, raise individual self-esteem and confidence, and widen horizons. (sportscotland, 2003: 7)

Fred Coalter (2007) reported, however, that evidence to support these seemingly functionalist views of sport is limited and/or based on dubious research. Despite such a recognition, Barrie Houlihan (1997: 113) observed that '[a]lmost without exception, industrialised and many developing states have, over the last thirty years, increased their funding for sport at a pace greater than that for most other services'. This unprecedented increase in funding has not abated even in times of global recession. Within Aotearoa New Zealand, Australia and England, for example, funding for sport over the last five years has increased at a faster rate than spending on health and education services. Government funding of sport in Aotearoa New Zealand, for instance, has more than doubled between 2007 ($NZ32 million) and 2012 ($NZ70 million).

In commenting on this increased funding of sport, Houlihan (1997) surmised that sport was not necessarily valued by governments because of its intrinsic qualities but due to its supposed ability to 'ameliorate or camouflage problems ranging from poor cardiovascular health and juvenile delinquency to low tourist volume' (Houlihan, 1997: 113). Houlihan, accordingly, believed that governments were not primarily interested in attempting to enhance a population's levels of happiness but in the political value of the alleged positive 'side-effects' of increased sport participation. Indeed, Sport New Zealand (2013b) states that they 'want young New Zealanders (aged 0–18) to develop a *love* of sport and recreation that leads to lifelong participation' (¶ 1; italics added for emphasis), suggesting that their prime concern is maximizing participation in sport.

The global encouragement of mass participation in sport has become an important public policy issue, with claims that sport participation can enhance public health, reduce anxiety and depression and enhance a sense of wellbeing. Yet, as governments have recognized, the key for gaining mass

Be Happy, Play Sport? 197

participation rests primarily upon individuals enjoying and gaining meaningful pleasures through sport. But do most people enjoy playing sport? And is sport a panacea for social and health problems?

In this chapter I critically review what is known about sport and its connections to pleasure/happiness, health and wellbeing and examine the issues surrounding the use of sport as a form of 'biopower'. Biopower, a term coined by Michel Foucault (1990), refers to the various techniques used by governments in attempts to foster the health and life of their populations. Biopower is a technology of power or a government mechanism of controlling or managing bodies (i.e. people). With the development of nation-states from the 18th century onward, Foucault argued that governments became concerned with fostering and controlling the biological features of a population. These features are tied to the body and related to issues of sexuality (e.g. population growth, pregnancy and sexually transmitted diseases, control of 'deviant' sexual practices), family relations and, more broadly, attempts to regulate various social practices, customs and the health and wellbeing of a population. Foucault (2007) suggested that biopower was a term that:

> ... somewhat vaguely (refers) ... to a number of phenomena that seem to me to be quite significant, namely, the set of mechanisms through which the basic biological features of the human species became the object of a political strategy, of a general strategy of power, or, in other words, how, starting from the 18th century, modern Western societies took on board the fundamental biological fact that human beings are a species. (Foucault, 2007: 1)

In this chapter I argue that governments are using sport as a form of biopower to foster the health, happiness and wellbeing of populations, but that this is a flawed strategy that produces a number of unintended and problematic consequences. To support this argument, I begin by examining the concept of subjective wellbeing (SWB), as this concept has become a prime focus of analysis within diverse disciplines (e.g. psychology, economics, politics, education, philosophy, sociology), including sport studies. I then review the limited literature associated with the intersections between sport and SWB, with the intention to understand whether it is prudent for governments to promote sport as a technique for enhancing a population's sense of wellbeing.

THE BIOPOLITICAL 'MEASUREMENT' OF
HAPPINESS/SUBJECTIVE WELLBEING

A growing body of researchers suggest that happiness is not just the product of positive outcomes but is also a state of being that is connected to 'better

198 *Richard Pringle*

health, better work performance, better social relationships and to more ethical behavior' (Kesebir and Diener, 2009: 66). In this respect, government policies that aim to promote happiness are often (uncritically) regarded as beneficial for individuals and societies and, correspondingly, an interest in *governing* happiness has grown in recent years. The United Kingdom's national wellbeing survey was undertaken in 2011 (Office for National Statistics, 2012), and the United Nations recently adopted a resolution for all member nations to give greater attention to happiness in their economic and social development policies (O'Brian, 2012).

Researchers (particularly psychologists) have tended to operationalize 'happiness' in relation to human flourishing and, more specifically, to the term *subjective wellbeing* (SWB): which refers to 'people's evaluations of their lives and encompasses both cognitive judgments of satisfaction and affective appraisals of moods and emotions' (Kesebir and Diener, 2009: 61). The concept of SWB does not offer a prescriptive definition of happiness but allows for subjective evaluations in relation to four prime components:

> . . . life satisfaction (global judgments of one's life), satisfaction with important life domains (satisfactions with one's work, health, marriage etc.), positive affect (prevalence of positive emotions and moods), and low levels of negative affect (prevalence of unpleasant emotions and moods). (Kesebir and Diener, 2009: 62)

Although the relationship between pleasure and SWB is not distinctively outlined, it is not difficult to imagine how experiencing of pleasure in sport could be linked to a prevalence of positive affects and emotions and perhaps, for some, to a broader sense of life satisfaction. At the same time, sporting displeasures could potentially work to decrease judgments of SWB.

Despite the recognition that SWB is a subjective judgment, researchers who have examined SWB have tended to adopt quantitative methods in an attempt to 'objectively' measure and correlate SWB with various socio-cultural factors. The Office for National Statistics (2012) in the UK, for example, surveyed 4000 respondents aged over 16 and found that the majority of people (75%) were satisfied with life, believed that there life was worthwhile (79.5%) and reported that they felt happy yesterday (71.3%).[1] These results are broadly similar to other surveys of happiness, which typically reveal that happiness trumps unhappiness by a three-to-one ratio. Additional findings suggested that older (aged 65–80) and younger people (aged 16–19) tended to be happier and less anxious than the middle aged; that those who were married or in civil unions and/or lived in a house with children considered their lives more worthwhile than those who did not; that females and males (despite differing socio-cultural expectations of how they should perform gender) were similarly satisfied with life; and that people living in Northern Ireland (which has suffered from ethno-nationalist and sectarian conflict for decades) reported greater levels of life satisfaction than those who lived in London.

These results could be interpreted as broadly comforting, given that they suggest that most people appear happy.[2] Yet the survey method, in conjunction with correlational analysis, has a number of well-known limitations dependent on one's paradigmatic position. Questions, for example, have been raised by researchers within the positivist paradigm about the validity of the constructs. Some individuals, for example, may be unhappy but, given the ambiguity of the term 'happiness', may rate themselves as happy. Postmodern scholars, on the other hand, simply reject that 'happiness' and 'life-satisfaction' can be measured and represented numerically, as they are complex and subjective social phenomena. Concern has also been raised about the limited depth of analysis afforded by the survey technique, as it does not take into account the nuances or context of how different people self-assess themselves. Darrin McMahon (2006), more broadly, concluded that the survey results of happiness/wellbeing have provided relatively few new insights with respect to the prime existential questions (e.g. how to obtain happiness and what constitutes the good life). More pointedly, McMahon claimed that these insights could have been readily obtained from reading the works of classical philosophers.

Despite these important limitations, SWB population surveys have become important tools of biopower and the results of such surveys are now being drawn upon to shape social policy, including policy related to sport participation. In the following section, I examine what is known about sport participation, health and SWB and how this knowledge is shaping social policy.

SPORT, SUBJECTIVE WELLBEING AND GOVERNMENTALITY

The biomedical health benefits of physical activities are well known. These benefits tend to be stated in terms of risk reduction; for example, regular bouts of moderate-intensity aerobic activity have been linked with reduced risk of sustaining cardiovascular disease, type-2 diabetes, and some cancers (Warburton, Nicol and Bredin, 2006). Numerous studies have also revealed a positive association between physical activity and positive affects. In a major review article, Kenneth Fox (1999) concluded that sufficient evidence supports the idea that exercise can be effective in managing depression, reducing levels of anxiety and, in some cases, improving physical self-perceptions and mood states. Recent research supports these contentions, but in a more cautious manner (e.g. Biddle and Mutrie, 2008; Galloway et al., 2006).[3] The links between health and SWB are, however, surprisingly tenuous. Ed Diener (2009), for example, found that physical health has little impact on an individual's SWB unless they are very ill, in which case SWB ratings are decreased, and that the 'healthy' typically take their health for granted rather than rejoice in their wellbeing.

200 *Richard Pringle*

The links between sport participation and SWB are also questionable. From an extensive review of literature, Susan Galloway, David Bell, Christine Hamilton and Adrienne Scullion (2006: 92) summarized that 'there is a lack of research on the contribution of sport to QOL (quality of life) and well-being' and 'most of the existing research relates to exercise, and even in this area there are significant gaps, and many of the studies undertaken have specific limitations'. They cautioned, however, against drawing from the physical activity literature and assuming that the findings would relate to sport.

The physical activities linked with health benefits are typically those that involve 'rhythmic, noncompetitive exercises in which individuals control and regulate their own body movements' (Coakley et al., 2009: 108). These types of physical activity are clearly different from that which occurs in many popular sports, within which high-speed movements associated with sudden changes in direction and acceleration, and the complex movements of other players, increase possibilities for injury. As such, the biomedical health benefits of sport have been judged as markedly less in comparison to rhythmic non-competitive forms of physical activity. In fact, given the high cost of sporting injuries, some epidemiologists now regard sporting injuries as a public health problem and are subsequently encouraging governments to adopt sport injury prevention policies within the broader health sector (e.g. see Finch, 2012). These policies, however, fall short of discouraging participation in particular sports. The generalized notion that participation in competitive sport is good for one's health is, nevertheless, being questioned. Ivan Waddington (2007), for example, stated:

> The health-related arguments in favour of regular and moderate physical activity are clear, but they are considerably less persuasive in relation to competitive, and especially contact, sport and very much less in relation to elite or professional sport. (Waddington, 2007: 2094)

Despite these cautionary observations, Galloway et al. (2006: 80) noted that key agencies for sport in the UK (e.g. **sport**scotland and Sport England), in the absence of sport-specific literature on wellbeing and health, 'have drawn on the wider exercise literature to underpin policy making'. Thus, governance policies to promote widespread sport participation as a strategy to promote health and pubic wellbeing are not typically based on studies that have examined the *actual* outcomes of sport participation. This, of course, is highly remiss.

Susan Galloway and colleagues (2006) tentatively suggested that if it is accepted that exercise is a part of sport, and that psychological wellbeing is an aspect associated with a quality of life, 'then it can be argued that sport has a role to play in the promotion of QOL' (Galloway et al., 2006: 87). Yet they further suggested that this was not a convincing argument, as psychological wellbeing is only one aspect of the complex array of factors

Be Happy, Play Sport? 201

associated with a quality of life or SWB (e.g. SWB is associated with factors such as social capital, social connections, sense of purpose to life, employment/income equality, positive affects and housing). In this manner, they did not believe that the exercise literature was particularly helpful for understanding how sport participation might impact SWB.

In the limited research that has examined sport and SWB, findings reveal a complex but limited relationship. William McTeer and James Curtis (1993) analyzed the connections between sport, physical activity and SWB and found that as levels of physical or sporting activity increased, so did feelings of wellbeing. The strength of this relationship was, however, markedly diminished when health status and involvement in social networks were included as controls. As such, they concluded that the sport, physical activity and wellbeing relationship was relatively weak and that other factors likely accounted for the increased feelings of wellbeing. They stated that the most important predictor of SWB was the degree of social interaction; that is, the greater the social interaction, regardless of sport or activity involvement, the higher the levels of SWB. They tentatively suggested:

> The finding that there is only a modest relationship between physical activity and psychological well being is better understood when we consider how little time each day is devoted to physical activity in comparison to other aspects of social life that seem to affect well being. The effects upon well being from circumstances concerning work (e.g., stress, alienation, unemployment) and the family (e.g., the burdens of domestic and paid work, parent/child conflict, or parental discord over childrearing and household duties), as well as economic circumstances . . . probably all have far more persistent effects upon one's psychological state than does a relatively brief bout with sport or exercise . . . (McTeer and Curtis, 1993: 409).

Susan Galloway and colleagues (2006: 92) similarly concluded that the benefits of sport are primarily associated with *other social factors* such as 'the social support, friendship and collective identity gained through participation'. Likewise, Richard Bailey and fellow researchers (2009) concluded, from an examination of physical education and school sport literature, that the prime social benefits gained (e.g. a sense of community, trust, empathy, responsibility and cooperation) were not necessarily related to the sporting or PE activities *per se* but to the social and educational processes inherent in movement participation. Accordingly, they stressed that the role of the teachers and coaches is paramount if one expects social benefits to accrue through sporting involvement. Indeed, they emphasized that social benefits are only likely to occur if there is credible leadership, a pedagogical emphasis on social interactions and learning processes and the youth are involved in decision-making processes. In other words, similar social benefits could be gained from participation in alternative activities, if the social context

202 *Richard Pringle*

was organized in a similar manner (such as related to drama, dance, art, music or outdoor recreation).

In partial response to the lack of robust evidence connecting sport with enhanced levels of SWB or other social benefits, Paul Downward and Samona Rasciute (2011) analyzed cross-sectional survey data to understand how the frequency and duration of participation in 67 different sporting activities influenced SWB. One of their (indirect) findings was that sport participation levels were found to be *very low* within the UK. For example, of the 28,117 respondents, less than 1% of them had participated in any one of the following sports in the four weeks prior to the survey: mountain biking, outdoor bowls, judo, karate, gymnastics, rugby league, rugby union, baseball/softball, hockey, netball, track and field, yachting, canoeing, windsurfing, climbing, volleyball, orienteering, triathlon, boxing, fencing, Frisbee, trampolining, shooting or pilates. The most popular activities were cycling (11%), health/fitness/gym (16%), keepfit classes (8%) and snooker/pool/billiards (8.6%). Yet most people do not necessarily conceptualize these exercise or recreational activities as sports. The most popular 'sports', in contrast, were outdoor football (including five-a-side and six-a-side) (6.8%), cricket (1.8%), tennis (3.3%), squash (1.6%) and basketball (1.3%). Yet these statistics, once again, indicate that the overwhelming majority of the general population had not actively participated in these sports over the four-week period of the survey.

Despite the general lack of participation in sport, Downward and Rasciute (2011: 345) concluded that their research 'demonstrates that sports participation has a positive association with the subjective wellbeing of the population, as measured by happiness . . .'. Yet this conclusion is dubious, as the overwhelming majority of the population did not actively participate in sport. A better conclusion, I surmise, would be: 'in relation to the small percentage of the population who participate in sport, there appears to be a positive association between participation and SWB'. But this does not mean that participation enhances SWB, as this correlational study does not confirm causality.

Similarly to McTeer and Curtis (1993), Downward and Rasciute found that the positive association with SWB was greater in sports that encouraged social interaction. They were nevertheless reticent to endorse the promotion of sport participation as an effective means for enhancing a population's SWB. McTeer and Curtis (1993: 346) concluded that further research needs to examine 'to whom the benefits accrue, how they link to any external benefits and costs, and the consequent levels of funding that might legitimately be committed to support sport as a policy objective'. I concur and suggest it is particularly important to find out to whom the benefits accrue, as if it is found that government promotion of sport typically works to support a small minority of people and if this minority is an already privileged section of the population, then the promotion of sport as a governing strategy to enhance levels of SWB needs to be questioned. Sport England (2013b), for

Be Happy, Play Sport? 203

example, reports that young men are much more likely than women to participate in sport, and participation is greatest amongst managerial/professional workers and lowest amongst manual workers and the unemployed.

More pointedly, I argue that if participation in sport has a positive association with SWB, then it seems reasonable to expect that a higher percentage of the population would regularly participate in sport. Yet survey evidence suggests that over half of the English population does not participate in any sports and that participation rates decrease with age (e.g. 69% of those aged over 26 do not participate) (Sport England, 2013b). The Australian Bureau of Statistics (2013) similarly reveals that the overwhelming majority of Australians are not active participants in team sports.[4] This evidence indirectly suggests that sport participation, for the majority of adults, does not enhance SWB or produce pleasure, as otherwise it would be expected that more people would participate.

Despite the lack of robust evidence that sport has any significant impact on a total population's wellbeing, a functionalist view of sport continues to underpin government investment in sport. Accordingly, governments continue to legitimate investment of large sums of public money in relation to quixotic beliefs that sport engenders national pride, integrates different socio-cultural groups, reduces crime, promotes public health, enhances wellbeing and produces a *feel good factor* or *pleasure* among the population (Hallmann, Breuer and Kühnreich, 2013). With respect to this last point, undoubtedly feelings of national pride and pleasure can be triggered by select sport performances or the hosting of international sporting tournaments (e.g. the London Olympics), yet these feelings have also been found to be somewhat transient and relatively small in overall consideration of an individual's rating of his/her SWB (see van Hilvoorde, Elling and Stokvis, 2010; Kavetsos and Szymanski, 2010).

In relation to the short term 'feel good effect', Kirstin Hallmann, Christoph Breuer and Benedikt Kühnreich (2013) conducted a survey within Germany to examine which groups of people gain the most from the sporting success of national teams/athletes. Perhaps surprisingly, given the assumed connections between sport and masculinities, they found that women, migrants and individuals with low levels of education and income gained the greatest feelings of happiness and national pride. Hallman and colleagues interpreted this finding by suggesting that those who are more privileged in a society (e.g. males with higher income and higher education) possibly have a greater range of activities or abilities that they can draw on to increase happiness and, correspondingly, are less affected by the transitory impact of national sporting success or failure. Hallman et al. (2013) did not specifically problematize the governmental promotion of sport but indirectly raised issues with sport enjoyment and existing social inequities between various groups.

In my view, these social inequities should be of fundamental concern if a government is interested in shifting a population's sense of wellbeing. Indeed,

204 *Richard Pringle*

the literature concerned with SWB suggests that various social inequalities/ injustices (e.g. as associated with income, sexualities, disability, illness, social capital) are factors that can potentially limit a populations and/or an individual's SWB (see Diener, 2009). Accordingly, various researchers have suggested that public policy that directs resources to select disadvantaged groups or to specific geographic regions is likely the most effective initiative to enhance a population's SWB (Cummins et al., 2009; Wilkinson and Pickett, 2010). There is *no* evidence, however, to suggest that attempts to use sport as a form of biopower has any positive impact on reducing inequities or inequalities between different social groups.

I am concerned, however, that the biopolitical promotion of sport could work to entrench existing inequities and sets of power relations and, correspondingly, impact negatively on SWB levels. To explain these concerns I draw from Valerie Harwood (2009), who encouraged critical exploration of how truths about the body and life are circulated via techniques of biopower. I argue, more specifically, that the promotion of national sporting teams and elite athletes and sport participation more broadly, via governance strategies, indirectly reinforces select body discourses (e.g. as associated with ability, gender, shape, size, sexualities, competition, worthiness, nationality and race). These various sets of discourses in turn mark and regulate particular bodies and athletic performances as normal or abnormal, which indirectly allows certain groups/individuals to gain social privileges over others. Thus, the biopolitical promotion of sport may be a factor in itself, which leads to some individuals/groups having less ability to exercise power and/or feel positive about their bodies/selves. This may seem a convoluted argument, yet if we draw on the now substantial body of sociological and pedagogical research concerned with sport/exercise, these concerns have very real substance.

Numerous studies have examined and found that the workings of discourses/power surrounding sport create divisions and inequities amongst groups and individuals. Sport indirectly works, as pertinent examples, to divide females from males (e.g. Hargreaves, 2000), able-bodied from disabled/injured (e.g. Howe, 2008; Smith and Sparkes, 2002), coordinated from the uncoordinated (e.g. Evans and Penney, 2008), dominant from marginalized forms of masculinities (e.g. Adams, 2011; Messner, 1992; Pringle and Markula, 2005;), straight from gay/queer (e.g. Caudwell, 2003; Cox and Thompson, 2000; Krane, 1996) and bodies of differing sizes (e.g. Gard and Wright, 2005; Sykes and McPhail, 2008). And although sport can work to challenge problematic sets of relations of power (e.g. in relation to the growth of female sport) it has, however, been more typically critiqued for its conservative political tendencies (see Fiske, 2005). At the least, therefore, I suggest that if we are interested in attempting to enhance a population's level of SWB, it is prudent to understand how the biopolitical promotion of sport in turn promotes select discourses and associated sets of power relations (e.g. amongst males/females, citizens/migrants, skilled/unskilled) and its potential impact on the wellbeing of select groups and individuals.

CRITICAL REFLECTIONS ON GOVERNING SWB VIA SPORT

With respect to questioning why sport is prioritized as a wellbeing/happiness strategy, I suggest there are lessons to be learned from Michael Gard and Jan Wright's (2005) meticulous analysis of the alleged obesity 'epidemic', in which they discussed the links between science, morality and ideology. They concluded that there were prime flaws in the epidemiological evidence that underpinned the concerns about obesity. They even illustrated how some epidemiologists would fail to show a link between obesity and poor health within their research but still conclude that more effort was needed to confront the 'obesity epidemic'. Thus, these researchers did not appear to believe their own evidence but, as Gard and Wright speculated, were driven by an existing ideology that positioned excess adipose tissue or fat as a social problem.

In a similar manner, I suggest that it is not empirical evidence that is driving the biopolitical promotion of sport, but discursive understandings of sport that promote an uncritical and unquestioning acceptance of the moral, social and health value of sport. Although the recent widespread governmental promotions of sport have likely been undertaken with good intentions, the *unquestioning acceptance* that sport is a force for social good needs to be challenged. For example, the promotion of sport as an activity that allegedly leads to good health, sound character and positive wellbeing acts to position sport participation as a moral imperative: correspondingly, individuals who do not enjoy participating in sport—perhaps those who are unskilled, unfit, uncompetitive or simply find sport painful or boring—are possibly at risk of understanding themselves as 'moral or health failures'. The non-sporting body in certain contexts is, accordingly, at risk of being marked as deviant or as unworthy.

Within schools, non-sporting boys risk social exclusion, harassment and bullying and correspondingly can feel dejected and unvalued (see Parker, 1996). This unfortunate link between non-sport participation and social exclusion has long existed, particularly amongst youthful males. Todd Crosset (1990), for example, contended that within the Victorian context, males who did not participate in sport indirectly risked becoming known as effeminate and unhealthy. Relatedly, weaker and non-sporting boys were disparaged as 'wankers' or 'saps'. The hierarchy of valued bodies is not just linked to gender but is also stratified via the intersections between race, class, age, size and sporting ability. Joanne Hill and Laura Azzarito (2012), relatedly, reported within their examination of valued bodies in physical education that:

> (I)n today's public health context, certain cohorts of young people are more likely than others to be identified as having 'bodies-at-risk', a discourse that fixes and homogenises minority young people identities as 'different', unhealthy and physically inactive. Evidence from national reports in the UK indicates that 'Other' girls, such as those from South

206 *Richard Pringle*

> Asian backgrounds, with low socio-economic status or with disabilities, have been identified as the least physically active and having the worst health status. . . . Rather than valued bodies—bodies that are healthy, sporting, physically active—'different' bodies are presented as 'deviant' from 'normal' white bodies and Western ways of knowing . . . (Hill and Azzarito, 2012: 264)

Akin to healthism (see Robert Crawford, 1980), I suggest that 'sportism' can be understood as an attempt by a government to use propaganda and ideological state institutions (e.g. schools, national sporting agencies, media) to encourage individuals to believe that their lives would be better if they played sport. The ideal or responsible citizen, correspondingly, is one who is thin, able-bodied, athletic and *enjoys* participating in sport. The non-sport participants, on the other hand, are at risk of being wellbeing failures. Thus, the promotion of sport as a biopolitical technique to enhance SWB can have unintended and negative consequences. Indeed, as Sara Ahmed (2010a: 41) argued, the governing of happiness can be fraught, as the 'promise of happiness . . . directs life in some ways rather than others', and this is not always in an individual's best interest.[5]

With a tinge of irony I also suggest that the discourse that informs that sport is 'good' for individuals simultaneously renders the biopolitical promotion of sport somewhat futile, as this discourse already works in specific contexts to actively encourage sport participation. Most parents/guardians, for example, encourage their young children to participate in sport. Likewise, the discursive contexts within schools also encourage and, at times, demand youthful sport participation. Hence, this invitatory sporting discourse (i.e. 'play sport, it is good for you') already circulates widely, so why does it need additional government promotion and funding?

FINAL WORDS

In this chapter, I have illustrated that governments are increasingly encouraging their populations to *enjoy* sport participation with the underpinning belief that this enjoyment will translate to physically active lifestyles and subsequent health and wellbeing benefits. Although the outcomes of these attempts to govern a population's wellbeing are currently under-researched, available evidence suggests that it is not a prudent strategy, as sporting participation does not come with any health or wellbeing guarantees. Moreover, if participants understand sport as a zero-sum game, as it is in elite sport, then victory can only be savored when the defeated know that they are defeated. Or, as 18th-century English poet William Cowper bemoaned: 'Detested sport, that owes its pleasures to another's pain'.

Many participants decide to stop playing, often in their youth, as they are frustrated with losing, physical pain, non-selection and inability to demonstrate skill (Butcher, Koenraad and Johns, 2002). For these individuals, withdrawal from sport is undertaken with a desire to help avoid displeasure. The consequence of promoting sport participation as a moral good, *without modification to how sport is played*, will not likely encourage these individuals back into sport and can have unintended and negative consequences, such as the castigation of non-sporting bodies in particular contexts (e.g. see Hill and Azzarito, 2012).

There are vast differences between the various sporting codes and respective cultures. Many competitive sports revolve around a participant's ability to tolerate pain (e.g. marathon running, rugby, American football, swimming, weightlifting, boxing, diving) with rewards being a sense of achievement, camaraderie or sensations of pleasure, but the 'costs' can be high. Michael Messner (1992) revealed that the average life expectancy of a professional American footballer was only 56 years. He suggested that it was not just the brutality of this high-speed collision sport, but the masculine culture of 'no pain no gain' that infiltrated the lives of the sportsmen and resulted in increased chances of early death (e.g. via car crashes, heart disease, violence, addiction, poor health care).

Biopolitical strategies to promote physical activity via sport simultaneously work to promote various sporting cultures, some of which have been linked to problematic sets of values (e.g. tolerance of pain, normalization of injuries, binge drinking, sexism, homophobia, hyper-masculinity). If governments desire to promote sport, they should, at the least, carefully consider which sports and associated cultures and values they wish to promote.

Although I readily acknowledge that sport participation, for a minority of individuals, can induce various pleasures and enhance the quality of their lives, for the majority this does not appear to be the case. Competitive sport fundamentally works as a dividing practice to mark bodies as different from each other (e.g. winners or losers, able or disabled, fit or unfit, male or female). If governments desire to enhance population happiness and SWB, it is more prudent to consider other political strategies, such as reducing income inequality, increasing the quality and availability of education, promoting democracy and peace, challenging prejudice and discrimination or targeting select groups via housing improvements or employment opportunities. The blanket call to encourage a population to participate in sport with a desire to encourage citizen wellbeing is a flawed biopolitical strategy.

NOTES

1. These broad results were obtained by asking respondents to answer the following four (seemingly simplistic) questions in relation to a (0–10) Likert scale:

   Overall, how satisfied are you with your life nowadays? Overall, to what extent do you feel the things you do in your life are worthwhile? Overall, how happy did you feel yesterday? Overall, how anxious did you feel yesterday?

208 *Richard Pringle*

2. In a similarly uncritical manner, the results could be interpreted to mean that dominant social practices (e.g. as associated with expectations to have children or be in an officially recognized and stable relationship) are worthy of pursuit, as they appear to be linked to enhanced levels of SWB. Yet such a conclusion is problematic, in part, as the direction of causality is impossible to determine. In other words, being married or having children might result from happiness as well as cause it. But perhaps more importantly, the simple act of performing accepted social practices might enhance SWB scores, as one simply feels 'good' through being accepted as normal.

3. Findings from intervention studies with older adults, however, appear more robust. Steriana Elavsky and colleagues (2005) concluded, for example, from their randomized controlled exercise study with older adults (M = 66.7 years) who increased their levels of physical activity, that they subsequently, over a five-year period, gained enhanced self-esteem, positive affect and life satisfaction.

4. There are many different ways that participation levels are calculated amongst populations, and survey results can appear to illustrate that a population is relatively active when the majority of citizens may not be overly active. For example, the Australian Bureau of Statistics (2013) survey of participation in sport and physical recreation reported that 63.6% of Australians were active (Australian Bureau of Statistics, 2013). Yet what this statistic meant was that 63.6% of those surveyed had participated in sport or physical recreation (e.g. walking for exercise, cycling, swimming) *at least once in the 12 months* prior to the survey. Thus, over a third of the population had not participated in any sport or physical recreation at all over a 12-month period. The survey further revealed, with respect to participation in the most popular team sports, that only 3.7% of males had participated in soccer (at least once over the last year), 2.8% in cricket and 2.6% in Australian Rules Football, and only 4.6% of females had participated in netball. Thus, only a small percentage of the Australian population is active participants in team sports (which are the sports most promoted within Schools).

5. To illustrate the complexity of promoting happiness, Sara Ahmed (2010) provided the example of a father who wanted his daughter, who identified as queer, to be 'happy'. The father believed that his daughter would not be happy in a queer relationship. Ahmed summarized:

> The father is unhappy as he thinks the daughter will be unhappy if she is queer. The daughter is unhappy as the father is unhappy with her being queer. The father witnesses the daughter's unhappiness as a sign of the truth of his position: that she will be unhappy because she is queer. The happy queer becomes unhappy at this point. In other words, the unhappy queer is made unhappy by the world that reads queers as unhappy. (Ahmed, 2010: 43)

Ahmed's vignette astutely illustrated that discourses of happiness (in this case the discourse or 'lay belief' that a queer relationship produces unhappiness), in and of themselves, have socially productive and political consequences. Ahmed correspondingly encouraged the need to critically interrogate the pursuit and monitoring of happiness.

Authors

Richard Pringle is an Associate Professor in Sport and Physical Education at the University of Auckland. He is the co-author of *Foucault, Sport and Exercise* (with Pirkko Markula) and co-editor of *Examining Sport Histories* (with Murray Phillips). He has served as the associate editor for the *Sociology of Sport Journal* and is currently on the editorial board of three international journals concerned with the sociology of sport, leisure and physical education.

Robert E. Rinehart, Associate Professor in Sport and Leisure Studies at the University of Waikato in Hamilton, Aotearoa New Zealand, has written *Inline Skating in Contemporary Sport: An Examination of Its Growth and Development* and *Players All: Performances in Contemporary Sport*. He has also co-edited (with Karen Barbour and Clive Pope) *Ethnographic Worldviews: Transformations and Social Justice* and (with Synthia Sydnor), *To the Extreme: Alternative Sports, Inside and Out*.

Jayne Caudwell is Reader in Sport, Gender and Sexualities at the University of Brighton. She is editor of *Sport, Sexualities and Queer Theory* (2006); *Women's Football in the UK* (2012) and co-editor of *Sexualities, Spaces and Leisure Studies* (2012). She is co-managing editor of the journal *Leisure Studies*.

References

Abbas, A. (2004) 'The embodiment of class, gender and age through leisure: a realist analysis of long distance running', *Leisure Studies*, 23(2): 159–175.

Adams, M.L. (2011) *Artistic Impressions: Figure Skating, Masculinity, and the Limits of Sport*, Toronto, Canada: University of Toronto Press.

Aftel, M. (2001) *Essence and Alchemy: A Book of Perfume*, London: Bloomsbury.

Ahmed, S. (2004) *The Cultural Politics of Emotion*, Edinburgh: Edinburgh University Press Ltd.

Ahmed, S. (2010a) 'Happy objects', in M. Gregg and G. Seigworth (eds.) *The Affect Theory Reader*, Durham, NC: Duke University Press.

Ahmed, S. (2010b) *The Promise of Happiness*, London: Duke.

Allen-Collinson, J. (2011) 'Feminist phenomenology and the woman in the running body', *Sport, Ethics and Philosophy*, 5(3): 297–313.

Allende, I. (2008[1991]) *The Infinite Plan*, trans. M.S. Peden, London: Harper Perennial.

Alon, R. (1996) *Mindful Spontaneity: Lessons in the Feldenkrais Method*, Berkeley, CA: North Atlantic Books.

'American shooter Libby Callahan' (2008) Online. Available HTTP: <http://www.2008.nbcolympics.com/shooting/news/newsid=207733.html> (accessed 25 March 2013).

Andrews, D. and Ritzer, G. (2007) 'The grobal in the sporting glocal', *Global Networks*, 7(2): 113–153.

Andrews, D.L. (2004) 'Sport in the late capitalist moment', in T. Slack (ed.) *The Commercialization of Sport*, London: Frank Cass.

Annas, J. (1987) 'Epicurus on pleasure and happiness', *Philosophical Topics,* 15(2): 5–21.

Annas, J. (1993) *The Morality of Happiness*, New York: Oxford University Press.

Anthony, J. (2008) 'George Foreman's record-shattering heavyweight championship win at age 45'. Online. Available HTTP: <http://anthonyj33.hubpages.com/hub/George-Foreman> (accessed 25 March 2013).

Archer, N.R. (2010) 'Ideological endzones: NFL films and the countersubversive tradition in American politics', *Open Access Dissertations*. Online. Available HTTP: <http://scholarworks.umass.edu/open_access_dissertations/217> (accessed 14 June 2013).

Aristotle (1962/350 BCE) *Nicomachean Ethics*, trans. M. Ostwald, Indianapolis: BobbsMerrill.

Atencio, M. and Beal, B. (2011) 'Beautiful losers: the symbolic exhibition and legitimization of outsider masculinity', *Sport in Society,* 14(1): 1–16.

Atkinson, M. (2008) 'Triathlon, suffering and exciting significance', *Leisure Studies*, 27(2): 165–180.

212 References

Atkinson, M. (2011) 'Physical cultural studies (redux)', *Sociology of Sport Journal*, 28: 135–44.

Australian Bureau of Statistics (2013) 'Culture and recreation'. Online. Available HTTP: <http://www.abs.gov.au/ausstats/abs@.nsf/Lookup/by%20Subject/1301.0~2012~Main%20Features~Sports%20and%20physical%20recreation~116> (accessed 15 May 2013).

Australian Sport Commission (2013) 'Government committed to keeping kids active'. Online. Available HTTP: <https://secure.ausport.gov.au/asc_internet/news/relea ses/archive/2013/story_538662_government_committed_to_keeping_kids_ active> (accessed 29 April 2013).

Avner, Z., Bridel, W., Eales, L., Glenn, N., Walker, R. L. and Peers, D. (2013) 'Moved to messiness: physical activity, feelings, and transdisciplinarity', *Emotion, Space and Society*. http://dx.doi.org/10.1016/j.emospa.2013.11.002

Bailey, R., Armour, K., Kirk, D., Jess, M., Pickup, I. and Sandford, R. (2009) 'The educational benefits claimed for physical education and school sport: an academic review', *Research Papers in Education*, 24(1): 1–27.

Bairner, A. (2012) 'For a sociology of sport', *Sociology of Sport Journal*, 29(1): 102–117.

Bakhtin, M. (1984) *Rabelais and His World*, trans. H. Iswolsky, Bloomington, IN: Indiana University Press.

Bale, J. (2004) *Running Cultures. Racing in Time and Space*, London: Routledge.

Barthes, R. (1972) *Mythologies*, New York: Hill and Wang.

Barthes, R. (1975[1973]) *The Pleasure of the Text*, trans. R. Miller, London: Macmillan.

Barthes, R. (2007) *What Is Sport?*, trans. R. Howard, New Haven, CT: Yale University Press.

Battin, M. P., Fisher, J., Moore, R. and Silvers, A. (1989) *Puzzles about Art: An Aesthetics Casebook*, New York: St. Martin's Press.

Baudrillard, J. (1989) *America,* trans. C. Turner, New York: Verso.

Baudrillard, J. (1994) *Simulacra and Simulation,* trans. S. F. Glaser, Ann Arbor, MI: University of Michigan Press.

Baudrillard, J. (2002) *The Spirit of Terrorism and Requiem for the Twin Towers*, New York: Verso.

Bauman, Z. (2003) *Liquid Love: On the Frailty of Human Bonds*, Cambridge, UK: Polity Press.

Beal, B. (1996) 'Alternative masculinity and its effects on gender relations in the subculture of skateboarding', *Journal of Sport Behavior*, 19(3): 204–20.

Beamish, R. and Ritchie, I. (2006) *Fastest, Highest, Strongest: A Critique of High-Performance Sport*, New York: Routledge.

Bentham, J. (1879) *The Principles of Morals and Legislation*, Oxford: Clarendon Press.

Berger, J. (2009) *Ways of Seeing*, New York: The Viking Press.

Berger, P. L. and Luckmann, T. (1966) *The Social Construction of Reality: A Treatise in the Sociology of Knowledge*, New York: Anchor Books.

Berstein, A. (2002) 'Is it time for a victory lap?: changes in the media coverage of women's sport', *International Review for the Sociology of Sport*, 37: 415–428.

Biddle, S.J.H. and Mutrie, N. (2008) *Psychology of Physical Activity: Determinants, Well-being, and Interventions,* 2nd ed, London: Routledge.

Blackman, L. (2008) *The Body: The Key Concepts*, Oxford: Berg.

Blanchard, C. M., Amiot, C. E., Perreault, S., Vallerand, R. J. and Provencher, P. (2009) 'Cohesiveness, coach's interpersonal style and psychological needs: their effects on self-determination and athletes' subjective well-being', *Psychology of Sport and Exercise*, 10(5): 545–551.

References 213

Boecker, H., Sprenger, T., Spilker, M. E., Henriksen, G., Koppenhoefer, M., Wagner, K. J., Valet, M., Berthele, A. and Tolle, T. R. (2008) 'The runner's high: opioidergic mechanisms in the human brain', *Cerebral Cortex*, 18(11): 2523–2531.

Booth, D. (1995a) 'Ambiguities in pleasure and discipline: the development of competitive surfing', *Journal of Sport History*, 22: 189–206.

Booth, D. (1995b) 'Sports policy in Australia: right, just and rational?', *The Australian Quarterly*, 67(1): 1–10.

Booth, D. (2004) 'Post-olympism? Questioning Olympic historiography', in J. Bale and C. Mette (eds.) *Post-Olympism? Questioning Sport in the Twenty-first Century*, Oxford: Berg.

Booth, D. (2008) '(Re) reading the surfers' bible: the affects of Tracks', *Continuum: Journal of Media & Cultural Studies*, 22(1): 17–35.

Booth, D. (2009) 'Politics and pleasure: the philosophy of physical education revisited', *Quest*, 61(2), 133–153.

Booth, D. (2011) *Surfing: The Ultimate Guide*, Santa Barbara, CA: ABC-CLIO.

Bordo, S. (1999) *The Male Body: A New Look at Men in Public and in Private*, New York: Farrar, Straus & Giroux.

Bourdieu, P. (1984) *Distinction: A Social Critique of the Judgement of Taste*, trans. R. Nice, Oxon: Routledge Kegan & Paul.

Bourriaud, N. (2009) *Michel Foucault: Manet and the Birth of the Viewer: Introduction to M. Foucault, Manet and the Object of Painting*, London: Tate Publishing.

Boxill, J. M. (1988) 'Beauty, sport, and gender', in W. J. Morgan and K. V. Meier (eds.) *Philosophic Inquiry in Sport*, Champaign, IL: Human Kinetics.

Bridel, W. (2010) 'Finish . . . whatever it takes: exploring pain and pleasure in the ironman triathlon: a socio-cultural analysis', unpublished doctoral thesis, Queen's University.

Broad, K. (2001) 'The Gendered Unapologetic: Queer Resistance and Transformation in Sport', *Sociology of Sport Journal*, 18(2): 181–203.

Brohm, J-M. (1978) *Sport: A Prison of Measured Time*, London: Pluto Press.

Brokaw, T. (1998) *The Greatest Generation*, New York: Random House.

Broudehoux, A. (2007) 'Spectacular Beijing: the conspicuous construction of an Olympic metropolis', *Journal of Urban Affairs*, 29: 383–399.

Bruce, T. (1998) 'Audience frustration and pleasure: women viewers confront televised women's basketball', *Journal of Sport & Social Issues*, 22(4): 373–97.

Burdsey, D. (2011) 'That joke isn't funny anymore: racial microaggressions, colourblind ideology and the mitigation of racism in English men's first-class cricket', *Sociology of Sport Journal*, 28(3): 261–283.

Burford, B. (1992) *Among the Thugs: The Experience, and the Seduction, of Crowd Violence*, New York: WW Norton & Co Inc.

Butcher, J., Lindner, K. J. and Johns, D. P. (2002) 'Withdrawal from competitive youth sport: a retrospective ten-year study', *Journal of Sport Behavior*, 25(2): 145–164.

Butler, J. (1990) *Gender Trouble and the Subversion of Identity*, New York: Routledge.

Caillois, R. (1961) *Man, Play and Games*, New York: The Free Press.

Carlson, J. (2010) 'The female significant in all-women's amateur roller derby', *Sociology of Sport Journal*, 27(4): 428–440.

'Carisbrook not giving up NZ great's ashes' (2010) 'NZPA'. Online. Available HTTP: <http://www.stuff.co.nz/sport/cricket/4016069/Carisbrook-not-giving-up-NZ-cricket-greats-ashes> (accessed 29 November 2013).

Carr, D. B., Bullen, B. A., Skrinar, G. S. Arnold, M. A., Rosenblatt, M., Beitins, I. Z., Martin, J. B. and McArthur, J. W. (1981) 'Physical conditioning facilitates the

214 References

exercise-induced secretion of beta-endorphin and beta-lipotropin in women', *The New England Journal of Medicine*, 305(10): 560.

Carver, R. (1981) *What We Talk about When We Talk about Love*, New York: Knopf.

Catalano, J. (2013) 'The beauty and art of body modification', *Ladybud*, Online. Available HTTP: <http://www.ladybud.com/2013/07/30/body-modification/> (accessed 28 October 2013).

Caudwell, J. (1999) 'Women's football in the United Kingdom: theorising gender and unpacking the Butch lesbian image', *Journal of Sport and Social Issues*, 23(4): 390–402.

Caudwell, J. (2003) 'Sporting gender: women's footballing bodies as sites/sights for the [re]articulation of sex, gender and desire', *Sociology of Sport Journal*, 20(4): 371–386.

Caudwell, J. (2006) 'Femme-fatale: re-thinking the femme-inine', in J. Caudwell (ed.) *Sport, Sexualities and Queer/Theory*, London: Routledge.

Caudwell, J. (2010) 'The jazz-sport analogue: passing notes on gender and sexuality', *International Review for the Sociology of Sport*, 45(2): 240–248.

Caudwell, J. (2011) '"Does your boyfriend know you're here?": The spatiality of homophobia in men's football culture in the UK', *Leisure Studies*, 30(2): 123–138.

Caudwell, J. (2012) '[Transgender] young men: gendered subjectivities and the physically active body', *Sport, Education and Society*, 1–17.

Caudwell, J. (2014) '"Feeling blue": the ordinary pleasures of mundane motion', *Qualitative Research in Sport, Exercise and Health*, (ahead of print), 1–12.

Celsi, R., Rose, R. and Leigh, T. (1993) 'An exploration of high-risk leisure consumption through skydiving', *The Journal of Consumer Research*, 20(1): 1–23.

Charmaz, K. (1991) *Good Days, Bad Days*, New Brunswick, NJ: Rutgers University Press.

Chase, L. (2006) '(Un)disciplined bodies: a Foucauldian analysis of women's rugby', *Sociology of Sport Journal*, 23: 229–247.

Chaudhri, S.K. and Jain, N.K. (2009) 'History of cosmetics', *Asian Journal of Pharmaceutics*, 3: 164–167.

'Clint Eastwood speaks out on Republican National Convention speech' (2012) Online. Available HTTP: <http://www.huffingtonpost.com/2012/09/15/clint-eastwood-rnc-speech_n_1886551.html> (accessed 17 September 2012).

Coakley, J. (2008) *Sports in Society: Issues and Controversies*, 10th ed, Boston: McGraw-Hill.

Coakley, J. (2011) 'Ideology doesn't just happen: sports and neoliberalism', *Journal of ALESDE*, 1(1): 67–84.

Coakley, J., Hallinan, C., Jackson, S. and Mewett, P. (2009) *Sports in Society: Issues and Controversies in Australia and New Zealand*, Sydney, Australia: McGraw-Hill.

Coalter, F. (2007) *A Wider Social Role for Sport: Who's Keeping the Score?*, London: Routledge.

Cole, C.L. (2000) 'Testing for sex or drugs', *Journal of Sport & Social Issues*, 24: 331–333.

Colebrook, C. (2006) 'Introduction', *Feminist Theory*, 7(2): 131–142.

Collins, Scott. (2012) 'London Olympics: NBC coverage most-watched TV event in U.S. history'. Online. Available HTTP: <http://www.latimes.com/entertainment/tv/showtracker/la-et-st-london-olympics-dubbed-mostwatched-event-in-us-history-by-nbc> (accessed 10 March 2013).

Connell, R.W. (1995) *Masculinities*, St. Leonards: Allen & Unwin.

Cope, B. and Kalantzis, M. (1999) *Teaching and Learning in the New World of Literacy: A Professional Development Program and Classroom Research Project: Participants' Resource Book*, Melbourne: RMIT University.

References 215

Coveney, J. and Bunton, R. (2003) 'In pursuit of the study of pleasure: implications for health research and practice', *Health: An Interdisciplinary Journal for the Social Study of Health, Illness and Medicine*, 7(2): 161–179.

Cowper, W. (1785) *The Works of William Cowper: His Life, Letters, and Poems.* Online. Available HTTP: <http://www.gutenberg.org/cache/epub/3698/pg3698. txt> (accessed 15 February 2012).

Cox, B., and Thompson, S. (2000) 'Multiple bodies: sportswomen, soccer and sexuality', *International Review for the Sociology of Sport*, 35(1): 5–20.

Crawford, G. (2004) *Consuming Sport: Fans, Sport and Culture*, London: Routledge.

Crawford, R. (1980) 'Healthism and the medicalization of everyday life', *International Journal of Health Services,* 10(3): 365–388.

'Cricket grounds' (2012) Online. Available HTTP: <http://www.scattering-ashes.co. uk/help-advice/law/cricket-grounds/> (accessed 10 March 2013).

Cross, G. S. (1990) *A Social History of Leisure Since 1600*, State College, PA: Venture Publishing.

Crosset, T. (1990) 'Masculinity, sexuality, and the development of early modern sport', in M. A. Messner and D. F. Sabo (eds.) *Sport, Men and the Gender Order: Critical Feminist Perspectives*, Champaign, IL: Human Kinetics.

Csíkszentmihályi, M. (1990) *Flow: The Psychology of Optimal Experience*, New York: Harper Collins Publishers.

Csíkszentmihályi, M. (1996) *Creativity: The Psychology of Discovery and Invention*, New York: HarperCollins Publishers.

Csíkszentmihályi, M. (1997) *Flow and the Psychology of Discovery and Invention.* New York: Harper Perennial.

Cumming, E. and Henry, W. E. (1961) *Growing Old: The Process of Disengagement*, New York: Basic Books.

Cummins, R. A., Lau, A. A., Mellor, D. and Stokes, M. A. (2009) 'Encouraging governments to enhance the happiness of their nation: step 1: understand subjective wellbeing', *Social Indicators Research*, 91(1): 23–36.

Cutri, C. (2006) *Riding the Wave*, Provo, UT: Brigham Young University.

Cutri, C. (2009) *Hanging Five*, Provo, UT: C. Cutri, Producer.

Dalziel, P. (2011) *The Economic and Social Value of Sport and Recreation to New Zealand*, Lincoln, NZ: Lincoln University.

Daniels, B. C. (1991) 'Did the puritans have fun? Leisure, recreation and the concept of pleasure in early New England', *Journal of American Studies*, 25(1): 7–22.

Davis, L. R. (1997) *The Swimsuit Issue and Sport: Hegemonic Masculinity in Sports Illustrated*, Albany, NY: State University of New York Press.

Davy, Z. (2012) 'Bodily aesthetic affects in tarns erotica: Towards a wider spectra of desire', paper presented at British Sociological Association Annual Conference, Leeds University, UK.

Dawson-Cook, S. (2007) 'The Feldenkrais method of somatic education', *American Fitness*, September/October: 16–17.

de Beauvoir, S. (1976[1949]) *The Second Sex*, London: Penguin.

de Coubertin, P. (2012) *Olympic Memoirs*. Online. Available HTTP: <http://www. la84 foundation.org/OlympicInformationCenter/OlympicReview/1977/ore113/ ore113q.pdf > (accessed 5 September 2012).

Debord, G. (1995[1967]) *The Society of the Spectacle,* trans. D. N. Smith, New York: Zone Books.

DeChaine, D. R. (2002) 'Affect and embodied understanding in musical experience', *Text and Performance Quarterly*, 22(2): 79–98.

Denzin, N. K. (1989) *Interpretive Interactionism*, Newbury Park, CA: Sage.

Denzin, N. K. (1991a) *Hollywood, Shot by Shot: Alcoholism in American Cinema*, New York: Aldine de Gruyter.

216   *References*

Denzin, N.K. (1991b) *Images of Postmodern Society: Social Theory and Contemporary Cinema*, Thousand Oaks, CA: Sage.

Denzin, N.K. (2001[1989]) *Interpretive Interactionism*, Thousand Oaks, CA: Sage Publications.

Denzin, N. K. (2010) *The Qualitative Manifesto: A Call to Arms*, Walnut Creek, CA: Left Coast Press.

Diener, E. (2009) 'Subjective well-being', in E. Diener (ed.) *The Science of Well-being: The Collected Works of Ed Diener*. London: Springer.

Diener, E. and Suh, E.M. (2000) 'Measuring subjective well-being to compare the quality of life of cultures', in E. Diener and E.M. Suh (eds.) *Culture and Subjective Well-being*, Cambridge, MA: MIT Press.

Dietrich, A. and McDaniel, W.F. (2004) 'Endocannabinoids and exercise', *British Journal of Sports Medicine*, 38(5): 536–541.

DiPietro, L. (2001) 'Physical activity in aging changes in patterns and their relationship to health and function', *The Journals of Gerontology Series A: Biological Sciences and Medical Sciences*, 56: 13–22.

Dishman, R.K. and O'Connor, P.J. (2009) 'Lessons in exercise neurobiology: the case of endorphins', *Mental Health and Physical Activity*, 2(1): 4–9.

Donmoyer, R. (2006) 'Take my paradigm . . . please! The legacy of Kuhn's construct in educational research', *International Journal of Qualitative Studies in Education*, 19(1): 11–34.

Donnelly, P. (2004) 'Sport and risk culture', in K. Young (ed.) *Sporting Bodies, Damaged Selves: Sociological Studies of Sports-Related Injury*, Bingley, UK: Emerald Group Publishing.

'Dortmund fans to offer support after the final whistle' (2008) Online. Available HTTP: <http://www.theroar.com.au/2008/12/12/dortmund-fans-to-offer-support-after-the-final-whistle/> (accessed 12 March 2013).

Douglas, P. (1996) 'The body and social theory in Connell's *Masculinities*', *Discourse: Studies in the Cultural Politics of Education*, 17(1): 107–114.

Downward, P. and Rasciute, S. (2011) 'Does sport make you happy? An analysis of the well-being derived from sports participation', *International Review of Applied Economics*, 25(3): 331–348.

Droney, D. (2010) 'The business of "getting up": street art and marketing in Los Angeles', *Visual Anthropology: Published in Cooperation with the Commission on Visual Anthropology*, 23(2): 98–114.

Duncan, M. and Brummett, B. (1989) 'Types and sources of spectating pleasure in televised sport', *Sociology of Sport Journal*, 6(3): 195–211.

Dunning, E., Murphy, P. and Williams, J. (1986) 'Spectator violence at football matches: towards a sociological explanation', *The British Journal of Sociology*, 37(2): 221–244.

Durkheim, E. (1976) *The Elementary Forms of the Religious Life*, trans. J.W. Swain, London: George Allen & Unwin Ltd.

Elavsky, S., McAuley, E., Motl, R.W., Marquez, D.X., Hu, L., Jerome, G.J. and Diener. E. (2005) 'Physical activity enhances long-term quality of life in older adults: efficacy, esteem, and affective influences', *Annals of Behavioral Medicine*, 30(2): 138–145.

Elias, N. (1986) 'Introduction', in N. Elias and E. Dunning (eds.) *Quest for Excitement: Sport and Leisure in the Civilizing Process*, Oxford, UK: Basil Blackwell.

Elias, N. and Dunning, E. (1986) *Quest for Excitement: Sport and Leisure in the Civilizing Process*, Oxford, UK: Basil Blackwell.

'Emotion classification' (2012) Online. Available HTTP: <http://en.wikipedia.org/wiki/Basic_emotions #Basic_and_complex_emotions> (accessed 10 December 2012).

References 217

Entine, J. (2008) *Taboo: Why Black Athletes Dominate Sports and Why We're Afraid to Talk about It*, New York: PublicAffairs.

Evans, J. and Davies, B. (2011) 'New directions, new questions? Social theory, education and embodiment', *Sport, Education and Society*, 16(3): 263–78.

Evans, J. and Penney, D. (2008) 'Levels on the playing field: the social construction of physical "ability" in the physical education curriculum', *Physical Education and Sport Pedagogy*, 13(1): 31–47.

Evers, C. (2006) 'How to surf', *Journal of Sport and Social Issues*, 30(3): 229–243.

Farred, G. (2002) 'Long distance love: growing up a Liverpool Football Club fan', *Journal of Sport and Social Issues*, 26(1): 6–24.

Feldenkrais, M. (1972) *Awareness Through Movement: Health Exercises for Personal Growth*, New York: HarperSanFrancisco.

Feldenkrais, M. (1981) *The Elusive Obvious*, Cupertino, CA: Meta Publications.

Feldman, F. (2004) *Pleasure and the Good Life: Concerning the Nature, Varieties, and Plausibility of Hedonism*, Oxford: Clarendon Press.

Feldman, F. (2007) 'Precis of pleasure and the good life: concerning the nature, varieties, and plausibility of hedonism', *Philosophical Studies*, 136: 405–408.

Ferreday, D. (2008) 'Showing the girl: the new Burlesque', *Feminist Theory*, 9(1): 47–65.

Finch, C.F. (2012) 'Getting sports injury prevention on to public health agendas–addressing the shortfalls in current information sources', *British Journal of Sports Medicine*, 46(1): 70–74.

Fincher, D. (2008) *The Curious Case of Benjamin Button*, Burbank, CA: The Kennedy.

Finley, N.J. (2010) 'Skating femininity: gender maneuvering in women's roller derby', *Journal of Contemporary Ethnography*, 39(4): 359.

Finn, G. (1994) 'Football violence: a societal psychological perspective', in R. Giulianotti, N. Bonney and M. Hepworth (eds.) *Football Violence and Social identity*, London: Routledge.

Fiske, J. (1991) *Understanding Popular Culture*, New York: Routledge.

Fiske, J. (2005) *Understanding Popular Culture*, London: Taylor & Francis.

Fitzgerald, F.S. (1953) *The Great Gatsby*, New York: Charles Scribner's Sons.

Fleming, D. and Sturm, D. (2011) *Media, Masculinities and the Machine: F1, Transformers, and Fantasizing Technology at Its Limits*, London: Continuum.

Fletcher, R. (2008) 'Living on the edge: the appeal of risk sports for the professional middle class', *Sociology of Sport Journal*, 25(3): 310–330.

Fonow, M. and Cook, J. (2005) 'Feminist methodology: new applications in the academy and public policy', *Signs: Journal of Women in Culture and Society*, 30(4): 2211–2236.

Foster, H. (ed.) (1983) *The Anti-aesthetic: Essays on Postmodern Culture*, Seattle, WA: Bay Press.

Foucault, M. (1985) *The Use of Pleasure: The History of Sexuality, Vol. 2*, London: Penguin Books.

Foucault, M. (1986) *The Care of the Self: History of Sexuality, Vol. 3*, New York: Pantheon.

Foucault, M. (1990a) *An Introduction: The History of Sexuality, Vol. 1*, trans. R. Hurley, New York: Vintage Books.

Foucault, M. (1990b) *The Use of Pleasure (Volume 2: The History of Sexuality)*, trans. R. Hurley, New York: Vintage Books.

Foucault, M. (1995) *Discipline and Punish: The Birth of the Prison*, New York: Random House.

Foucault, M. (2007) *Security, Territory and Population: Lectures at the Collège de France*, trans. G. Burchell, Basingstoke: Palgrave Macmillian.

218 *References*

Foucault, M. (2009) *Manet and the Object of Painting*, London: Tate Publishing.

Fox, K. (1999) 'The influence of physical activity on mental well-being', *Public Health Nutrition*, 2(3a): 411–418.

Fox, K.M. and Walker, G. (2002) 'Reconsidering the relationship between flow and feminist ethics: a response', *Leisure studies*, 21(1): 15–26.

Freeland, C.A. (1998) *Feminist Interpretations of Aristotle*, University Park, PA: Penn State University Press.

Freud, S. (1921) *Beyond the Pleasure Principle*, London: Hogarth Press.

Freud, S. (2010[1930]) *Civilization and Its Discontents*, New York: WW Norton & Company.

Frijda, N.H. and Parrott, W.G. (2011) 'Basic emotions or ur-emotions?', *Emotion Review*, 3(4): 406–415.

Frith, S. (1982) 'Music for pleasure', *Mass Communication Review Yearbook*, 3: 495–503.

Frith, S. and Street, J. (1992) 'Rock Against Racism and Red Wedge: from music to politics, from politics to music', *Rockin'the Boat: Mass Music and Mass Movements*, 67–80.

Frueh, J. (1991) 'The fear of flesh that moves', *High Performance*, 55: 70–71.

Fukuyama, F. (1989) 'The end of history?', *The National Interest*, 16: 3–18.

Galloway, S., Bell, D., Hamilton, C. and Scullion, A.C. (2006) 'Well-being and quality of life: measuring the benefits of culture and sport-a literature review and think piece', *Scottish Executive Social Research*. Online. Available HTTP: <http://www.scotland.gov.uk.>

Gantz, W. and Wenner, L.A. (1991) 'Men, women, and sports: Audience experiences and effects', *Journal of Broadcasting & Electronic Media*, 35(2): 233–243.

Gard, M. and Wright, J. (2005) *The Obesity Epidemic: Science, Morality and Ideology*, London: Routledge.

Genet. (1966[1949]) *The Thief's Journal*, London: Penguin.

Gergen, K.J. and Gergen, M.M. (2000) 'The new aging: self construction and social values', in K.W. Schaie and J. Hendricks (eds.) *The Evolution of the Aging Self: The Societal Impact on the Aging Process*, New York: Springer.

Gibson, O. (2011) 'London Olympics security to be boosted by 13,500 troops'. Online. Available HTTP: <http://www.guardian.co.uk/sport/2011/dec/15/london-olympics-security-boosted-troops?newsfeed=true>.

'Golden oldie: Hopkins beats George Foreman's record and wins major title at the age of 46!' (2011) Online. Available HTTP: <http://www.dailymail.co.uk/sport/othersports /article-1389654/Bernard-Hopkins-beats-George-Foremans-record-wins-major-title-age-46.html> (accessed 25 March 2013).

Gieseck, J. and Madden, J. (2007) *'The Sydney Olympics, Seven Years On: An Ex-post Dynamic CGE Assessment'*, Melbourne: Centre of Policy Studies/IMPACT Centre.

Gillette, P.J. (2005) *The Complete Marquis de Sade*, Los Angeles, CA: Holloway House Publishing.

Gilligan, C. (1992) *In A Different Voice: Psychological Theory and Women's Development*, Cambridge, MA: Harvard University Press.

Giroux, H. (2012) 'Coda: why faculty should join Occupy Movement protesters on college campuses', in N.K. Denzin and M.D. Giardina (eds.) *Qualitative Inquiry and the Politics of Advocacy*, Walnut Creek, CA: Left Coast Press.

Giroux, H.A. (2011) *Education and the Crisis of Public Values: Challenging the Assault on Teachers, Students, and Public Education*, New York: Peter Lang.

Giulianotti, R. (2005) *Sport: A Critical Sociology*, Cambridge, UK: Polity Press.

Giulianotti, R. and Klauser, F. (2010) 'Security governance and sport mega-events: toward an interdisciplinary research agenda', *Journal of Sport and Social Issues*, 34(1): 49–61.

References 219

Giulianotti, R. and Robertson, R. (2004) 'The globalization of football: a study in the glocalization of the "serious life"', *The British Journal of Sociology*, 55(4): 545–568.

Gobeil, M. (1965) 'Interviews: Simone de Beauvoir, the art of fiction, No. 35', trans. B. Frechtman, *Paris Review*, 34. Online. Available HTTP: <http://www.theparisreview.org/interviews/4444/the-art-of-fiction-no-35-simone-de-beauvoir> (accessed 9 May 2013).

Gold, J. and Gold, M. (2010) 'Olympic cities: regeneration, city rebranding and changing urban agendas', in V. Girginov (ed.) *The Olympics: A Critical Reader*, London: Routledge.

Gold, T. (2004) *Living Wabi Sabi*, Kansas City, KN: Andrews McMeel Publishing.

Goldlust, J. (1987) *Playing for Keeps: Sport, the Media and Society*, Melbourne: Longman Cheshire.

Goldman, R. and Papson, S. (2000) *Nike Culture: The Sign of the Swoosh*, London: Sage.

Gosset, K. (2014) 'Inconvenience store', Radio New Zealand National. Online. Available HTTP: <http://www.radionz.co.nz/national/programmes/afternoons/audio/2588937/nz-society-inconvenience-store> (accessed 14 March 2014).

Grant, B. C. (2001) '"You're never too old": beliefs about physical activity and playing sport in later life', *Ageing and Society*, 21(6): 777–798.

Grant, B. C. and Kluge, M. A. (2007) 'Exploring "other body(s)" of knowledge: getting to the heart of the story about aging and physical activity', *Quest*, 59(4): 398–414.

Greer, G. (1970) *The Female Eunuch*, London: Harper Collins.

Griffin, M. (2010) 'Setting the scene: hailing women into a running identity', *Qualitative Research in Sport, Exercise and Health*, 2(2): 153–174.

Griggs, G., Leflay, K. and Groves, M. (2012) '"Just watching it again now still gives me goose bumps!": examining the mental postcards of sport spectators', *Sociology of Sport Journal*, 29(1): 89–101.

Gross, L. (2012) 'Sijo'. Online. Available HTTP: <www.ahapoetry.com/sijo.htm> (accessed 9 November 2012).

Grossberg, L. (1992) 'Is there a fan in the house?: the affective sensibility of fandom', in L. Lewis (ed.) *The Adoring Audience: Fan Culture and Popular Media*, London: Routledge.

Grossberg, L. (2010) 'Affects future: rediscovering the virtual in the actual', in M. Gregg and G. Seigworth (eds.) *The Affect Theory Reader*, Durham, NC: Duke University Press.

Gubrium, J. F. and Holstein, J. A. (2003) 'The everyday visibility of the aging body', in C. A. Faircloth (ed.) *Aging Bodies: Images and Everyday Experience*, Walnut Creek, CA: AltaMira Press.

Guiterman, A. (1921) *A Ballad-maker's Pack*, New York: Harper and Brothers.

Guttmann, A. (1996) *The Erotic in Sports,* New York: Columbia University Press.

'Gymbit' (2008) 'Age is just a number', Online. Available HTTP: <http://www.gymbits.com/inspiration/age-is-just-a-number/> (accessed 28 November 2013).

Hallmann, K., Breuer, C. and Kühnreich, B. (2013) 'Happiness, pride and elite sporting success: what population segments gain most from national athletic achievements?', *Sport Management Review*, 16(2): 226–235.

Hargreaves, J. (2000) *Heroines of Sport: The Politics of Difference and Identity*, London: Routledge.

Harris, D. K. (2007) *The Sociology of Aging*, 3rd ed, Lanham, MD: Rowman & Littlefield Publishers.

Harvey, D. (2005) *A Brief History of Neoliberalism*, Oxford: Oxford University Press.

Harwood, V. (2009) 'Theorizing biopedagogies', in J. Wright and V. Harwood (eds.) *Biopolitics and the 'Obesity Epidemic': Governing Bodies*, New York: Routledge.

220 References

Hebdige, D. (1979) *Subculture: The Meaning of Style*, London: Routledge.

Hemmings, C. (2005) 'Invoking affect: cultural theory and the ontological turn' *Cultural Studies,* 19(5): 548–67.

Hill, J. and Azzarito, L. (2012) 'Representing valued bodies in PE: a visual inquiry with British Asian girls', *Physical Education & Sport Pedagogy*, 17(3): 263–276.

Hitchens, C. (2007) *The Portable Atheist: Essential Readings for the Non-believer,* Philadelphia: De Capo Press.

Hoberman, J. (1995) 'Toward a theory of Olympic internationalism', *Journal of Sport History*, 22(1): 1–37.

Hoberman, J. (2011) 'The myth of sport as a peace-promoting political force', *The SAIS Review of International Affairs*, 3(1): 17–29.

Hockey, J. (2005) 'Knowing the route: distance runner's mundane knowledge', *Sociology of Sport Online,* 7(1). Online. Available HTTP: <http://physed.otago.ac.nz/sosol> (accessed 19 January 2013)

Hockey, J. (2006) 'Sensing the run: the senses and distance running', *Senses and Society*, 1(1): 183–202.

Hoeller, S. A. (2014) 'The Gnostic world view: a brief summary of Gnosticism'. Online. Available HTTP: <http://www.gnosis.org/gnintro.htm> (accessed 13 April 2014).

Hogan, K. and Norton, K. (2000) 'The "price" of Olympic gold', *Journal of Science and Medicine in Sport*, 3(2): 203–218.

Holt, J. (2006) 'Oh, joy [Review of the book *Happiness: A history*]', Online. Available HTTP: <http://www.nytimes.com/2006/02/12/books/review/12holt.html?pagewanted=all&_r=0> (accessed 22 April 2013).

Horne, J. (2007) 'The four 'knowns' of sports mega-events', *Leisure Studies*, 26(1): 81–96.

Houlihan, B. (1997) 'Sport, national identity and public policy', *Nations and Nationalism,* 3(1): 113–137.

Howe, D. (2008) *The Politics of the Paralympic Games*, London: Routledge.

Huber, G. (ed.) (1997) *Healthy Aging, Activity and Sports—Proceedings*, Heidelberg, Germany: Health Promotion Publications.

Hughes, N. and Rogers, S. (2012) 'The oldest, youngest, biggest and smallest Olympians'. Online. Available HTTP: <http://au.businessinsider.com/the-oldest-youngest-biggest-and-smallest-olympians-2012–8> (accessed 26 March 2013).

Hughes, R. and Coakley, J. (1991) 'Positive deviance among athletes: the implications of overconformity to the sport ethic', *Sociology of Sport Journal*, 8(4): 307–325.

Huizinga, J. (1955) *Homo Ludens,* Boston: Beacon Press.

Huizinga, J. (1970/1938) *Homo Ludens: A Study of the Play Element in Culture*, London: Routledge & Kegan Paul.

Humberstone, B. (2011) 'Embodiment and social and environmental action in nature-based sport: spiritual spaces', *Leisure Studies*, 30(4): 495–512.

Humberstone, B. and Stan, I. (2012) 'Nature and well-being in outdoor learning: authenticity or performativity', *Journal of Adventure Education & Outdoor Learning*, 12(3): 183–197.

Ignatow, G. (2012) 'Mauss's lectures to psychologists: a case for holistic sociology', *Journal of Classical Sociology*, 12(1): 3–21.

Immordino-Yang, M. H. and Damasio, A. (2007) 'We feel, therefore we learn: the relevance of affective and social neuroscience to education', *Mind, Brain, and Education*, 1(1): 3–10.

International Olympic Committee (1994) *Olympic Charter.* Online. Available HTTP: <http://www.olympic.org/Documents/Olympic%20Charter/Olympic_Charter_through_time/1994-Olympic_Charter_Sept94.pdf> (accessed 20 December 2011)

References   221

International Olympic Committee (2004a) *Celebrate Humanity Booklet.* Online. Available HTTP: <www.olympic.org/Documents/Reports/EN/en_report_808.pdf> (accessed 20 December, 2011).

International Olympic Committee (2004b) *Olympic Charter*, Lausanne, Switzerland.

Internet Encyclopedia of Philosophy (2013) Online. Available HTTP: <http://www.iep.utm.edu/cyren/> (accessed 19 March 2013).

Irigaray, L. (1985) *This Sex Which is Not One*, New York: Cornell University Press.

Iso-Ahola, S. E., Jackson, E. and Dunn, E. (1994) 'Starting, ceasing, and replacing leisure activities over the life-span', *Journal of Leisure Research*, 26(3): 227–249.

Ives, K. (2010) *Cixous, Irigaray, Kristeva. The Jouissance of French Feminism*, 4th ed, Maidstone: Crescent Moon Publishing.

Izard, C., Kagan, J. and Zajonc, R. (eds.) (1984) *Emotions, Cognition, and Behaviour*, Cambridge, UK: Cambridge University Press.

Jackson, S. (2000) 'Joy, fun and flow state in sport', in Y. Hanin (ed.) *Emotions in Sport*, Champaign, IL: Human Kinetics.

Jackson, S. A. and Kimiecik, J. C. (2008) 'The flow perspective for optimal experience in sport and physical activity', in T. Horn (ed.) *Advances in Sport Psychology*, 3rd ed, Champaign, IL: Human Kinetics.

Janzen, M. D. (2008) 'The women of Agabagaya: education and post-development theory', *Canadian Journal of Education / Revue canadienne de l'éducation*, 31(1): 8–31.

Jeffrey, B. and Troman, G. (2004) 'Time for ethnography', *British Educational Research Journal*, 30(4): 535–548.

Jeffreys, S. (2005) *Beauty and Misogyny: Harmful Cultural Practices in the West*, London: Routledge.

Jennings, A. (2011) 'Investigating corruption in corporate sport: the IOC and FIFA', *International Review for the Sociology of Sport*, 46(4): 387–398.

Jones, I. (2000) 'A model of serious leisure identification: the case of football fandom', *Leisure Studies*, 19(4): 283–298.

Jones, K. W. (2008) 'Female fandom: identity, sexism, and men's professional football in England', *Sociology of Sport Journal*, 25(4): 516–537.

Kashdan, T. B., Biswas-Diener, R. and King, L. A. (2008) 'Reconsidering happiness: the costs of distinguishing between hedonics and eudaimonia', *The Journal of Positive Psychology*, 3(4): 219–233.

Kavetsos, G. and Szymanski, S. (2010) 'National well-being and international sports events', *Journal of Economic Psychology*, 31(2): 158–171.

Kay, J. and Laberge, S. (2003) 'Oh say can you ski? Imperialistic construction of freedom in Warren Miller's Freeriders', in R. E. Rinehart and S. Sydnor (eds.) *To the Extreme: Alternative Sports Inside and Out*, Albany, NY: State University of New York Press.

Kelly, P. J. (1990) 'Utilitarian strategies in Bentham and John Stuart Mill', *Utilitas*, 2(2): 245–66.

Kennedy, E., Pussard, H. and Thornton, A. (2006) '"Leap for London"? Investigating the affective power of the sport spectacle', *World Leisure*, 3: 6–21.

Kesebir, P. and Diener, E. (2009) 'In pursuit of happiness: empirical answers to philosophical questions', in E. Deiner (ed.) *The Science of Well-being: The Collected Works of Ed Diener*, London: Springer.

Kidd, B. (2010) 'Human rights and the Olympic movement after Beijing', *Sport in Society*, 13(5): 901–910.

King, A. (1997) 'The postmodernity of football hooliganism', *The British Journal of Sociology*, 48(4): 576–593.

Kingsbury, P. (2008) 'Did somebody say jouissance? On Slavoj Žižik, consumption, and nationalism', *Emotion, Space and Society*, 1: 48–55.

222 References

Kjellström, R. (1974) 'Senilicide and invalidicide among the Eskimos', *Folk*, 16: 117.

Kleinman, S. and Copp, M. A. (1993) *Emotions and Fieldwork*, London: Sage.

Klugman, M. (2009) *Passion Play: Love, Hope and Heartbreak at the Footy*, Melbourne: Hunter Publishers.

Klugman, M. (2013) 'It's that feeling sick in my guts that I think I like the most: sport, pleasure, and embodied suffering', in R. Pringle and M. Phillips (eds.) *Sport History and Postmodernism as Social Theory*, Morgantown, WV: Fitness Information Technology.

Kohe, G. (2010) 'Disrupting the rhetoric of the rings: a critique of Olympic idealism in physical education', *Sport, Education and Society*, 15(4): 479–494.

Kohn, A. (1992) *No Contest: The Case against Competition*, Boston: Houghton Mifflin Company.

Krane, V. (1996) 'Lesbians in sport: toward acknowledgment, understanding, and theory', *Journal of Sport and Exercise Psychology*, 18: 237–246.

Kreft, L. (2013) 'Aesthetics of the beautiful game', *Soccer & Society*, 1–23.

Kretchmar, R.S. (1994) *Practical Philosophy of Sport*, Champaign, IL: Human Kinetics.

Krishnan, A. (2009) *Five Strategies for Practising Interdisciplinarity*, Southampton, UK: ESRC National Centre for Research Methods: NCRM Working Paper Series.

Kristeva, J., Jardine, A. and Blake, H. (1981) 'Women's time', *Signs*, 7(1): 13–35.

Kroker, A., Kroker, M. and Cook, D. (eds.) (1989) *Panic Encyclopedia: The Definitive Guide to the Postmodern Scene*, New York: St. Martin's Press.

Kuhn, T.S. (1996) *The Structure of Scientific Revolutions*, 3rd ed, Chicago: The University of Chicago Press.

Kupritz, V.W. (1998) 'Privacy in the workplace: the impact of building design', *Journal of Environmental Psychology*, 18(4): 341–356.

Lacan, J. (1972–3) *Encore*. Seminar.

Lama, D. and Cutler, H.C. (1998) *The Art of Happiness: A Handbook for Living*, Sydney: Hachette Australia.

Larsson, H. (2012) 'Materialising bodies: there is nothing more material than a socially constructed body', *Sport, Education and Society*, 1–15, iFirst Article. DOI: 10.1080/13573322.2012.722550

Latour, B. (2005) *Reassembling the Social: An Introduction to Actor-network Theory*, Oxford: Oxford University Press.

Laurendeau, J. (2006) 'He didn't go in doing a skydive: sustaining the illusion of control in an edgework activity', *Sociological Perspectives*, 49(4): 583–605.

Laurendeau, J. (2008) 'Gendered risk regimes: a theoretical consideration of edgework and gender', *Sociology of Sport Journal*, 25(3): 293–309.

Laurendeau, J. (2012) *Base Jumping: The Ultimate Guide*, Santa Barbara, CA: ABC-CLIO.

Law, J. (2004) *After Method: Mess in Social Science Research*, London: Routledge.

Le Breton, D. (2000) 'Playing symbolically with death in extreme sports', *Body and Society*, 6(1): 1–11.

Leedy, G. (2009) 'I can't cry and run at the same time: women's use of distance running', *Journal of Women and Social Work*, 24(1): 80–93.

Lenskyj, H. (2010) 'Olympic impacts on bid and host cities', in V. Girginov (ed.) *The Olympics: A Critical Reader*, London: Routledge.

Leont'ev, A. (1981) *Problems of the Development of Mind*, Moscow: Progress Press.

Levenson, R., Soto, J. and Pole, N. (2007) 'Emotion, biology, and culture', in S. Kitayama and D. Cohen (eds.) *Handbook of Cultural Psychology*, New York: Guilford Press.

Levin, J. (1997) 'Her marathon', in J. Sandoz (ed) *A Whole Other Ball Game: Women's Literature on Women's Sport*, New York: Noonday Press.

References 223

Lewis, P. (2013) 'Boxing: Tua retires after defeat'. Online. Available HTTP: <http://www.nzherald.co.nz/sport/news/article.cfm?c_id=4&objectid=11158469> (accessed 28 November 2013).

Liljeström, M. and Paasonen, S. (2010) 'Introduction: feeling differences—affect and feminist readings', in M. Liljeström and S. Paasonen (eds.) *Working with Affect in Feminist Readings,* London: Routledge.

Lindsay-Abaire, D. (2006) *Rabbit Hole,* New York: Theatre Communications Group.

Litsky, F. (2007) 'Al Oerter, Olympic discus champion, is dead at 71'. Online. Available HTTP: <http://www.nytimes.com/2007/10/01/sports/othersports/01cnd-oerter.html?_r=0&pagewanted=print> (accessed 25 March 2013).

Locke, J. (1823) *The Works of John Locke,* London: Thomas Davison, Whitefriars.

Lowe, B. (1977) *The Beauty of Sport: A Cross-disciplinary Inquiry,* New York: Prentice-Hall.

Lowenthal, D. (1985) *The Past is a Foreign Country,* Cambridge, UK: Cambridge University Press.

Lupton, D. (1998) *The Emotional Self,* London: Sage.

Lykken, D and Tellegen, A. (1996) 'Happiness is a stochastic phenomenon', *Psychological Science,* 7(3): 186–189.

Lyman, S.M. (1987) 'From matrimony to malaise: men and women in the American film, 1930–1980', *International Journal of Politics, Culture, and Society,* 1(2): 263–290.

Lyng, S. (1990) 'Edgework: a social psychological analysis of voluntary risk taking', *The American Journal of Sociology,* 95(4), 851–886.

Lyng, S. (2005a) 'Edgework and the risk-taking experience', in S. Lyng (ed.) *Edgework: The Sociology of Risk-taking,* New York: Routledge.

Lyng, S. (2005b) 'Sociology at the edge: social theory and voluntary risk taking', in S. Lyng (ed.) *Edgework: The Sociology of Risk-taking,* New York: Routledge.

Lyotard, J-F. (1984) 'Adrift', in R. McKeon (ed.) *Driftworks,* New York: Foreign Agents Series.

Lyotard, J-F. (1994) *Lessons on the Analytic of the Sublime,* trans. E. Rottenberg, Palo Alto, CA: Stanford University Press.

Madrigal, R. (2006) 'Measuring the multidimensional nature of sporting event performance consumption', *Journal of Leisure Research,* 38: 267–292.

Maffesoli, M. (1993) *The Shadow of Dionysus: A Contribution to the Sociology of the Orgy,* trans. C. Linse and M.K. Palmquist, Albany, NY: SUNY Press.

Magdalinski, T. (2009) *Sport, Technology and the Body: The Nature of Performance,* New York: Routledge.

Maguire, J. (1992) 'Towards a sociological theory of sport and the emotions: a process-sociological perspective', in E. Dunning and C. Rojek (eds.) *Sport and Leisure in the Civilising Process: Critique and Counter-critique,* London: Macmillan.

Maguire, J.S. (2008) 'Leisure and the obligation of self-work: an examination of the fitness field', *Leisure Studies,* 27(1): 59–75.

Maguire, J., Barnard, S., Butler, K. and Golding, P. (2010) '"Celebrate humanity" or "consumers?": a critical evaluation of a brand in motion', in V. Girginov (ed.) *The Olympics: A Critical Reader,* London: Routledge.

Maguire, J., Jarvie, G., Mansfield, L. and Bradley, J. (eds.) (2002) *Sport Worlds: A Sociological Perspective,* Champaign, IL: Human Kinetics.

Maitland, K. (1997) 'The loveliness of the long distance runner', in J. Sandoz (ed) *A Whole Other Ball Game: Women's Literature on Women's Sport,* New York: Noonday Press.

224 References

Maivorsdotter, N. and Quennerstedt, M. (2012) 'The act of running: a practical epistemology analysis of aesthetic experience in sport', *Qualitative Research in Sport, Exercise and Health*, 4(3): 362–381.

Marcuse, H. (1961) *Eros and Civilization: A Philosophical Inquiry into Freud*, Boston: Beacon Press.

Markula, P. and Denison, J. (2000) 'See spot run: movement as an object of textual analysis', *Qualitative Inquiry*, 6(3): 406–431.

Markula, P. and Silk, M. (2011) *Qualitative Research for Physical Culture*, London: Palgrave Macmillan.

Markula-Denison, P. and Pringle, R. (2006) *Foucault, Sport and Exercise: Power, Knowledge and Transforming the Self*, Oxon: Routledge.

Martin, A. (2003) 'Introduction: Luce Irigaray and the culture of difference', *Theory, Culture and Society*, 20(3): 1–12.

Martin, A. and Leberman, S. (2004) 'Adventure the Czech way', *New Zealand Journal of Outdoor Education: Ko Tane Mahuta Pupuke*, 1(3): 65–85.

Martin, M. (2011) 'The (im)possible sexual difference: representations from a rugby union setting', *International Review for the Sociology of Sport*, 47(2): 183–199.

Massumi, B. (1995) 'The autonomy of affect', *Cultural Critique*, 31: 83–109.

Massumi, B. (2002) *Parables for the Virtual: Movement, Affect, Sensation*, London: Duke University Press.

Maynard, M. and Purvis, J. (eds.) (1994) *Researching Women's Lives from A Feminist Perspective*, London: Taylor and Francis.

McCullough, S. (2010) 'Body like a rocket: performing technologies of naturalization', *Thirdspace: A Journal of Feminist Theory and Culture*, 9(2): 1–28.

McFarlin, K. (2012) 'What is endemic advertising? Small business by demand media'. Online. Available HTTP: <http://smallbusiness.chron.com/endemic-adver tising-10527.html> (accessed 23 July 2012).

McKay, J., Gore, J.M. and Kirk, D. (1990) 'Beyond the limits of technocratic physical education', *Quest*, 42(1): 52–76.

McLoughlin, C. (2010) 'Playing with numbers: quantification and jouissance in the New York Marathon', *Anthropological Theory*, 10(1–2): 75–80.

McLuhan, M. (1988) *Laws of Media: The New Science*, Toronto, Canada: University of Toronto Press.

McMahon, D.M. (2006) *Happiness: A History*, New York: Grove Press.

McNamee, M. (ed.) (2007) *Philosophy, Risk and Adventure Sports*, Oxon: Routledge.

McTeer, W. and Curtis, J. (1993) 'Sport and physical activity and subjective well being: national panel data for the US', *International Review for the Sociology of Sport*, 28(4): 397–412.

McWillian, E. (1999) 'Laughing within reason: on pleasure, women, and academic performance', paper presented at the Annual Meting of the American Educational Research Association, Montreal, Quebec, Canada.

Merrill, J. and Wann, D.L. (2011) 'An examination of sport fandom in Australia: socialization, team identification, and fan behaviour', *International Review for the Sociology of Sport*, 46(4): 456–470.

Messner, M.A. (1992) *Power at Play: Sports and the Problem of Masculinity*, Boston: Beacon Press.

Meštrović, S. (1992) *Durkheim and Postmodern Culture*, New York: Aldine de Gruyter.

Miah, A. (2010) *Genetically Modified Athletes: Biomedical Ethics, Gene Doping and Sport*, New York: Routledge.

Michaelis, V. (2008) 'Today's Olympians aim to prove age is just a number'. Online. Available HTTP: <http://usatoday30.usatoday.com/sports/olympics/beijing/2008-07-24-older-athletes_N.htm> (accessed 23 March 2013).

References 225

Miller, P. C. (1994) 'Desert asceticism and "the body from nowhere"', *Journal of Early Christian Studies*, 2(2): 137–153.

Miller, T. (2002) *Sportsex*, Philadelphia: Temple University Press.

Miller, T., Lawrence, G. A., Mckay, J. and Rowe, D. (2004) 'Sports media sans frontiers', in D. Rowe (ed.) *Critical Readings: Sport, Culture and the Media*, Maidenhead, UK: Open University Press.

Millington, B. and Wilson, B. (2010) 'Media consumption and the contexts of physical culture: methodological reflections on a "third generation" study of media audiences', *Sociology of Sport Journal*, 27(1): 20–53.

Mills, C. W. (1959) *The Sociological Imagination*, Oxford: Oxford University Press.

Møller, Verner. (2007) 'Walking the edge', in M. McNamee (ed.) *Philosophy, Risk and Adventure Sports*, Oxon: Routledge.

Moor, L. (2007) 'Sport and commodification: a reflection on key concepts', *Journal of Sport & Social Issue*, 31(2): 128–142.

Morgan, W. P. (1985) 'Affective beneficence of vigorous physical activity', *Medicine & Science in Sports & Exercise*, 17: 94–100.

Murakami, H. (2008) *What I Talk about When I Talk about Running*, trans. P. Gabriel, London: Vintage Books.

Nathanson, D. L. (1992) *Shame and Pride: Affect, Sex, and the Birth of the Self*, New York: W.W. Norton.

Nietzsche, F. W. (1998[1872]) *Twilight of the Idols, or, How to Philosophize with A Hammer*, trans. D. Large, Oxford: Oxford University Press.

Nietzsche, F., Geuss, R. and Speirs, R. (eds.) (1999) *Nietzsche: The Birth of Tragedy and Other Writings*, Cambridge, UK: Cambridge University Press.

Nikora, L. W., Rua, M. and Te Awekotuku, N. (2003) 'In your face: wearing Moko— Māori facial marking in today's world', paper presented at the *Tatau/Tattoo: Embodied Art and Cultural Exchange Conference*, Victoria University, Wellington.

'Oakley Men's Store' (2012) Online. Available HTTP: <http://www.oakley.com/products/4883/26258> (accessed 5 September 2012).

'Oakley Sports' (2012) Online. Available HTTP <http://www.oakley.com/sports> (accessed 5 September 2012).

O'Brian, C. (2012) 'Sustainable happiness and well-being: future directions for positive psychology', *Psychology*, 3(12a): 1196–1201.

O'Connor, B. and Boyle, R. (1993) 'Dallas with balls: televized sport, soap opera and male and female pleasures', *Leisure Studies*, 12(2): 107–119.

O'Connor, B and Klaus, E. (2000) 'Pleasure and meaningful discourse: an overview of research issues', *International Journal of Cultural Studies*, 3(3): 369–387.

O'Malley, P. and Valverde, M. (2004) 'Pleasure, freedom and drugs: the uses of "pleasure" in liberal governance of drug and alcohol consumption', *Sociology*, 38(1): 25–42.

Obrador-Pons, P. (2007) 'A Haptic geography of the beach: naked bodies, vision and touch', *Social & Cultural Geography*, 8(1): 123–141.

Office for National Statistics (2012) 'Analysis of experimental subjective well-being data from the annual population survey'. Online. Available HTTP: <http://www.ons.gov.uk/ons/dcp171776_257882.pdf> (accessed 6 June 2013).

Olivier, S. (2006) 'Moral dilemmas of participation in dangerous leisure activities', *Leisure Studies*, 25(1): 95–109.

Olstead, R. (2011) 'Gender, space and fear: a study of women's edgework', *Emotion, Space and Society*, 4(2): 86–94.

Olympic (2012a) 'Best of London 2012'. Online. Available HTTP: <http://www.youtube.com/watch?v=TbsXUJITa40> (accessed 21 August 2012).

Olympic (2012b) 'Athletics Men's 100m Final Full Replay—London 2012 Olympic Games—Usain Bolt'. Online. Available HTTP: <http://www.youtube.com/watch?v=2O7K-8G2nwU> (accessed 5 August 2012).

226   References

Ormrod, J. (2009) 'On the edge: leisure, consumption and the representation of adventure sports—Introduction', in J. Ormrod and B. Wheaton (eds.) *On the Edge: Leisure, Consumption and the Representation of Adventure Sports (LSA 104)*, Eastbourne, UK: Leisure Studies Association.

Orwell, G. (1970) 'The sporting spirit', in S. Orwell and I. Angus (eds.) *In Front of Your Nose: The Collected Essays, Journalism and Letters of George Orwell*, Harmondsworth: Penguin.

Ott, B. (2010) 'The visceral politics of V for Vendetta: on political affect in cinema', *Critical Studies in Media Communication*, 27(1): 39–54.

Owen, J. (2005) 'Estimating the cost and benefit of hosting Olympic Games: what can Beijing expects from its 2008 Games?', *The Industrial Geographer*, 3(1): 1–18.

Papoulias, C. and Callard, F. (2010) 'Biology's gift: interrogating the turn to affect', *Body & Society*, 16(1): 29–56.

Parker, A. (1996) 'The construction of masculinity within boys' physical education', *Gender and Education*, 8(2): 141–157.

Partington, S., Partington, E. and Olivier, S. (2009) 'The dark side of flow: a qualitative study of dependence in big wave surfing', *The Sport Psychologist*, 23: 170–185.

'Pat Ngohol What's your boggle?' New Romantic: A Global Collective. Online. Available HTTP: <http://newromantic.com.au/?page_id=16> (accessed 23 July 2012).

Patel, G. (2013) 'Courteney Cox: fighting my age is "a constant daily vicious battle"'. Online. Available HTTP: <http://emag.co.uk/courteney-cox-fighting-age-constant-daily-vicious-battle/6428> (accessed 6 September 2013).

Pater, W. (1966) 'From studies in the history of the renaissance', in K. Beckson (ed.) *Aesthetes and Decadents of the 1890s: An Anthology of British Poetry and Prose*, New York: Vintage Books.

Pavlidis, A. (2012) 'From Riot Grrrls to roller derby? Exploring the relations between gender, music and sport', *Leisure Studies*, 31(2): 165–176.

Pavlidis, A. and Fullagar, S. (2013) 'Becoming roller derby grrrls: exploring the gendered play of affect in mediated sport cultures', *International Review for the Sociology of Sport*, 48(6): 673–688.

Penn, A. (1970) *Little Big Man*, Los Angeles, CA: Stockbridge-Hiller Productions.

Peralta, S. (2001) *Dogtown and Z Boys*, Culver City, CF: Agi Orsi Productions.

Phillips, J.B. (2009) 'Mid week'. Online. Available HTTP: <http://wanganui2009.nzmg.com/mid-week-2> (accessed 23 January 2014).

Pierce, E.F., Eastman, M., Tripathi, H.L., Olson, K.G. and Dewey, W. (1993) 'ß-Endorphin response to endurance exercise: relationship to exercise dependence', *Perceptual and Motor Skills*, 77(3): 767–770.

Plunkett, J. (2012) 'BBC's Olympics coverage secured more than a third of all viewers'. Online. Available HTTP: <http://www.guardian.co.uk/media/2012/aug/15/bbc-olympics-coverage-third-viewers?newsfeed=true.> (accessed 5 January 2013).

Plutchik, R. (1980) 'A general psychoevolutionary theory of emotion', *Theories of Emotion,* 1.

Poole, G. (2012) '*Rabbit Hole*: staging grieving bodies', paper presented at Contemporary Ethnography Across the Disciplines (CEAD), Hamilton, NZ.

Pope, S. (2010) 'Like pulling down Durham Cathedral and building a brothel: women as "new consumer" fans?', *International Review for the Sociology of Sport*, 46(4): 471–487.

Pope, S. (2012) '"The Love of My Life": the meaning and importance of sport for female fans', *Journal of Sport and Social Issues*, 37(2): 176–195.

Pringle, R. (2009) 'Defamiliarizing heavy-contact sport: a critical examination of rugby, discipline and pleasure', *Sociology of Sport Journal*, 26: 211–234.

References 227

Pringle, R. (2012) 'Debunking Olympic sized myths: government investment in Olympism in the context of terror and the risk society', *Educational Review*, 64(3): 303–16.

Pringle, R. and Hickey, C. (2010) 'Negotiating masculinities via the moral problematization of sport', *Sociology of Sport Journal*, 27: 115–138.

Pringle, R. and Markula, P. (2005) 'No pain is sane after all: a Foucauldian analysis of masculinities and men's rugby experiences', *Sociology of Sport Journal*, 22(4): 472–497.

Probyn, E. (2004) 'Shame in the habitus', *The Sociological Review*, 52(2): 224–248.

Probyn, E. (2005) *Blush: Faces of Shame*, Minneapolis, MN: University of Minnesota Press.

Probyn, E. (2010) 'Writing shame', in M. Gregg and G. Seigworth (eds.) *The Affect Theory Reader*, Durham, NC: Duke University Press.

Pronger, B. (1999) 'Outta my end zone: sport and the territorial anus', *Journal of Sport and Social Issues*, 23(4): 373–389.

Putnam, R. D. (1995) 'Bowling alone: America's declining social capital', *Journal of Democracy*, 6(1): 65–78.

'Raglan kitesurfing' (2013) Online. Available HTTP: <http://www.raglankitesurfing.com/ozone/46-edge-7m.html> (accessed 7 April 2013).

Ramazanoglu, C. and Holland, J. (2002) *Feminist Methodology: Challenges and Choices*, London: Routledge.

Rand, E. (2012) *Red Nails, Black Skates, Gender, Cash, and Pleasure on and off the Ice*, London: Duke University Press.

Real, M. (2010) 'Who owns the Olympics? Political economy and critical moments in the modern games', in V. Girginov (ed.) *The Olympics: A Critical Reader*, London: Routledge.

Riefenstahl, L. (1938) *Olympia*, Berlin: Olympia-Film.

Richardson, L. (2000) 'New writing practices in qualitative research', *Sociology of Sport Journal*, 17(1): 5–20.

Rinehart, R. E. (1998a) *Players All: Performances in Contemporary Sport*, Bloomington, IN: Indiana University Press.

Rinehart, R. E. (1998b) 'Inside of the outside: Pecking orders within alternative sport at ESPN's 1995 "The eXtreme Games"', *Journal of Sport and Social Issues*, 22(4): 398–415.

Rinehart, R. E. (1998c) 'Skating', Waikato Journal of Education, 4: 55–63.

Rinehart, R. E. (1999) '"Babes", boards, and balance: women as co-opted sports model in extreme sports', *Annual North American Society for Sport Sociology Conference*, Cleveland, Ohio.

Rinehart, R. E. (2003) 'Dropping into sight: commodification and co-optation of in-line skating', in R. E. Rinehart and S. Sydnor (eds.) *To the Extreme: Alternative Sports, Inside and Out*, Albany, NY: State University of New York Press.

Rinehart, R. E. (2005) '"Babes" and boards: opportunities in the New Millennium?', *Journal of Sport and Social Issues*, 29(3): 233–255.

Rinehart, R. E. (2010a) 'Poetic sensibilities, humanities, and wonder: toward an e/affective sociology of sport', *Quest*, 62(2): 184–201.

Rinehart, R. E. (2010b) 'Sport performance in four acts: players, workers, audience, and immortality', *Qualitative Inquiry*, 16(3): 197–199.

Rinehart, R. E. (2010c) 'Performing sport: re-visioning sport practices in an age of global discord', *International Review of Qualitative Research*, 2(4): 445–455.

Rinehart, R. E. and Grenfell, C. (2002) 'BMX spaces: children's grass roots' courses and corporate-sponsored tracks', *Sociology of Sport Journal*, 19(3): 302–314.

Rinehart, R. E. and Sydnor, S. (eds.) (2003) *To the Extreme: Alternative Sports, Inside and Out*, Albany, NY: Suny Press.

228 References

Ritzer, G. (1993) *The McDonaldization of Society: An Investigation into the Changing Character of Contemporary Social Life*, Newbury Park, CA: Pine Forge Press.

Ritzer, G. (2005) *Enchanting A Disenchanted World: Revolutionizing the Means of Consumption,* 2nd ed, Thousand Oaks, CA: Pine Forge Press.

Ritzer, G. (2006) 'Globalization and McDonaldization: does it all amount to . . . nothing?', in G. Ritzer (ed.) *McDonaldization: The Reader*, 2nd ed, Thousand Oaks, CA: Pine Forge Press.

Rose, A. and Friedman, J. (1997) 'Television sports as mas(s)culine cult of distraction', in A. Baker and T. Boyd (eds.) *Out of Bounds: Sports, Media and the Politics of Identity*, Bloomington, IN: Indiana University Press.

Rose, G. (2012) *Visual Methodologies: An Introduction to Researching with Visual Materials*, 3rd ed, Los Angeles, CA: Sage.

Rowe, D. (2004) *Sport, Culture and the Media: The Unruly Trinity,* 2nd ed, Maidenhead, UK: Open University Press.

Roy, G. (2013) 'Taking emotions seriously: feeling female and becoming-surfer through UK surf space', *Emotion, Space and Society*, http://dx.doi.org/10.1016/j.emospa.2013.07.004.

Ruddock, A. (2005) 'Let's kick racism out of football-and the lefties too! Responses to Lee Bowyer on a west ham web site', *Journal of Sport & Social Issues*, 29(4): 369–385.

Russell, B. (1945) *A History of Western Philosophy and Its Connection with Political and Social Circumstances from the Earliest Times to the Present Day*, New York: Simon & Schuster.

Sachs, M. (1980) 'The runner's high', paper presented at the Annual Convention of the *American Alliance for Health, Physical Education, Recreation and Dance,* Detroit, MI.

Sage, G. H. (1990) *Power and Ideology in American Sport: A Critical Perspective*, Champaign, IL: Human Kinetics.

Said, E. W. (1979) *Orientalism*, New York: Vintage Books.

Salter, M. A. (1996) 'The post-classic Highland Maya ball game: a view from symbolic anthropology', in F. van der Merwe (ed.) *Sport as Symbol, Symbol as Sport: Proceedings of the 3rd ISHPES Congress*, Berlin: Academia Verlag.

Sandell, K. (2012) 'Outdoor recreation in change–What about Sweden?', *Scandinavian Journal of Hospitality and Tourism*, 10(3): 291–309.

Saville, S. J. (2008) 'Playing with fear: parkour and the mobility of emotion', *Social & Cultural Geography*, 9(8): 891–914.

Sawhney, S. (2006) 'Feminism and hybridity round table', *Surfaces,* 7(113): 3–12.

Schimmack, U. (2001) 'Pleasure, displeasure, and mixed feelings: are semantic opposites mutually exclusive?', *Cognition and Emotion*, 15(1): 81–97.

Schumacher, E. F. (1975) *Small Is Beautiful: Economics as If People Mattered*, New York: Perennial Library.

Šebek, L. (2004) 'Developing the ability of adventure', *Proceedings from the International Symposium: Outdoor Sports Education (Czech Republic)*, 78–81.

Sedgwick, E. and Frank, A. (1995) 'Shame in the cybernetic fold: reading Silvan Tomkins', *Critical Inquiry*, 21(2): 496–522.

Seidler, V. J. (2001) 'Jean-Francois Lyotard', in A. Elliot and T. Brian (eds.) *Profiles in Contemporary Social Theory*, Thousand Oaks, CA: Sage Publications.

Seigworth, G. and Gregg, M. (2010) 'An inventory of shimmers', in M. Gregg and G. Seigworth (eds.) *The Affect Theory Reader*, Durham & London: Duke University Press.

Serres, M. (2008) *The Five Senses: A Philosophy of Mingled Bodies*, New York: Continuum Press.

References   229

Sforzo, G. A., Seeger, T.F., Pert, C.B., Pert, A. and Dotson, C.O. (1986) 'In vivo opioid receptor occupation in the rat brain following exercise', *Medicine and Science in Sports and Exercise*, 18: 380–384.

Shaviro, S. (1993) *The Cinematic Body*, Minneapolis, MN: University of Minnesota Press.

Shaw, C. and Chase, M. (1989) *The Imagined Past: History and Nostalgia*, Manchester: Manchester University Press.

Shelley, J. (2009) 'The concept of the aesthetic', in *Stanford Encyclopedia of Philosophy*. Online. Available HTTP: < http://plato.stanford.edu/entries/aesthetic-concept/> (accessed 7 December 2012).

Sheppard, A. (1989) *Aesthetics: An Introduction to the Philosophy of Art*, Oxford: Oxford University Press.

Shilling, C. (1997) 'The body and difference', in K. Woodward (ed.) *Identity and Difference: Culture, Media and Identities,* London: Sage Publications.

Shilling, C. (2002) 'The two traditions in the sociology of emotions', in J. Barbalet (ed.) *Emotions and Sociology*, Oxford, UK: Blackwell Publishing.

Shouse, E. (2005) 'Feeling, emotion, affect', *M/C Journal*, 8(6): 1215–1217.

Silk, M. and Andrews, D. (2012) 'Sport and the neoliberal conjuncture: complicating the consensus', in D. Andrews and M. Silk (eds.) *Sport and Neoliberalism: Politics, Consumption, and Culture*, Philadelphia: Temple University Press.

Silk, M. L. (2008) 'Mow my lawn', *Cultural Studies: Critical Methodologies*, 8(4): 477–478.

Silk, M. L., Andrews, D. L. and Mason, D. S. (2005) 'Encountering the field: sports studies and qualitative research', in D. Andrews, D. S. Mason and M. L. Silk (eds.) *Qualitative Methods in Sports Studies,* London: Berg.

Sillitoe, A. (1958) *The Loneliness of the Long Distance Runner*, London: Star Books.

Simmons, D. R. (1997) *Ta Moko: The Art of Māori Tattoo*, Auckland, NZ: Reed Publishers.

Smallwood, J. (2013) 'In extreme sports, the X-factor is death'. Online. Available HTTP: <http://articles.philly.com/2013-02-03/sports/36723401_1_extreme-sports-snowmobile-backflip> (accessed 28 April 2014).

Smith, S. (2000) 'British nonelite road running and masculinity', *Masculinities*, 3(2): 187–208.

Sorek, T. (2003) 'Arab football in Israel as an "integrative enclave"', *Ethnic and Racial Studies*, 3, 422–450.

Sotirin, P. (2010) 'Autoethnographic mother-writing: advocating radical specificity', *Journal of Research Practice*, 6(1). Online. Available HTTP: <http://jrp.icaap.org/index.php/jrp/article/view/220/189> (accessed 31 August 2012).

Sparkes, A. and Smith, B. (2002) 'Sport, spinal cord injury, embodied masculinities, and the dilemmas of narrative identity', *Men and Masculinities*, 4(3): 258–285.

Sparkes, A. and Smith, B. (2012) 'Embodied research methodologies and seeking the senses in sport and physical culture: a fleshing out of problems and possibilities', *Research in the Sociology of Sport*, 6: 167–190.

Sport England (2013a) 'Sport and You'. Online. Available HTTP: <http://www.sportengland.org/sport-you/> (accessed 29 April 2014).

Sport England (2013b) 'Who plays sport?' Onlilne. Available HTTP: <http://www.sportengland.org/research/who-plays-sport/national-picture/who-plays-sport> (accessed 26 July 2013).

Sport New Zealand (2013) 'Young people'. Online. Available HTTP: <http://www.sportnz.org.nz/en-nz/young-people/.> (accessed 29 April 2013).

Sportscotland (2003) *Sport 21 2003–2007: The National Strategy for Sport*, Edinburgh Sportscotland.

230   *References*

Steiner, W. (1995) *The Scandal of Pleasure: Art in An Age of Fundamentalism*, Chicago: University of Chicago Press.

Stern, D. N. (1985) *The Interpersonal World of the Infant*, New York: Basic Books.

Stewart, B. (2005) 'Channelling passion or manufacturing identity? Managing fans in the Australian Football League', in M. Nicholson (ed.) *Fanfare: Spectator Culture and Australian Rules Football*, Melbourne: Australian Society for Sports History.

Stewart, K. (2007) *Ordinary Affects*, Durham, NC: Duke University Press.

Stewart, S. (1993) *On Longing: Narratives of the Miniature, the Gigantic, the Souvenir, the Collection*, Durham, NC: Duke University Press.

Stoltenberg, J. (1990) *Refusing to Be A Man: Essays on Sex and Justice*, New York: Meridian.

Stone, B. (2009) 'Running man', *Qualitative Research in Sport and Exercise*, 1(1): 67–71.

Stranger, M. (1999) 'The aesthetics of risk: a study of surfing', *International Review for the Sociology of Sport*, 34(3): 265–276.

Stranger, M. (2011) *Surfing Life: Surface, Substructure and the Commodification of the Sublime*, Surrey, UK: Ashgate Publishing.

Straughan, E.R. (2012) 'Touched by water: the body in scuba diving', *Emotion, Space and Society*, 5(2): 19–26.

Storms, C. E. (2008) '"There's no sorry in roller derby": a feminist examination of identity of women in the full contact sport of roller derby', *The New York Sociologist*, 3: 68–87.

Sturm, D. (2012) 'Masculinities, affect and the (re)place(ment) of stardom in Formula One fan leisure practices', *Annals of Leisure Research*, 14(2–3): 224–241.

Sutton-Smith, B. (1997) *The Ambiguity of Play*, Cambridge, MA: Harvard University Press.

Sykes, H. (2011) *Queer Bodies: Sexualities, Genders, and Fatness in Physical Education*, Oxford: Peter Lang.

Sykes, H. and McPhail, D. (2008) 'Unbearable lessons: contesting fat phobia in physical education', *Sociology of Sport Journal*, 25(1): 66–96.

Tapp, A. (2004) 'The loyalty of football fans—we'll support you evermore?', *Database Marketing & Customer Strategy Management*, 11(3): 203–215.

Te Awekotuku, N. (2013) 'Māori culture: Ta moko: significance of Māori tattoos'. Online. Available HTTP: <http://www.newzealand.com/travel/media/features/maori-culture/maori_ta-moko-significance_feature.cfm> (accessed 28 October 2013).

Te Rangikāheke, W.M., Grey, G. and Simmons, D.R. (2007) *Ta Moko: The Art of Māori Tattoo*, Wellington: New Zealand Electronic Text Collection (Te Pūhikotuhi o Aotearoa).

Tester, K. (1989) 'The pleasure of the rich is the labour of the poor: some comments on Norbert Elias' "An Essay on Sport and Violence"', *Journal of Historical Sociology*, 2(2): 161–172.

The Universal Declaration of Human Rights (2012) Online. Available HTTP: <http://www.un.org/en/documents/udhr/> (accessed 9 January 2012).

Thomas, D. (1968a) 'The force that through the green fuse drives the flower', in M.H. Abrams, E.T. Donaldson, H. Smith, R.M. Adams, S.H. Monk, G.H. Ford and D. Daiches (eds.) *Norton Anthology of English Literature*, New York: W.W. Norton & Co.

Thomas, D. (1968b) 'Do not go gentle into that good night', in M.H. Abrams, E.T. Donaldson, H. Smith, R.M. Adams, S.H. Monk, G.H. Ford and D. Daiches (eds.) *Norton Anthology of English Literature*, New York: W.W. Norton & Co.

Thorpe, H. (2005) 'Jibbing the gender order: females in the snowboarding culture', *Sport in Society*, 8(1): 76–100.

References 231

Thorpe, H. (2011) *Snowboarding Bodies in Theory and Practice*, Hampshire, UK: Palgrave Macmillan.

Thorpe, H. (2012a) 'Moving bodies beyond the social/biological divide: toward theoretical and transdisciplinary adventures', *Sport, Education and Society*, 19(5): 1–21.

Thorpe, H. (2012b) 'Sex, drugs and snowboarding: (il)legitimate definitions of taste and lifestyle in a physical youth culture', *Leisure Studies*, 31(1): 33–51.

Thorpe, H. and Rinehart, R. (2010) 'Alternative sport and affect: non-representational theory examined', *Sport in Society*, 13(7–8): 1268–1291.

Thrift, N. (2004) 'Intensities of feeling: toward a spatial politics of affect', *Geografiska Annaler*, 86(b): 57–78.

Thrift, N. (2008) *Non-representational Theory: Space, Politics, Affect*, London: Routledge.

Tiger, L. (1992) *The Pursuit of Pleasure*, New Brunswick, NJ: Transaction Publishers.

Tinning, R. and Fitzclarence, L. (1992) 'Postmodern youth culture and the crisis in Australian secondary school physical education', *Quest*, 44(3): 287–303.

Tomlinson, A. (2004) 'The Disneyfication of the Olympics? Theme parks and freakshows of the body', in J. Bale and M. Christensen (eds.) *Post-Olympism? Questioning Sport in the Twenty-first Century*, Oxford: Berg.

Tompkins, S. (1995) *Exploring Affect: The Selected Writings of Silvan S. Tompkins*. New York: Cambridge University Press.

Toohey, K. (2008) 'Terrorism, sport and public policy in the risk society', *Sport in Society*, 11(4): 429–442.

Toohey, K. and Veal, A.J. (2007) *The Olympic Games: A Social Science Perspective*, Oxfordshire, UK: Cab International.

Tucker Center for Research on Girls & Women in Sport (2007) *The 2007 Tucker Center Research Report, Developing Physically Active Girls: An Evidence-based Multidisciplinary Approach*, University of Minnesota, MN: Author.

Tulle, E. (2007) 'Running to run: embodiment, structure and agency amongst veteran elite runners', *Sociology*, 41(2): 329–346.

Turner, B. (1984) *The Body and Society*, Oxford: Blackwell.

Ullman, H.K., Wade, J.P., Edney, L.A., Franks, F.M., Horner, C.A., Howe, J.T. and Brendley, K. (1996) *Shock and Awe: Achieving Rapid Dominance*, Washington, DC: National Defense University.

UNESCO. (1978) *International Charter of Physical Education and Sport*. Online. Available HTTP: <http://portal.unesco.org/en/ev.phpURL_ID=13150&URL_DO=DO_TOPIC&URL_SECTION=201.html> (accessed 28 April 2014).

Van Dalen, D.B. and Bennett, B.L. (1971) *A World History of Physical Education: Cultural, Philosophical, Comparative*, 2nd ed, Englewood Cliffs, NJ: Prentice Hall.

Van Hilvoorde, I., Elling, A. and Stokvis, R. (2010) 'How to influence national pride? The Olympic medal index as a unifying narrative', *International Review for the Sociology of Sport*, 45(1): 87–102.

van Ingen, C. (2004) 'Therapeutic landscapes and the regulated body in the Toronto front runners', *Sociology of Sport Journal*, 21(3): 253–269.

Vātsyāyana, M. (2009) *Kamasutra: A New, Complete English Translation of the Sanskrit Text: With Excerpts from the Sanskrit Jayamangala Commentary of Yashodhara Indrapada, the Hindi Jaya Commentary of Devadatta Shastri, and Explanatory Notes by the Translators*, Oxford: Oxford University Press.

Veblen, T. (1979/1899) *The Theory of the Leisure Class*, New York: Penguin Books.

Verkaaik, O. (2003) 'Fun and violence: ethnocide and the effervescence of collective aggression', *Social Anthropology*, 11(1): 3–22.

Vertinsky, P. (2009) 'Mind the gap (or mending it): qualitative research and interdisciplinarity in kinesiology', *Quest*, 61: 39–51.

232 References

Waddington, I. (2007) 'Sport and health: a sociological perspective', in G. Ritzer (ed.) *Encyclopedia of Sociology*, London: Blackwell.

Wagg, S. (2011) '"They can't stop us laughing": politics, leisure and the comedy business', in P. Bramham and S. Wagg (eds.) *The New Politics of Leisure and Pleasure*, London: Palgrave.

Walford, G. (1991) 'Researching the city technology college, Kingshurst', in G. Walford (ed.) *Doing Educational Research*, London: Routledge.

Walford, G. (2001) 'Site selection within comparative case study and ethnographic research', *Compare: A Journal of Comparative and International Education*, 31(2): 151–164.

Walker, J. J., Golub, S. A., Bimbi, D. S. and Parsons, J. T. (2012) 'Butch bottom-femme top? An exploration of lesbian stereotypes', *Journal of Lesbian Studies*, 16(1): 90–107.

Wankel, L. (1997) '"Strawpersons", selective reporting, and inconsistent logic: a response to Kimiecik and Harris's analysis of enjoyment', *Journal of Sport and Exercise Psychology*, 19: 98–109.

Warburton, D.E.R., Nicol, C.W. and Bredin, S.S.D. (2006) 'Health benefits of physical activity: the evidence', *Canadian Medical Association Journal*, 174(6): 801–809.

Warner, M. (1999) *The Trouble with Normal: Sex, Politics, and the Ethics of Queer Life*, Cambridge, MA: Harvard University Press.

Warraq, I. (2007) *Defending the West: A Critique of Edward Said's Orientalism*, Amherst, NY: Prometheus Books.

Wattchow, B. and Brown, M. (2011) *A Pedagogy of Place: Outdoor Education for A Changing World*, Victoria, Australia: Monash University Publishing.

Wellard, I. (2012) 'Body-reflexive pleasures: exploring bodily experiences within the context of sport and physical activity', *Sport, Education and Society*, 17(1): 21–33.

Wenn, S.R. (2000) 'Riding into the sunset: Richard Pound, Dick Ebersol, and long-term Olympic television contracts', in K.B. Wamsley, S.G. Marten, G.H. MacDonald and R.K. Barney (eds.) *Bridging Three Centuries: Intellectual Crossroads and the Modern Olympic Movement, Fifth International Symposium for Olympic Research*, London: International Centre for Olympic Studies.

Wenner, L. (ed.) (1998) *Media Sport*, London: Routledge.

Wensing, E. and Bruce, T. (2003) 'Bending the rules: media representations of gender during an international sporting event', *International Review for the Sociology of Sport*, 38: 387–396.

Weston, R.J. (2004) 'Essential oils of the leaves of the *Raukaua* genus (Araliaceae)', *Verlag der Zeitschrift für Naturforschung*, 59c: 35–38.

Wetherell, M. (2012) *Affect and Emotion: A New Social Science Understanding*, Los Angeles, CA: Sage.

Whannel, G. (1992) *Fields in Vision: Television Sport and Cultural Transformation*, London: Routledge.

Whannel, G. (1993) 'Sport and popular culture: the temporary triumph of process over product', *Innovation: The European Journal of Social Science Research*, 6(3): 341–49.

Wheaton, B. (2000) '"Just do it": Consumption, commitment, and identity in the windsurfing subculture, *Sociology of Sport Journal*, 17(3): 254–274.

Wheaton, B. (ed.) (2004) *Understanding Lifestyle Sport: Consumption, Identity and Difference*, London: Routledge.

Wheaton, B. (2007) 'After sport culture: rethinking sport and post-subcultural theory', *Journal of Sport and Social Issues*, 31(3): 283–307.

Wheaton, B. and Tomlinson, A. (1998) 'The changing gender order in sport?: the case of windsurfing subcultures', *Journal of Sport and Social Issues*, 22(3): 252–274.

References 233

Wiesel, E. (1960) *Night*, New York: Bantam Books.

Wilde, O. (1891) *The Picture of Dorian Gray*, Oxford: Oxford University Press.

Wilkinson, R. and Pickett, K. (2010) *The Spirit Level: Why Equality Is Better for Everyone*, London: Penguin UK.

Wilkinson, S. (1988) 'The role of reflexivity in feminist psychology', *Women's Studies International Forum*, 11(5): 493–502.

Williams, R. (1977) *Marxism and Literature*, Oxford: Oxford University Press.

Willis, Paul. (1994) 'Women in sport ideology', in S. Birrell and C. Cole (eds.) *Women, Sport, and Culture*, Champaign, IL: Human Kinetics.

Wilson, B. and Sparks, R. (1999) 'Impacts of black athlete media portrayals on Canadian youth', *Canadian Journal of Communication*, 24(4): 589–627.

Wilson, S. (2012) 'Belarus shot putter stripped of Olympic gold'. Online. Available HTTP: <http://timesleader.com/stories/Belarus-shot-putter-stripped-of-Olympic-gold,190874> (accessed 5 March 2013).

Wilson, T. D. and Gilbert, D. T. (2005) 'Affective forecasting: knowing what to want', *Current Directions in Psychological Science*, 14(3): 131–134.

Wolf, N. (1991) *The Beauty Myth: How Images of Beauty are Used Against Women*, London: Vintage.

Wollstonecraft, M. (1992) *A Vindication of the Rights of Women*, London, UK: Penguin.

Woolf, V. (1985) *Moments of Being: A Collection of Autobiographical Writing*, 2nd ed, San Diego, CA: Harcourt.

Wright, J. and Dewar, A. (1997) 'On pleasure and pain: women speak out about physical activity', in G. Clarke and B. Humberstone (eds.) *Researching Women and Sport*, London: MacMillan Press.

Yu, L. (2012) 'Written in a carefree mood', trans. B. Watson. Online. Available HTTP: <http://poetrychina.net/wp/poets/lu_yu/3> (accessed 3 September 2012).

Zakaria, I. (2012) 'Ibn Sina on "Pleasure and Happiness"', *Advances in Natural and Applied Sciences*, 6(8): 1283–1286.

Žižek, S. (1994) *The Metastases of Enjoyment: On Women and Causality*. London: Verso.

Author Index

Ahmed, Sara 8, 77–8, 100, 103, 122, 140, 196, 206, 208, 211
Allen-Collinson, Jacqueline 98, 211
Allende, Isabel 13, 19, 211
Andrews, David L. 116, 139, 140, 184, 190, 211
Annas, Julia 13, 14, 23, 27, 211
Aristotle 2, 7, 29, 31, 32, 40, 58, 211
Atencio, Matthew 155, 163–4, 211
Atkinson, Michael 43, 98, 102, 107, 113, 211
Azzarito, Laura 205–7, 220

Bairner, Alan 98, 212
Bakhtin, Mikhail 7, 15–17, 22, 34–5, 40, 67, 212
Bale, John 99, 101–3, 108, 212
Barthes, Roland 7, 35, 73, 75–6, 118–21, 127, 145, 151, 212
Battin, Margaret P. 153–4, 158, 178, 212
Baudrillard, Jean 10, 105, 157, 159, 189, 192–3, 212
Baumann, Zygmunt 10
Beal, Beck 155, 162–4, 193, 211, 212
Beamish, Robert 116, 120–1, 212
Benjamin, Walter 10, 95, 157–8
Bennett, Bruce L. 28, 231
Bentham, Jeremy 2–3, 7, 22, 36, 40, 212
Berger, John 152, 212
Booth, Douglas xi, 3, 45, 49, 56, 63, 116–18, 122, 130, 213
Bordo, Susan 5, 213
Bourdieu, Pierre 18, 102, 110, 151, 154, 159, 160, 188, 213
Brohm, Jean-Marie 99, 213
Bruce, Toni 117, 213
Brummett, Barry 44, 117, 134–5, 216

Burdsey, Daniel 148, 213
Butler, Judith 63, 213

Caillois, Roger 26, 180, 213
Carlson, Jennifer 68–70, 213
Carver, Raymond 106, 214
Caudwell, Jayne C. i, xi, 67, 71, 134, 140, 156, 182, 192–3, 204, 209
Charmaz, Kathy 88, 214
Chase, Laura 35, 214
Cixous, Hélène 8, 66, 72–6, 79, 221
Coakley, Jay 19–20, 95, 116–17, 119, 164, 169, 172, 200, 214
Coalter, Fred 196, 214
Cole, CL 121, 214
Colebrook, Claire 66–8, 214
Connell, Raewyn W. 51, 54–6, 63, 214
Crosset, Todd 205, 215
Csíkszentmihályi, Mihaly 44, 58–63, 158, 215
Cumming, Elaine 91, 215
Curtis, James 201–2, 224
Cutri, Chris 156, 161–2, 215

Dalai Lama 2, 31, 222
de Beauvoir, Simone 66, 74, 190, 215
Debord, Guy 18, 160, 215
de Coubertin, Pierre 162, 215
Deleuze, Gilles 22, 45, 89, 123
Denison, Jim 98, 224
Denzin, Norman K. 26, 82, 100, 136, 139, 155, 157, 181–2, 193, 215–16
Diener, Ed 28–9, 36, 198–9, 204, 216, 221
Donnelly, Peter 45, 47, 216
Downward, Paul 202, 216
Duncan, Margaret Carlisle 44, 117, 134–5, 216

236 *Author Index*

Dunning, Eric 8, 42, 44–8, 133, 216, 223
Durkheim, Emile 42, 163, 178, 216, 224

Eisenberg, Arlo 186–8
Elias, Norbert 8, 42, 44–8, 64, 216, 230
Epicurus 13–14, 22–3, 27, 211
Evans, John 43, 204, 217
Evers, Clifton 45, 63, 217

Farred, Grant 134, 142, 144–5, 149, 217
Feldenkrais, Moshe 84, 211, 215, 217
Ferreday, Debra 68, 217
Finley, Nancy 68–70, 217
Fiske, John 35, 45, 204, 217
Fitzgerald, F. Scott 190–1, 217
Foster, Hal 178, 217
Foucault, Michel 1, 7, 10, 15, 18, 22, 27–8, 32–4, 40, 51, 62–3, 78, 154–5, 165, 197, 209, 213, 217–18, 224
Freeland, Cynthia 32, 218
Freud, Sigmund 2, 7, 22, 38–40, 47, 73, 75, 77, 218, 224
Frith, Simon 47, 131, 218

Galloway, Susan 199–210, 218
Gard, Michael 204–5, 218
Gergen, Kenneth J. 82, 218
Gergen, Mary M. 82, 218
Gilligan, Carol 84, 218
Giroux, Henry A. 185, 189, 213, 218
Giulianotti, Richard 45, 116, 119, 131, 135, 217–19
Gold, Taro 87, 91, 93, 219
Grant, Bevan C. 80, 86, 219
Gross, Larry E. 91–3, 219
Grossberg, Lawrence 118, 130, 219
Gubrium, Jaber F. 88, 219
Guiterman, Arthur 84, 219

Harwood, Valerie 10, 204, 219
Hebdige, Dick 70, 220
Henry, William Earl 91, 215
Hitchens, Christopher 3, 26, 220
Hoberman, John 37, 116, 220
Holstein, James A. 86, 88, 219
Holt, Jim 39, 58, 220
Houlihan, Barrie 196, 220
Hughes, Robert 19, 164, 169, 172, 220

Huizinga, Johan 7, 18, 21–2, 30–3, 33, 48, 220
Humberstone, Barbara 63, 189, 220

Irigaray, Luce 8, 22, 66, 72–6, 79, 221, 224

Kant, Immanuel 48, 153
Kay, Joanne 187, 221
Kennedy, Eileen 117–18, 130–1, 221
Klugman, Matthew 60, 135, 222
Kohn, Alfie 84–5, 222
Kretchmar, R. Scott 29, 30, 222
Kristeva, Julia 8, 22, 66, 72–6, 79, 221–2
Kroker, Arthur 182, 192, 222
Kuhn, Thomas S. 15, 216, 222

Lacan, Jacques 22, 73, 75–7, 222
Larsson, Håkan 49, 62–3, 222
Laurendeau, Jason 45–7, 222
Law, John 6, 11, 177, 193
Lenskyj, Helen 116, 118, 222
Leont'ev, Alexei 91, 222
Levin, Jennifer 97–8, 103, 110–11, 222
Locke, John 7, 36, 223
Lowe, Benjamin 22, 84, 151, 223
Lowenthal, David 178, 223
Lu Yu 83, 90, 233
Lupton, Deborah 43–4, 223
Lyng, Stephen 39, 45–7, 182–3, 223
Lyotard, Jean-François 22, 48, 123–4, 130, 223

Maffesoli, Michel 14, 223
Maguire, Joseph 1, 29, 43, 45, 118–20, 223
Marcuse, Herbert 7, 38–40, 224
Markula, Pirkko 18, 98, 136, 204, 209, 224, 227
Marx, Karl 38, 46, 73, 178, 233
Massumi, Brian 51, 56, 109, 122–3, 224
Mauss, Marcel 42, 220
McTeer, William 201–2, 224
Messner, Michael 204, 207, 215, 224
Miller, Toby 25, 62, 135, 225
Mills, C. Wright 6, 95, 225
Murakami, Haruki 88–9, 94, 102–3, 106–7, 111, 225

Nietzsche, Friedrich 7, 28, 33, 40, 196, 225

Author Index 237

Orwell, George 14, 226
Ott, Brian 9, 118–19, 122, 124–5, 128, 226

Pater, Walter 153, 156–8, 190, 226
Pavlidis, Adele 63, 68–70, 226
Penney, Dawn 204, 217
Peralta, Stacy 187, 226
Pringle, Richard i, xi, 18, 35, 45, 51, 116, 204, 209, 222, 224, 226–7
Probyn, Elspeth 16, 42, 51, 123, 227
Putnam, Robert 183, 227

Rand, Erica 71–2, 140, 149, 227
Rasciute, Samona 202, 216
Richardson, Laurel 136, 227
Riefenstahl, Leni 162, 227
Rinehart, Robert E. i, xi, 22, 45, 63, 84, 89, 98, 114, 125, 130, 159, 164, 166, 178, 183, 186, 188–9, 193–4, 209, 221, 227, 231
Ritchie, Ian 116, 120–1, 212
Ritzer, George 27, 184–5, 211, 228
Rose, Gillian 160, 228
Ruddock, Andy 133–4, 145–6, 148–9, 228
Russell, Bertrand 32, 228

Sade, Marquis de 23, 172, 218
Sage, George 4, 228
Sedgwick, Eve 51, 56, 123, 228
Serres, Michel 152, 228
Sheppard, Anne 153, 178, 229
Shilling, Chris 29, 62, 229
Silk, Michael 116, 134, 136, 139–40, 224, 229
Sillitoe, Alan 97–9, 229
Smith, Brett 51–2, 204, 229
Socrates 3
Sotirin, Patty 89, 229
Sparkes, Andrew 51–2, 204, 229
Spinoza, Baruch 123, 152

Steiner, Wendy 22–3, 230
Stewart, Kathleen 151, 178, 230
Stewart, Susan 178, 230
Stranger, Mark 45–6, 48–9, 230
Sturm, Damion 135, 217, 230
Sutton-Smith, Brian 84, 230
Sydnor, Synthia 45, 209, 221, 227
Sykes, Heather 76–7, 204, 230

Thomas, Dylan vi, 84–6, 90, 230
Thorpe, Holly 43, 45, 56, 63, 193, 230–1
Thrift, Nigel 51, 56, 177, 193, 231
Tinning, Richard 185, 231
Tomkins, Silvan 122–3, 152, 228
Toohey, Kristine 116, 118, 131, 231
Tulle, Emmanuelle 98, 102, 113, 231
Turner, Brian 55, 231

U T'ak 92

Van Dalen, Deobold B. 28, 231
Veal, Tony 116, 231

Waddington, Ivan 200, 232
Wankel, Leonard 60–1, 232
Warner, Michael 16–17, 232
Wellard, Ian 63, 232
Wetherell, Margaret 9, 20–2, 49, 51, 56–7, 105, 110–11, 113, 123, 163, 232
Whannel, Garry 117–18, 232
Wheaton, Belinda 169, 187–8, 193, 226, 232
Wolf, Naomi 65–6, 233
Wollstonecraft, Mary 7, 22, 37, 40, 65–6, 233
Wright, Janice 44, 204–5, 218

Yon Son-do 92

Zakaria, Idris 21, 233
Žižek, Slavos 73, 76, 233

Subject Index

activity theory 91
aesthetics 151–79; and beauty 10, 22, 64–7, 84; and pleasure 2, 22, 24, 64–7, 113, 119, 139, 152; universality in 140, 152
affect theories 122–5, 211
affect(s): alienation and 180–94; flattening of 157, 160, 182–3, 189–90; multi-dimensionality of 170; patterns in 126–30, 159, 163; politics of 125, 128
affective resonance 123–4, 126, 129–30
aging 80–96; and pleasure 6, 8, 28, 55, 83, 91; and sport 80, 87, 93, 167, 169
alternative sport 10, 162–3, 180–94
anhedonia 180–94
Apollonian 33
art: and the aesthetic 10, 12, 22–3, 25, 84, 86–7, 89, 100, 112, 125, 151–79, 190; and skateboarding 151–79
ascetics 25
avant-garde 163–4

Barthesian 75
BASE jumping/skydiving 2, 45–8
Beautiful Losers 155
biology 5, 8, 42, 44, 49–57, 62–3
biopower 10, 197–9, 204
body-reflexive pleasures 8, 54–61
body/bodily 7–8, 10, 16–17, 21–8, 30, 34, 42–63, 64–71, 77, 79–96, 98–114, 120–4, 148, 152, 156, 172, 175, 182, 197, 200, 204–5
Bolt, Usain 127, 159
Bowl-a-Rama 153–64

capital, cultural/social 18, 46, 102, 105–10, 113, 155, 164, 183, 185, 201, 204
carnival/carnivalesque 34–5, 64, 67, 78, 127
Christian/Christianity 7, 15–18, 28, 32–5, 93
civic disengagement 91, 183
commodification 184–93
competition 3, 8, 37, 41, 59, 82, 85–9, 94, 97, 99, 106, 119, 121, 133, 151, 153, 157, 162, 164, 190
consumerism 130, 156, 184; advertising in 193; endemics/non-endemics 162
creativity 44, 91, 107, 112
Cyrenaics 3

death 40, 45–6, 55, 60, 73, 82–94, 114, 151, 207
Deleuzean 22, 45, 89, 123
Dewey, John 156
Dionysius 33
disengagement theory 91

edgework 46–50, 61, 182–3
embodiment 6, 40, 54, 66, 68–9, 74, 76–7, 88, 98, 102, 107, 109, 161, 172
emotions i, 6, 29–30, 42, 44, 47–8, 108, 112–14, 122–6, 129–30, 133, 138, 142, 146, 149, 152, 159, 198
endorphins 52–4, 57
enlightenment 7, 36, 39
epiphanies 26, 155, 182
ethnography 6, 9, 48, 62, 100, 161–4, 194

240 *Subject Index*

eudaimonia 29, 31, 62
extreme sports 41, 45, 163, 183, 185, 193

fandom 9, 130–1, 133–51
feminism 6, 8, 64–79
figurational sociology 46
flow state 57–61
Foucauldian 62–3

Gnosticism 27
governmentality 10, 199–207
governments/-al 2–3, 10–11, 17, 20, 36–9, 116, 119, 185–9, 195–207
grobal/glocal 181, 184–6

happiness 2–3, 7–8, 10–11, 13, 18, 21, 23, 27–32, 36–40, 57–60, 78, 85–6, 103, 108, 113–14, 148, 191, 195–207
health 10, 53, 83, 89, 108, 114, 119, 161, 186, 195–206
healthism 206
hedonic calculus 36
hedonism 3, 7, 18–21, 24, 27, 86, 135, 156, 183
Hellenites 13

Inconvenience Store, The 12
interdisciplinary studies 42–4, 61–3
International Olympic Committee (IOC) 116, 119–21, 125, 128–9, 162

Jefferson, Thomas 2–3, 37
jouissance 7, 13, 18, 35, 66, 72–7, 103, 117

lifestyle sports 187–8
local/global 184, 185
love 4, 25, 26, 30, 50, 62, 70–1, 88, 93, 106, 128, 132–50, 151–78, 192–3, 196
Love + Guts 151–79

Manet, Édouard 154–6, 158, 165
Māori 81
masculinity 207
materiality 49, 54–5, 62, 155
media 2, 5, 9, 24, 46, 48, 53, 59, 75, 86, 94, 101, 116–32, 133, 135, 137, 148, 150, 163, 182, 185, 188, 190–2, 206
messiness, in social research 6, 67, 77
myth 67, 118–22, 127–30, 187

NASSS 4
neoliberal 2, 10, 65, 116–17, 130, 185–9
normalization 2, 207
nostalgia 10, 164–70, 181

obesity 205
Olympics 6, 9, 37, 56, 80, 94, 116–32, 159, 178, 203
outdoor challenge activities 180, 183–9, 191, 202

pain and suffering 2, 4–6, 10, 13–14, 19–20, 24, 26–7, 34–7, 40–2, 47–8, 52, 73, 77, 84, 88, 107, 126, 134, 140, 152, 165, 170–3, 205–7
philosophies: asceticism 34; Cyrenaicism 3; "Eastern" 8, 58, 80, 83, 87, 91–5; epicureanism 3, 27; Gnosticism 27; stoicism 109, 172
pleasure, attempts to define it 1–2, 12–28, 29–30, 39–40
poetic sensibility 89, 125
postmodern/postmodernism 45–6, 48–9, 57, 81, 157, 163, 165, 178, 182, 185, 190, 192–3, 199
poststructural 1, 4, 21, 45, 49, 64, 73, 75, 89, 183
psychology 2, 5, 8, 42–4, 57–63

quality of life 83, 196, 200–1
queer theory 9, 16–17, 24, 62, 64, 68, 70–1, 76–7, 134, 136–50

Raglan, Aotearoa/NZ 5, 103, 105, 187
risk 172, 180–3, 199, 205–6
rowing 102, 111
runner's high 52–4, 62
running 4–6, 9, 52–4, 62, 89, 97–115, 207

senilicide 82
senses/sensory 14, 19–27, 33, 51, 81, 88–9, 109, 122, 130, 151, 156–7, 185
sex/sexuality 6–10, 17, 21, 23, 28, 33–4, 37, 40, 52, 54–5, 58–9, 62–79, 80, 82, 97–8, 101–3, 107, 121, 134–50, 154, 170, 173, 176–7, 180, 197, 204
shame 7, 16–17, 24, 42, 130, 152
sijo 83, 91–3
simulacra 157
skateboarding 10, 98, 151–79, 187

Subject Index   241

sportism 206
stress 47, 58, 108, 149, 152, 201
subjective wellbeing (SWB) 2, 10,
    197–208
sublime 12, 19, 46, 48–9, 85, 92–3,
    120–1, 127, 151, 181
summum bonum principle 19
surfing 2, 5, 12, 19, 41, 46, 49,
    59–60, 156, 158, 187

theory/theorizing 1–2, 8, 41–63, 66, 122
thrill sports, vertigo aspect of 26, 180

time (compression/commodification)
    182, 189–93
Tour de France 119–21
transnational 2, 120

viewing pleasure 36, 60, 116–32,
    134–5, 155, 177

Wabi Sabi 83, 87–93
women, and sporting pleasure 203

X-Games 45, 186